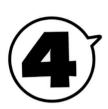

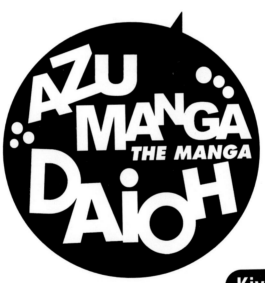

AZU MANGA DAIOH

THE MANGA

Kiyohiko Azuma

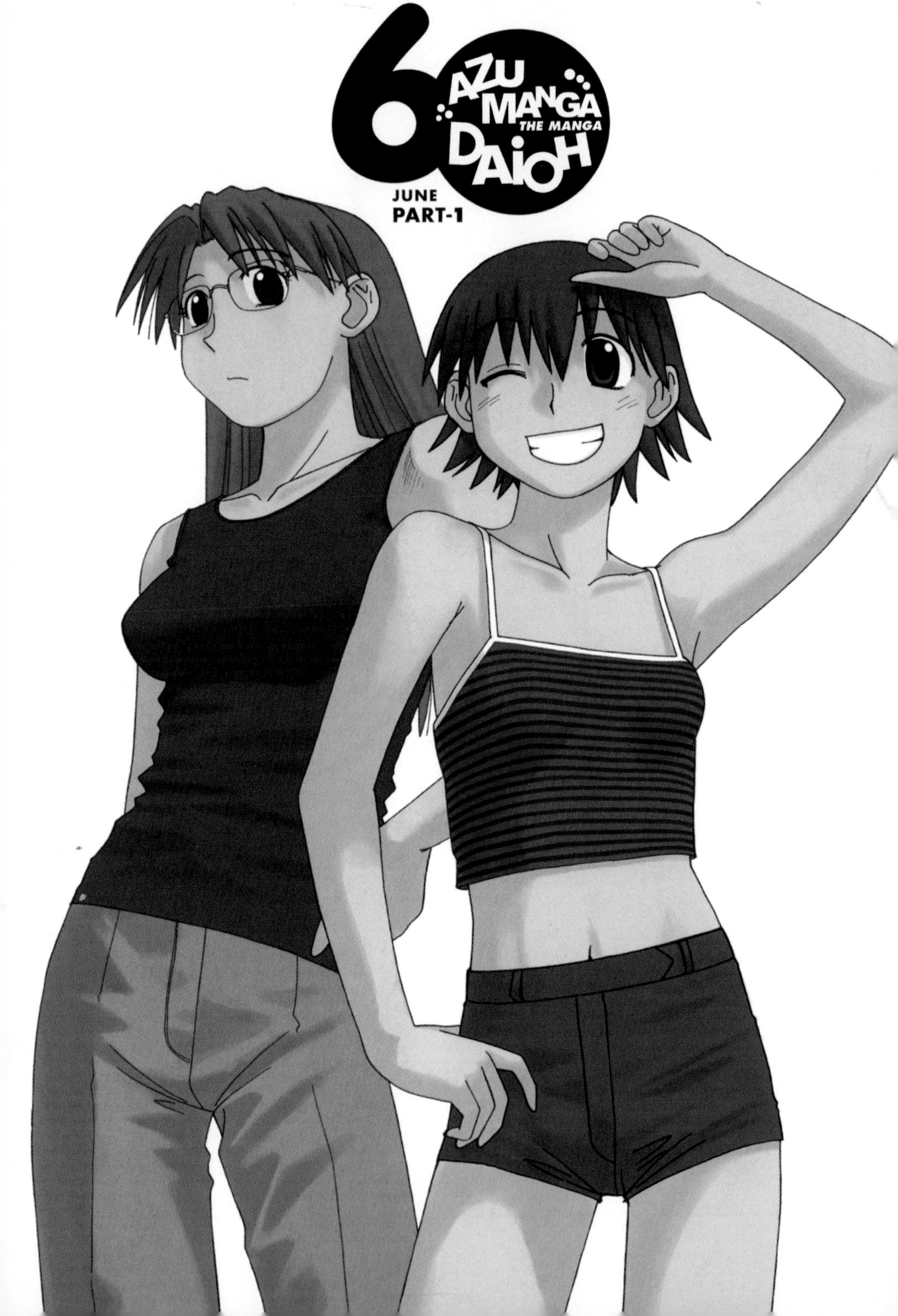
6
AZU MANGA
THE MANGA
DAIOH
JUNE
PART-1

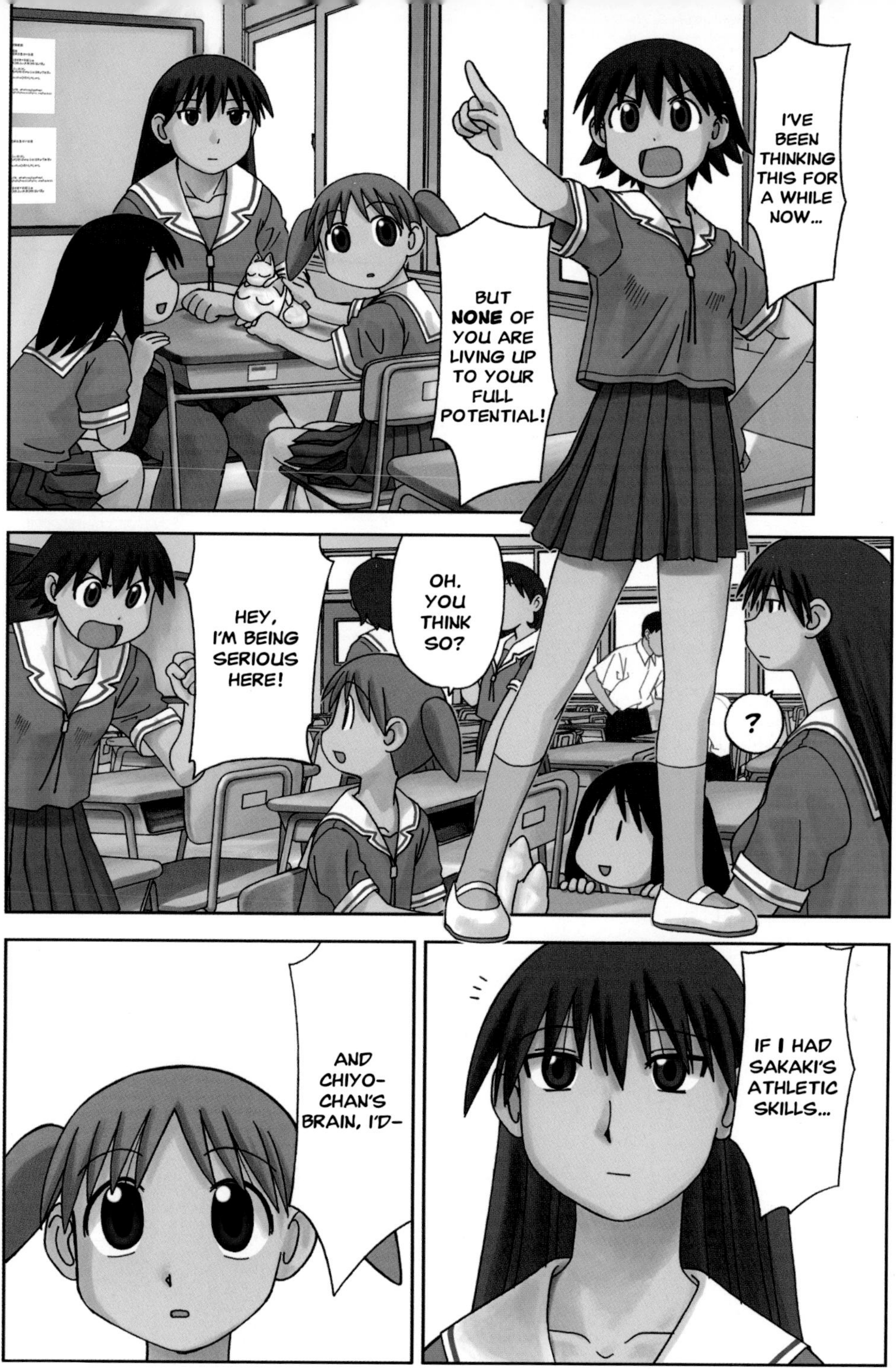
I'VE BEEN THINKING THIS FOR A WHILE NOW...
BUT **NONE** OF YOU ARE LIVING UP TO YOUR FULL POTENTIAL!
?
OH. YOU THINK SO?
HEY, I'M BEING SERIOUS HERE!
IF I HAD SAKAKI'S ATHLETIC SKILLS...
AND CHIYO-CHAN'S BRAIN, I'D-

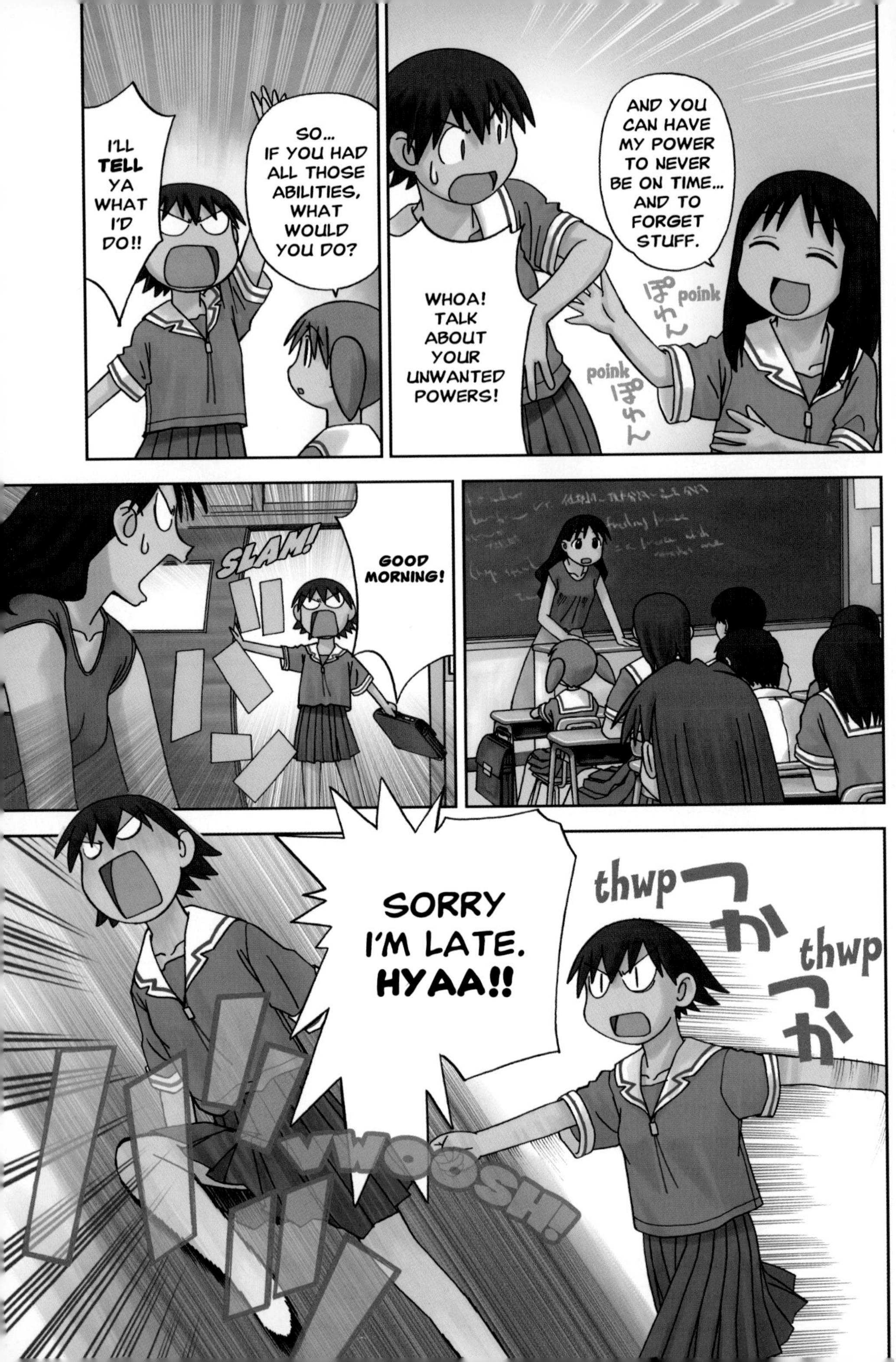
AND YOU CAN HAVE MY POWER TO NEVER BE ON TIME... AND TO FORGET STUFF.
ぽわん poink
poink ぽわん
WHOA! TALK ABOUT YOUR UNWANTED POWERS!
SO... IF YOU HAD ALL THOSE ABILITIES, WHAT WOULD YOU DO?
I'LL **TELL** YA WHAT I'D DO!!
GOOD MORNING!
SLAM!
thwp つか
thwp つか
SORRY I'M LATE. **HYAA!!**
VWOOSH!

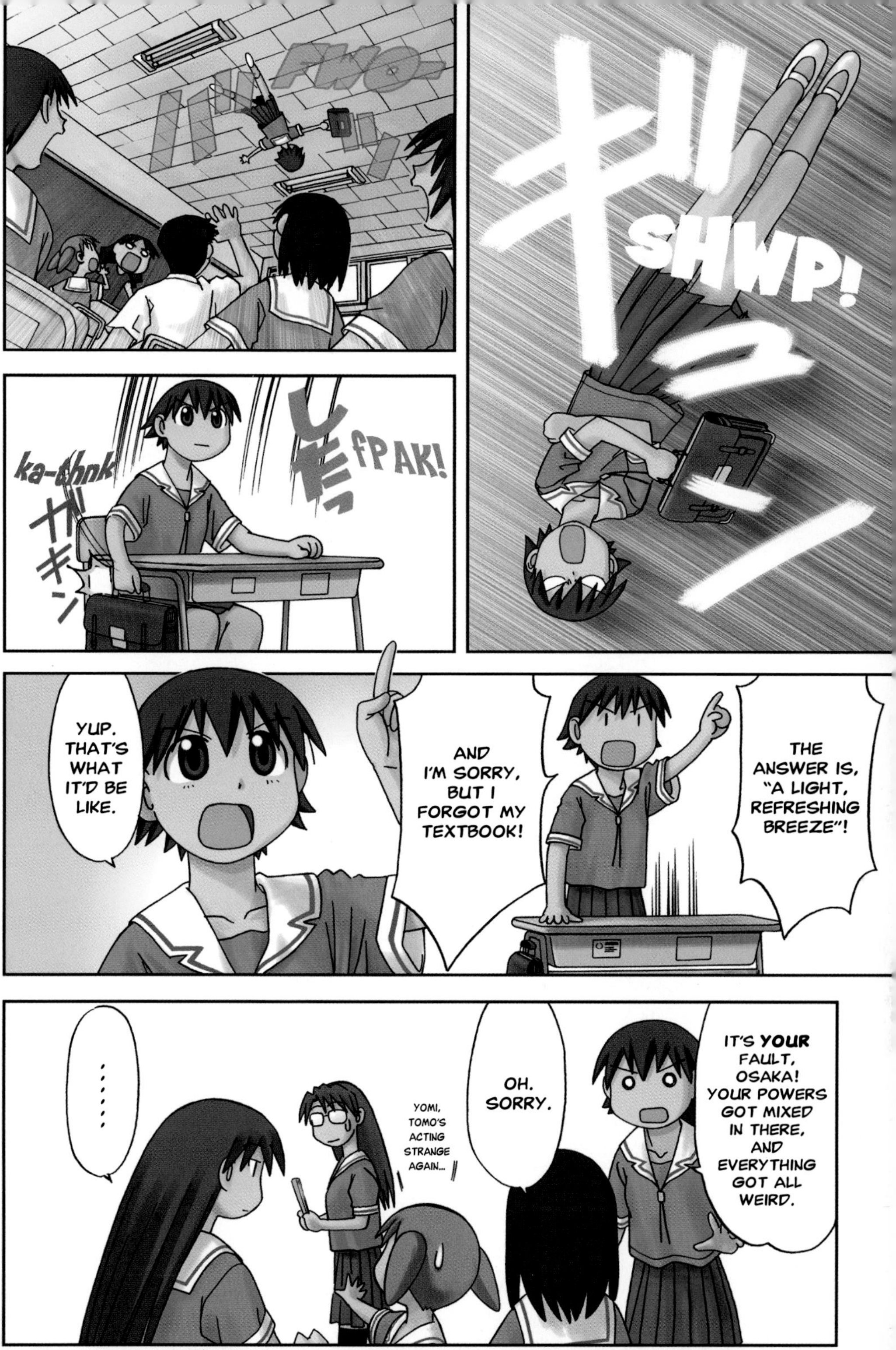
SHWP!
FWO-
ka-thnk
fPAK!
THE ANSWER IS, "A LIGHT, REFRESHING BREEZE"!
AND I'M SORRY, BUT I FORGOT MY TEXTBOOK!
YUP. THAT'S WHAT IT'D BE LIKE.
IT'S **YOUR** FAULT, OSAKA! YOUR POWERS GOT MIXED IN THERE, AND EVERYTHING GOT ALL WEIRD.
OH. SORRY.
YOMI, TOMO'S ACTING STRANGE AGAIN...
......

DON'T NEED 'EM

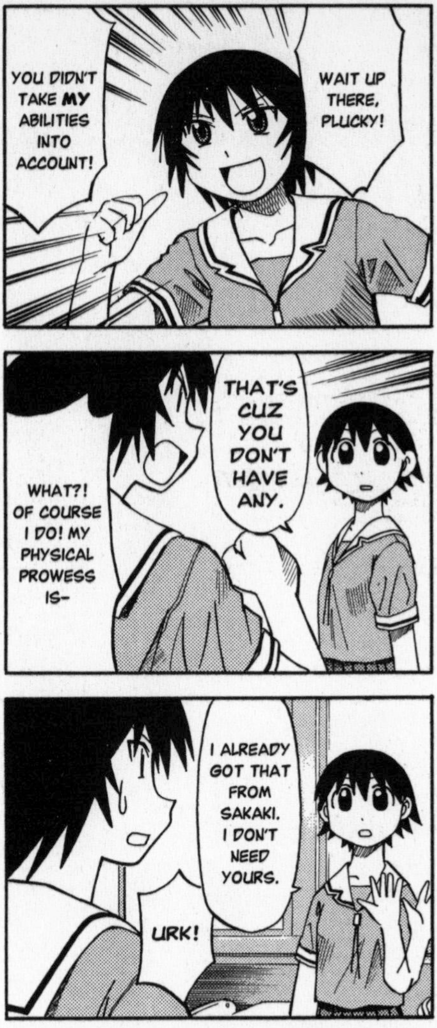
WAIT UP THERE, PLUCKY!
YOU DIDN'T TAKE MY ABILITIES INTO ACCOUNT!
THAT'S CUZ YOU DON'T HAVE ANY.
WHAT?! OF COURSE I DO! MY PHYSICAL PROWESS IS-
I ALREADY GOT THAT FROM SAKAKI. I DON'T NEED YOURS.
URK!
YOU WANT ME TO SHARE SOME OF MY GENIUS POWERS WITH YOU?
HEY! DON'T SOUND LIKE YOU'RE FEELIN' SORRY FOR ME!

THE GOOD DAUGHTER

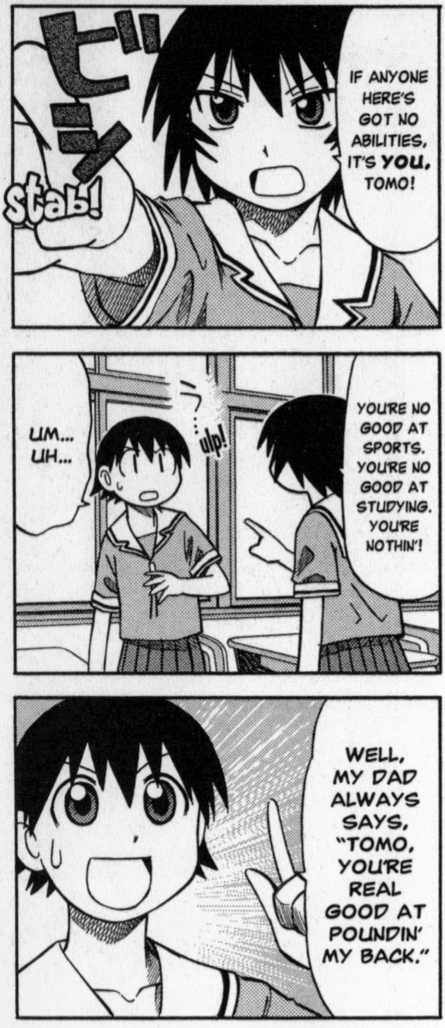
IF ANYONE HERE'S GOT NO ABILITIES, IT'S YOU, TOMO!
stab!
YOU'RE NO GOOD AT SPORTS. YOU'RE NO GOOD AT STUDYING. YOU'RE NOTHIN'!
ulp!
UM... UH...
WELL, MY DAD ALWAYS SAYS, "TOMO, YOU'RE REAL GOOD AT POUNDIN' MY BACK."
OH. WELL, THAT'S GOOD. I'M GLAD.
HEY! DON'T SOUND LIKE YOU'RE FEELIN' SORRY FOR ME!

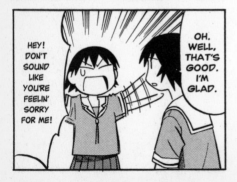

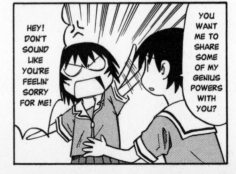

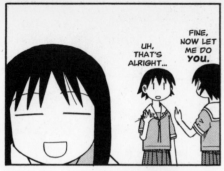

A SLIGHT ERROR

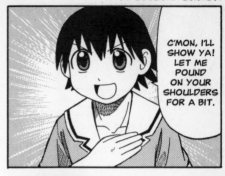

C'MON, I'LL SHOW YA! LET ME POUND ON YOUR SHOULDERS FOR A BIT.
WELL, IF YOU INSIST...
UNDER-STOOD!
HYAAAA!
FWACK!
カッ
Ungrh. I think my aim was a little off.
Ow...

NECOSAKA

FINE, NOW LET ME DO YOU.
UH, THAT'S ALRIGHT...
MAN, THIS SURE IS CUTE.
YEAH, IT'S NECOCONECO.

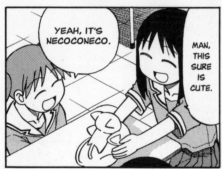

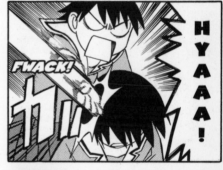

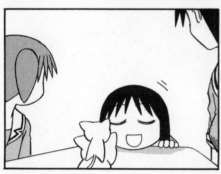

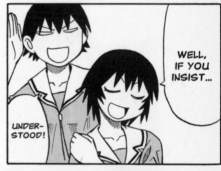

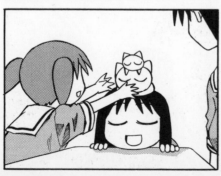

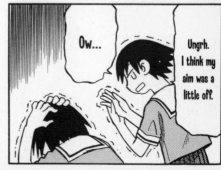

WHOOPS!

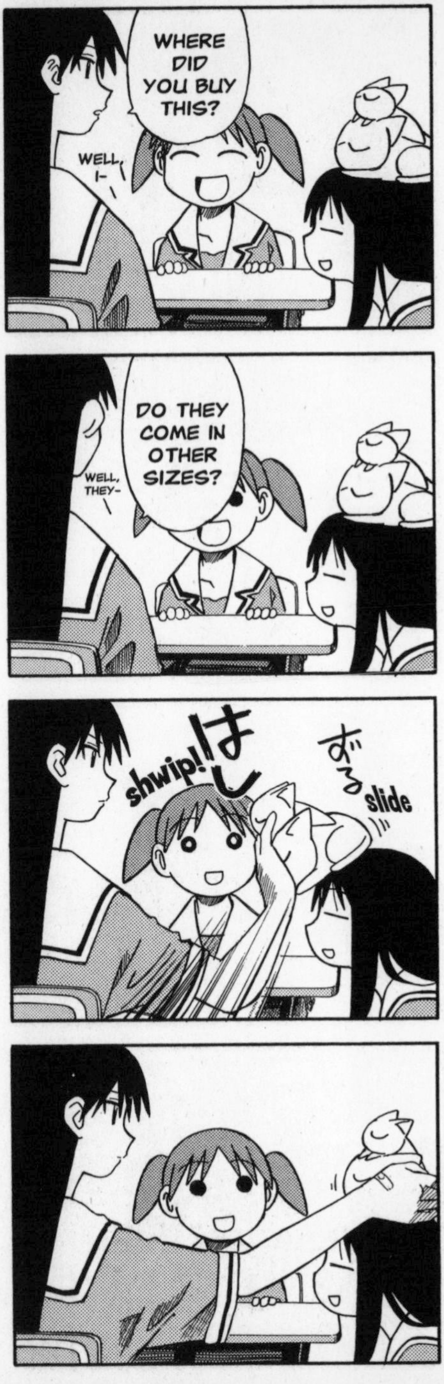
WHERE DID YOU BUY THIS?
WELL, I-
DO THEY COME IN OTHER SIZES?
WELL, THEY-
ずる slide
はし shwip!

NO GOOD

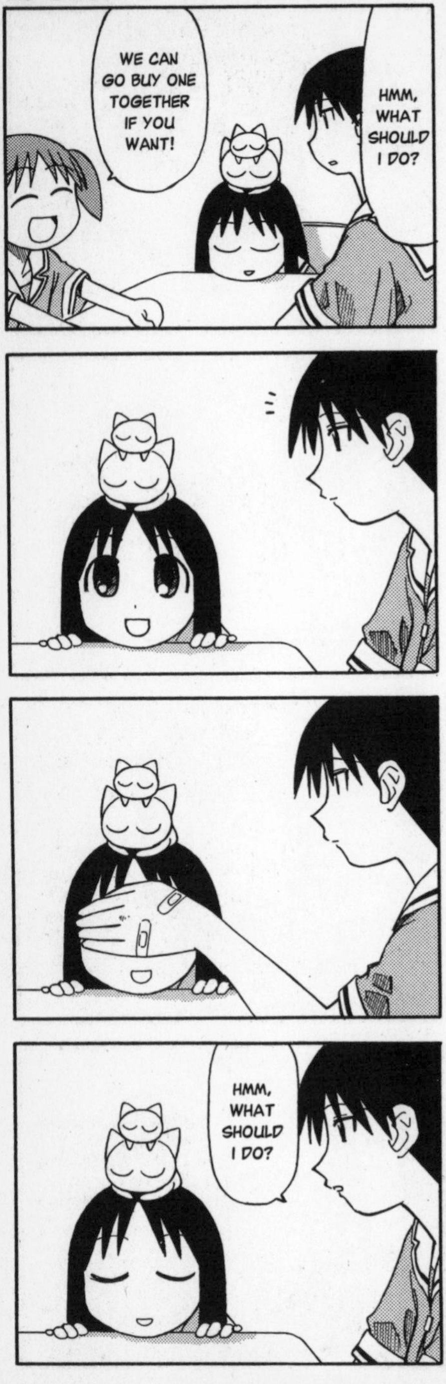
HMM, WHAT SHOULD I DO?
WE CAN GO BUY ONE TOGETHER IF YOU WANT!
HMM, WHAT SHOULD I DO?

AN AID TO UNDERSTANDING

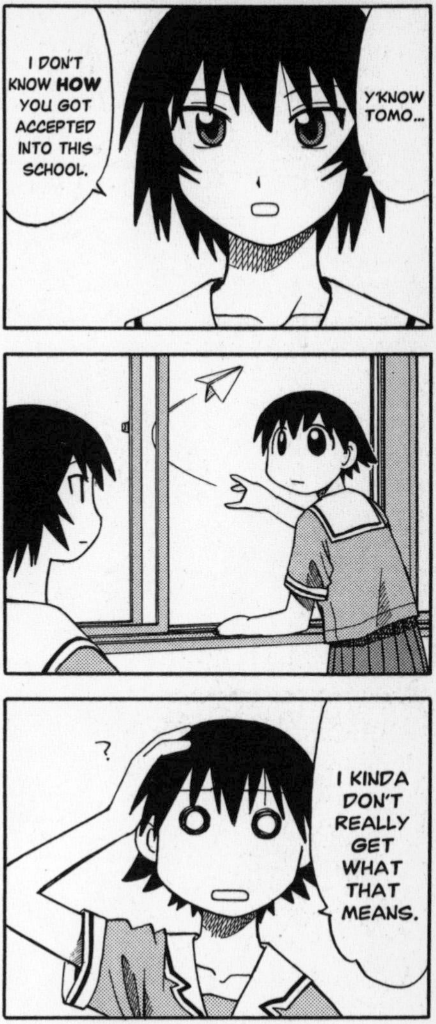
Y'KNOW TOMO...
I DON'T KNOW **HOW** YOU GOT ACCEPTED INTO THIS SCHOOL.
I KINDA DON'T REALLY GET WHAT THAT MEANS.
?
WOULD YOU MIND SAYIN' THAT IN **ENGLISH** FOR ME?
ENGLISH ?!

ENGLISH

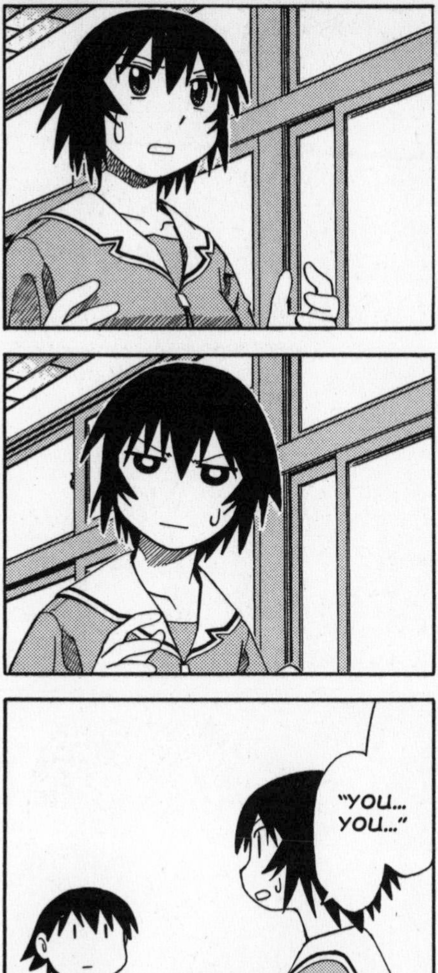
"YOU... YOU..."
"YOU ARE... A... **FOOL!**"
WHAAT?!

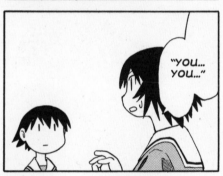

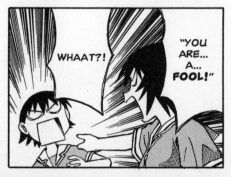

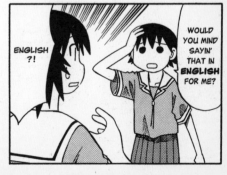

TRANSLATION

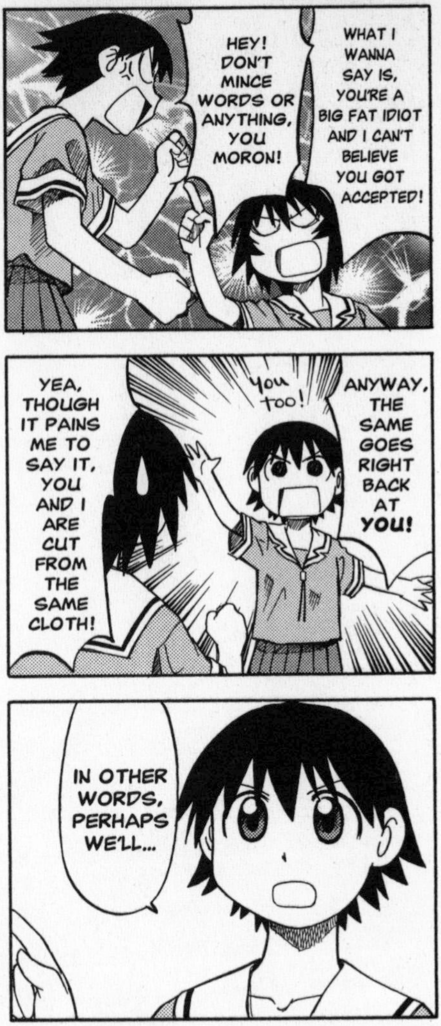

WHAT I WANNA SAY IS, YOU'RE A BIG FAT IDIOT AND I CAN'T BELIEVE YOU GOT ACCEPTED!
HEY! DON'T MINCE WORDS OR ANYTHING, YOU MORON!
ANYWAY, THE SAME GOES RIGHT BACK AT YOU!
You too!
YEA, THOUGH IT PAINS ME TO SAY IT, YOU AND I ARE CUT FROM THE SAME CLOTH!
IN OTHER WORDS, PERHAPS WE'LL...
BOTH SQUEAK BY ON OUR ENTRANCE EXAMS, TOO.
OH. HEY, YEAH...
ARE YOU HEARING YOURSELVES?

IN TOMO'S RECOLLECTION...

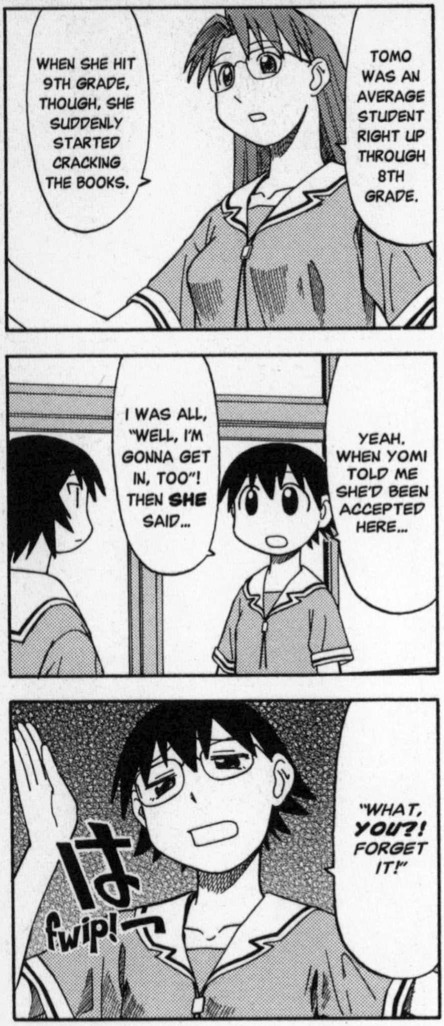

TOMO WAS AN AVERAGE STUDENT RIGHT UP THROUGH 8TH GRADE.
WHEN SHE HIT 9TH GRADE, THOUGH, SHE SUDDENLY STARTED CRACKING THE BOOKS.
YEAH. WHEN YOMI TOLD ME SHE'D BEEN ACCEPTED HERE...
I WAS ALL, "WELL, I'M GONNA GET IN, TOO"! THEN SHE SAID...
"WHAT, YOU?! FORGET IT!"
は
fwip!
AND OTHER STUFF LIKE THAT.
MAN, THAT'D BE ENOUGH TO TICK ANYONE OFF! WHAT A WENCH!
MY GLASSES...

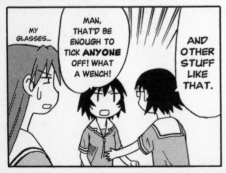

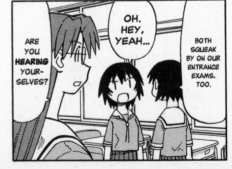

AAH, THE MEMORIES

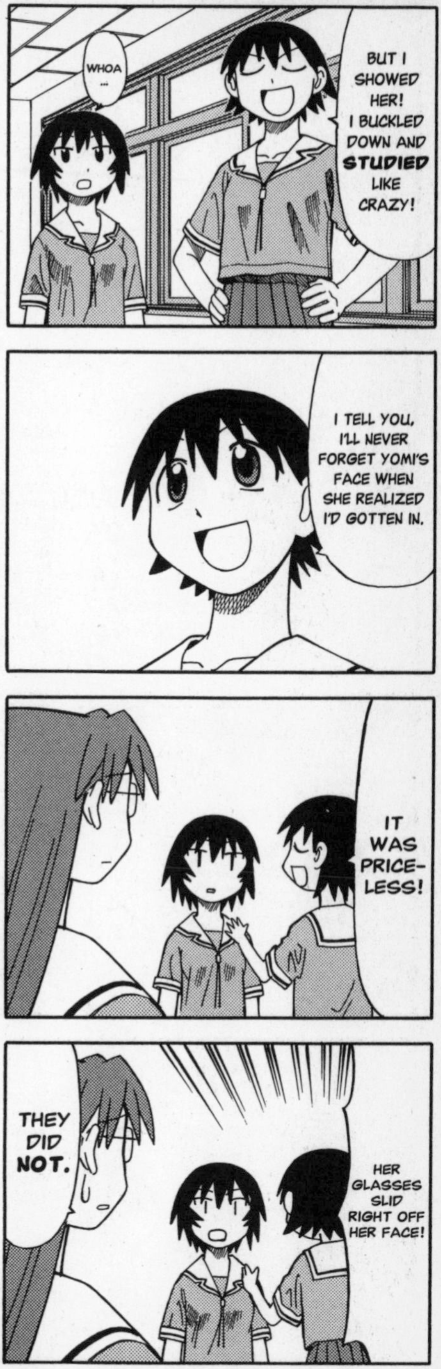
BUT I SHOWED HER! I BUCKLED DOWN AND **STUDIED** LIKE CRAZY!
WHOA ...
I TELL YOU, I'LL NEVER FORGET YOMI'S FACE WHEN SHE REALIZED I'D GOTTEN IN.
IT WAS PRICE-LESS!
HER GLASSES SLID RIGHT OFF HER FACE!
THEY DID **NOT.**

PRAISE ME!

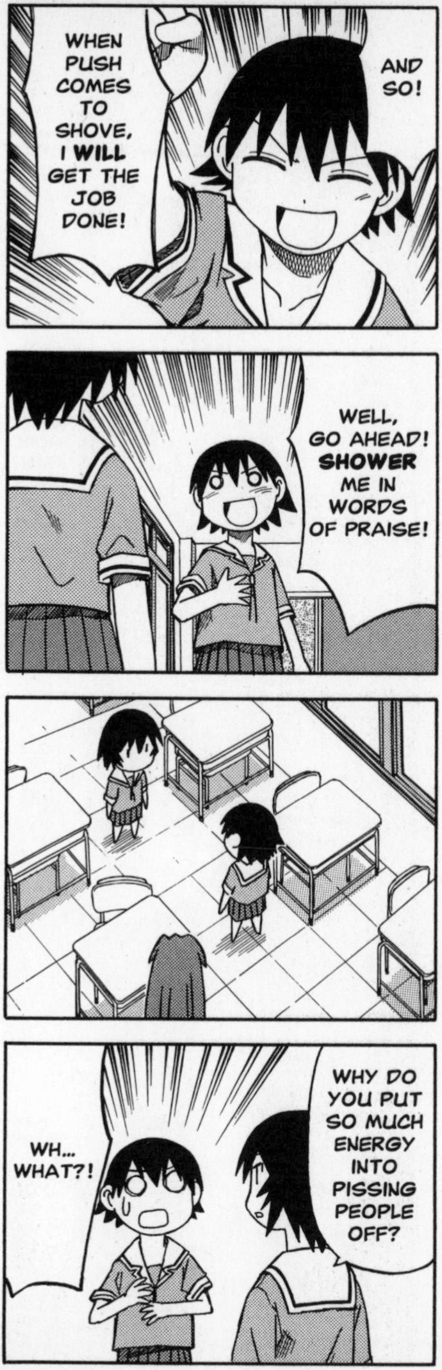
AND SO!
WHEN PUSH COMES TO SHOVE, I **WILL** GET THE JOB DONE!
WELL, GO AHEAD! **SHOWER** ME IN WORDS OF PRAISE!
WHY DO YOU PUT SO MUCH ENERGY INTO PISSING PEOPLE OFF?
WH... WHAT?!

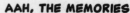

FUHGEDDABOUTIT

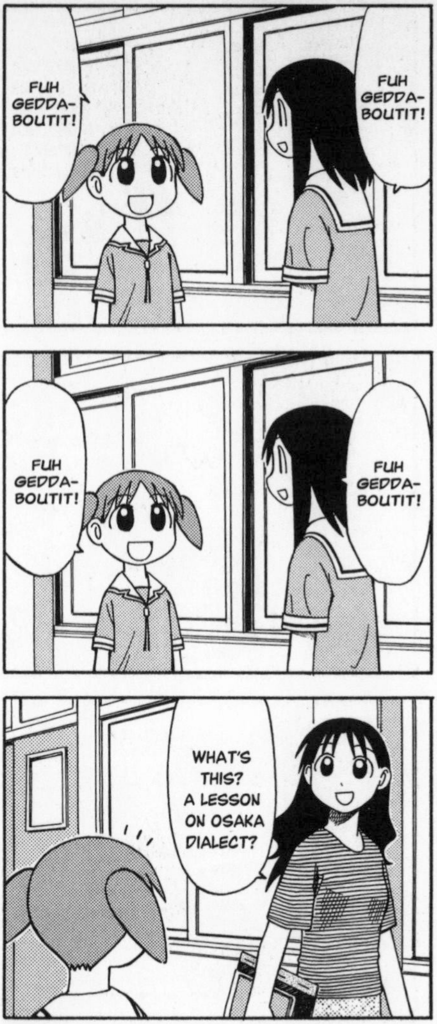
FUH GEDDA-BOUTIT!
FUH GEDDA-BOUTIT!
FUH GEDDA-BOUTIT!
FUH GEDDA-BOUTIT!
WHAT'S THIS? A LESSON ON OSAKA DIALECT?
FUH GEDDA-BOUTIT!
WHA?!

CONTAGION

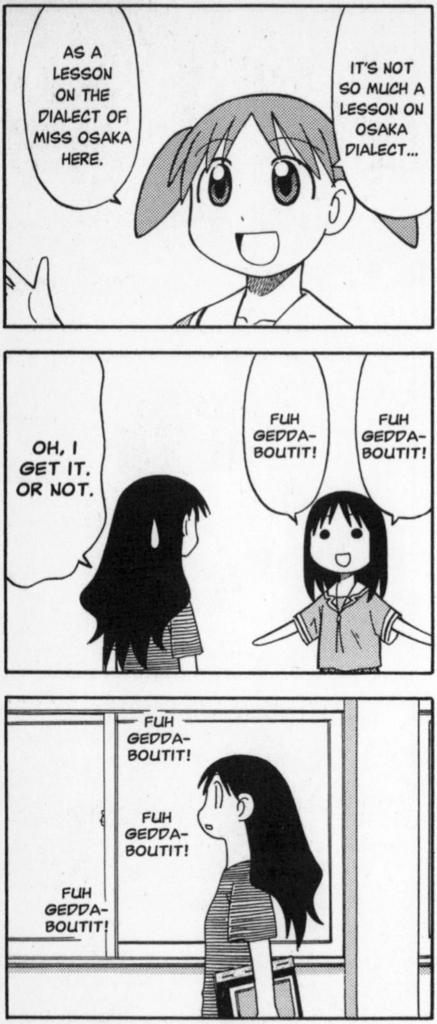
IT'S NOT SO MUCH A LESSON ON OSAKA DIALECT...
AS A LESSON ON THE DIALECT OF MISS OSAKA HERE.
FUH GEDDA-BOUTIT!
FUH GEDDA-BOUTIT!
OH, I GET IT. OR NOT.
FUH GEDDA-BOUTIT!
FUH GEDDA-BOUTIT!
FUH GEDDA-BOUTIT!
HEY! IT WAS **YOU** WHO DIDN'T LOCK UP THE LANGUAGE LAB, WASN'T IT?
A LITTLE WHILE AGO.
FUH GEDDA-BOUTIT!

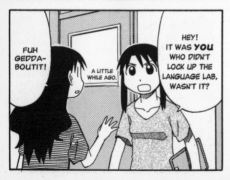

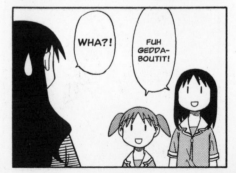

HIDE AND GO CAT?

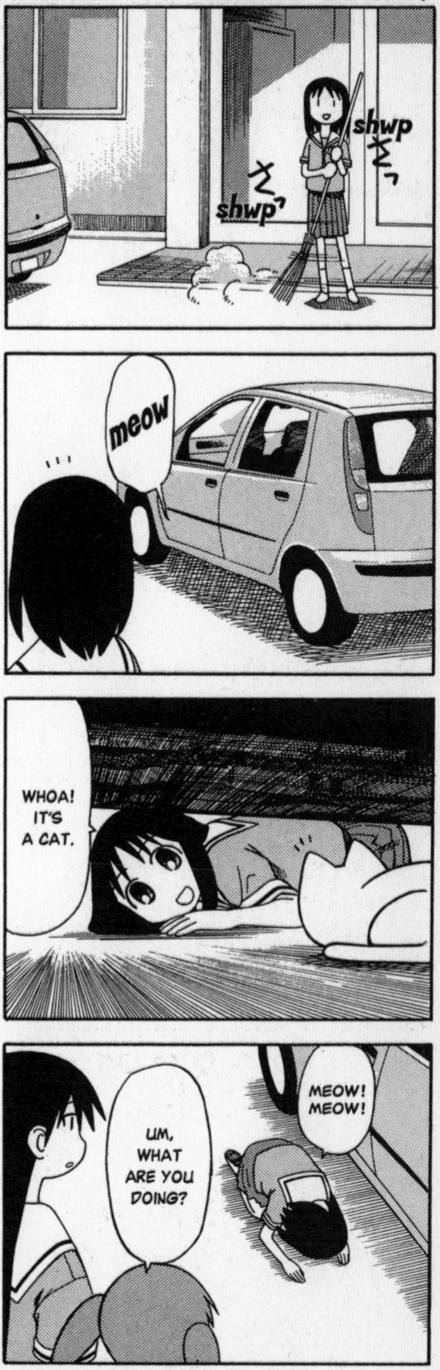
shwp
shwp
meow
WHOA! IT'S A CAT.
MEOW! MEOW!
UM, WHAT ARE YOU DOING?

GONE FISHING

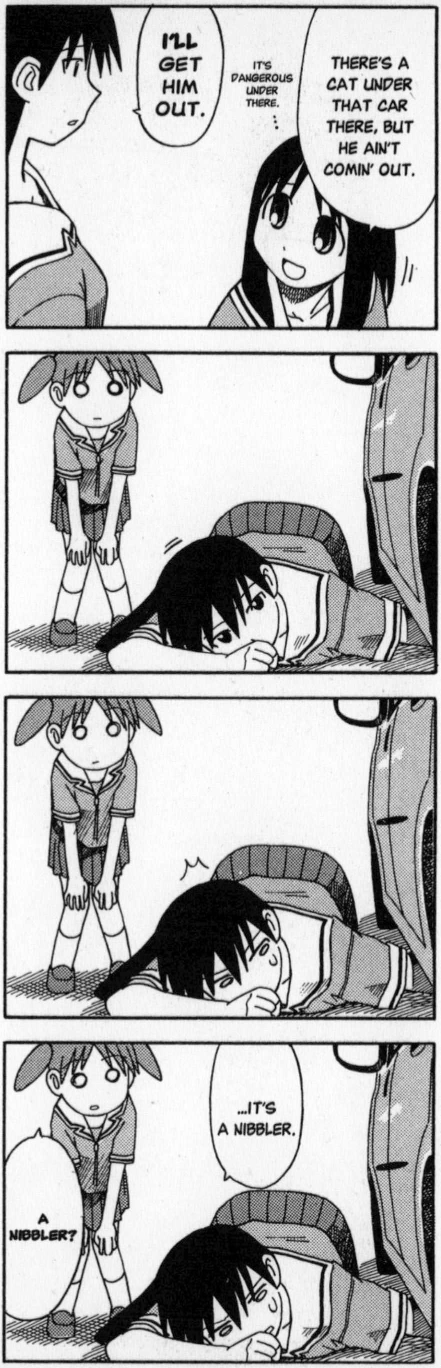
THERE'S A CAT UNDER THAT CAR THERE, BUT HE AIN'T COMIN' OUT.
IT'S DANGEROUS UNDER THERE. ...
I'LL GET HIM OUT.
...IT'S A NIBBLER.
A NIBBLER?

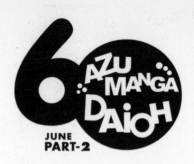

6 AZU MANGA DAIOH

JUNE
PART-2

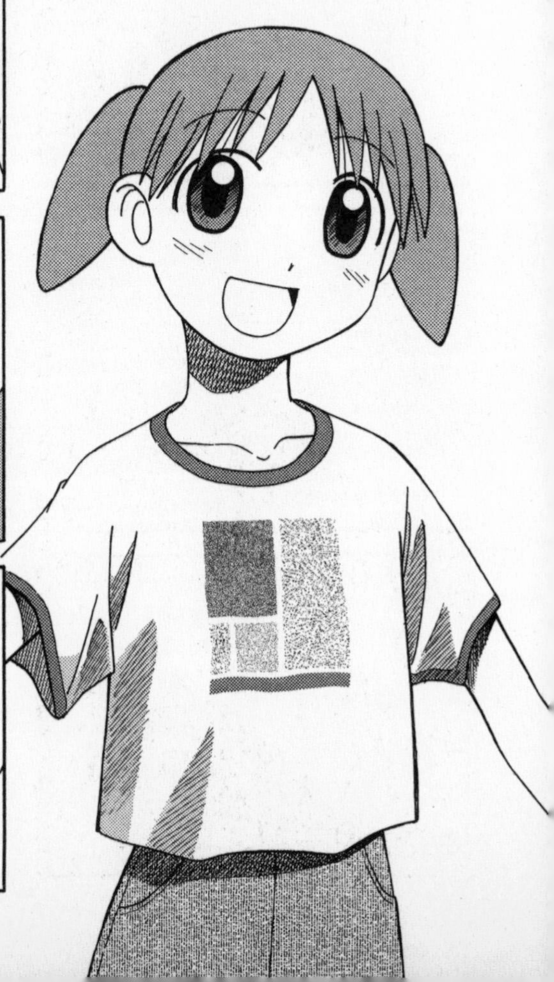

THE NEW CHIYO

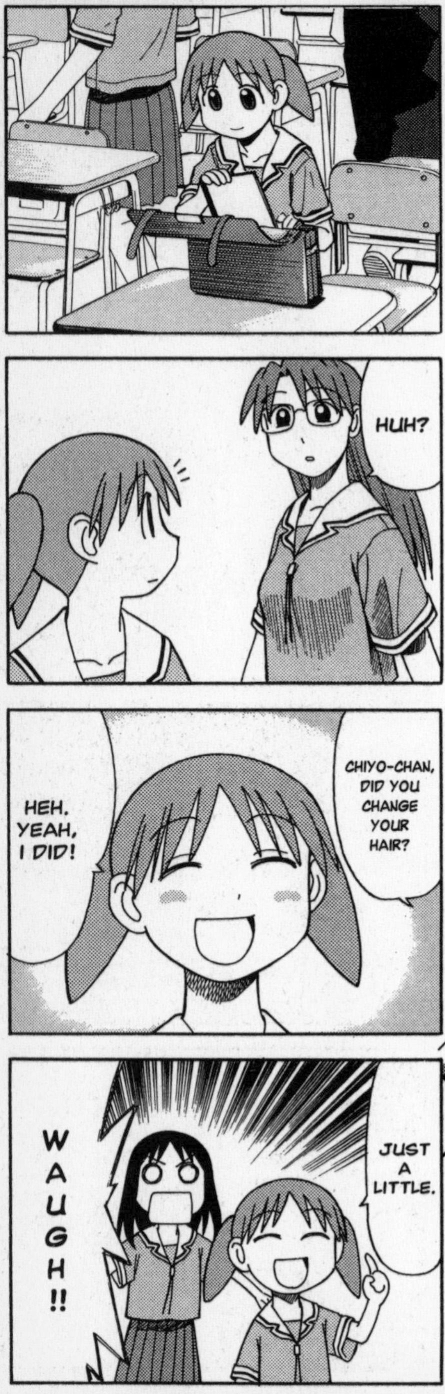
HUH?
CHIYO-CHAN, DID YOU CHANGE YOUR HAIR?
HEH. YEAH, I DID!
JUST A LITTLE.
WAUGH!!

THE HECK'S GOIN' ON?!

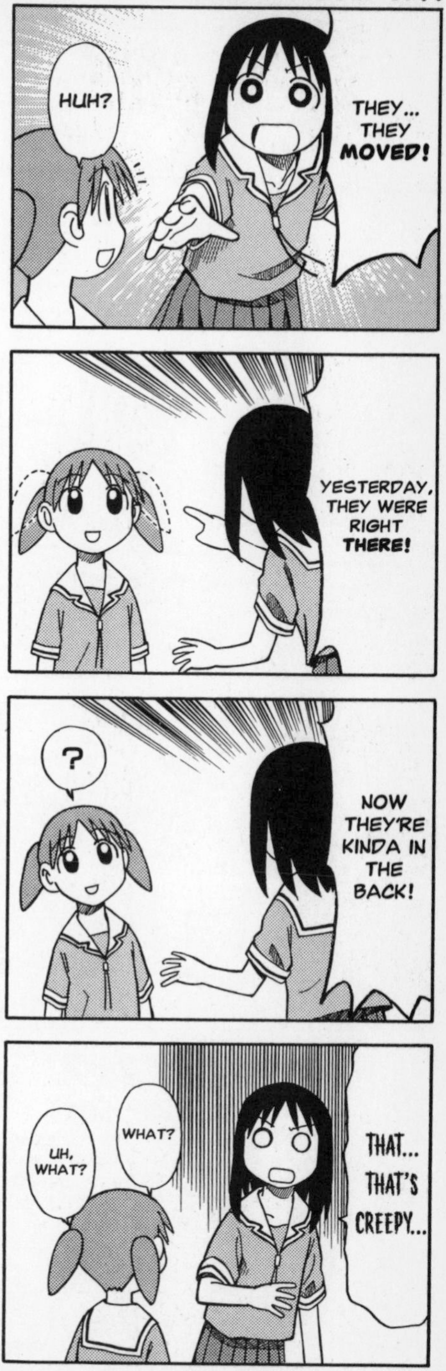

THEY... THEY MOVED!
HUH?
YESTERDAY, THEY WERE RIGHT THERE!
NOW THEY'RE KINDA IN THE BACK!
?
THAT... THAT'S CREEPY...
WHAT?
UH, WHAT?

WHAT ARE YOU TALKING ABOUT?

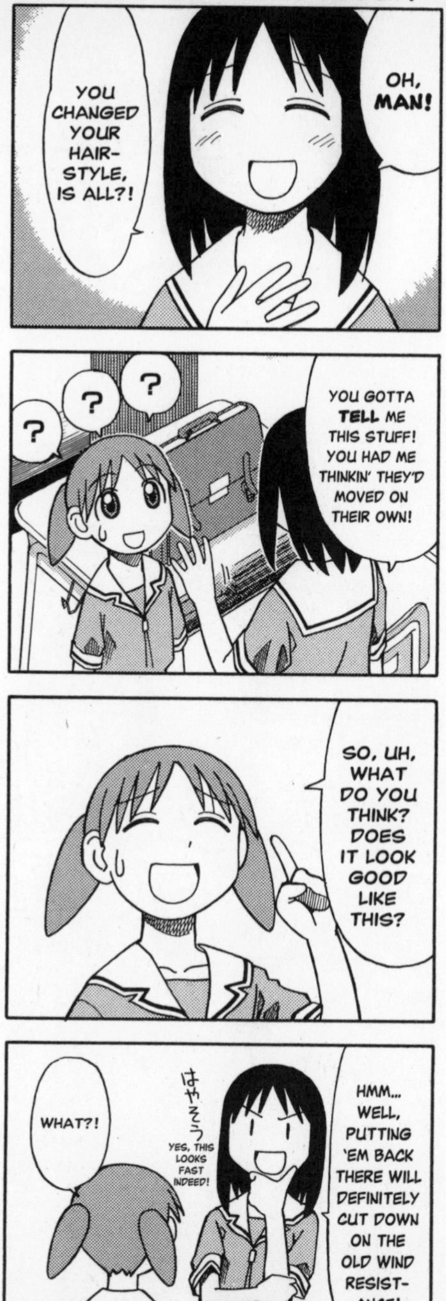

OH, MAN!
YOU CHANGED YOUR HAIR-STYLE, IS ALL?!
YOU GOTTA TELL ME THIS STUFF! YOU HAD ME THINKIN' THEY'D MOVED ON THEIR OWN!
?
?
?
SO, UH, WHAT DO YOU THINK? DOES IT LOOK GOOD LIKE THIS?
HMM... WELL, PUTTING 'EM BACK THERE WILL DEFINITELY CUT DOWN ON THE OLD WIND RESIST-ANCE!
はやそう
YES, THIS LOOKS FAST INDEED!
WHAT?!

I WONDER WHERE I SHOULD GO...

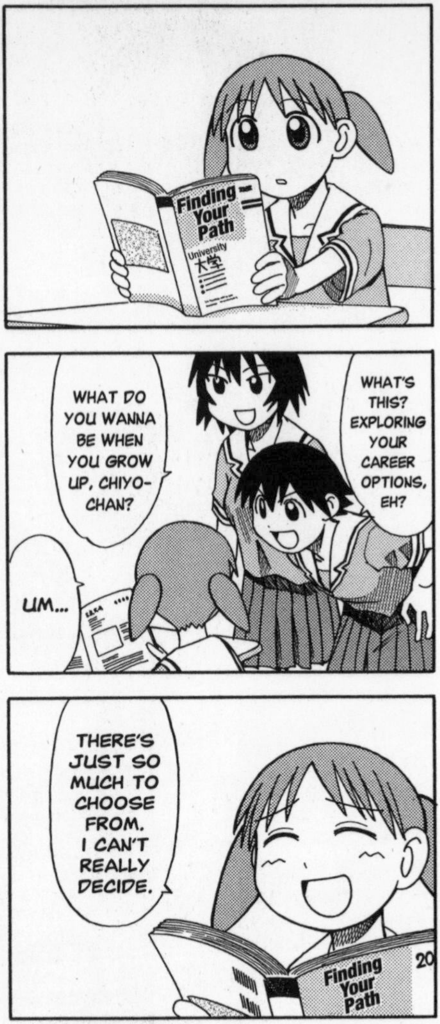

WHAT'S THIS? EXPLORING YOUR CAREER OPTIONS, EH?
WHAT DO YOU WANNA BE WHEN YOU GROW UP, CHIYO-CHAN?
UM...
THERE'S JUST SO MUCH TO CHOOSE FROM. I CAN'T REALLY DECIDE.
WHAT ABOUT YOU, TOMO? WHAT DO YOU WANT TO DO?
WHAT, ME?
I WANNA WORK FOR THE ICPO.

THE DREAM

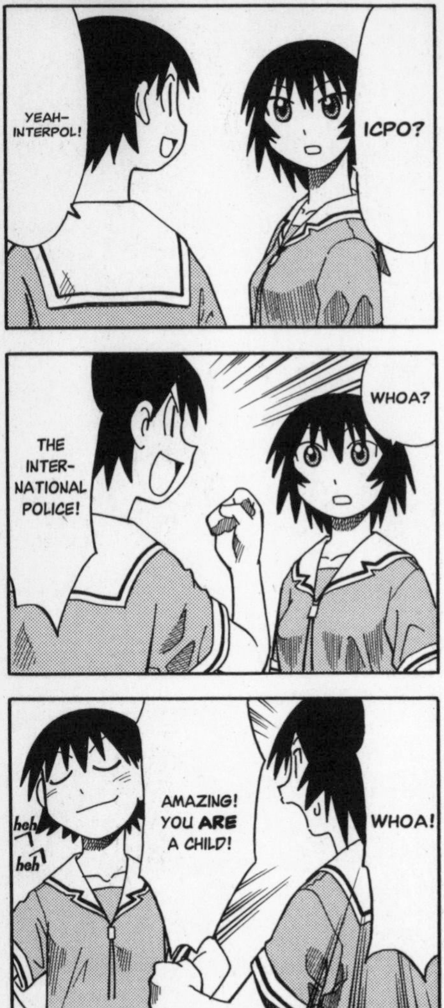

ICPO?
YEAH–INTERPOL!
WHOA?
THE INTER-NATIONAL POLICE!
WHOA!
AMAZING! YOU ARE A CHILD!
heh heh
I WONDER IF THERE EVEN IS AN INTERPOL. I THOUGHT IT WAS ONLY IN THE MOVIES.
WHAT? YOU MEAN IT ISN'T REAL?!

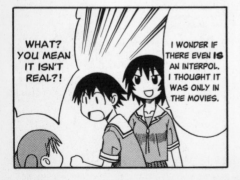

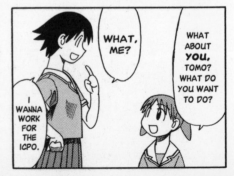

A MYSTERIOUS ORGANIZATION

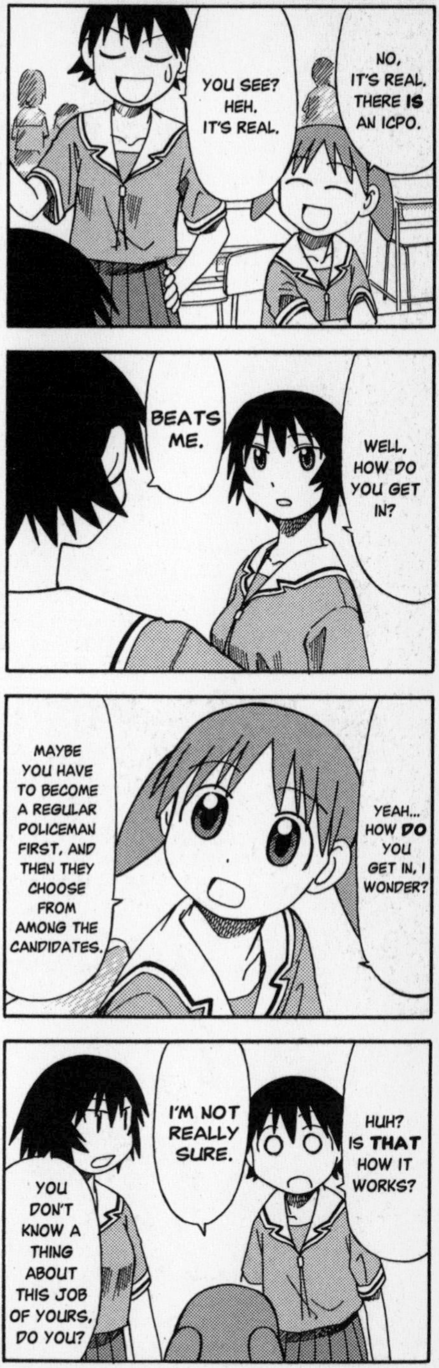
NO, IT'S REAL. THERE IS AN ICPO.
YOU SEE? HEH. IT'S REAL.
WELL, HOW DO YOU GET IN?
BEATS ME.
YEAH... HOW DO YOU GET IN, I WONDER?
MAYBE YOU HAVE TO BECOME A REGULAR POLICEMAN FIRST, AND THEN THEY CHOOSE FROM AMONG THE CANDIDATES.
HUH? IS THAT HOW IT WORKS?
I'M NOT REALLY SURE.
YOU DON'T KNOW A THING ABOUT THIS JOB OF YOURS, DO YOU?

I'LL SHOW YOU ALL!

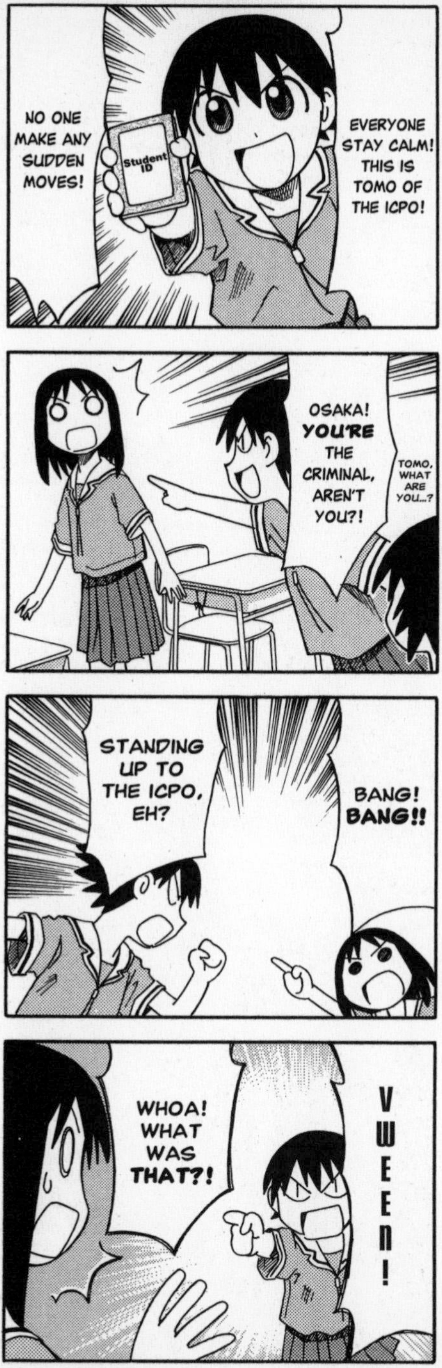
EVERYONE STAY CALM! THIS IS TOMO OF THE ICPO!
Student ID
NO ONE MAKE ANY SUDDEN MOVES!
TOMO, WHAT ARE YOU...?
OSAKA! YOU'RE THE CRIMINAL, AREN'T YOU?!
BANG! BANG!!
STANDING UP TO THE ICPO, EH?
VWEEN!
WHOA! WHAT WAS THAT?!

ANTICIPATION

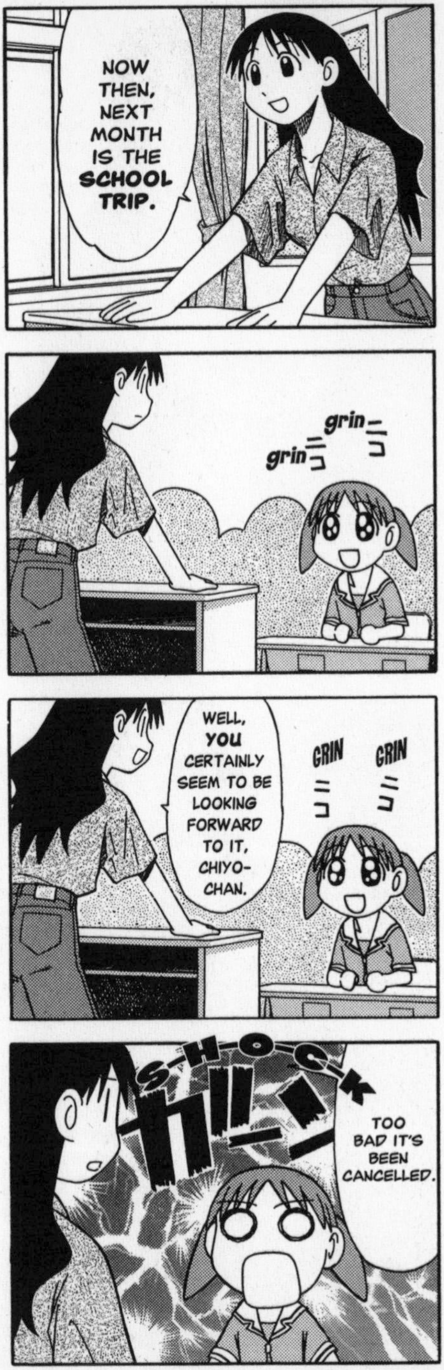
NOW THEN, NEXT MONTH IS THE SCHOOL TRIP.
grin grin
WELL, YOU CERTAINLY SEEM TO BE LOOKING FORWARD TO IT, CHIYO-CHAN.
GRIN GRIN
S-H-O-C-K
TOO BAD IT'S BEEN CANCELLED.

WITHERS AWAY

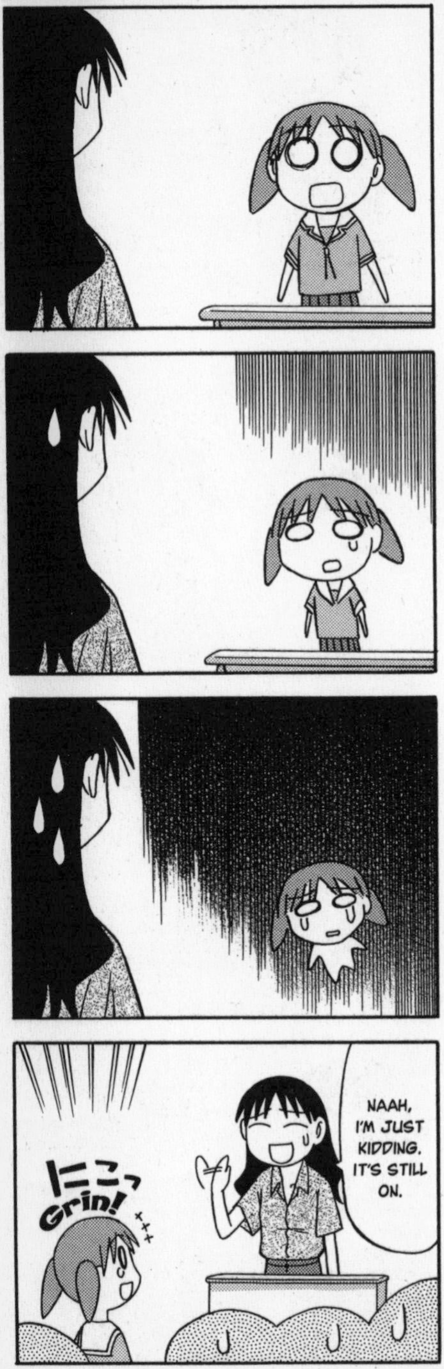
NAAH, I'M JUST KIDDING. IT'S STILL ON.
にこっ
Grin!

KINDA

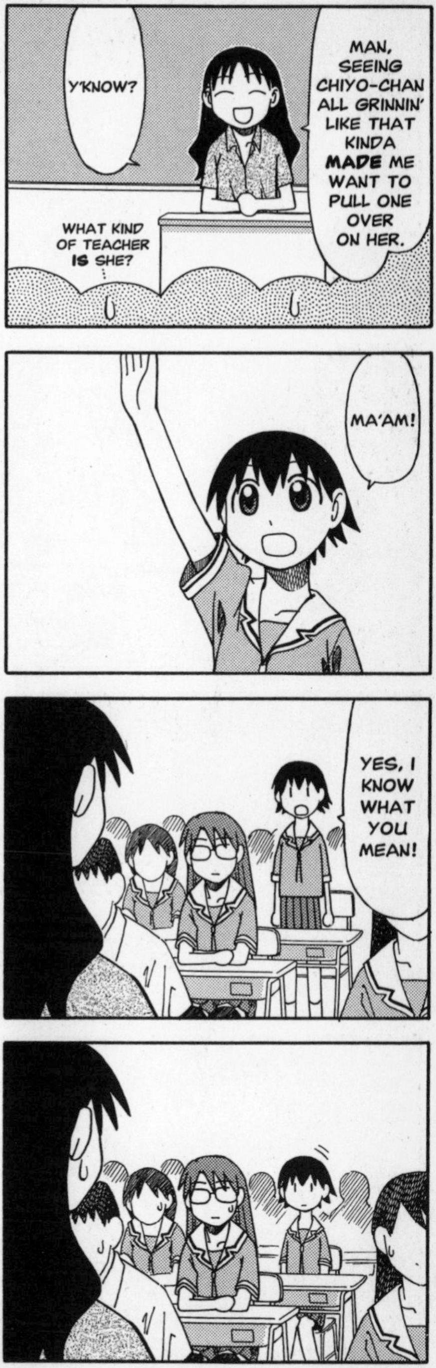
MAN, SEEING CHIYO-CHAN ALL GRINNIN' LIKE THAT KINDA MADE ME WANT TO PULL ONE OVER ON HER.
Y'KNOW?
WHAT KIND OF TEACHER IS SHE?
MA'AM!
YES, I KNOW WHAT YOU MEAN!

THE PROPHECY

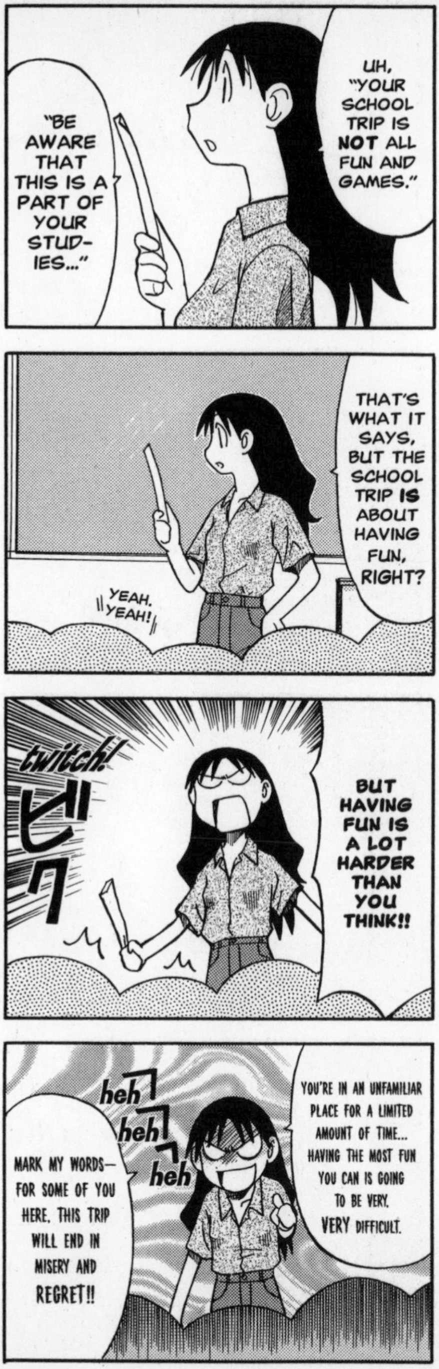
UH, "YOUR SCHOOL TRIP IS NOT ALL FUN AND GAMES."
"BE AWARE THAT THIS IS A PART OF YOUR STUDIES..."
THAT'S WHAT IT SAYS, BUT THE SCHOOL TRIP IS ABOUT HAVING FUN, RIGHT?
YEAH. YEAH!
BUT HAVING FUN IS A LOT HARDER THAN YOU THINK!!
twitch!
ビク
YOU'RE IN AN UNFAMILIAR PLACE FOR A LIMITED AMOUNT OF TIME... HAVING THE MOST FUN YOU CAN IS GOING TO BE VERY, VERY DIFFICULT.
heh heh heh
MARK MY WORDS— FOR SOME OF YOU HERE, THIS TRIP WILL END IN MISERY AND REGRET!!

POINT ONE

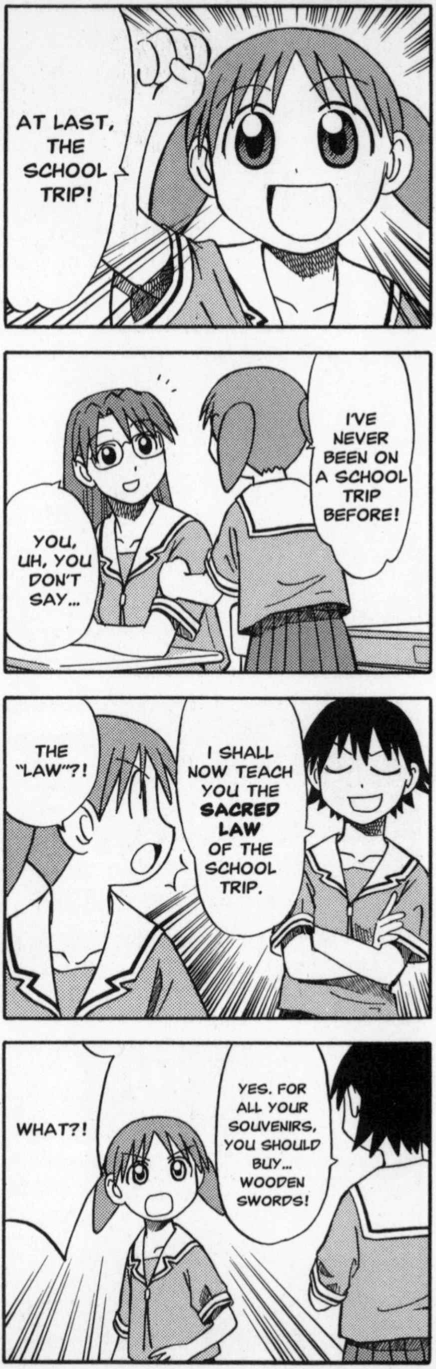
AT LAST, THE SCHOOL TRIP!
I'VE NEVER BEEN ON A SCHOOL TRIP BEFORE!
YOU, UH, YOU DON'T SAY...
I SHALL NOW TEACH YOU THE **SACRED LAW** OF THE SCHOOL TRIP.
THE "LAW"?!
YES. FOR ALL YOUR SOUVENIRS, YOU SHOULD BUY... WOODEN SWORDS!
WHAT?!

A PREMONITION OF FAILURE

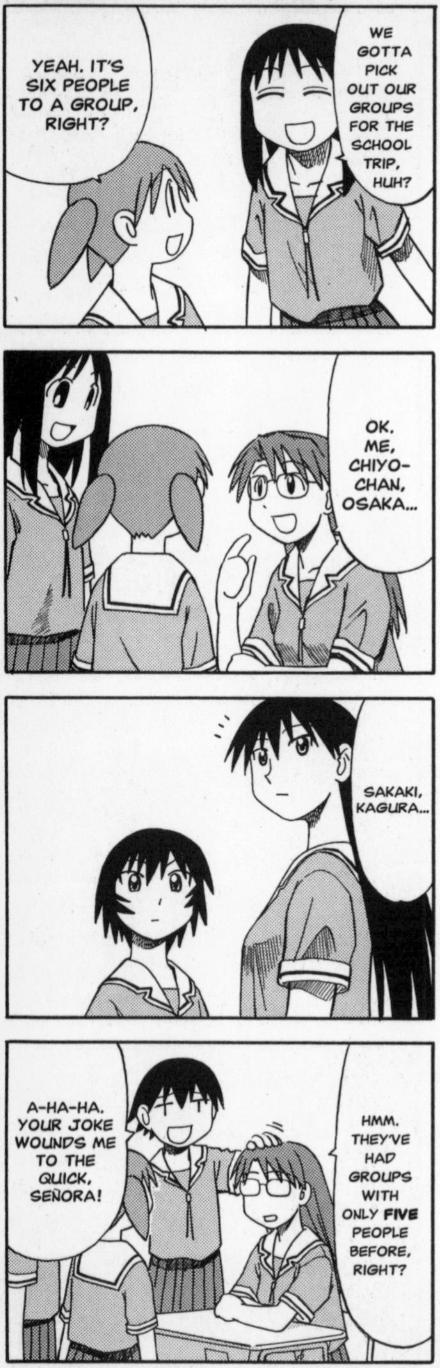
WE GOTTA PICK OUT OUR GROUPS FOR THE SCHOOL TRIP, HUH?
YEAH. IT'S SIX PEOPLE TO A GROUP, RIGHT?
OK. ME, CHIYO-CHAN, OSAKA...
SAKAKI, KAGURA...
HMM. THEY'VE HAD GROUPS WITH ONLY **FIVE** PEOPLE BEFORE, RIGHT?
A-HA-HA. YOUR JOKE WOUNDS ME TO THE QUICK, SEÑORA!

EXCITED

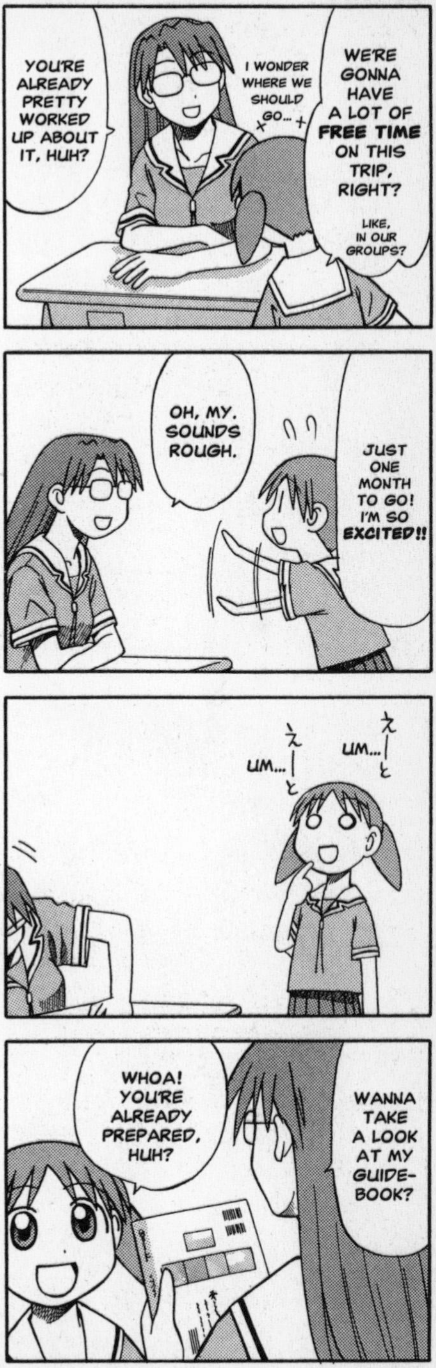
WE'RE GONNA HAVE A LOT OF FREE TIME ON THIS TRIP, RIGHT?
LIKE, IN OUR GROUPS?
I WONDER WHERE WE SHOULD GO...
YOU'RE ALREADY PRETTY WORKED UP ABOUT IT, HUH?
JUST ONE MONTH TO GO! I'M SO EXCITED!!
OH, MY. SOUNDS ROUGH.
えーと
UM...
えーと
UM...
WANNA TAKE A LOOK AT MY GUIDE-BOOK?
WHOA! YOU'RE ALREADY PREPARED, HUH?

TO BE CONTINUED

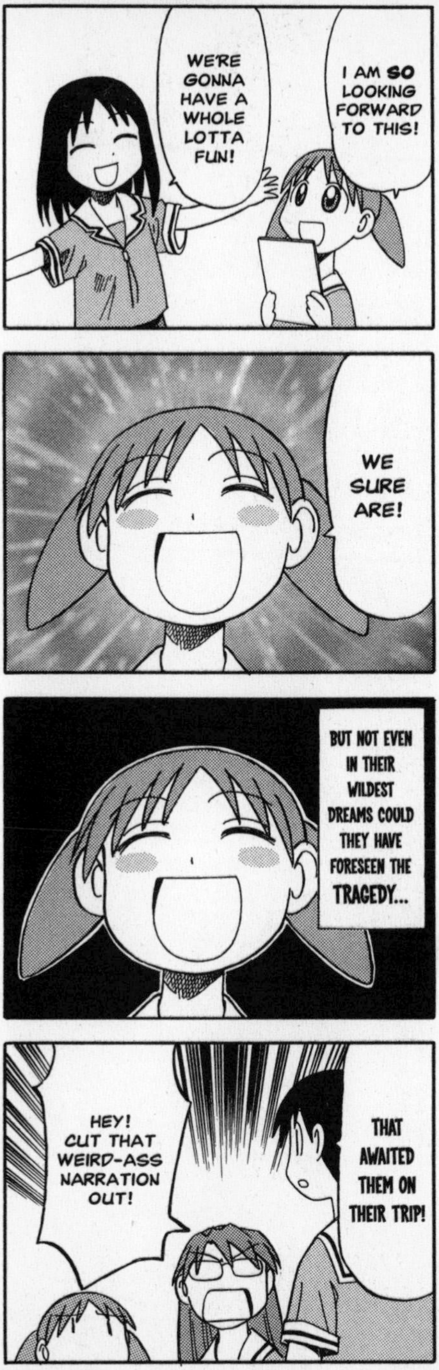
I AM SO LOOKING FORWARD TO THIS!
WE'RE GONNA HAVE A WHOLE LOTTA FUN!
WE SURE ARE!
BUT NOT EVEN IN THEIR WILDEST DREAMS COULD THEY HAVE FORESEEN THE TRAGEDY...
THAT AWAITED THEM ON THEIR TRIP!
HEY! CUT THAT WEIRD-ASS NARRATION OUT!

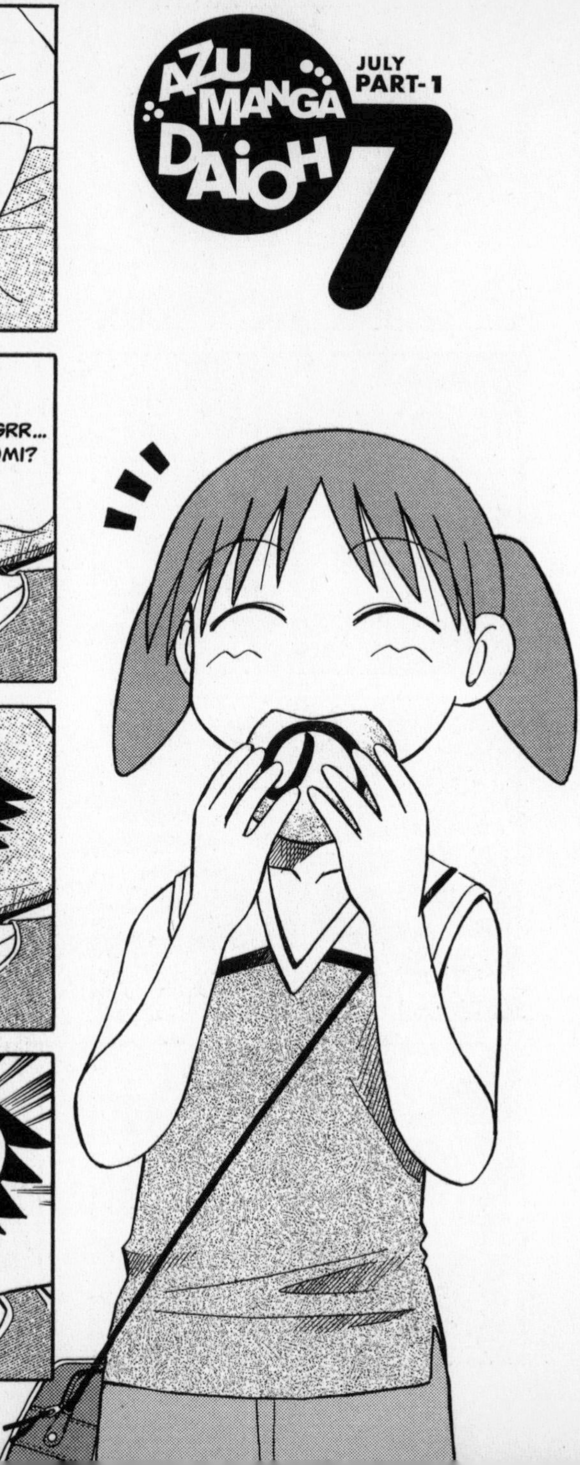
AZU MANGA DAIOH 7
JULY PART-1

THE WAKEUP CALL

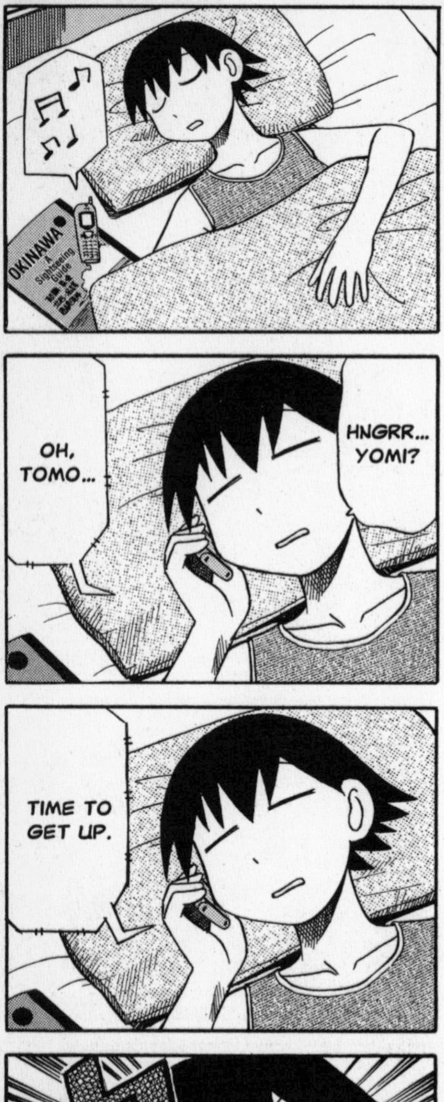
OKINAWA
HNGRR... YOMI?
OH, TOMO...
TIME TO GET UP.
HNGRAR!

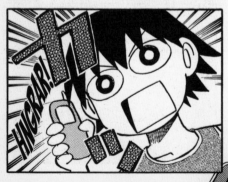

THE AIRPORT

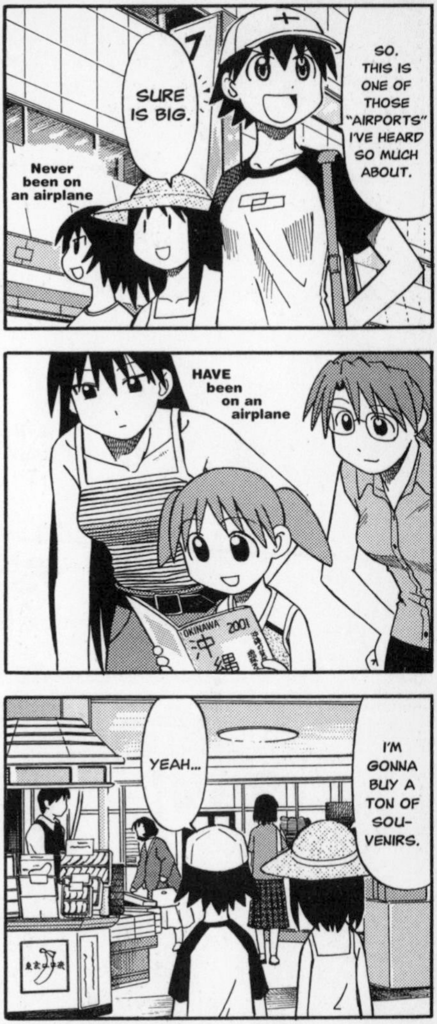
SO. THIS IS ONE OF THOSE "AIRPORTS" I'VE HEARD SO MUCH ABOUT.
SURE IS BIG.
Never been on an airplane
HAVE been on an airplane
OKINAWA 2001 沖縄
I'M GONNA BUY A TON OF SOU-VENIRS.
YEAH...
LOOK! MY FIRST AIRPORT SOU-VENIR!
WHOA, YOU BOUGHT ONE ALREADY?!

GO!

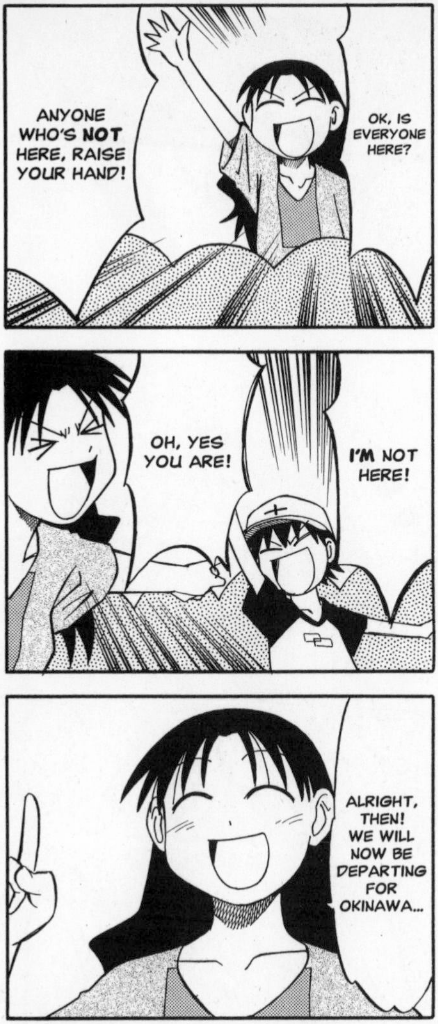
OK, IS EVERYONE HERE?
ANYONE WHO'S **NOT** HERE, RAISE YOUR HAND!
I'M NOT HERE!
OH, YES YOU ARE!
ALRIGHT, THEN! WE WILL NOW BE DEPARTING FOR OKINAWA...
AND UNTIL WE ARRIVE BACK AT OUR HOMES, WE ARE **OFFICIALLY** ON VACATION!
SOME-BODY'S CARRIED AWAY...
ALREADY?!

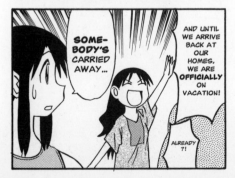

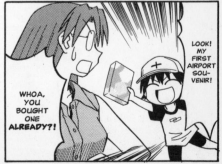

TO THE SKIES

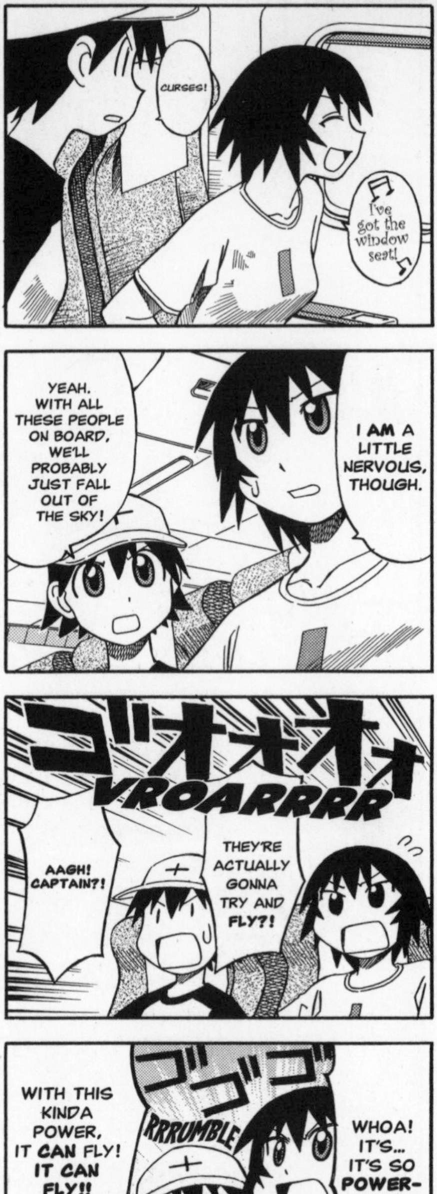
I've got the window seat!
CURSES!
I AM A LITTLE NERVOUS, THOUGH.
YEAH. WITH ALL THESE PEOPLE ON BOARD, WE'LL PROBABLY JUST FALL OUT OF THE SKY!
ゴオオオォ
VROARRRR
THEY'RE ACTUALLY GONNA TRY AND FLY?!
AAGH! CAPTAIN?!
ゴゴゴ
RRRUMBLE
WHOA! IT'S... IT'S SO POWER-FUL!
WITH THIS KINDA POWER, IT CAN FLY! IT CAN FLY!!
WILL YOU TWO SHUT UP?

GREAT

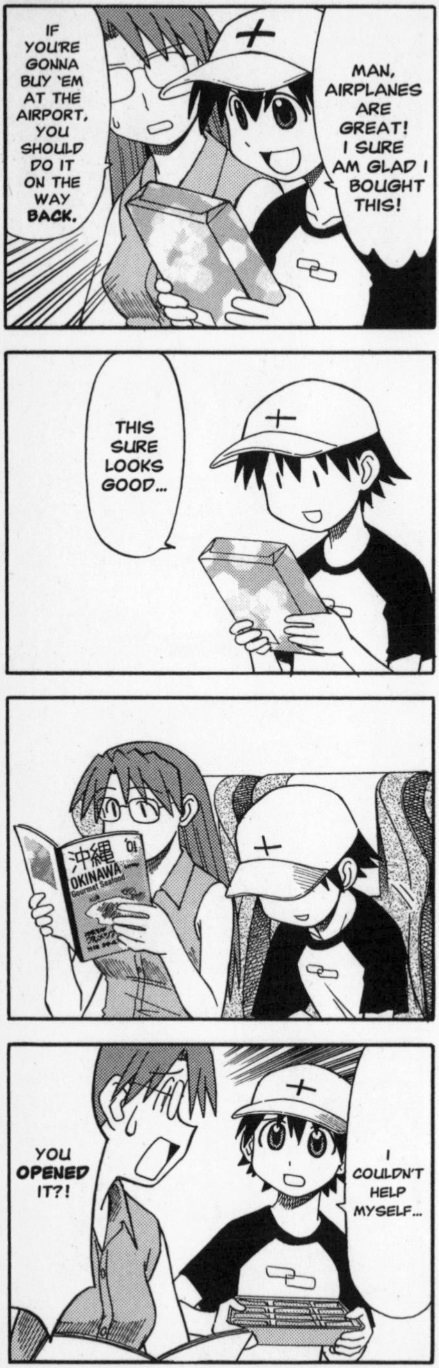
MAN, AIRPLANES ARE GREAT! I SURE AM GLAD I BOUGHT THIS!
IF YOU'RE GONNA BUY 'EM AT THE AIRPORT, YOU SHOULD DO IT ON THE WAY BACK.
THIS SURE LOOKS GOOD...
沖縄
OKINAWA
Gourmet Seafood
I COULDN'T HELP MYSELF...
YOU OPENED IT?!

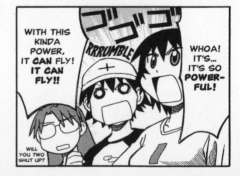

BURSTING WITH EXCITEMENT

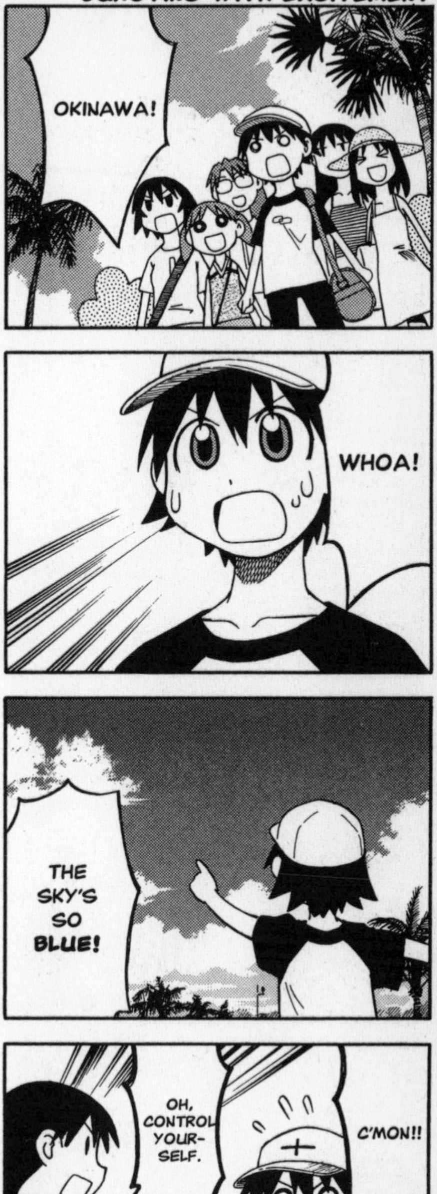
OKINAWA!
WHOA!
THE SKY'S SO **BLUE!**
C'MON!!
OH, CONTROL YOURSELF.

DONE HER HOMEWORK

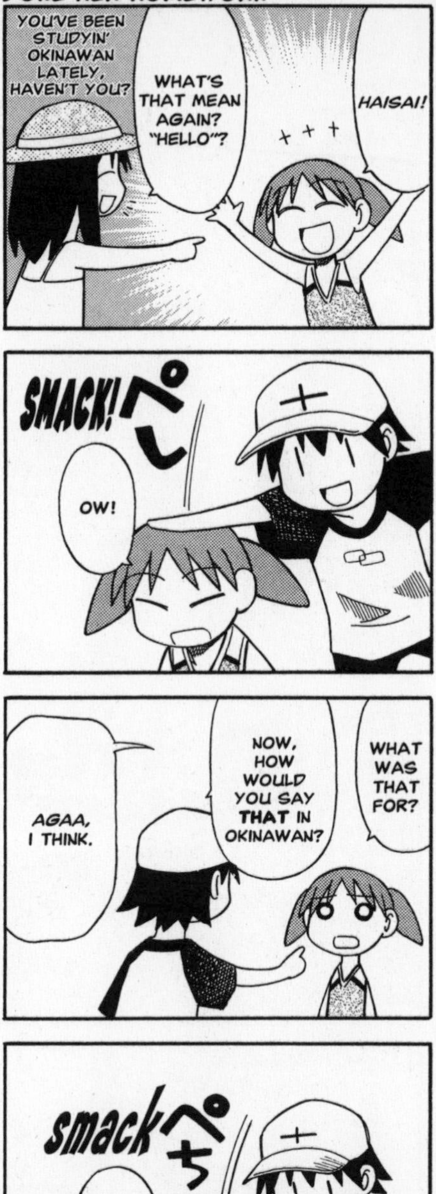
HAISAI!
WHAT'S THAT MEAN AGAIN? "HELLO"?
YOU'VE BEEN STUDYIN' OKINAWAN LATELY, HAVEN'T YOU?
SMACK! ぺし
OW!
WHAT WAS THAT FOR?
NOW, HOW WOULD YOU SAY **THAT** IN OKINAWAN?
AGAA, I THINK.
smack ぺち
OW!

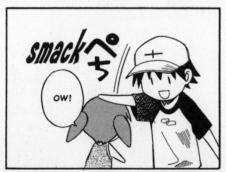

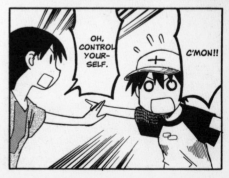

SHURI CASTLE

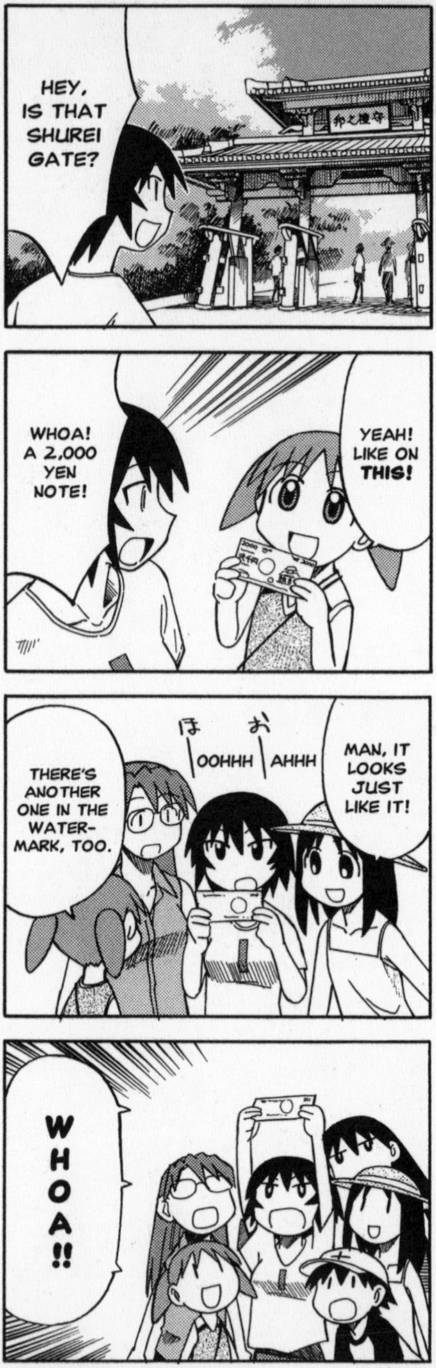
HEY, IS THAT SHUREI GATE?
YEAH! LIKE ON THIS!
WHOA! A 2,000 YEN NOTE!
MAN, IT LOOKS JUST LIKE IT!
お AHHH
ほ OOHHH
THERE'S ANOTHER ONE IN THE WATER-MARK, TOO.
WHOA!!

IT'S A *SHISA*

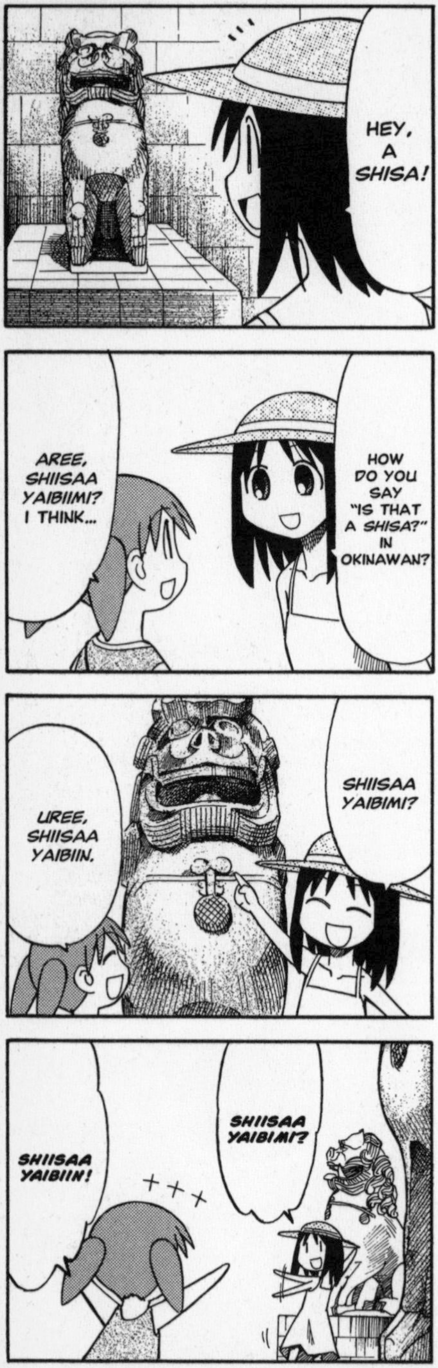
HEY, A *SHISA*!
HOW DO YOU SAY "IS THAT A *SHISA*?" IN OKINAWAN?
AREE, SHIISAA YAIBIIMI? I THINK...
SHIISAA YAIBIMI?
UREE, SHIISAA YAIBIIN.
SHIISAA YAIBIMI!?
SHIISAA YAIBIIN!

IT'S NOT A *SHISA*

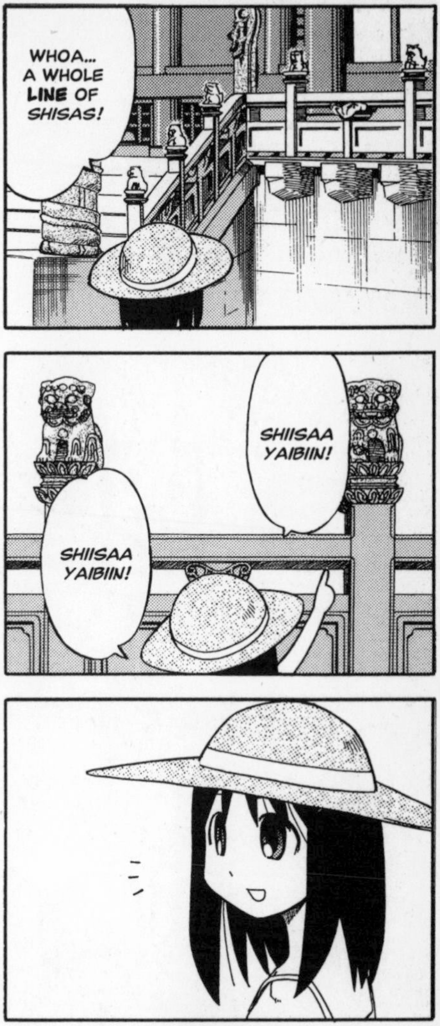
WHOA... A WHOLE LINE OF SHISAS!
SHIISAA YAIBIIN!
SHIISAA YAIBIIN!
?
SHIISAA YAIBIIMI?
AREE, SHIISAA AIBIRAN!

CHA

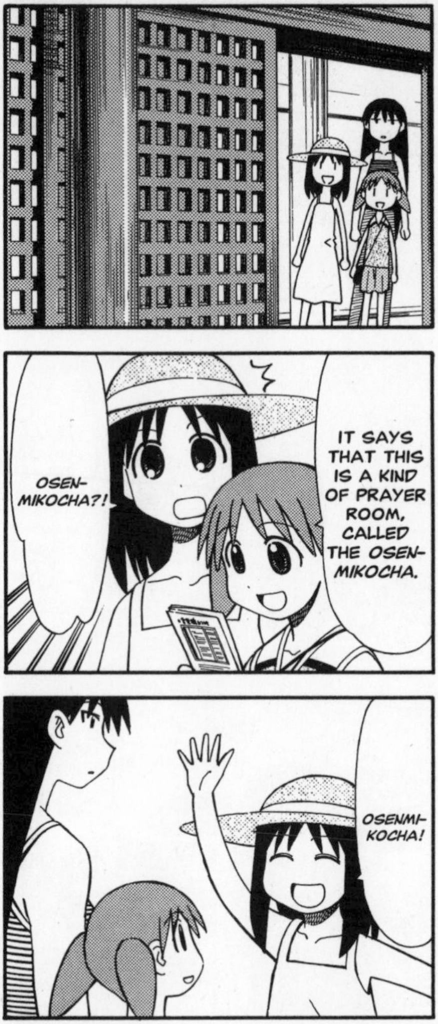
IT SAYS THAT THIS IS A KIND OF PRAYER ROOM, CALLED THE OSEN-MIKOCHA.
OSEN-MIKOCHA?!
OSENMI-KOCHA!
AHA HAHA!
BWA HAHAHA!
?

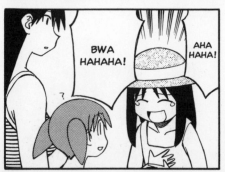

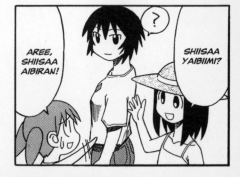

FUNNYBONE

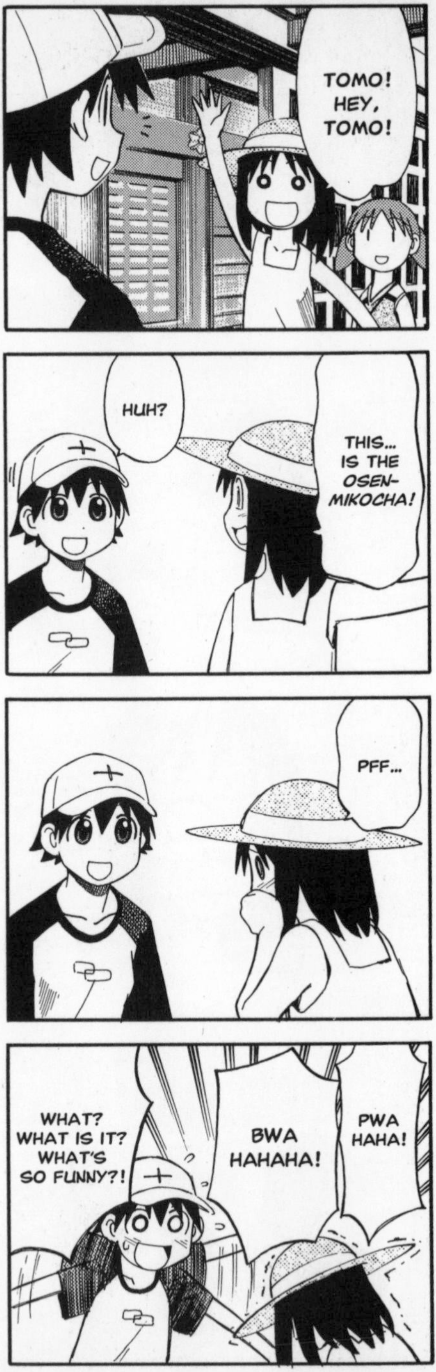
TOMO! HEY, TOMO!
THIS... IS THE OSEN-MIKOCHA!
HUH?
PFF...
PWA HAHA!
BWA HAHAHA!
WHAT? WHAT IS IT? WHAT'S SO FUNNY?!

ALL YOU CAN EAT

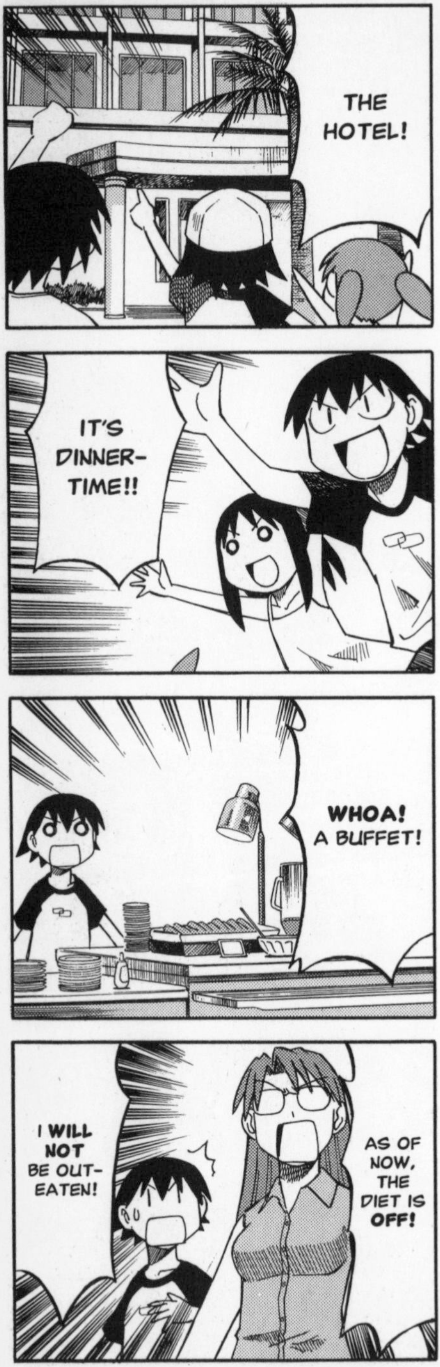
THE HOTEL!
IT'S DINNER-TIME!!
WHOA! A BUFFET!
AS OF NOW, THE DIET IS OFF!
I WILL NOT BE OUT-EATEN!

CHAMPURU

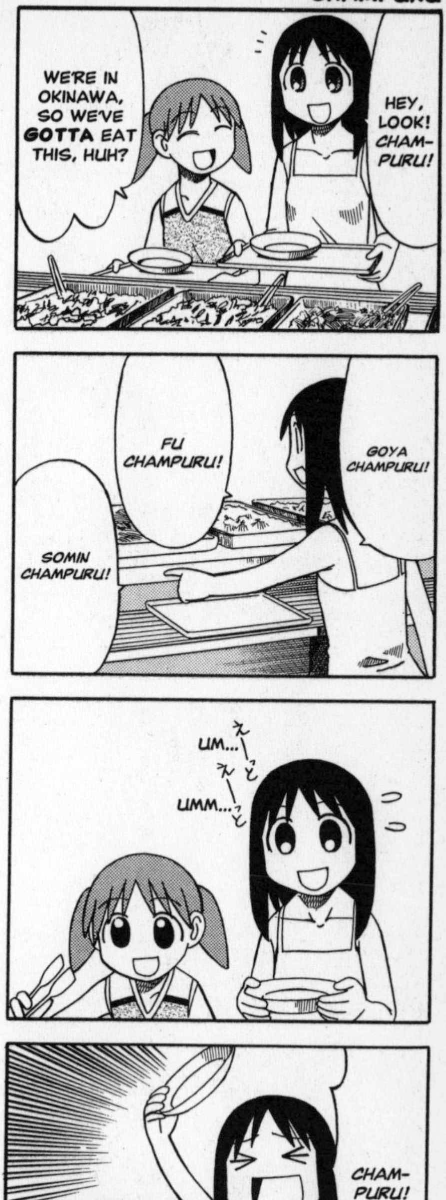
HEY, LOOK! CHAM-PURU!
WE'RE IN OKINAWA, SO WE'VE **GOTTA** EAT THIS, HUH?
GOYA CHAMPURU!
FU CHAMPURU!
SOMIN CHAMPURU!
えーと
UM...
えーっと
UMM...
CHAM-PURU!

STUFFED TO THE GILLS

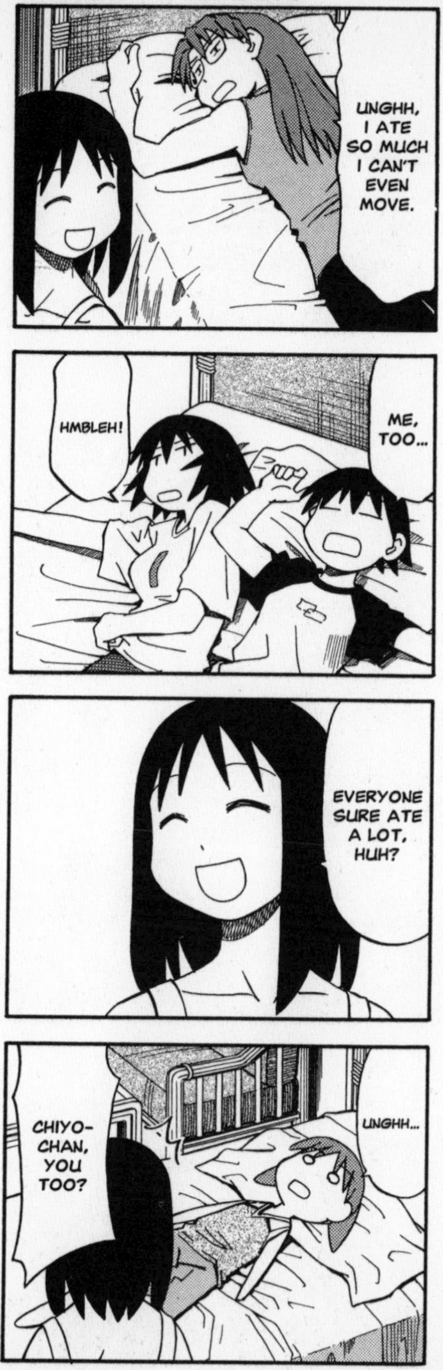
UNGHH, I ATE SO MUCH I CAN'T EVEN MOVE.
ME, TOO...
HMBLEH!
EVERYONE SURE ATE A LOT, HUH?
UNGHH...
CHIYO-CHAN, YOU TOO?

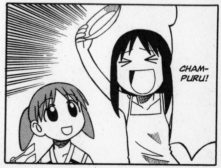

THE ELEPHANT

Man-
zamo
CLIFF! C... CLIFF!
SO... SCARY.
HEY CHIYO-CHAN!
YOU'RE SO TALL! YOU'RE SO TALL!
HNGYAHHH!

DAVY JONES' LOCKER

NEXT UP,
OUR TRIAL DIVING LESSON!
FOR THIS ACTIVITY, I'LL BE PARTICIPATING ALONG WITH YOUR GROUP.
お OH...
IT'S TOTALLY OUR FIRST TIME DIVING! IT'LL TOTALLY BE A LOT OF FUN!
RIGHT?!
ACTUALLY, UM, I'VE BEEN DIVING BEFORE...
YOU LITTLE RUNT! INTO THE OCEAN YOU GO!
AIII!

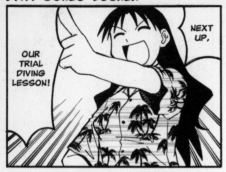

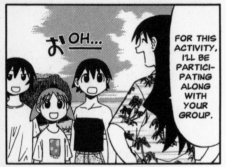

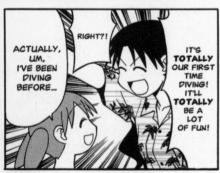

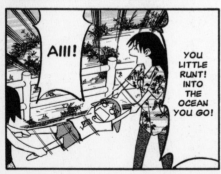

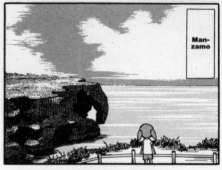

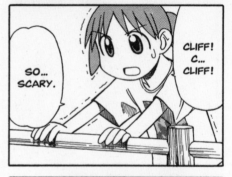

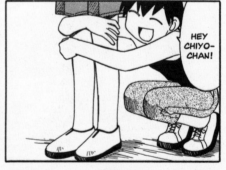

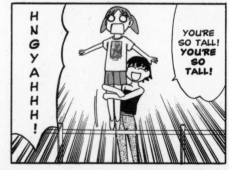

THE FRUIT OF THE SEA

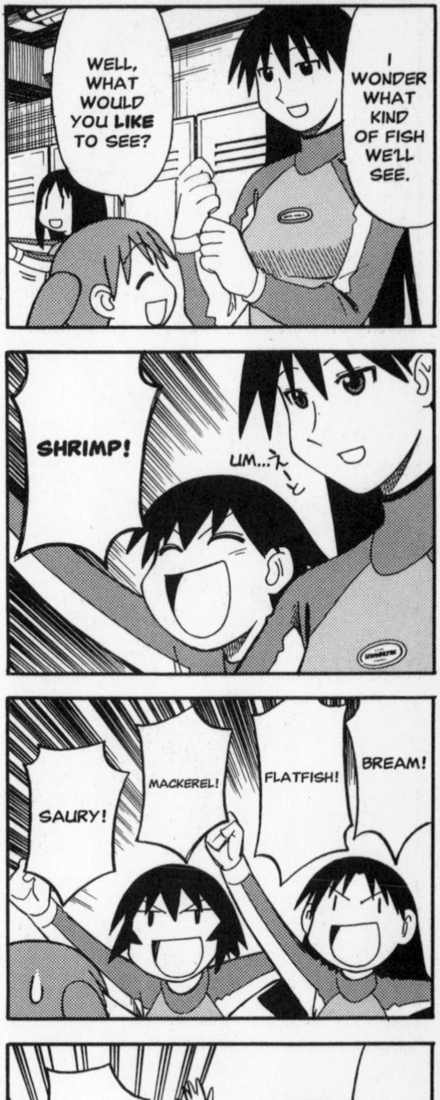

I WONDER WHAT KIND OF FISH WE'LL SEE.
WELL, WHAT WOULD YOU LIKE TO SEE?
UM...
SHRIMP!
BREAM!
FLATFISH!
MACKEREL!
SAURY!
SALMON ROE!
WHA-?

GOT 'EM!

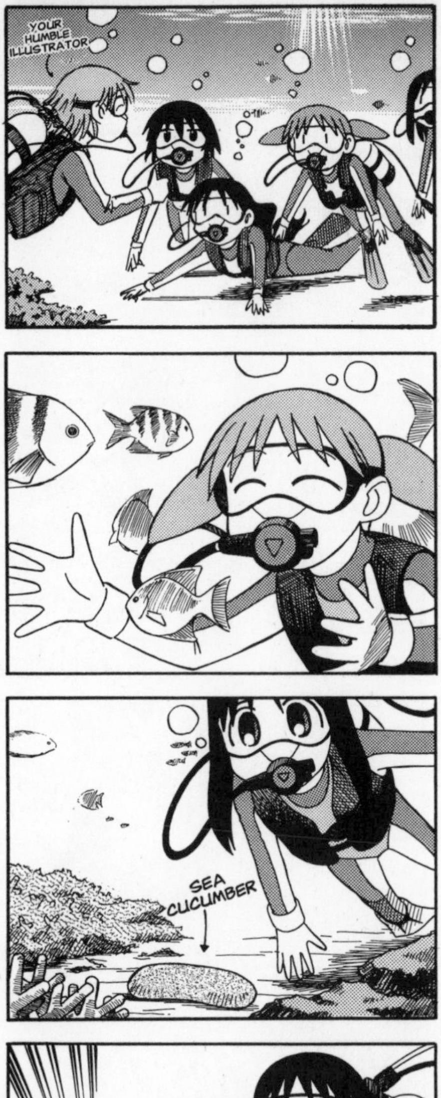

YOUR HUMBLE ILLUSTRATOR
SEA CUCUMBER

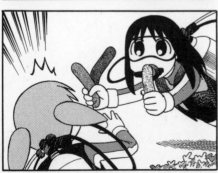

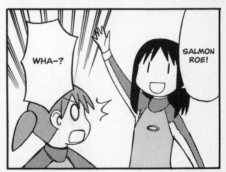

CHIYO-CHAN CAN EAT IT, TOO

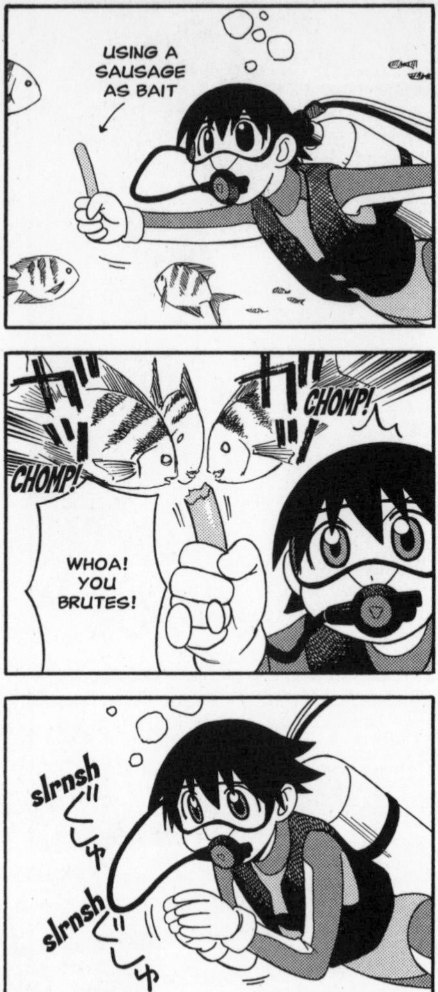
USING A SAUSAGE AS BAIT
CHOMP!
CHOMP!
WHOA! YOU BRUTES!
slrnsh
slrnsh
bwsh!

TOTALLY

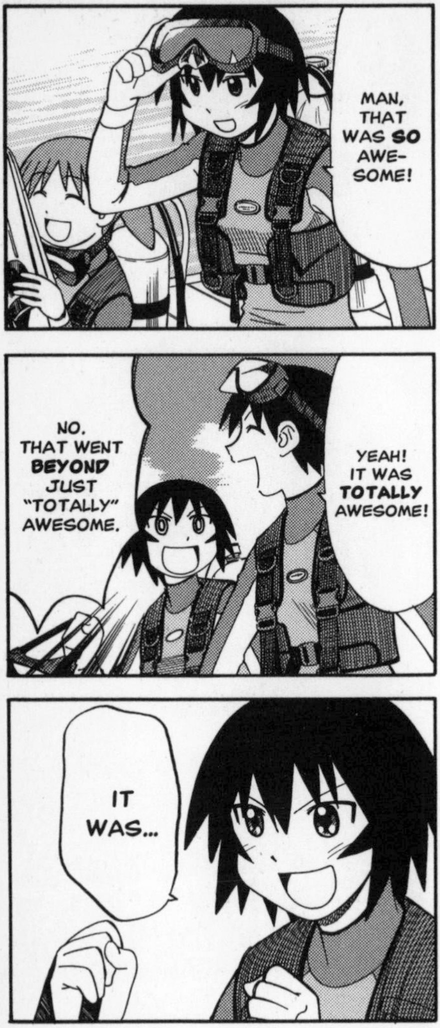
MAN, THAT WAS **SO** AWE-SOME!
YEAH! IT WAS **TOTALLY** AWESOME!
NO. THAT WENT **BEYOND** JUST "TOTALLY" AWESOME.
IT WAS...
SO...
SO AWESOME!

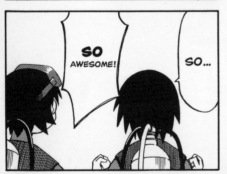

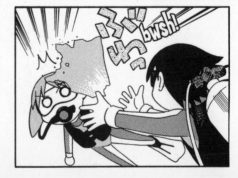

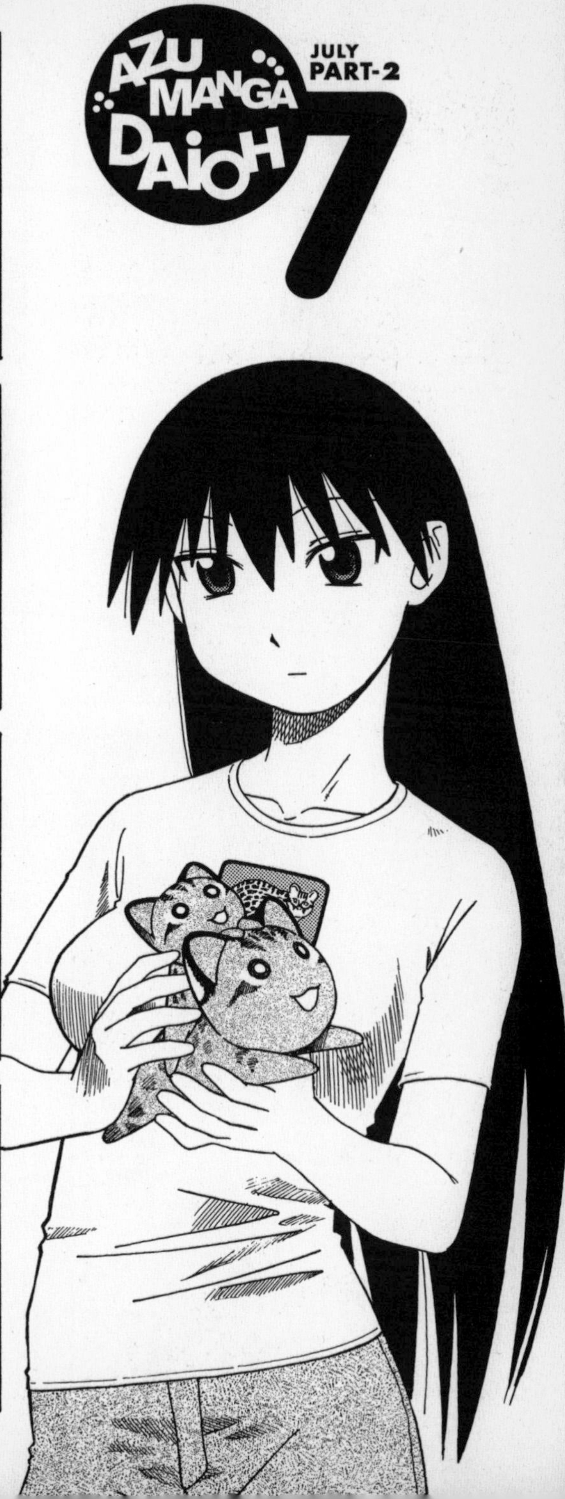
AZUMANGA DAIOH
JULY PART-2
7

BUY THIS!

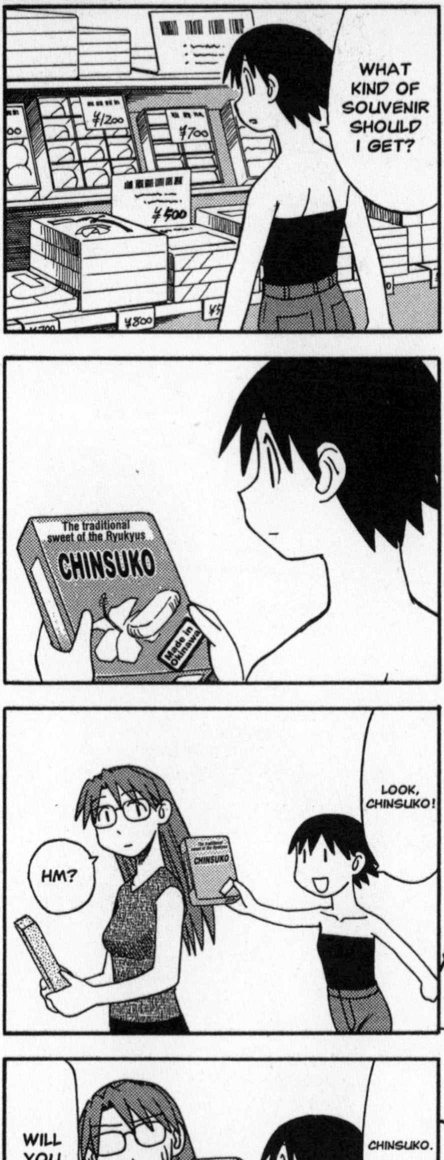
WHAT KIND OF SOUVENIR SHOULD I GET?
The traditional sweet of the Ryukyus
CHINSUKO
Made in Okinawa
LOOK, CHINSUKO!
HM?
CHINSUKO.
CHINSUKO!
WILL YOU SHUT UP?

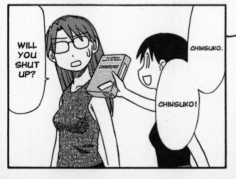

THAT'S THE BEST ONE

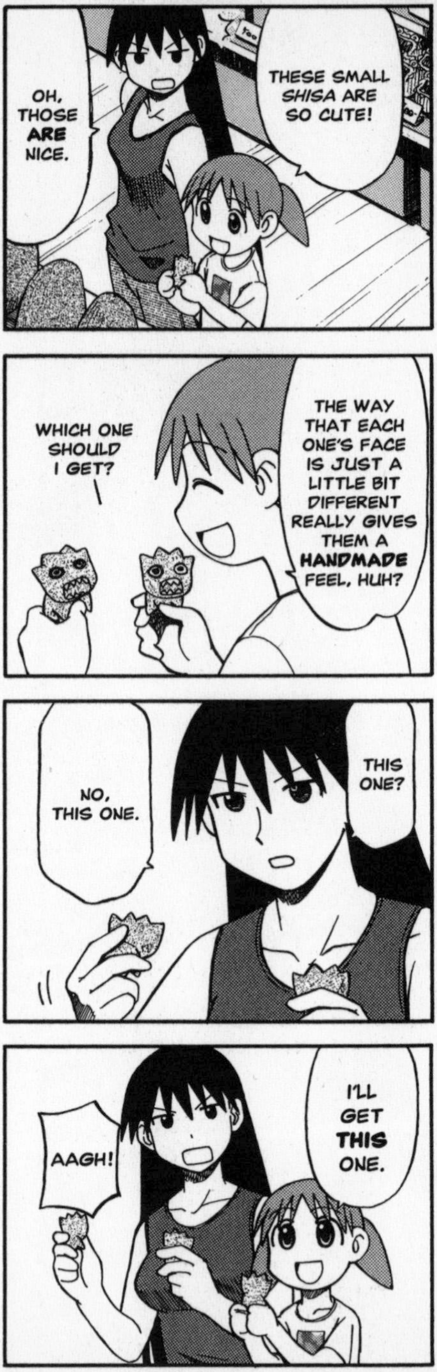
THESE SMALL SHISA ARE SO CUTE!
OH, THOSE **ARE** NICE.
THE WAY THAT EACH ONE'S FACE IS JUST A LITTLE BIT DIFFERENT REALLY GIVES THEM A **HANDMADE** FEEL, HUH?
WHICH ONE SHOULD I GET?
THIS ONE?
NO, THIS ONE.
I'LL GET **THIS** ONE.
AAGH!

DONUTS

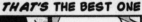

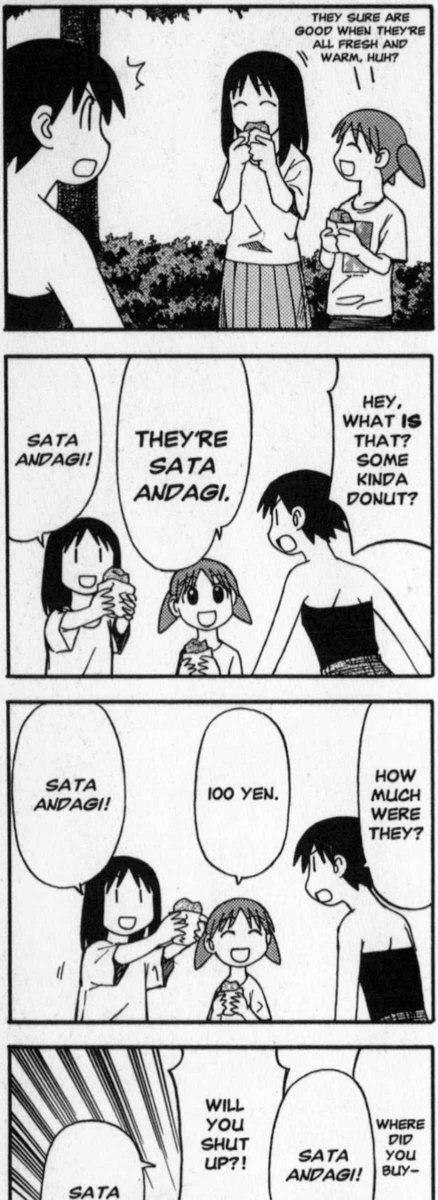
THEY SURE ARE GOOD WHEN THEY'RE ALL FRESH AND WARM, HUH?
HEY, WHAT **IS** THAT? SOME KINDA DONUT?
THEY'RE SATA ANDAGI.
SATA ANDAGI!
HOW MUCH WERE THEY?
100 YEN.
SATA ANDAGI!
WHERE DID YOU BUY-
SATA ANDAGI!
WILL YOU SHUT UP?!
SATA ANDAGI!!

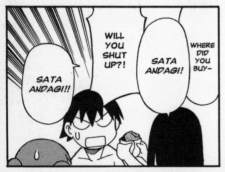

THE ISLAND OF DREAMS

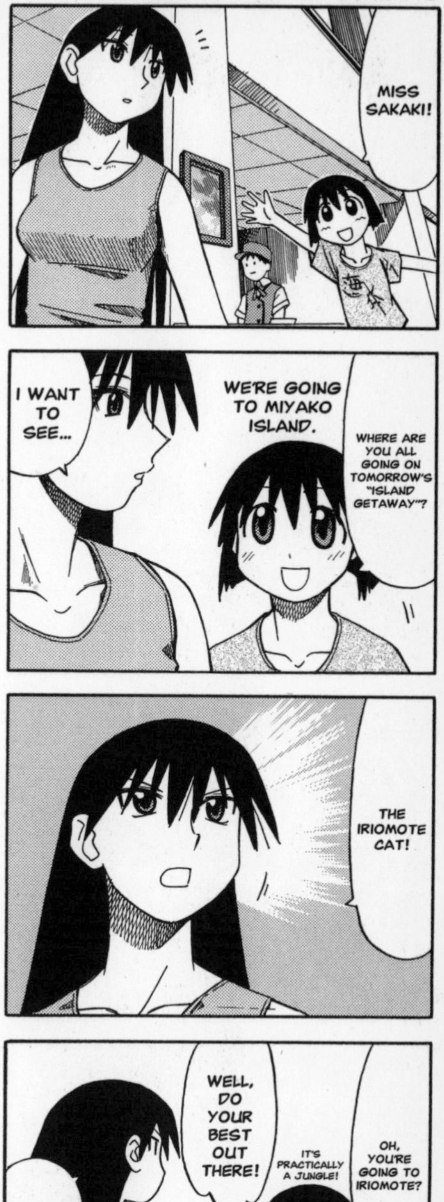
MISS SAKAKI!
WHERE ARE YOU ALL GOING ON TOMORROW'S "ISLAND GETAWAY"?
WE'RE GOING TO MIYAKO ISLAND.
I WANT TO SEE...
THE IRIOMOTE CAT!
OH, YOU'RE GOING TO IRIOMOTE?
IT'S PRACTICALLY A JUNGLE!
WELL, DO YOUR BEST OUT THERE!
OH, I WILL!

TWINS

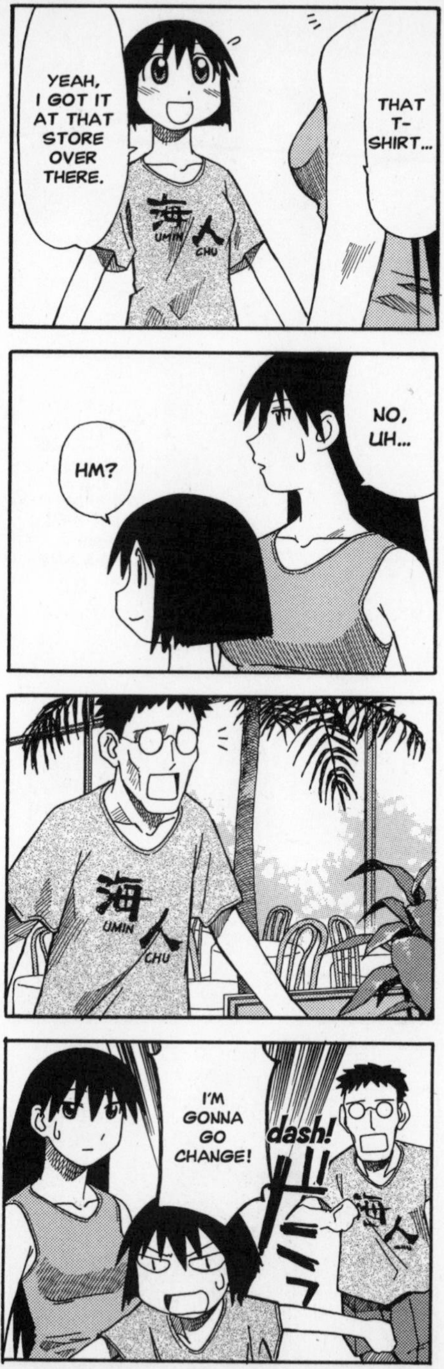
THAT T-SHIRT...
YEAH, I GOT IT AT THAT STORE OVER THERE.
海人
UMIN
CHU
NO, UH...
HM?
海人
UMIN
CHU
dash!
I'M GONNA GO CHANGE!

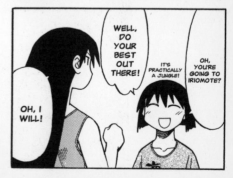

THE UNDISCOVERED COUNTRY

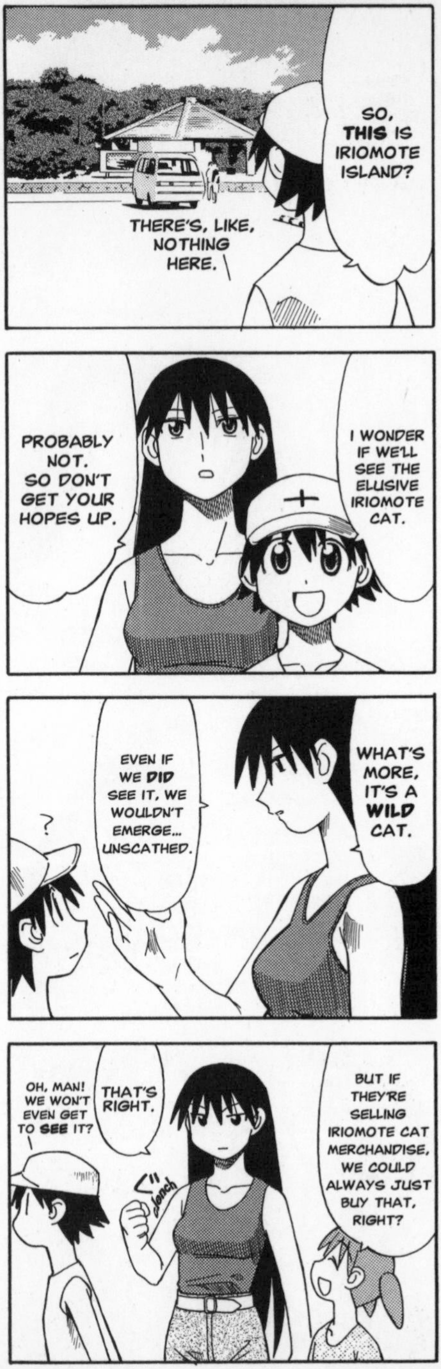
SO, THIS IS IRIOMOTE ISLAND?
THERE'S, LIKE, NOTHING HERE.
I WONDER IF WE'LL SEE THE ELUSIVE IRIOMOTE CAT.
PROBABLY NOT. SO DON'T GET YOUR HOPES UP.
WHAT'S MORE, IT'S A WILD CAT.
EVEN IF WE DID SEE IT, WE WOULDN'T EMERGE... UNSCATHED.
?
BUT IF THEY'RE SELLING IRIOMOTE CAT MERCHANDISE, WE COULD ALWAYS JUST BUY THAT, RIGHT?
clench
THAT'S RIGHT.
OH, MAN! WE WON'T EVEN GET TO SEE IT?

DESTINY

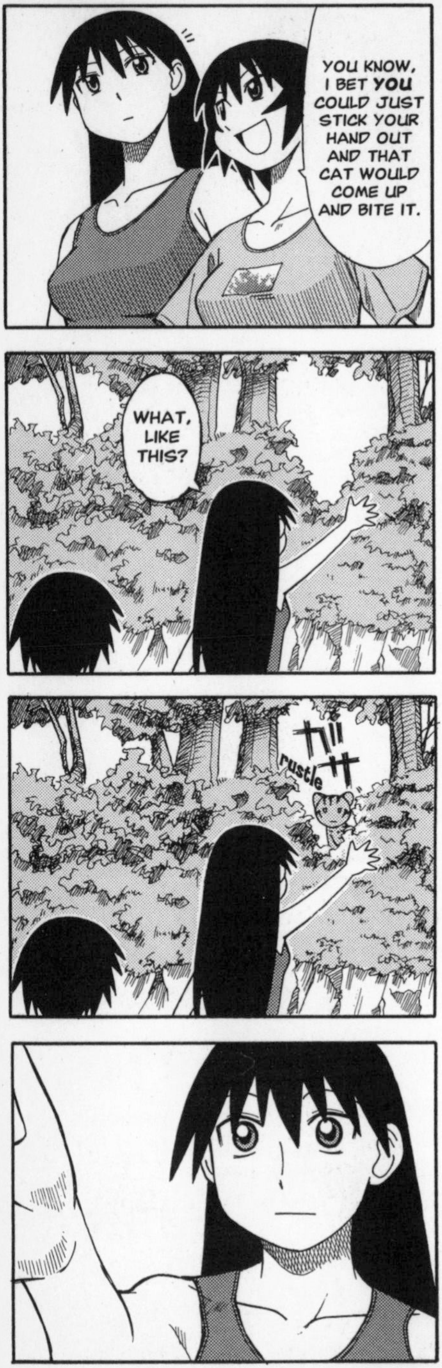
YOU KNOW, I BET YOU COULD JUST STICK YOUR HAND OUT AND THAT CAT WOULD COME UP AND BITE IT.
WHAT, LIKE THIS?
rustle

A SHINING RAY OF LIGHT

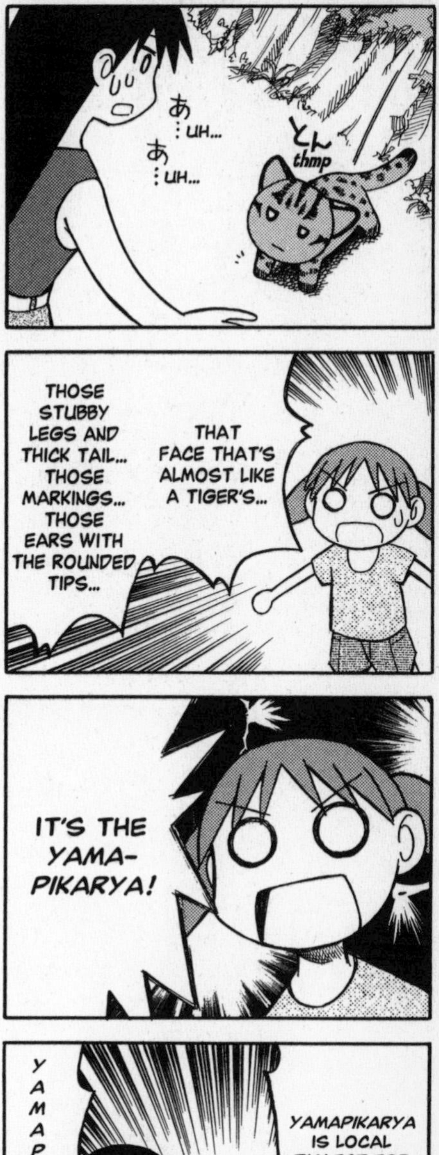
あ…UH...
あ…UH...
とん thmp
THAT FACE THAT'S ALMOST LIKE A TIGER'S...
THOSE STUBBY LEGS AND THICK TAIL... THOSE MARKINGS... THOSE EARS WITH THE ROUNDED TIPS...
IT'S THE YAMA-PIKARYA!
YAMAPIKARYA IS LOCAL DIALECT FOR "IRIOMOTE CAT."
YAMAPIKARYA!!

FRIEND

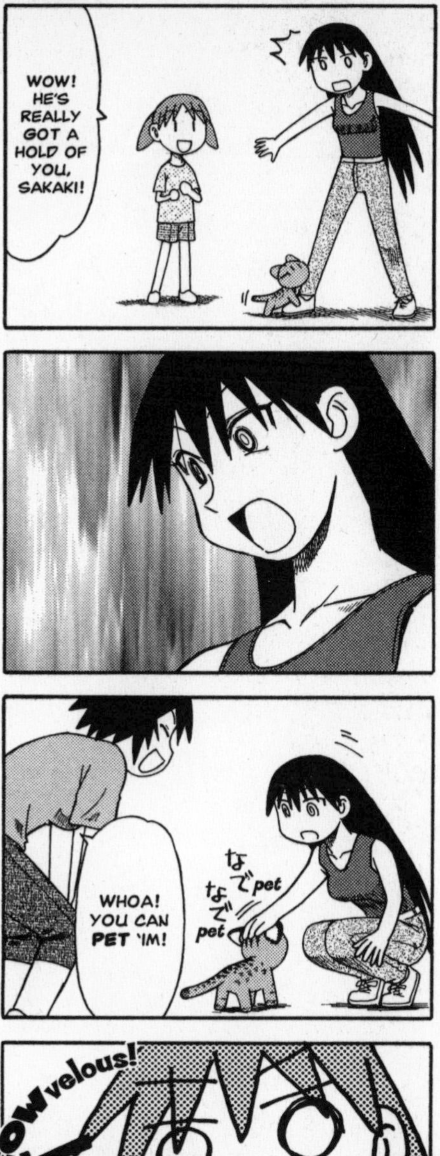
WOW! HE'S REALLY GOT A HOLD OF YOU, SAKAKI!
なで pet
なで pet
WHOA! YOU CAN PET 'IM!
にゃーとぴ
MEOWvelous!

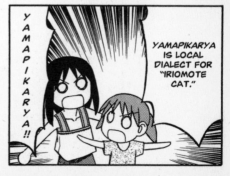

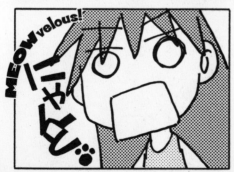

THE CAT THAT LIVES IN THE MOUNTAINS

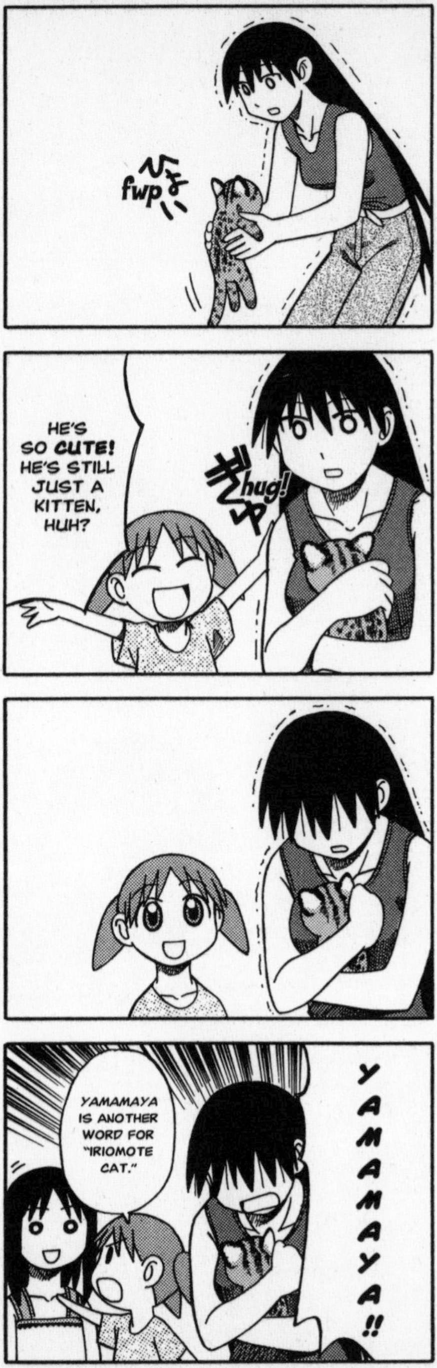
ひょい
fwp
HE'S SO CUTE! HE'S STILL JUST A KITTEN, HUH?
ぎゅ
hug!
YAMAMAYA!!
YAMAMAYA IS ANOTHER WORD FOR "IRIOMOTE CAT."

THE SIGHTS WE SAW TOGETHER

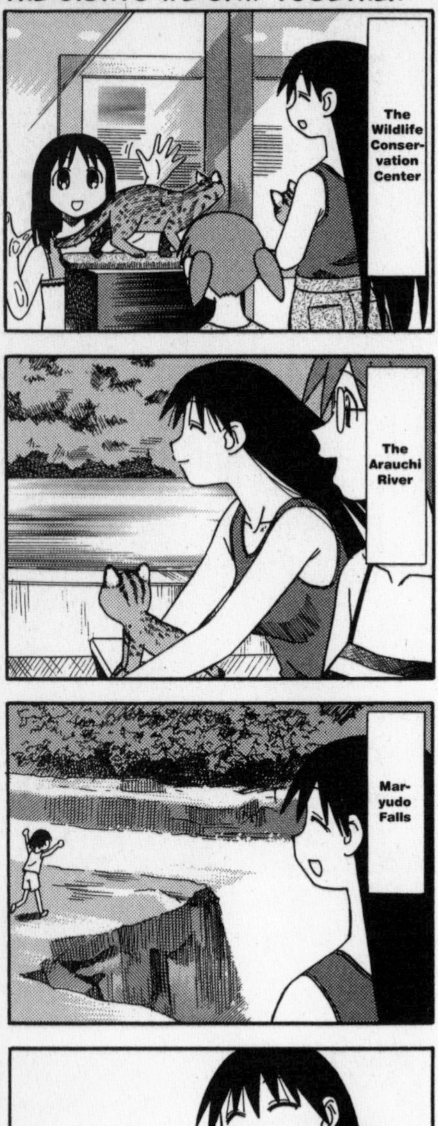
The Wildlife Conservation Center
The Arauchi River
Maryudo Falls

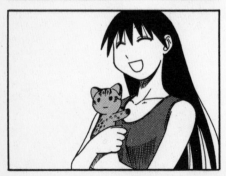

LIVE IN THE WILD!

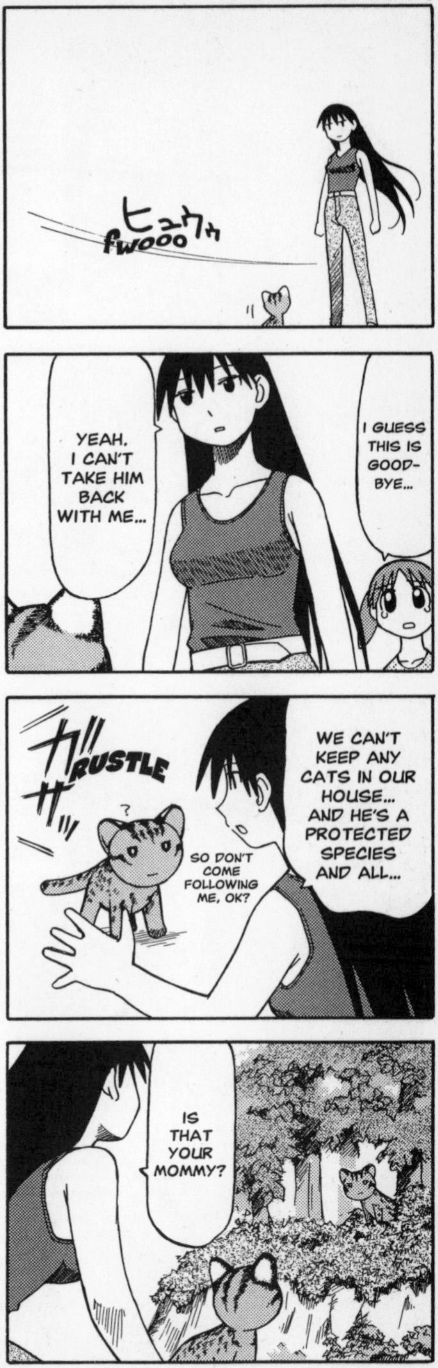
ヒュウゥ
fwooo
I GUESS THIS IS GOOD-BYE...
YEAH. I CAN'T TAKE HIM BACK WITH ME...
WE CAN'T KEEP ANY CATS IN OUR HOUSE... AND HE'S A PROTECTED SPECIES AND ALL...
ガサッ
RUSTLE
?
SO DON'T COME FOLLOWING ME, OK?
IS THAT YOUR MOMMY?

GOODBYE

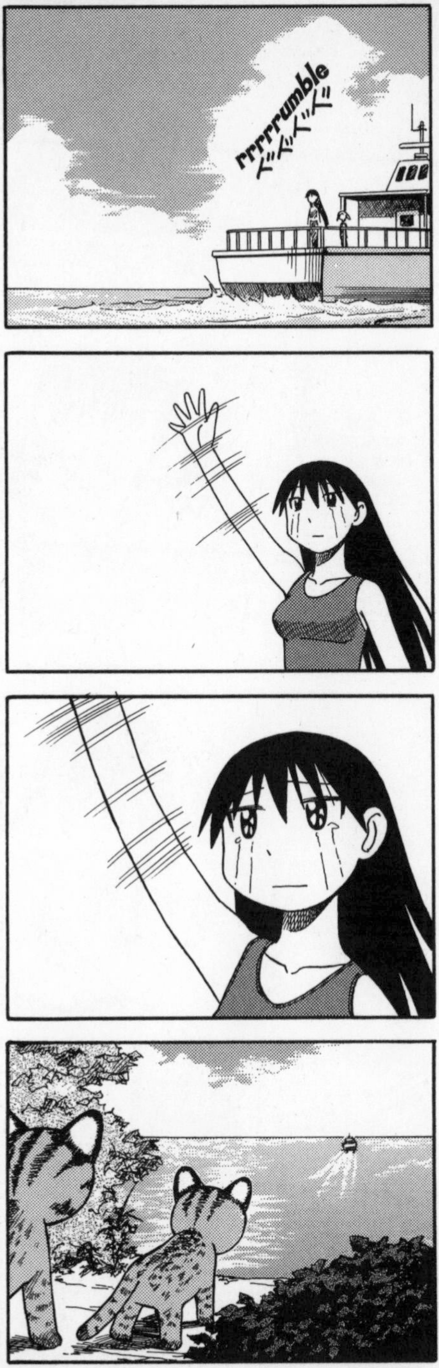
rrrrrumble

THE BEACH AND THE WATERMELON

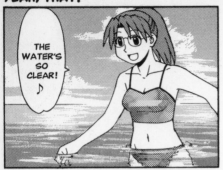

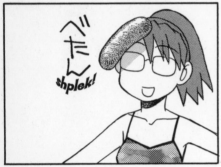

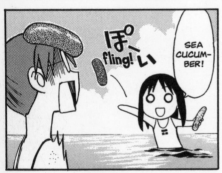

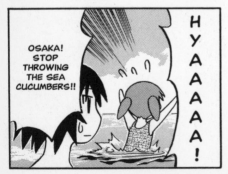

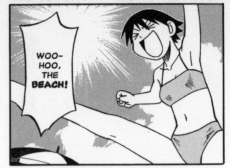

WOO-HOO, THE **BEACH!**
IT'S WATER-MELON-SPLITTING TIME!
WE DIDN'T BRING ONE.
WHAAT?!
WELL, ISN'T THERE **ANYTHING** WE CAN SPLIT?
A PINEAPPLE? THERE ARE PINEAPPLES HERE, RIGHT?!
WHY IS SHE SO DETERMINED TO SPLIT SOMETHING?
BEATS ME.

YEAH, THAT!

THE WATER'S SO CLEAR! ♪
べたん
shplek!
SEA CUCUMBER!
ぽ〜い
fling!
HYAAAAAA!
OSAKA! STOP THROWING THE SEA CUCUMBERS!!

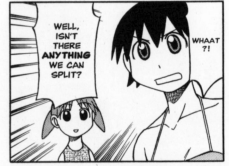

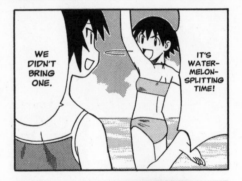

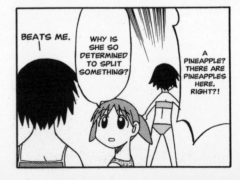

THE SOUVENIR

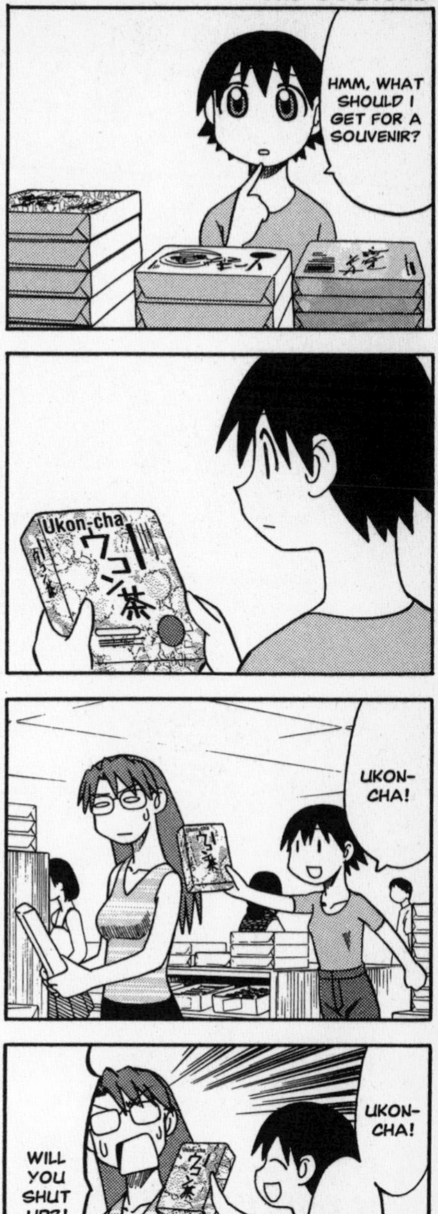
HMM, WHAT SHOULD I GET FOR A SOUVENIR?
Ukon-cha
ウコン茶
UKON-CHA!
UKON-CHA!
WILL YOU SHUT UP?!
UKON-CHA!

OKINAWA

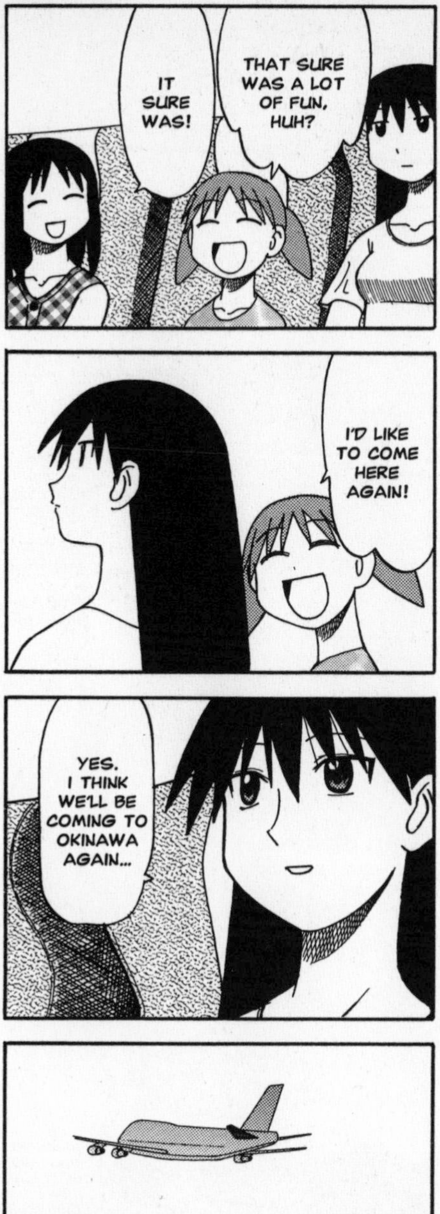
THAT SURE WAS A LOT OF FUN, HUH?
IT SURE WAS!
I'D LIKE TO COME HERE AGAIN!
YES. I THINK WE'LL BE COMING TO OKINAWA AGAIN...

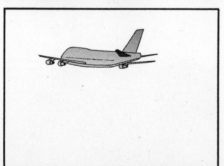

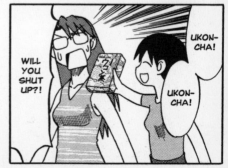

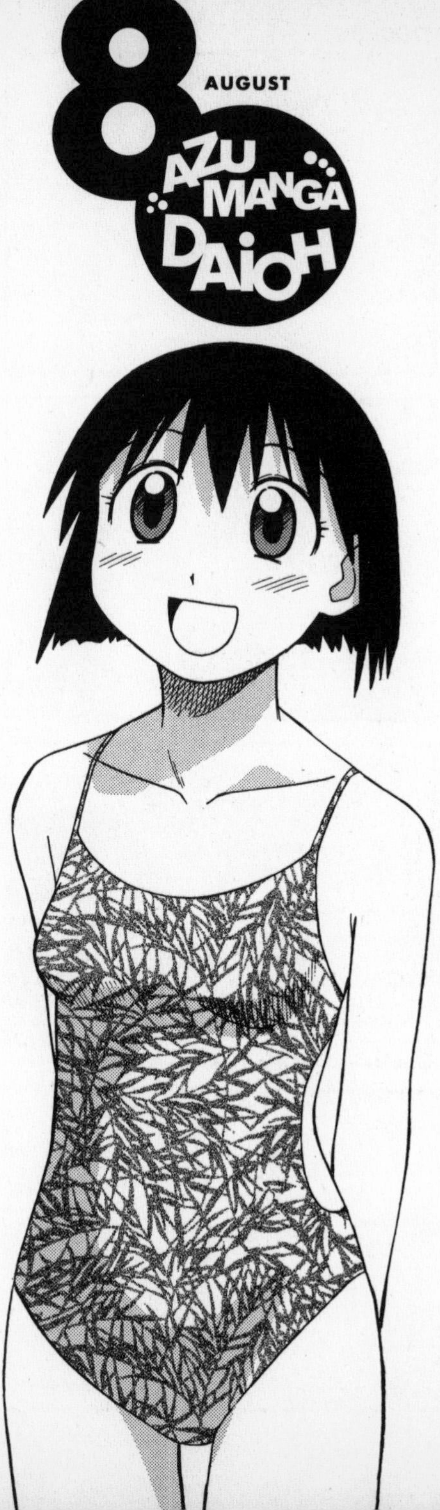
8
AUGUST
AZU MANGA DAIOH

NICE!

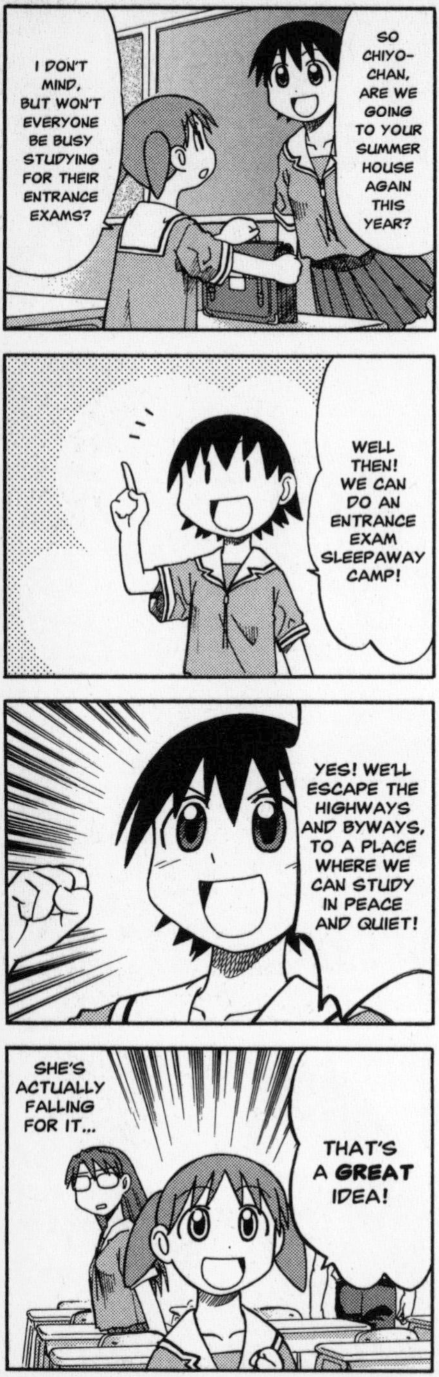
SO CHIYO-CHAN, ARE WE GOING TO YOUR SUMMER HOUSE AGAIN THIS YEAR?
I DON'T MIND, BUT WON'T EVERYONE BE BUSY STUDYING FOR THEIR ENTRANCE EXAMS?
WELL THEN! WE CAN DO AN ENTRANCE EXAM SLEEPAWAY CAMP!
YES! WE'LL ESCAPE THE HIGHWAYS AND BYWAYS, TO A PLACE WHERE WE CAN STUDY IN PEACE AND QUIET!
THAT'S A **GREAT** IDEA!
SHE'S ACTUALLY FALLING FOR IT...

THANK YOU

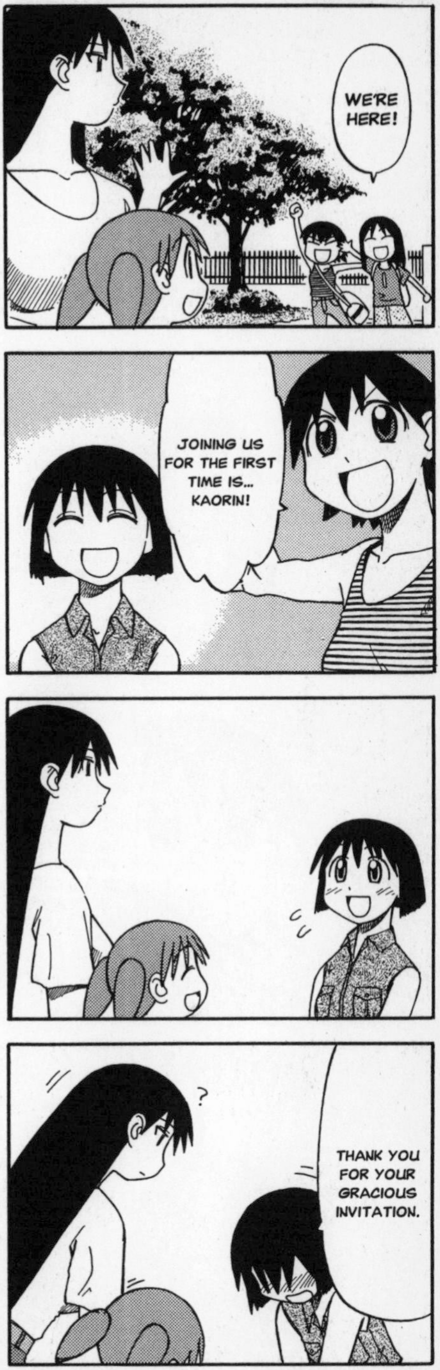
WE'RE HERE!
JOINING US FOR THE FIRST TIME IS... KAORIN!
THANK YOU FOR YOUR GRACIOUS INVITATION.

THIS ONE

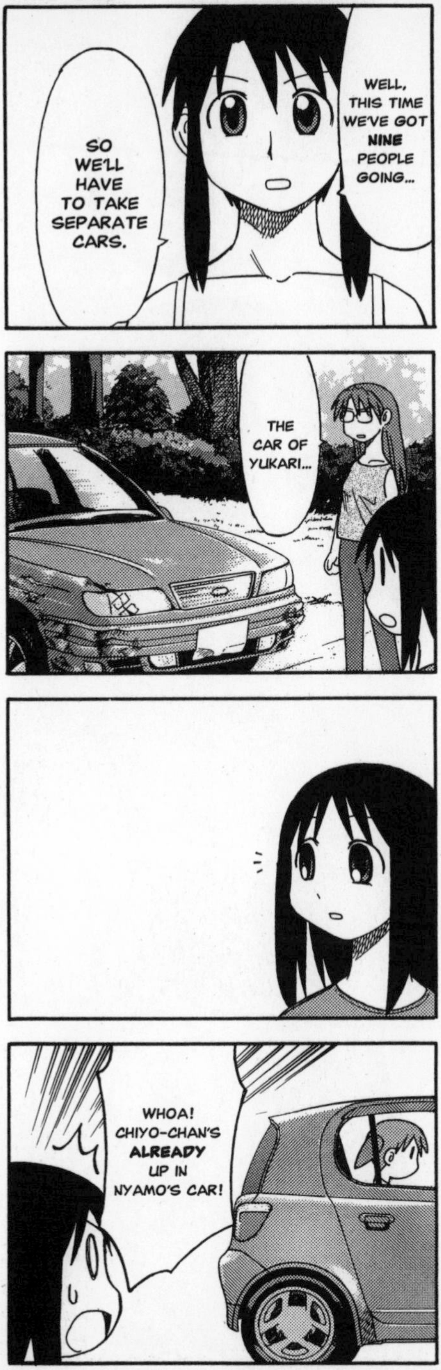
WELL, THIS TIME WE'VE GOT NINE PEOPLE GOING...
SO WE'LL HAVE TO TAKE SEPARATE CARS.
THE CAR OF YUKARI...
WHOA! CHIYO-CHAN'S ALREADY UP IN NYAMO'S CAR!

TO THE BITTER END

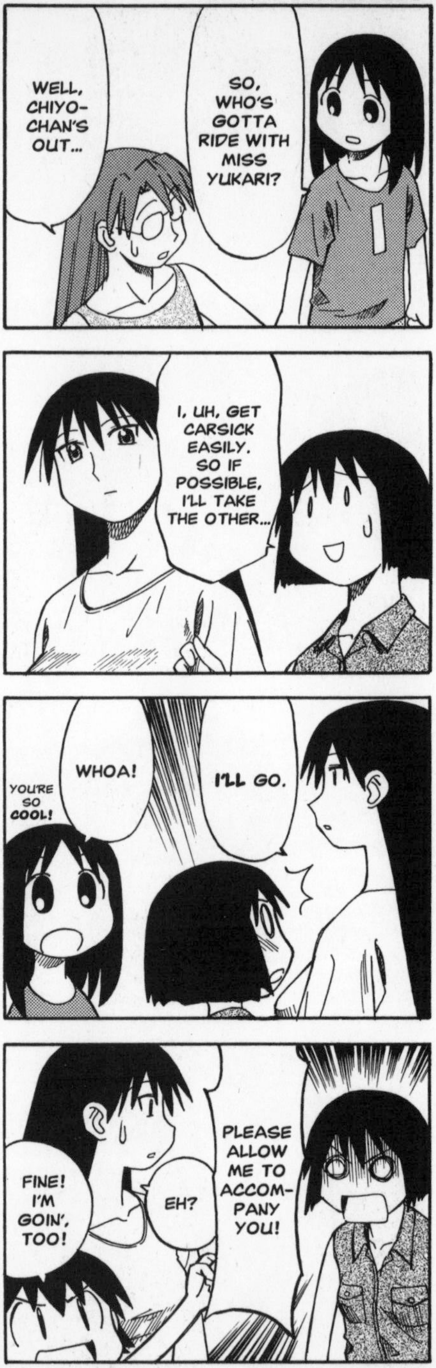
SO, WHO'S GOTTA RIDE WITH MISS YUKARI?
WELL, CHIYO-CHAN'S OUT...
I, UH, GET CARSICK EASILY. SO IF POSSIBLE, I'LL TAKE THE OTHER...
I'LL GO.
WHOA!
YOU'RE SO COOL!
PLEASE ALLOW ME TO ACCOMPANY YOU!
EH?
FINE! I'M GOIN', TOO!

THIS ONE

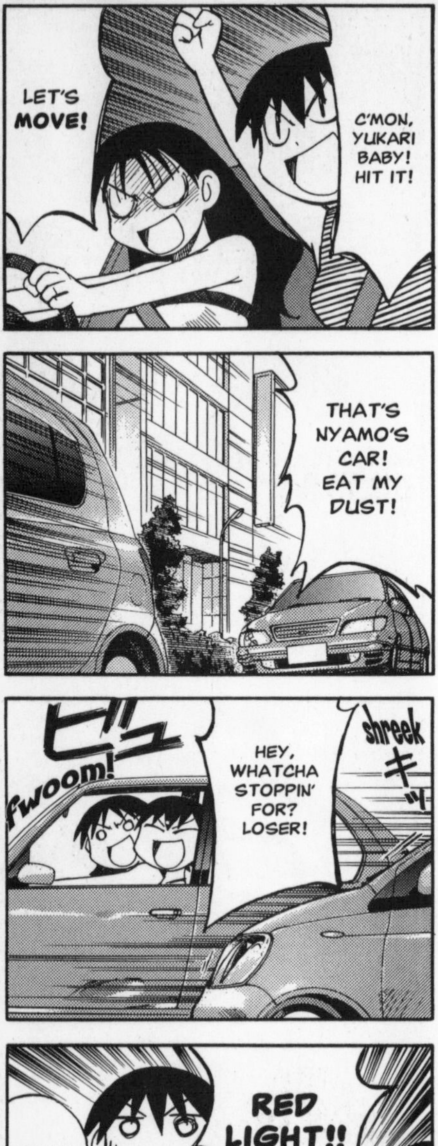
C'MON, YUKARI BABY! HIT IT!
LET'S MOVE!
THAT'S NYAMO'S CAR! EAT MY DUST!
shreek
キッ
HEY, WHATCHA STOPPIN' FOR? LOSER!
fwoom!
ビュ
RED LIGHT!!
HUH?

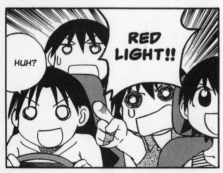

CARELESS

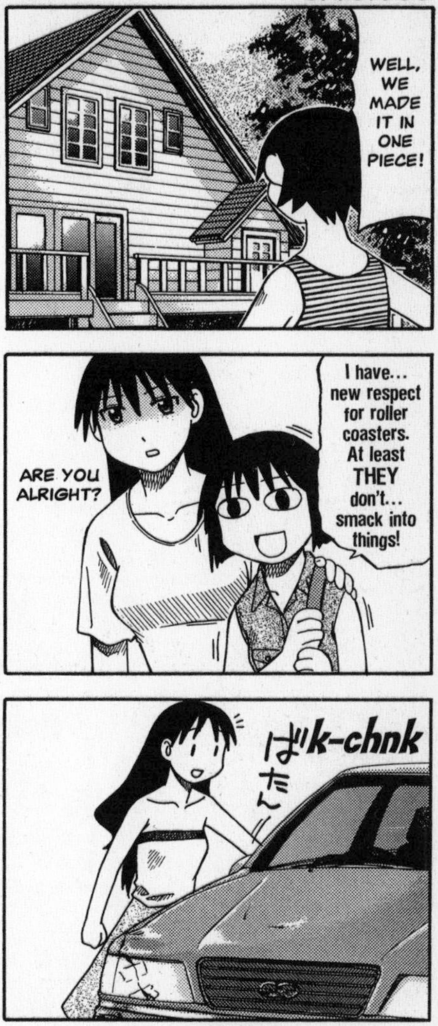
WELL, WE MADE IT IN ONE PIECE!
I have… new respect for roller coasters. At least THEY don't… smack into things!
ARE YOU ALRIGHT?
ばたん
k-chnk
HER SIDE MIRROR WAS... THAT WAY THE WHOLE TIME?!
くい
creak!

ROLLIN'

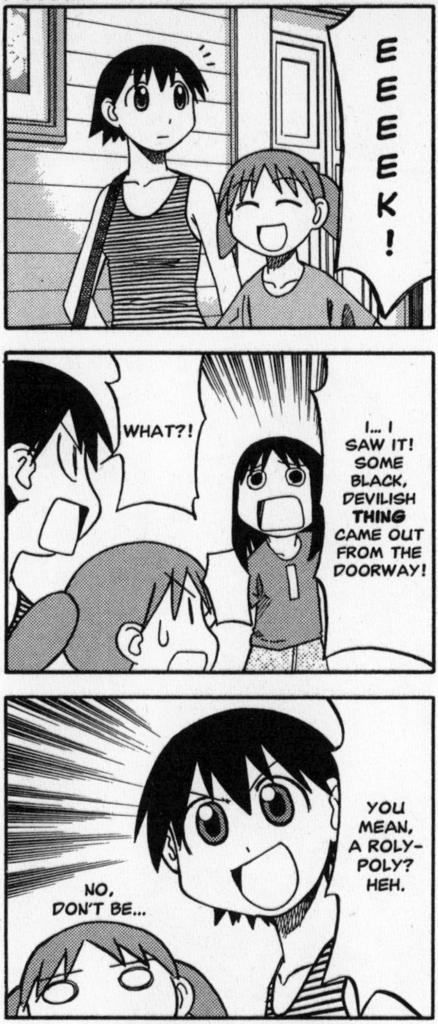
EEEEK!
I... I SAW IT! SOME BLACK, DEVILISH THING CAME OUT FROM THE DOORWAY!
WHAT?!
YOU MEAN, A ROLY-POLY? HEH.
NO, DON'T BE...
YEAH! A ROLY-POLY!
WHAT?! ARE YOU FOR REAL?

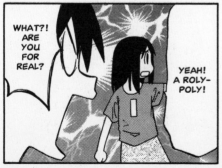

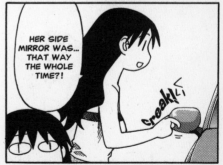

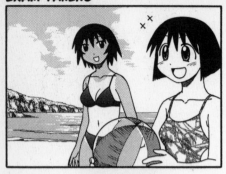

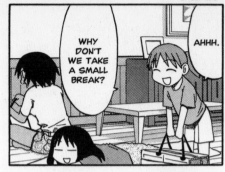

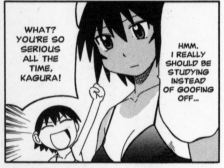

DUPED

AHHH.
WHY DON'T WE TAKE A SMALL BREAK?
WELL, LET'S HEAD TO THE BEACH!
YOU'RE IN YOUR BATHING SUIT **ALREADY?**
UM, I THOUGHT THIS WAS SUPPOSED TO BE AN "ENTRANCE EXAM SLEEPAWAY CAMP."
NAH, THAT WAS A LIE.
YOU DON'T BEAT AROUND THE BUSH, DO YOU?

EXAM TAKERS

HMM. I REALLY SHOULD BE STUDYING INSTEAD OF GOOFING OFF...
WHAT? YOU'RE SO SERIOUS ALL THE TIME, KAGURA!
STILL, THAT DOESN'T MEAN WE CAN JUST BLOW OFF THE TEST!
AAH, WHAT-EVER. LET'S JUST HAVE FUN!
YOU ARE SOMETHIN' ELSE, YOU KNOW THAT?

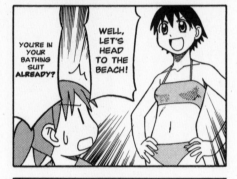

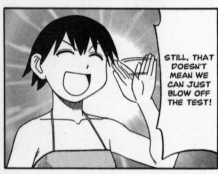

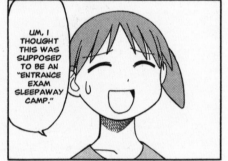

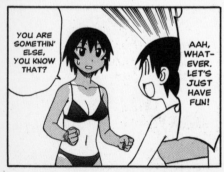

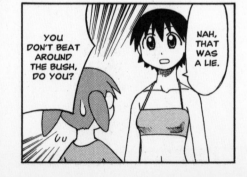

TOO LITTLE, TOO LATE?

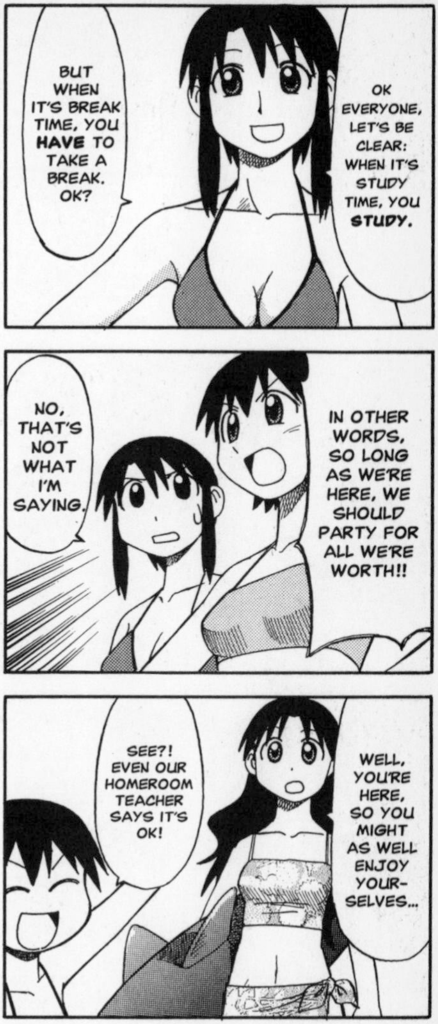
OK EVERYONE, LET'S BE CLEAR: WHEN IT'S STUDY TIME, YOU **STUDY.**
BUT WHEN IT'S BREAK TIME, YOU **HAVE** TO TAKE A BREAK. OK?
IN OTHER WORDS, SO LONG AS WE'RE HERE, WE SHOULD PARTY FOR ALL WE'RE WORTH!!
NO, THAT'S NOT WHAT I'M SAYING.
WELL, YOU'RE HERE, SO YOU MIGHT AS WELL ENJOY YOURSELVES...
SEE?! EVEN OUR HOMEROOM TEACHER SAYS IT'S OK!
'CUZ EVEN IF YOU **DO** STUDY, THERE'S NO WAY
YOU'LL PASS THAT TEST.
UH... YOU THINK SO?

THE PROBLEM

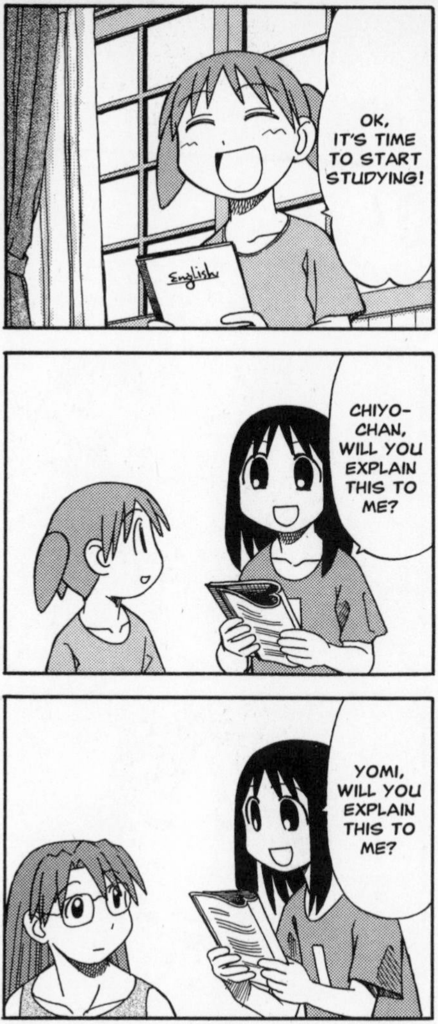
OK, IT'S TIME TO START STUDYING!
English
CHIYO-CHAN, WILL YOU EXPLAIN THIS TO ME?
YOMI, WILL YOU EXPLAIN THIS TO ME?
MISS YUKARI, WILL YOU-
ARE YOU EVEN **USING** THAT BRAIN OF YOURS?

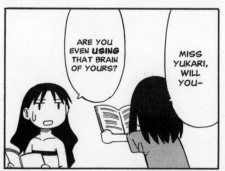

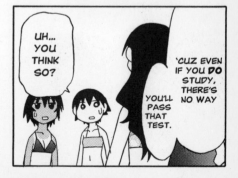

MISS KUROSAWA

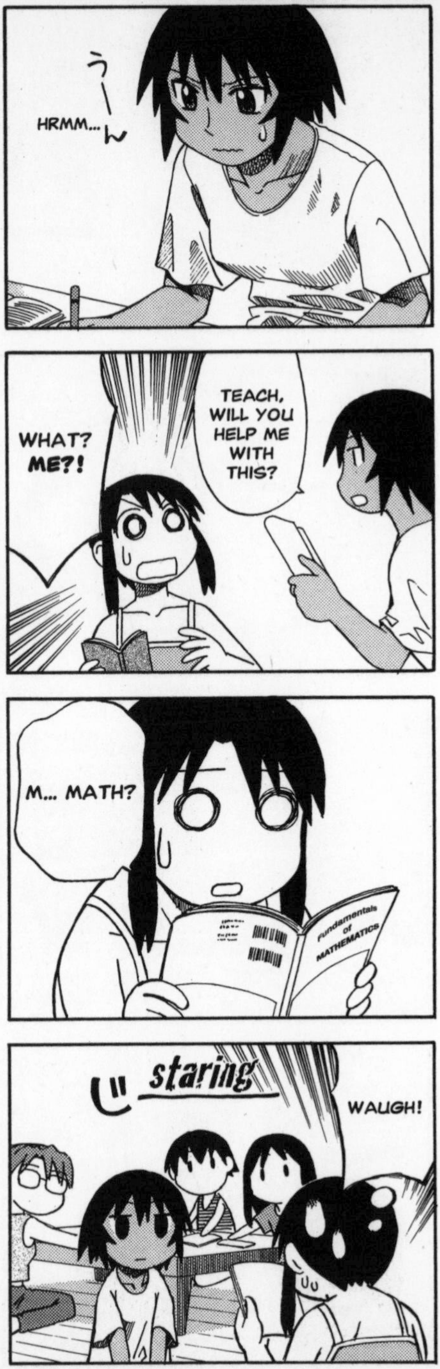
うーん
HRMM...
TEACH, WILL YOU HELP ME WITH THIS?
WHAT? ME?!
M... MATH?
Fundamentals of MATHEMATICS
WAUGH!
じ
staring

NO IDEA

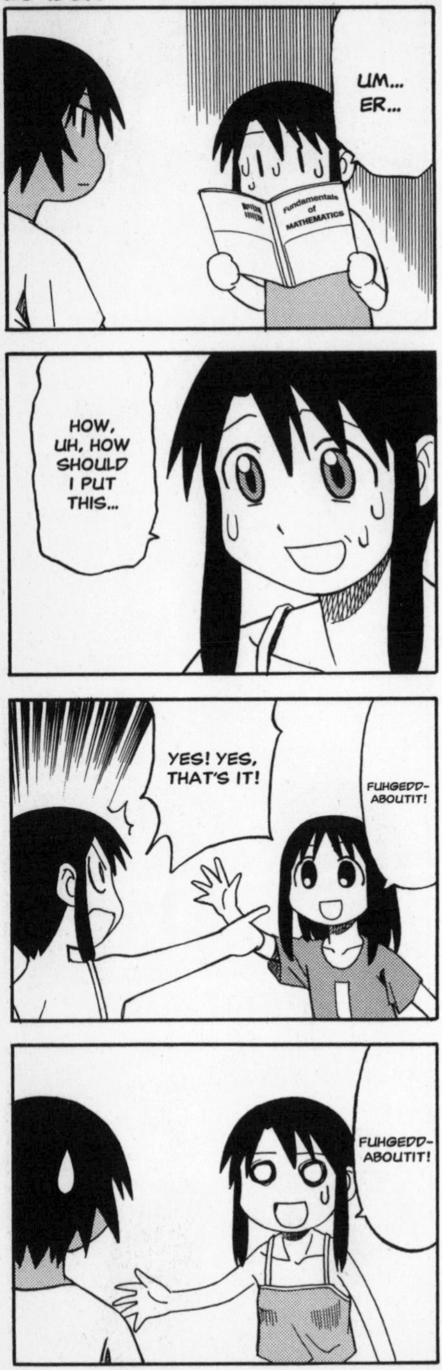
UM... ER...
Fundamentals of MATHEMATICS
HOW, UH, HOW SHOULD I PUT THIS...
FUHGEDD-ABOUTIT!
YES! YES, THAT'S IT!
FUHGEDD-ABOUTIT!

THE TEACHER

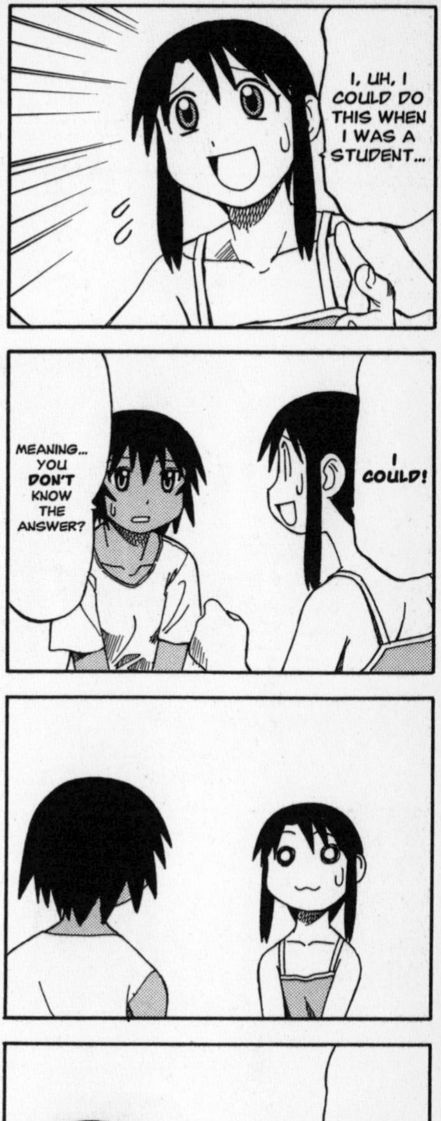
I, UH, I COULD DO THIS WHEN I WAS A STUDENT...
I COULD!
MEANING... YOU **DON'T** KNOW THE ANSWER?
THASS-RIGHT.

YUKARI TAKES CENTER STAGE

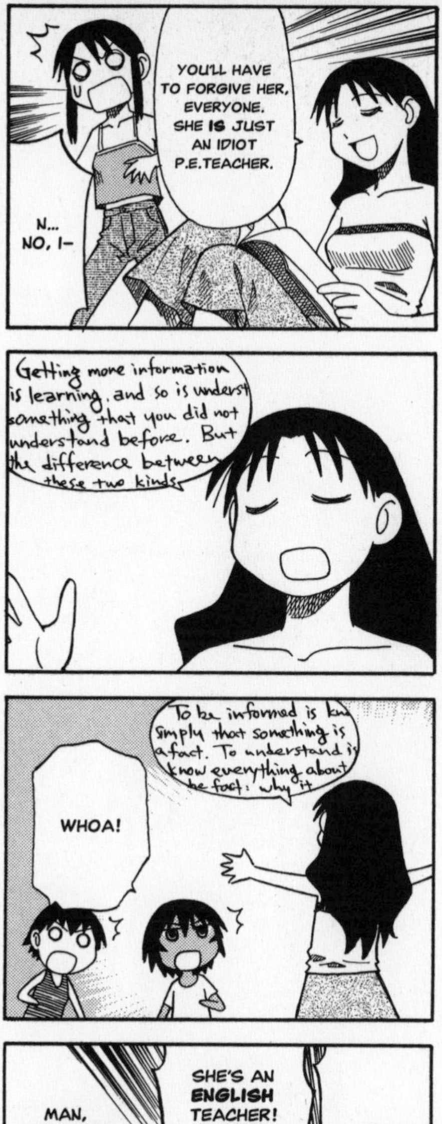
YOU'LL HAVE TO FORGIVE HER, EVERYONE. SHE **IS** JUST AN IDIOT P.E.TEACHER.
N... NO, I–
Getting more information is learning, and so is underst something that you did not understand before. But the difference between these two kinds
To be informed is kn simply that something is a fact. To understand is know everything about the fact: why it
WHOA!
D... DON'T BE FOOLED!
SHE'S AN **ENGLISH** TEACHER! THERE'S NOTHING GREAT ABOUT HER BEING ABLE TO SPEAK IT!
MAN, YUKARI IS **GREAT!**

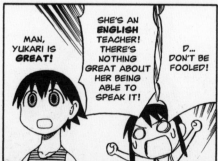

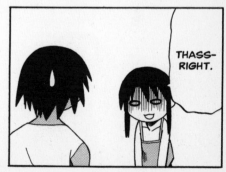

SAVING FACE

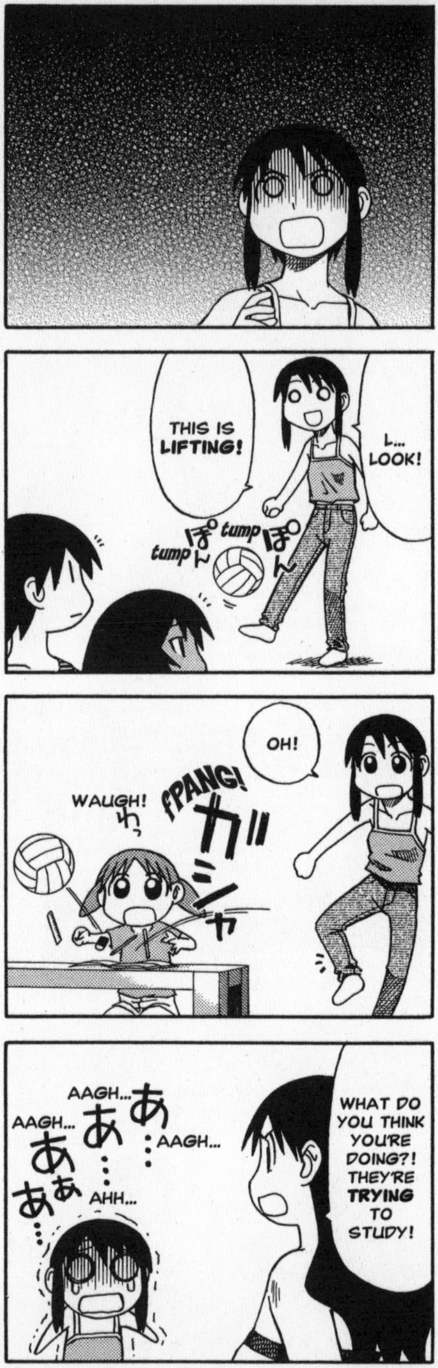

L... LOOK!
THIS IS LIFTING!
tump ぽん
tump ぽん
OH!
FPANG! ガシャ
WAUGH! わっ
WHAT DO YOU THINK YOU'RE DOING?! THEY'RE TRYING TO STUDY!
AAGH... あ
AAGH... あ
AAGH... あ
AHH... あ

DEJECTED

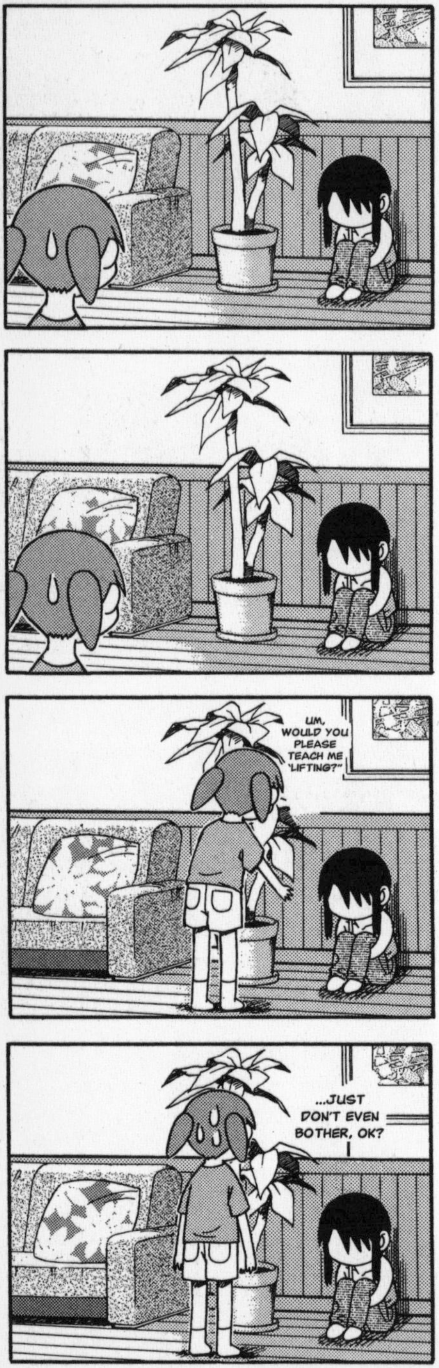

UM, WOULD YOU PLEASE TEACH ME "LIFTING?"
...JUST DON'T EVEN BOTHER, OK?

A CLEAR SHOT

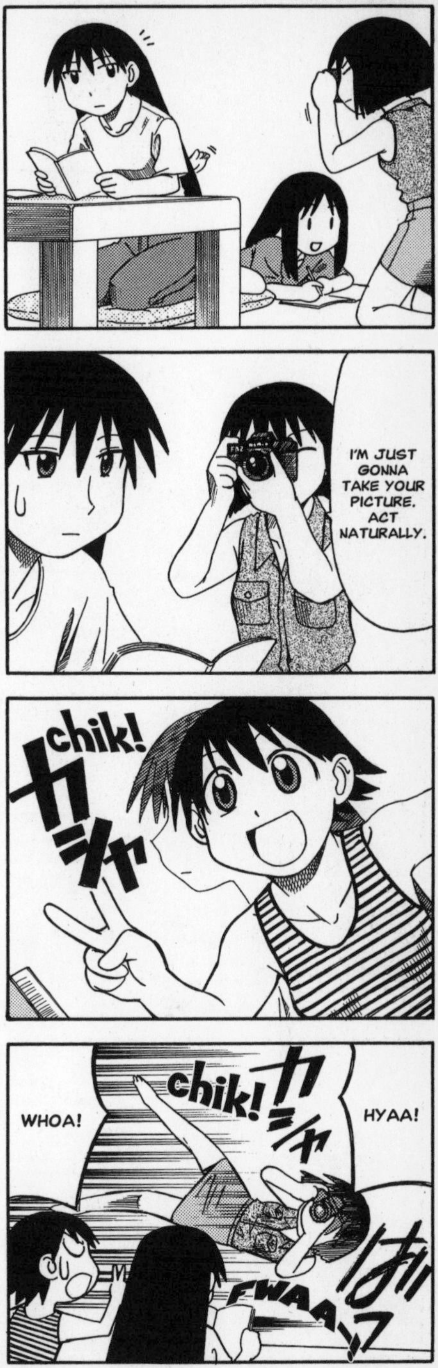
I'M JUST GONNA TAKE YOUR PICTURE. ACT NATURALLY.
chik!
カシャ
HYAA!
chik!
カシャ
WHOA!
はっ
FWAA-!?

SUMMER ROUTINE

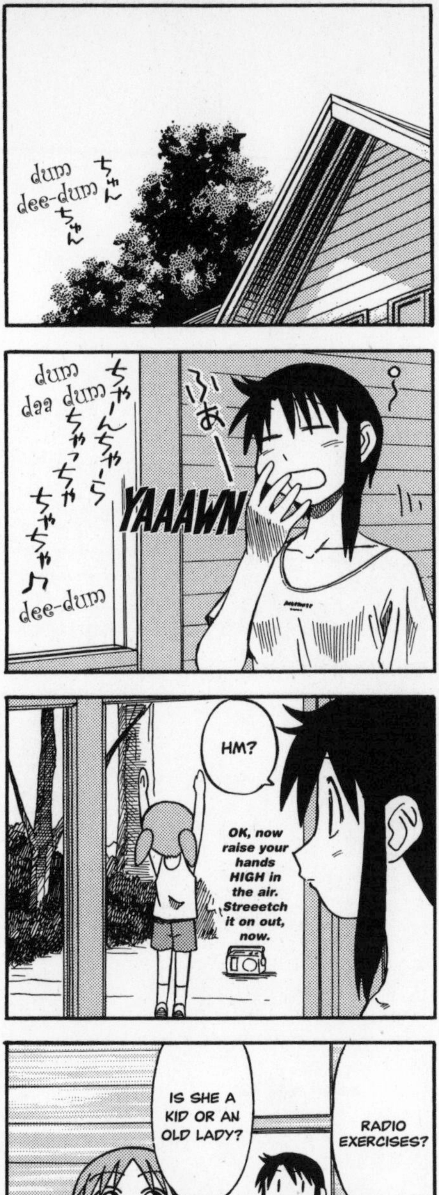
ちゃん ちゃん
dum dee-dum
ちゃーんちゃら ちゃっちゃ ちゃちゃ♪
dum daa dum dee-dum
ふぉー
YAAAWN
HM?
OK, now raise your hands HIGH in the air. Streeetch it on out, now.
RADIO EXERCISES?
IS SHE A KID OR AN OLD LADY?

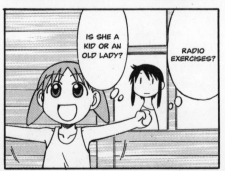

THE STAMP BOOK

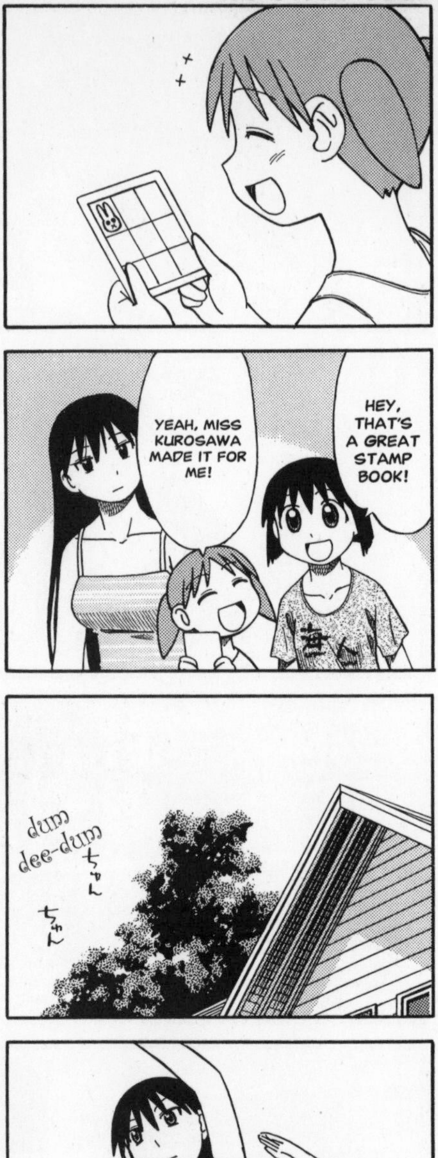
HEY, THAT'S A GREAT STAMP BOOK!
YEAH, MISS KUROSAWA MADE IT FOR ME!
dum dee-dum
ちゃんちゃん

HALF-AWAKE

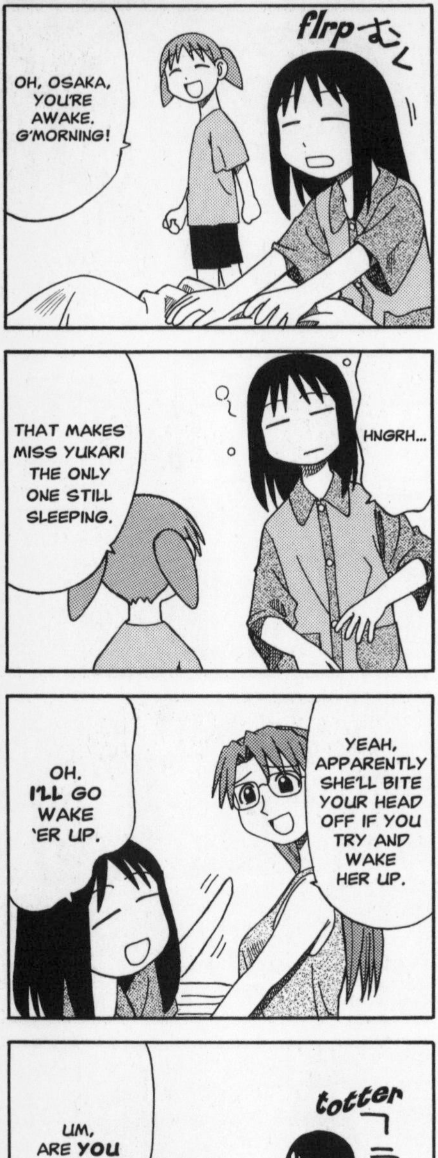
flrp むく
OH, OSAKA, YOU'RE AWAKE. G'MORNING!
HNGRH...
THAT MAKES MISS YUKARI THE ONLY ONE STILL SLEEPING.
YEAH, APPARENTLY SHE'LL BITE YOUR HEAD OFF IF YOU TRY AND WAKE HER UP.
OH. I'LL GO WAKE 'ER UP.
totter
UM, ARE YOU EVEN UP, OSAKA?

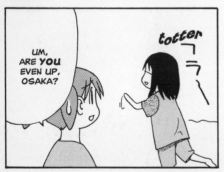

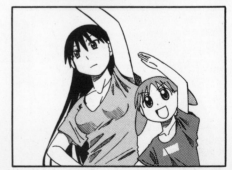

RISE-N-SHINE

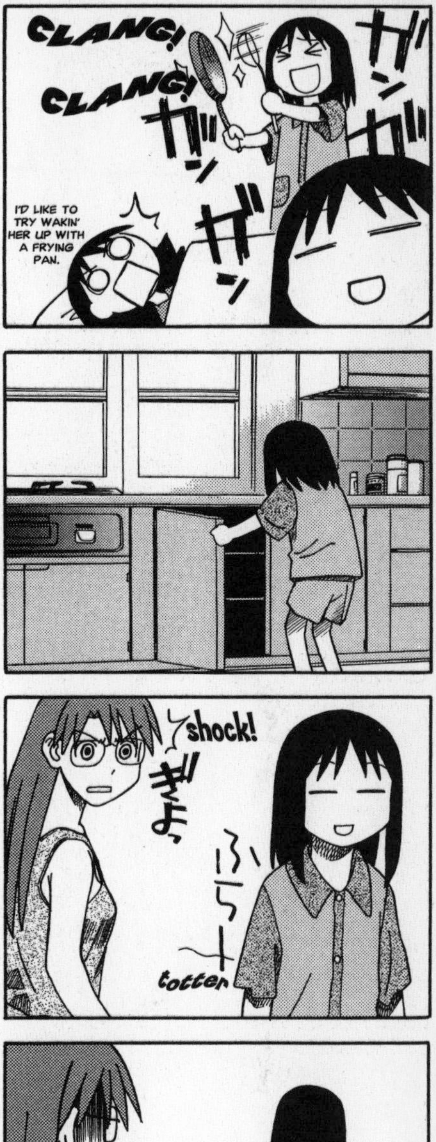
CLANG!
CLANG!
I'D LIKE TO TRY WAKIN' HER UP WITH A FRYING PAN.
shock!
ぎょ
ふらー
totter

FAILURE

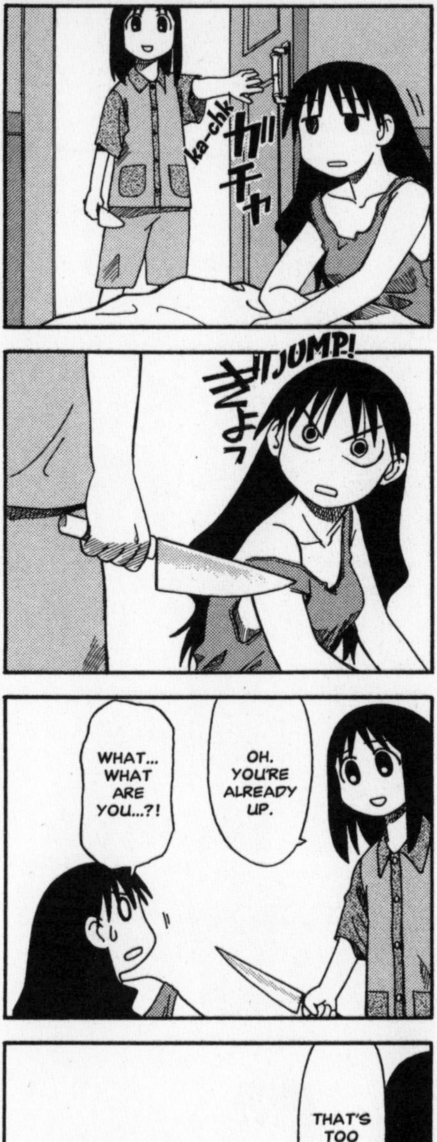
ka-chk
ガチャ
JUMP!
ぎょっ
OH. YOU'RE ALREADY UP.
WHAT... WHAT ARE YOU...?!
THAT'S TOO BAD.

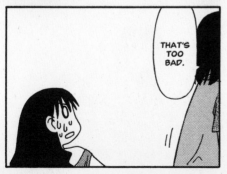

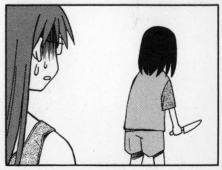

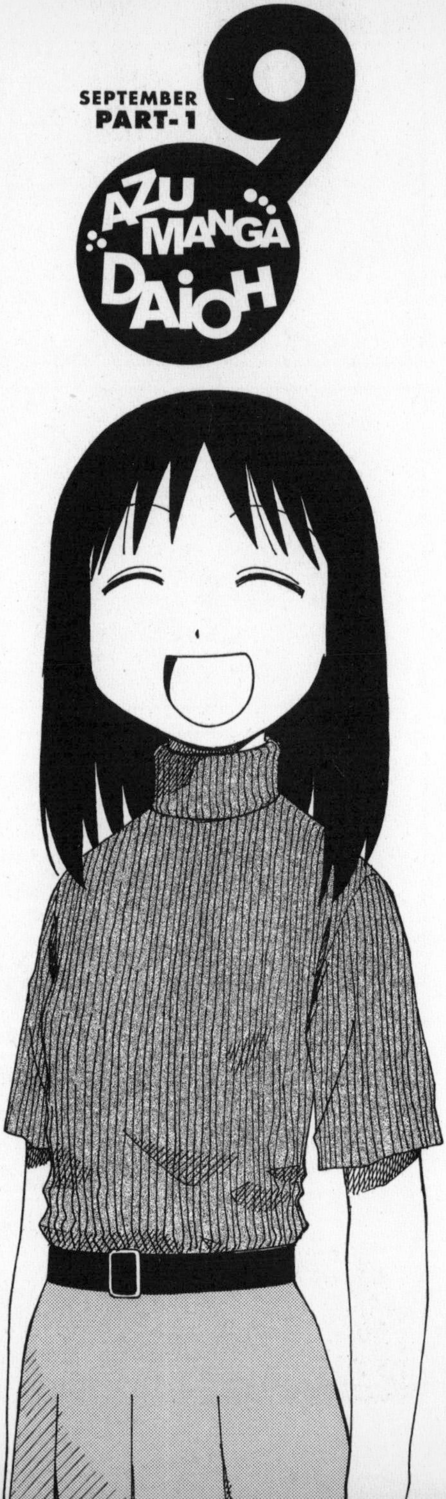
SEPTEMBER
PART-1
9
AZU MANGA DAIOH

IT'S NOT OVER YET

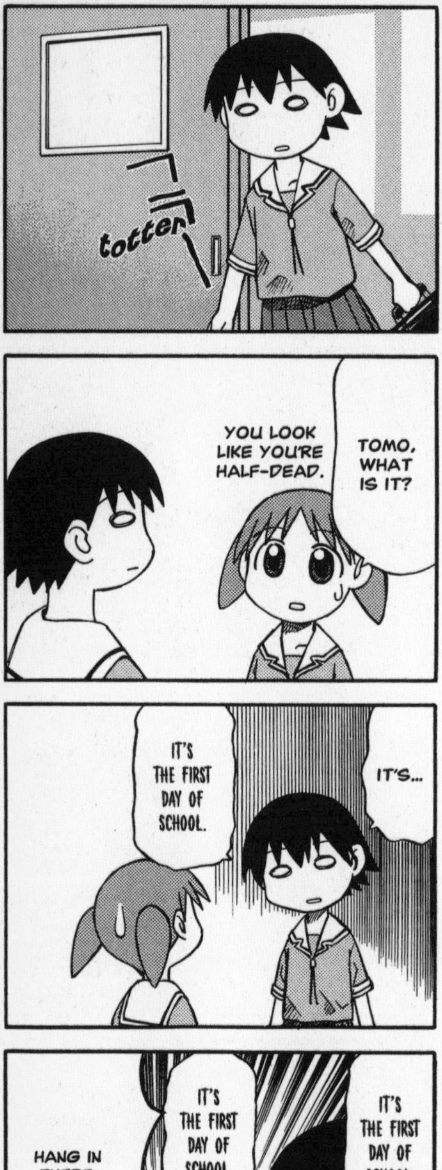
totter
TOMO, WHAT IS IT?
YOU LOOK LIKE YOU'RE HALF-DEAD.
IT'S...
IT'S THE FIRST DAY OF SCHOOL.
IT'S THE FIRST DAY OF SCHOOL.
IT'S THE FIRST DAY OF SCHOOL.
HANG IN THERE, TOMO! WE'RE ALREADY IN THE SECOND SEMESTER!

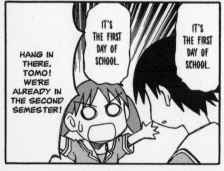

CONFUSED

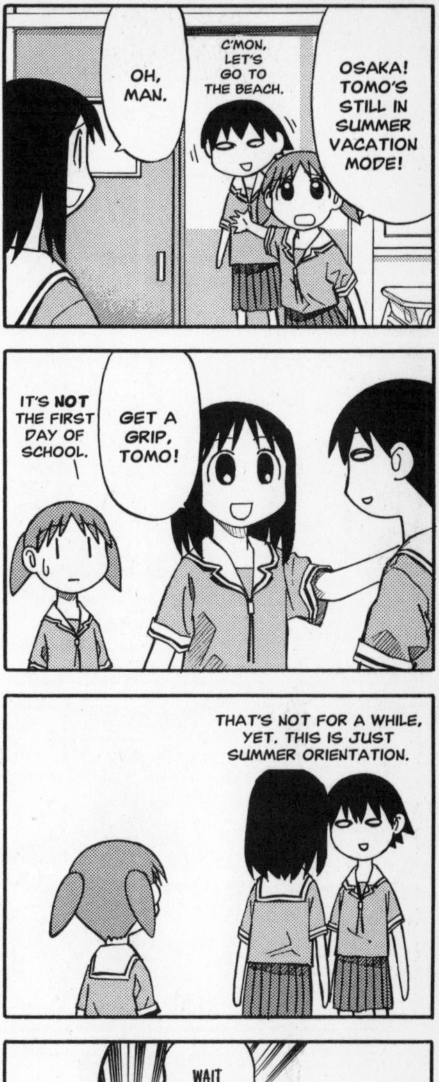
OSAKA! TOMO'S STILL IN SUMMER VACATION MODE!
C'MON, LET'S GO TO THE BEACH.
OH, MAN.
GET A GRIP, TOMO!
IT'S **NOT** THE FIRST DAY OF SCHOOL.
THAT'S NOT FOR A WHILE, YET. THIS IS JUST SUMMER ORIENTATION.
WAIT. IT IS THE FIRST DAY OF SCHOOL.
OH, NO!

THE TRICK

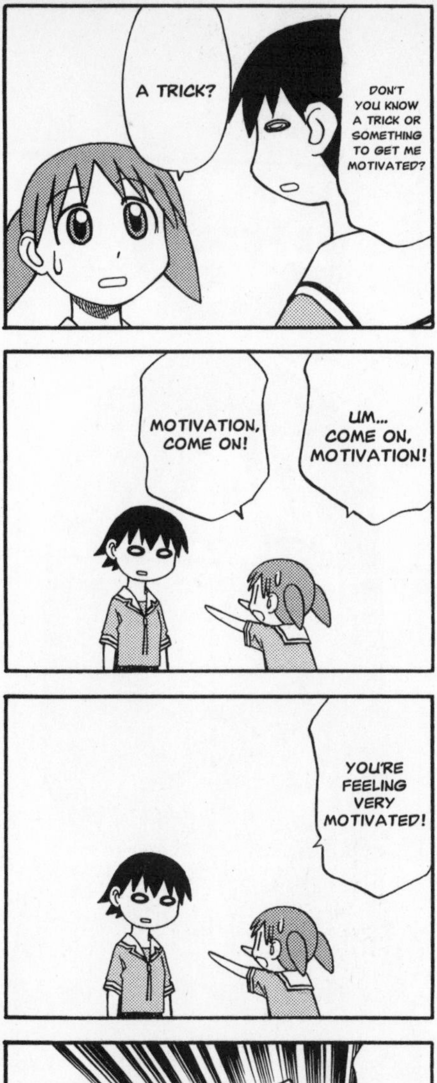
DON'T YOU KNOW A TRICK OR SOMETHING TO GET ME MOTIVATED?
A TRICK?
UM... COME ON, MOTIVATION!
MOTIVATION, COME ON!
YOU'RE FEELING VERY MOTIVATED!
MOTIV-ATION...
HUH?!
AAGH! M... MOTIVATION! COME ON!

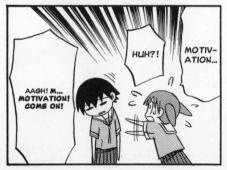

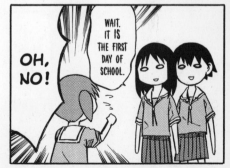

NO GOOD

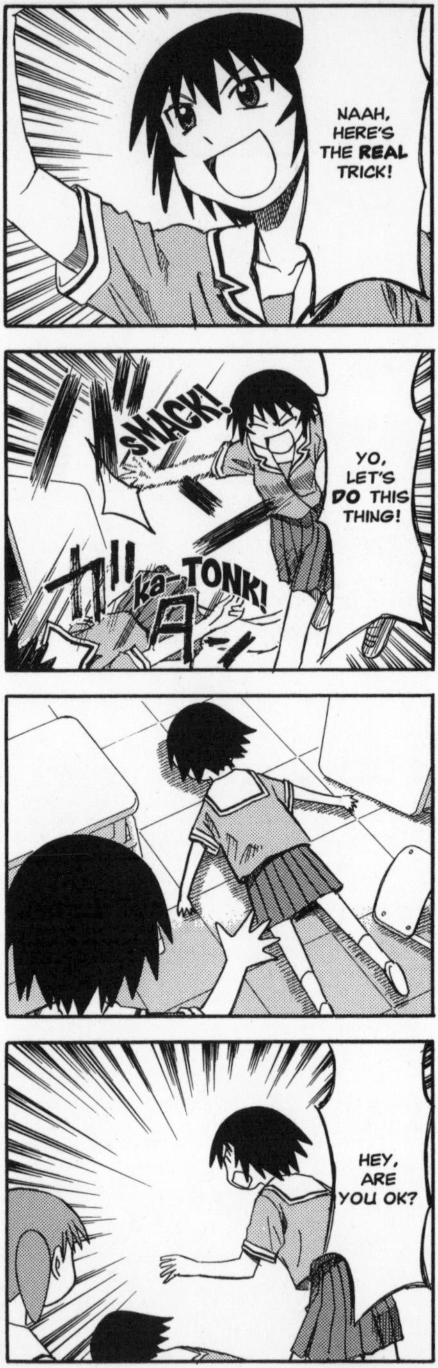
NAAH, HERE'S THE **REAL** TRICK!
SMACK!
YO, LET'S **DO** THIS THING!
ka-TONK!
HEY, ARE YOU OK?

ANOTHER SHOT

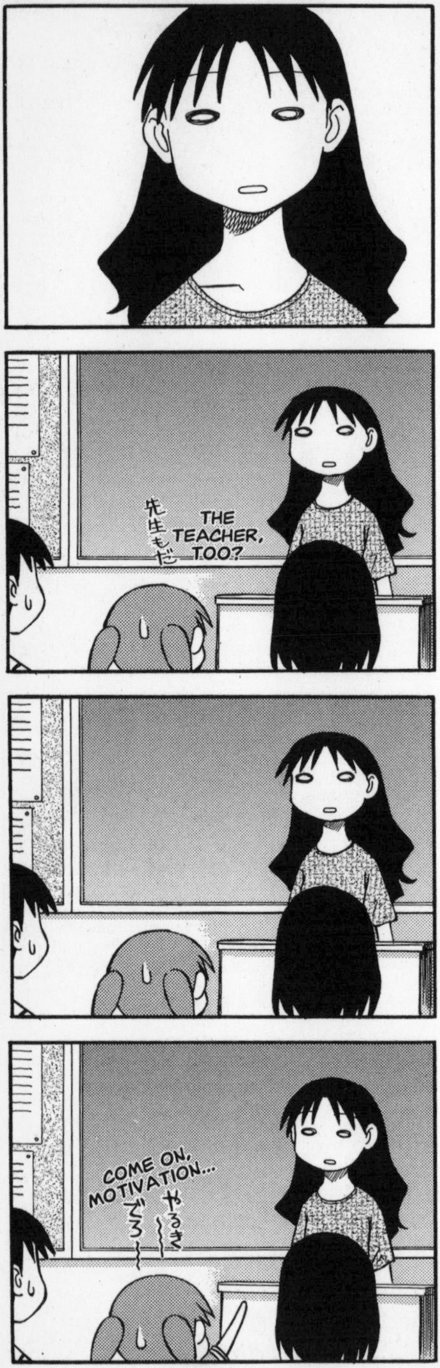
THE TEACHER, TOO?
先生もだ
COME ON, MOTIVATION...
やるき〜〜でろ〜〜

THE RETURN

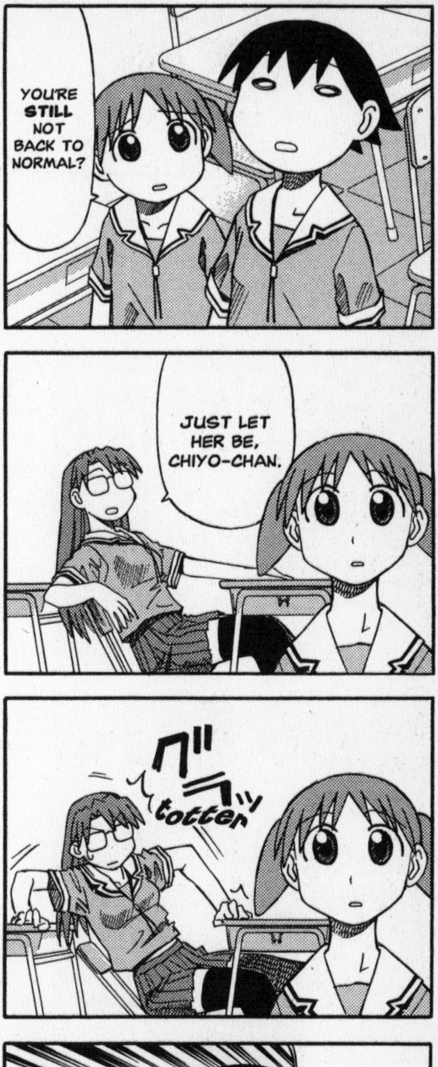
YOU'RE **STILL** NOT BACK TO NORMAL?
JUST LET HER BE, CHIYO-CHAN.
グラッ
totter
HA! YOU ALMOST FELL RIGHT NOW, DIDN'TCHA? DIDN'TCHA?!
bwoosh!

MILK

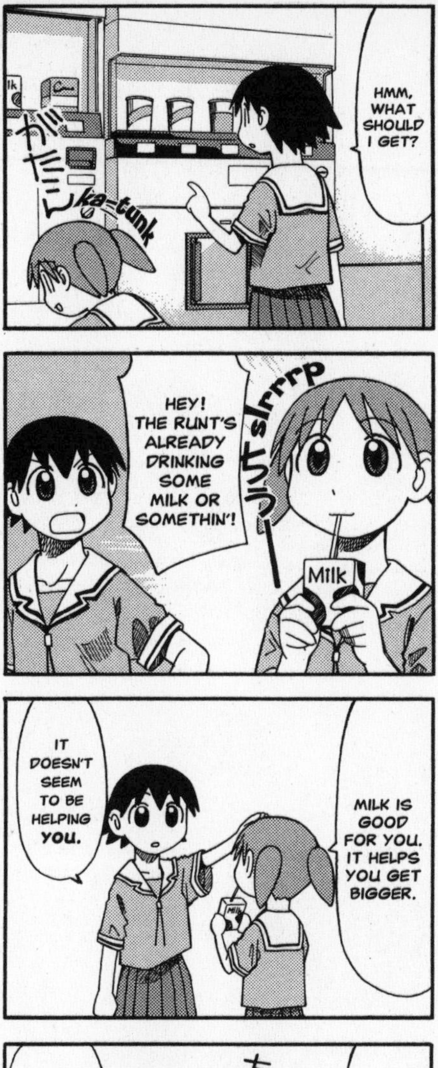
HMM, WHAT SHOULD I GET?
ka-tunk
slrrrp
HEY! THE RUNT'S ALREADY DRINKING SOME MILK OR SOMETHIN'!
Milk
MILK IS GOOD FOR YOU. IT HELPS YOU GET BIGGER.
IT DOESN'T SEEM TO BE HELPING **YOU.**
AND IT TASTES GREAT, EVEN HOT.
slrrrp
IT'S BEEN A WHILE... IS IT REALLY **THAT** GOOD?

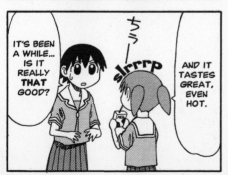

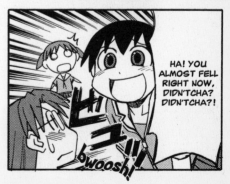

STOP!

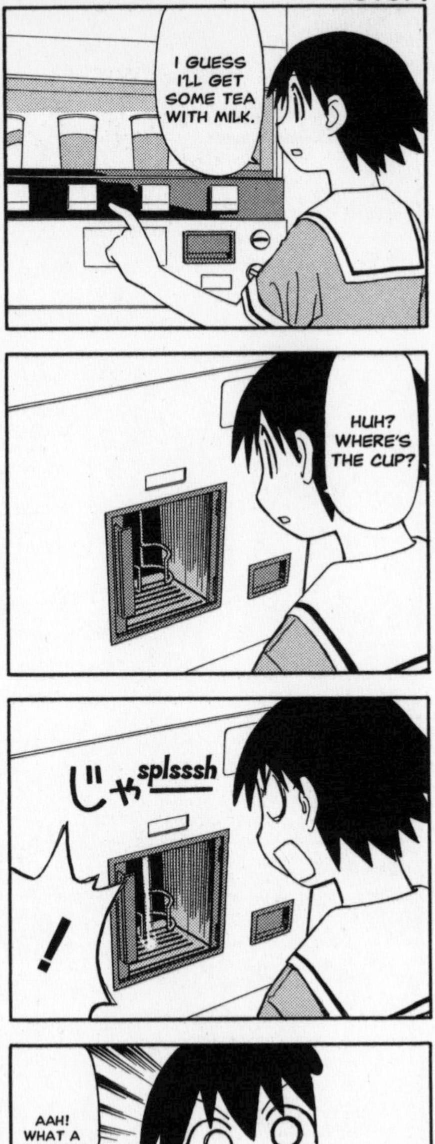
I GUESS I'LL GET SOME TEA WITH MILK.
HUH? WHERE'S THE CUP?
じゃ splsssh
!
WAUUGH! STOP, STOP!
AAH! WHAT A TRAGEDY!

BETRAYAL

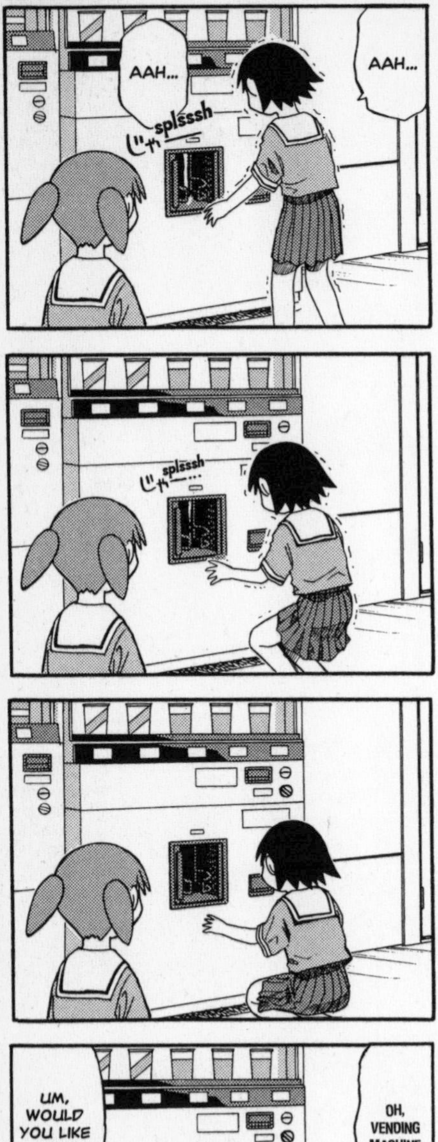
AAH...
AAH...
じゃ splsssh
じゃ splsssh...
OH, VENDING MACHINE I BELIEVED IN YOU!
UM, WOULD YOU LIKE SOME OF MY MILK?

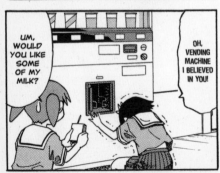

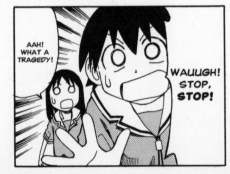

MISERY LOVES COMPANY

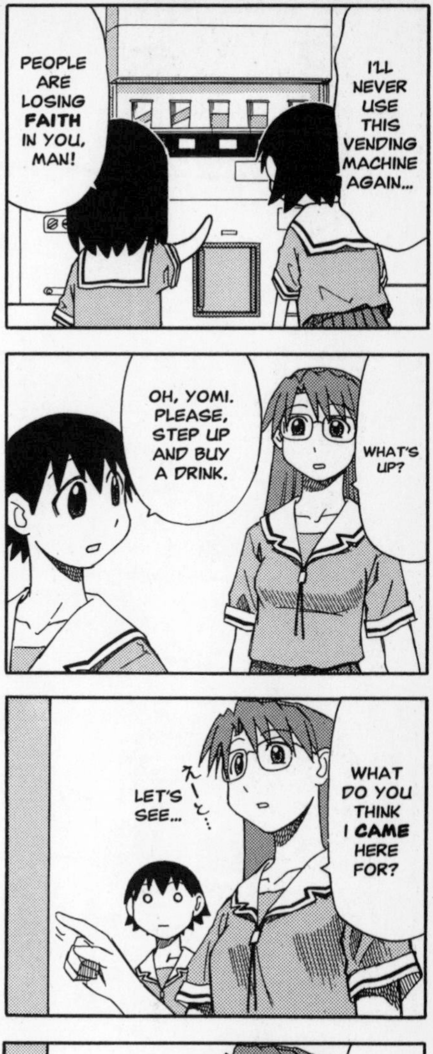
I'LL NEVER USE THIS VENDING MACHINE AGAIN...
PEOPLE ARE LOSING **FAITH** IN YOU, MAN!
WHAT'S UP?
OH, YOMI. PLEASE, STEP UP AND BUY A DRINK.
WHAT DO YOU THINK I **CAME** HERE FOR?
えーと…
LET'S SEE...
I GUESS I'LL GET SOME TEA WITH MILK.

MY DRINK...

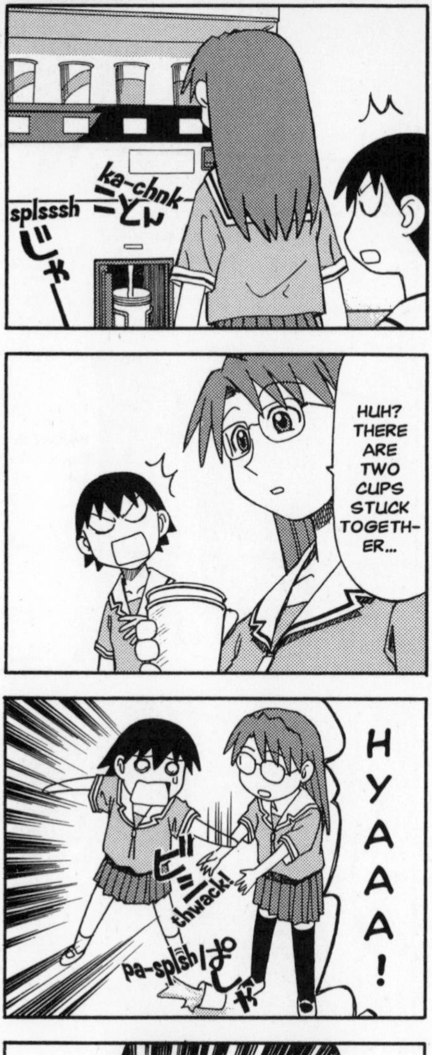
ka-chnk
ごとん
splsssh
じゃー
HUH? THERE ARE TWO CUPS STUCK TOGETH-ER...
HYAAAA!
ビシ
thwack!
pa-splsh
ぱしゃ
WHA-?!
WHY? **WHY?!**

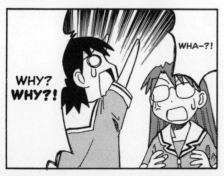

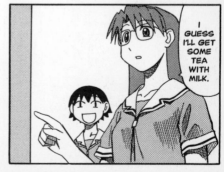

CAUGHT IN THE ACT

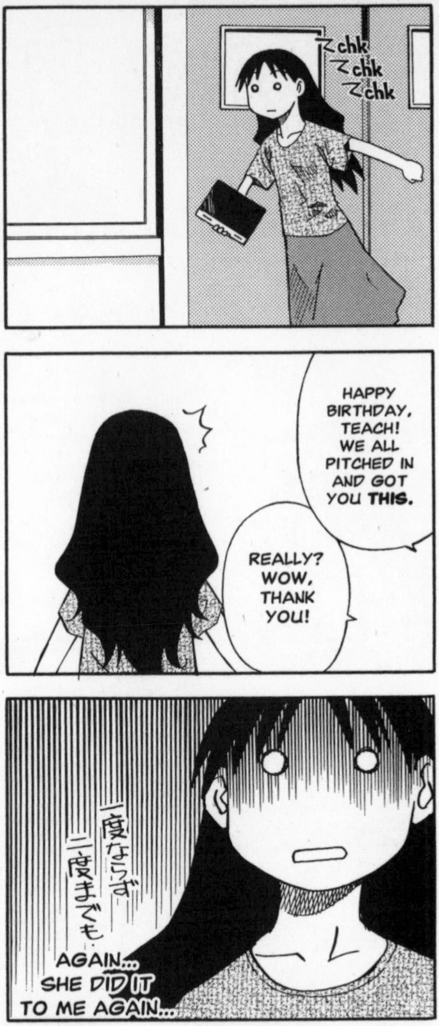
chk
chk
chk
HAPPY BIRTHDAY, TEACH! WE ALL PITCHED IN AND GOT YOU THIS.
REALLY? WOW, THANK YOU!
一度ならず二度までも
AGAIN... SHE DID IT TO ME AGAIN...
KUROSAWA!!
WAUGH!

WHO CARES?

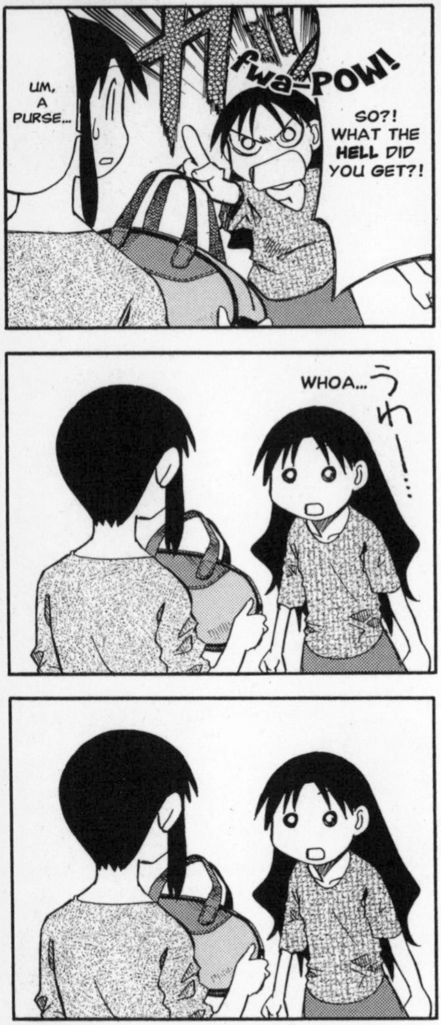
fwa-POW!
SO?! WHAT THE HELL DID YOU GET?!
UM, A PURSE...
WHOA... うわー!...
WHO CARES?! I'VE ALREADY GOT A PURSE!
Y... YEAH...

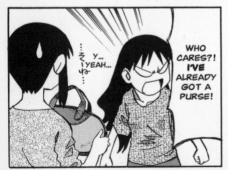

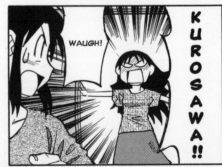

THE ASSERTION

LET ME TELL YA SOMETHIN'– SHE'S BETTER OFF **WITHOUT** A PURSE!
WHAT? WHY?
SHE'S **EVIL**, I TELL YOU!
WHAT ?!

SORRY, TEACHER

まる聞こえ
Hearing every word
Y...YOU KNOW WHAT? THIS YEAR, WE...
YEAH, WE DIDN'T GET HER ANYTHING. AGAIN.
WELL, WHAT ARE WE **SUPPOSED** TO DO? HER BIRTHDAY'S RIGHT IN THE MIDDLE OF SUMMER VACATION.
WE SHOULD STILL GET HER SOMETHING, THOUGH.
PRESENTS?! HA! WHO NEEDS 'EM?!
WE'RE SO SORRY...

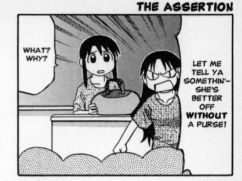

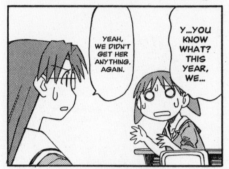

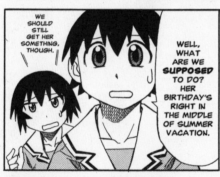

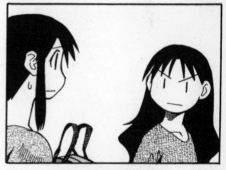

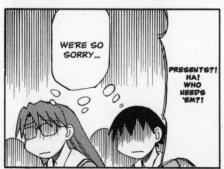

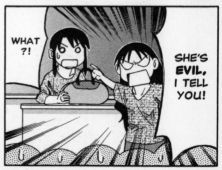

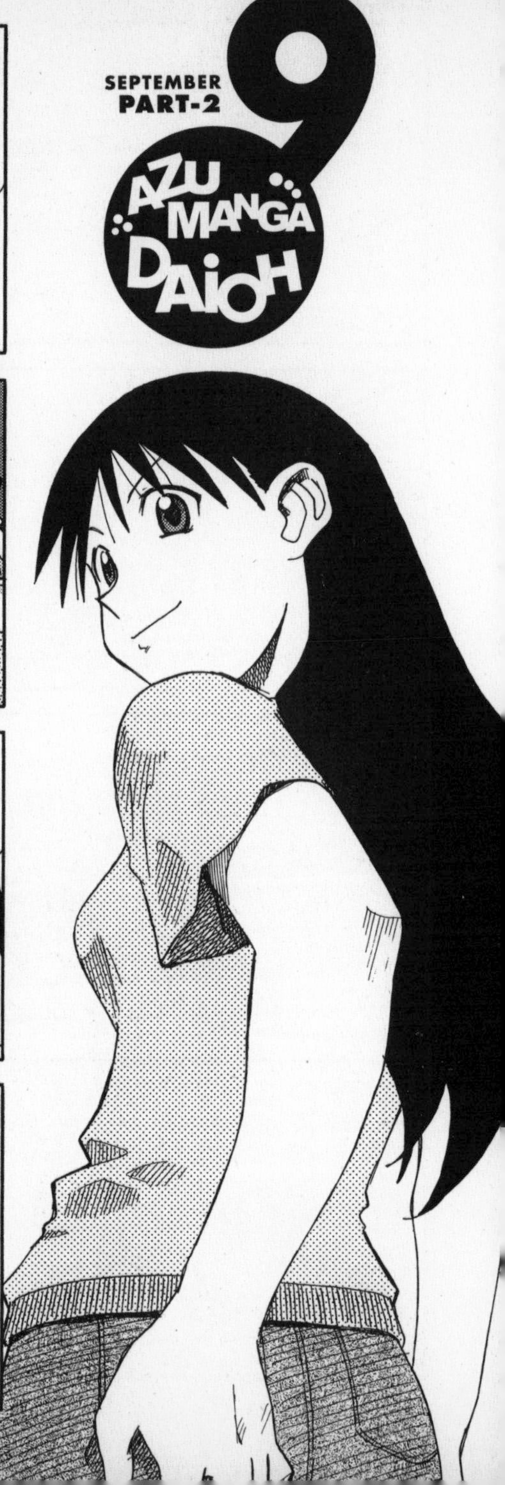
SEPTEMBER
PART-2
9
AZU MANGA DAIOH

THE FOLLOW-UP

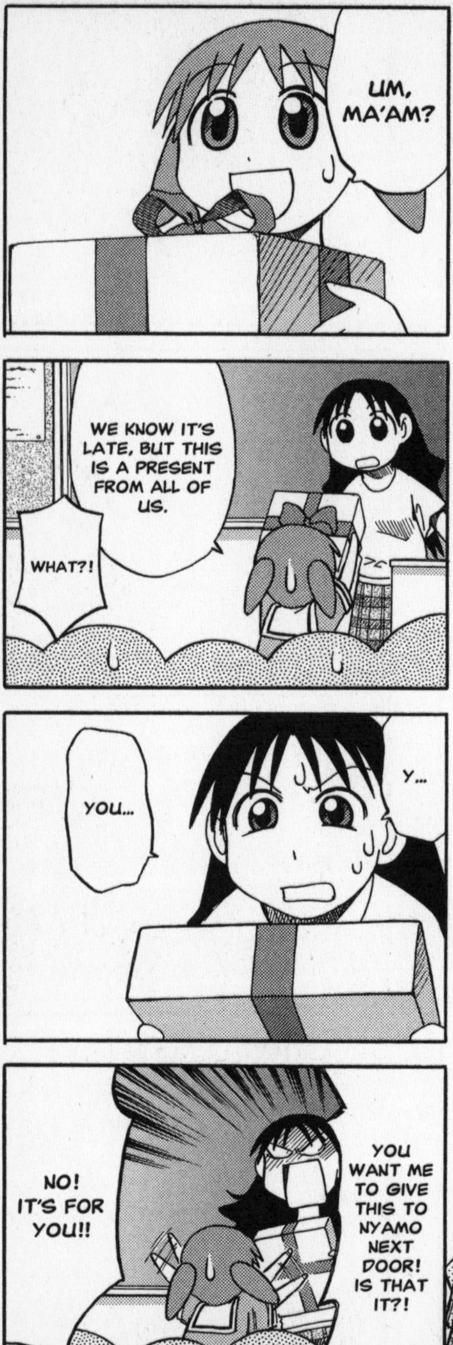
UM, MA'AM?
WE KNOW IT'S LATE, BUT THIS IS A PRESENT FROM ALL OF US.
WHAT?!
Y...
YOU...
YOU WANT ME TO GIVE THIS TO NYAMO NEXT DOOR! IS THAT IT?!
NO! IT'S FOR YOU!!

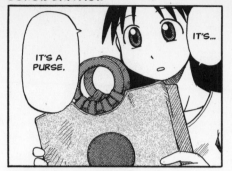

YUKARI'S BIRTHDAY

A PRESENT?
私の
FOR ME?
プレゼント…？
HAPPY BIRTH-DAY TO YOU!
HAPPY BIRTH-DAY TO YOU!!
ビク
wince
HAPPY BIRTH-DAY DEAR...
YUKARI!!!
HAPPY BIRTH-DAY TO YOU!!!
IS SHE... HAPPY?

CONSIDERATION

IT'S...
IT'S A PURSE.
IF YOU'LL EXCUSE ME FOR A MOMENT!
HUH?!
SLAM!
SHE WENT TO GO SHOW IT OFF TO NYAMO'S CLASS, DIDN'T SHE?
WELL, SHE LIKED IT. I GUESS THAT'S THE MOST IMPORTANT THING...

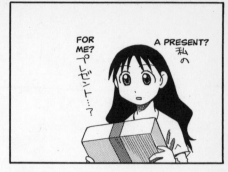

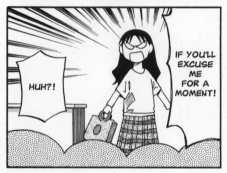

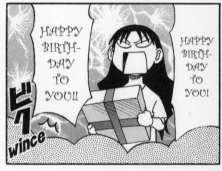

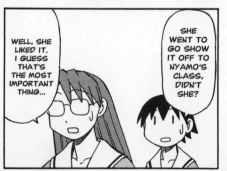

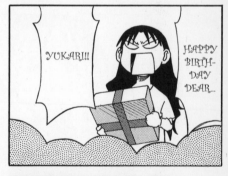

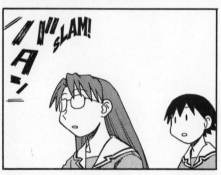

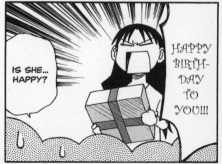

GOOD LUCK, CHIYO-CHAN

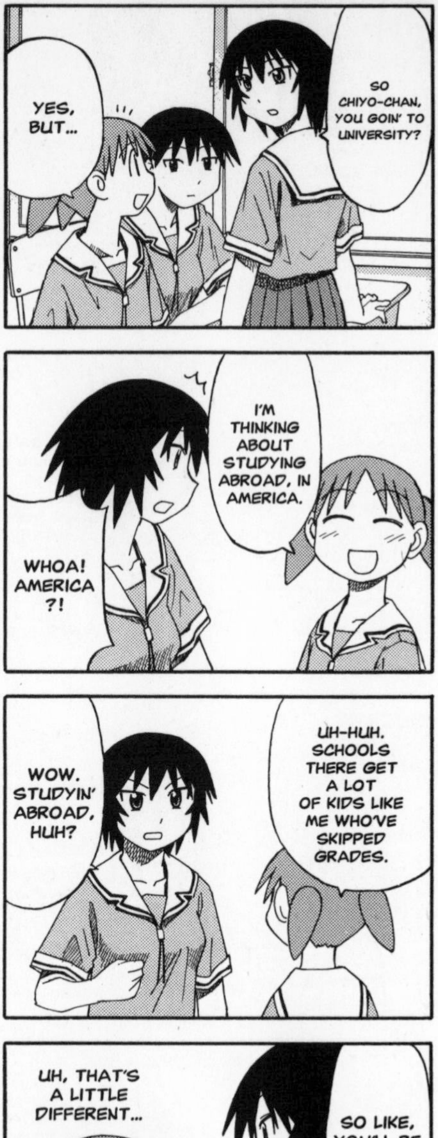
SO CHIYO-CHAN, YOU GOIN' TO UNIVERSITY?
YES, BUT...
I'M THINKING ABOUT STUDYING ABROAD, IN AMERICA.
WHOA! AMERICA?!
UH-HUH. SCHOOLS THERE GET A LOT OF KIDS LIKE ME WHO'VE SKIPPED GRADES.
WOW. STUDYIN' ABROAD, HUH?
SO LIKE, YOU'LL BE THE NEXT ICHIRO OR SASAKI, HUH?
UH, THAT'S A LITTLE DIFFERENT...

WORRY

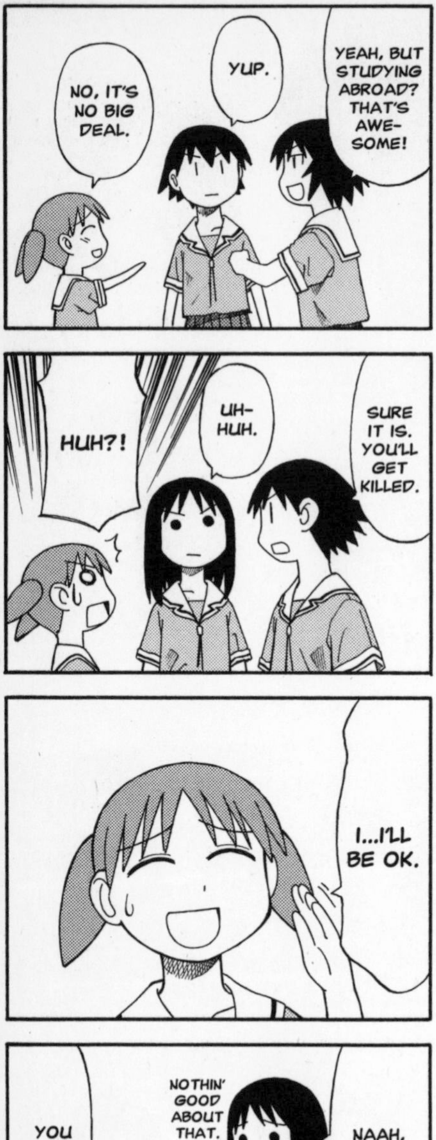
YEAH, BUT STUDYING ABROAD? THAT'S AWE-SOME!
YUP.
NO, IT'S NO BIG DEAL.
SURE IT IS. YOU'LL GET KILLED.
UH-HUH.
HUH?!
I...I'LL BE OK.
NAAH, YOU'RE GONNA GET SHOT.
NOTHIN' GOOD ABOUT THAT.
YOU REALLY THINK I'LL...

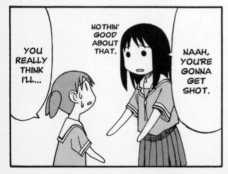

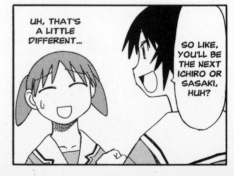

EXTREMELY WORRIED

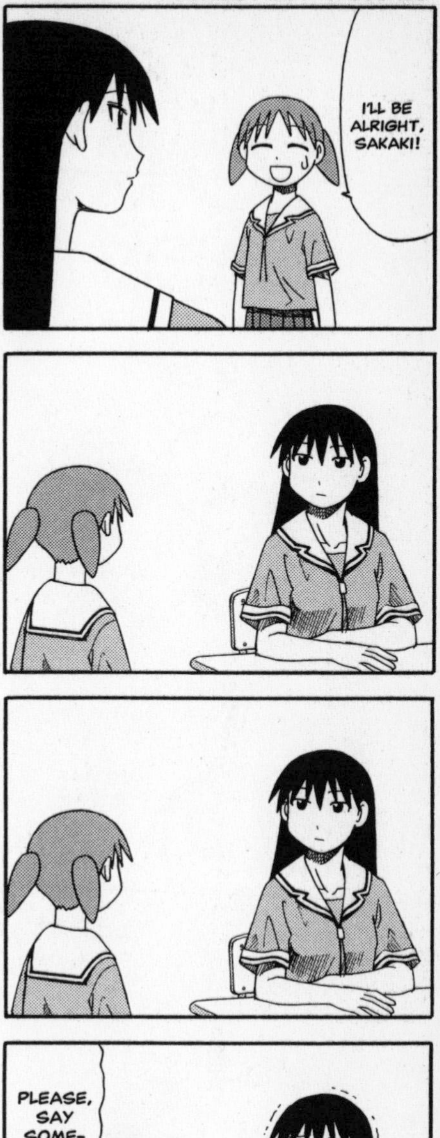
I'LL BE ALRIGHT, SAKAKI!
PLEASE, SAY SOME-THING!

YOU PASS!

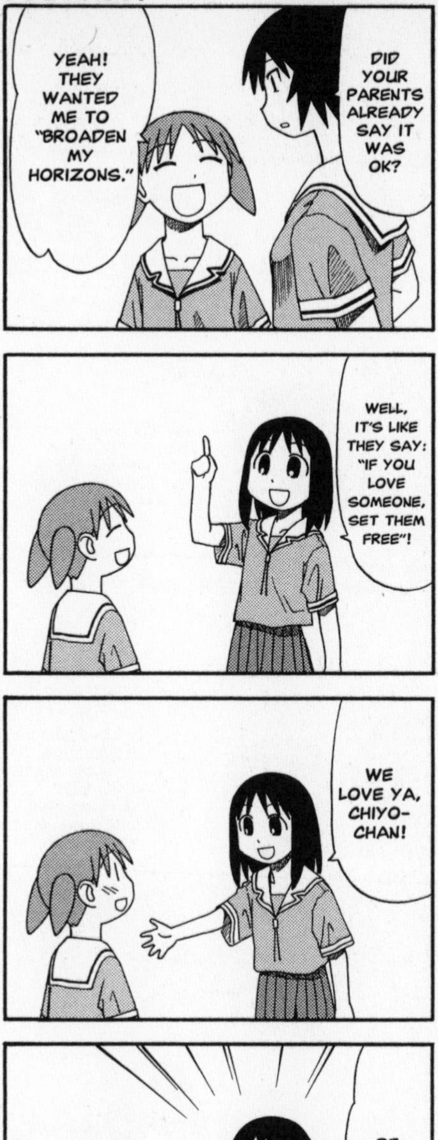
DID YOUR PARENTS ALREADY SAY IT WAS OK?
YEAH! THEY WANTED ME TO "BROADEN MY HORIZONS."
WELL, IT'S LIKE THEY SAY: "IF YOU LOVE SOMEONE, SET THEM FREE"!
WE LOVE YA, CHIYO-CHAN!
BE FREE!

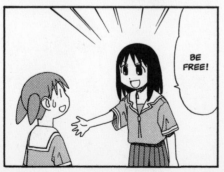

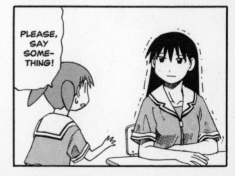

THE CHILD PRESIDENT

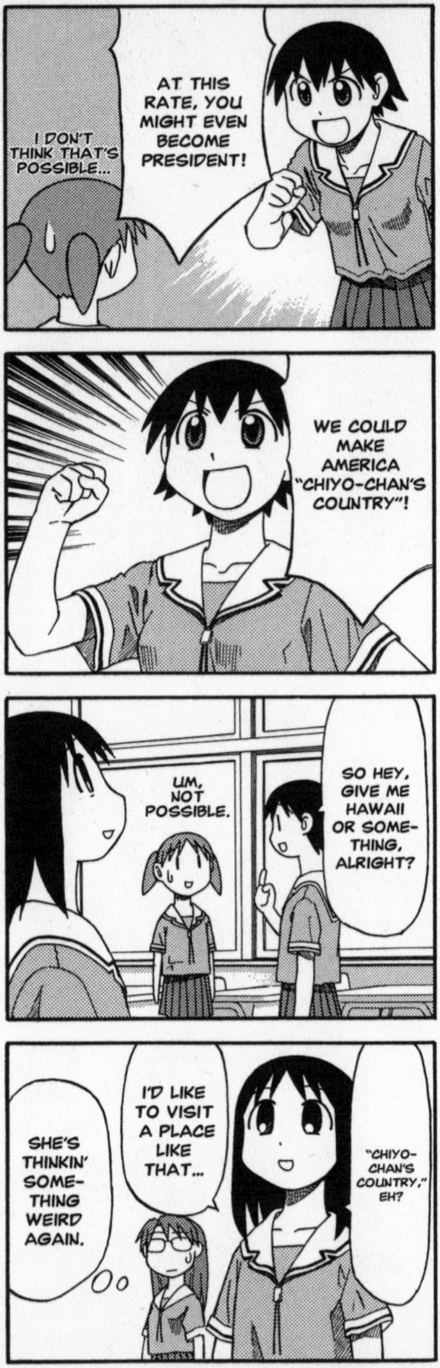
AT THIS RATE, YOU MIGHT EVEN BECOME PRESIDENT!
I DON'T THINK THAT'S POSSIBLE...
WE COULD MAKE AMERICA "CHIYO-CHAN'S COUNTRY"!
SO HEY, GIVE ME HAWAII OR SOMETHING, ALRIGHT?
UM, NOT POSSIBLE.
"CHIYO-CHAN'S COUNTRY," EH?
I'D LIKE TO VISIT A PLACE LIKE THAT...
SHE'S THINKIN' SOMETHING WEIRD AGAIN.

CHIYO-CHAN'S COUNTRY

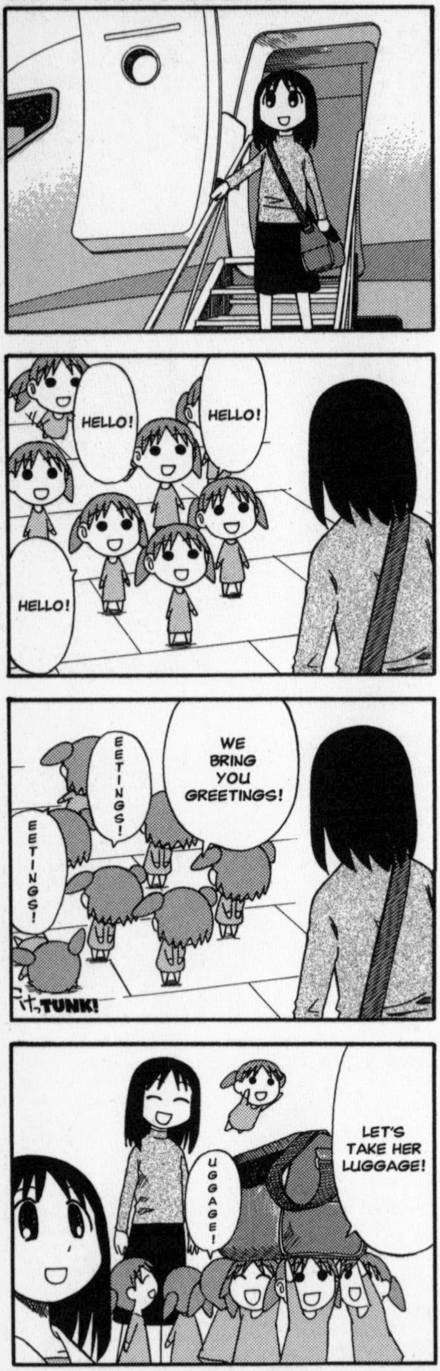
HELLO!
HELLO!
HELLO!
WE BRING YOU GREETINGS!
EETINGS!
EETINGS!
TUNK!
LET'S TAKE HER LUGGAGE!
UGGAGE!

CELEBRATE AMERICA

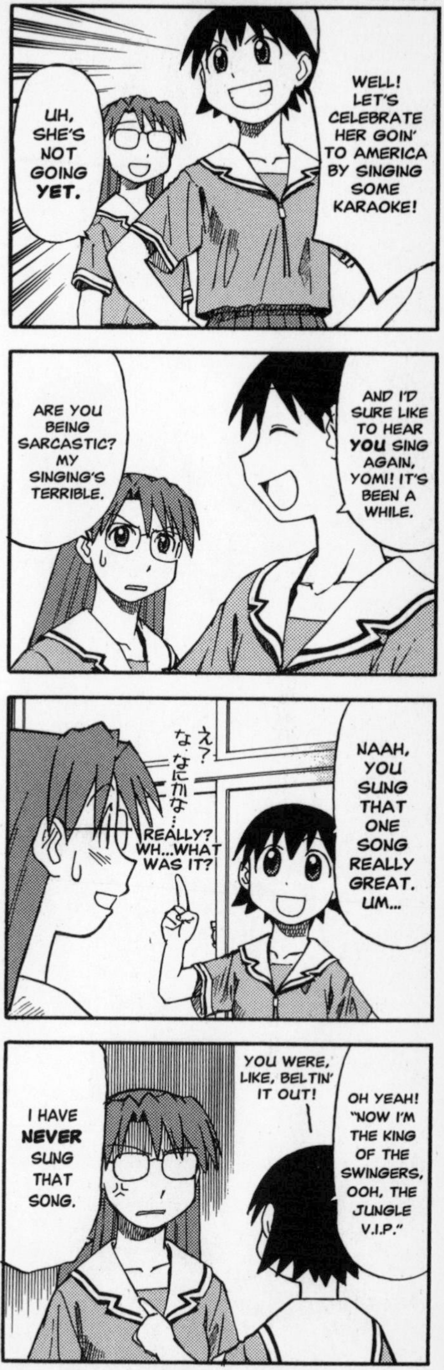
WELL! LET'S CELEBRATE HER GOIN' TO AMERICA BY SINGING SOME KARAOKE!
UH, SHE'S NOT GOING YET.
AND I'D SURE LIKE TO HEAR YOU SING AGAIN, YOMI! IT'S BEEN A WHILE.
ARE YOU BEING SARCASTIC? MY SINGING'S TERRIBLE.
NAAH, YOU SUNG THAT ONE SONG REALLY GREAT. UM...
えっ？な なにかな…
REALLY? WH...WHAT WAS IT?
OH YEAH! "NOW I'M THE KING OF THE SWINGERS, OOH, THE JUNGLE V.I.P."
YOU WERE, LIKE, BELTIN' IT OUT!
I HAVE NEVER SUNG THAT SONG.

THE TYPHOON

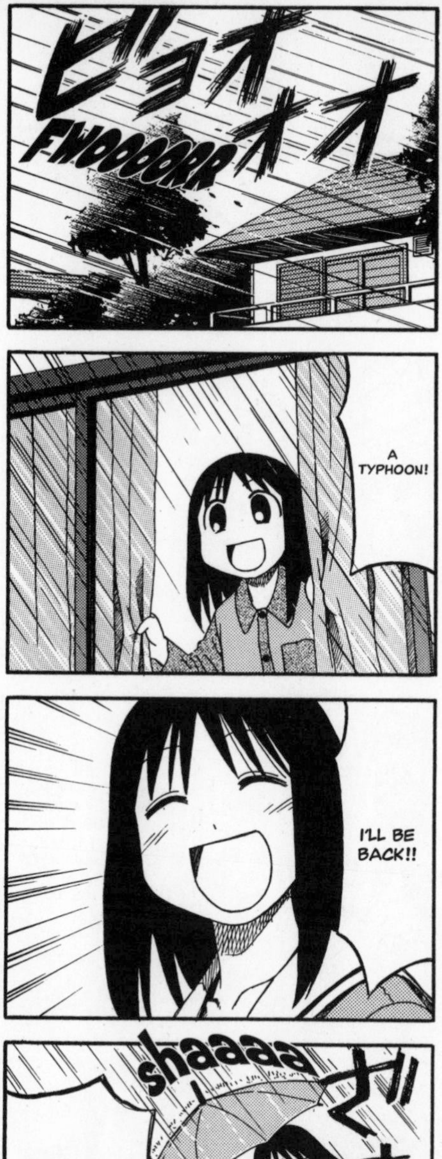
ビョオオオ
FWOOOORRR
A TYPHOON!
I'LL BE BACK!!
shaaaa
ざー
あああ
WHOA! OH, MAN!!

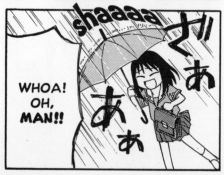

RISK MANAGEMENT

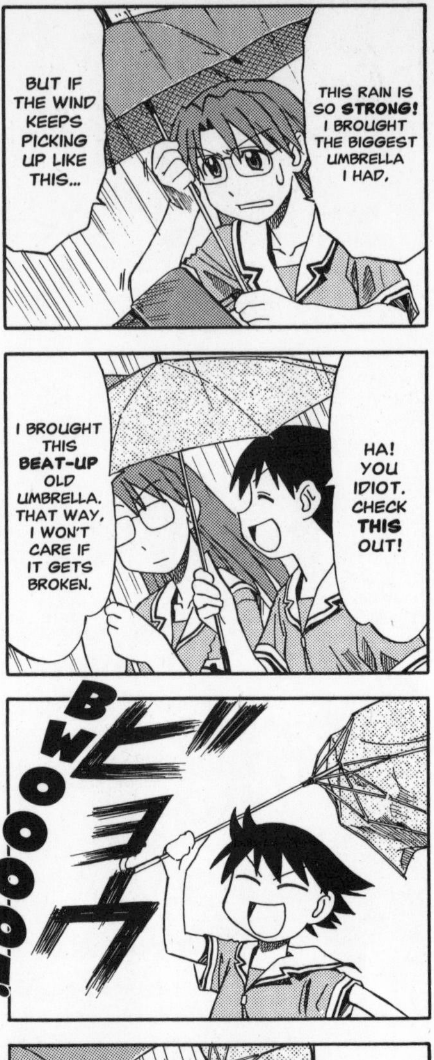
THIS RAIN IS SO STRONG! I BROUGHT THE BIGGEST UMBRELLA I HAD,
BUT IF THE WIND KEEPS PICKING UP LIKE THIS...
HA! YOU IDIOT. CHECK THIS OUT!
I BROUGHT THIS BEAT-UP OLD UMBRELLA. THAT WAY, I WON'T CARE IF IT GETS BROKEN.
BWOOOOOO!!
WAUGH! IT'S BROKEN!!
IDIOT.

DRENCHED

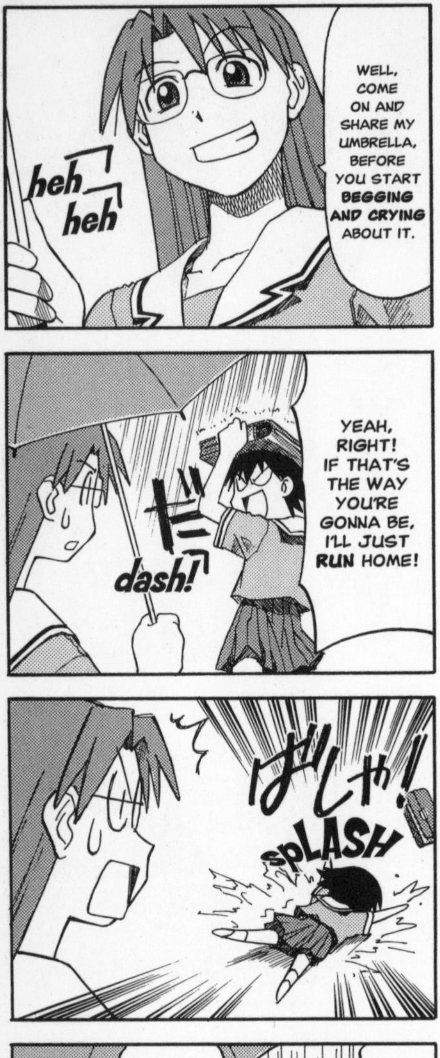
WELL, COME ON AND SHARE MY UMBRELLA, BEFORE YOU START BEGGING AND CRYING ABOUT IT.
heh heh
YEAH, RIGHT! IF THAT'S THE WAY YOU'RE GONNA BE, I'LL JUST RUN HOME!
ダッ
dash!
ばしゃ!
sPLASH
C'MON. LET ME SHARE YOUR UMBRELLA...
drenched
どろー
OK, OK. JUST STOP CRYING.

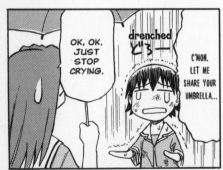

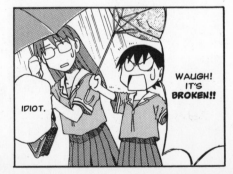

TOGETHER

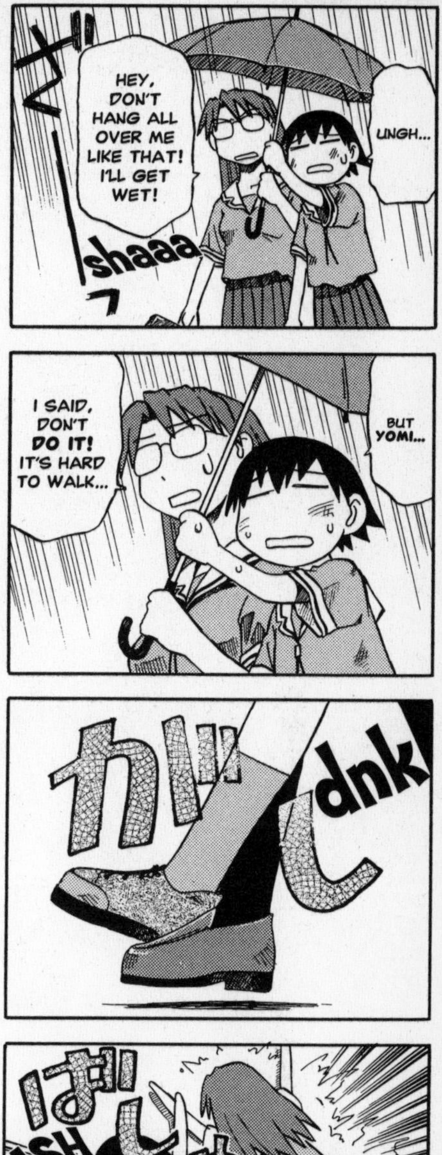
HEY, DON'T HANG ALL OVER ME LIKE THAT! I'LL GET WET!
UNGH...
shaaa
I SAID, DON'T DO IT! IT'S HARD TO WALK...
BUT YOMI...
dnk
SPLASH

THE TYPHOON

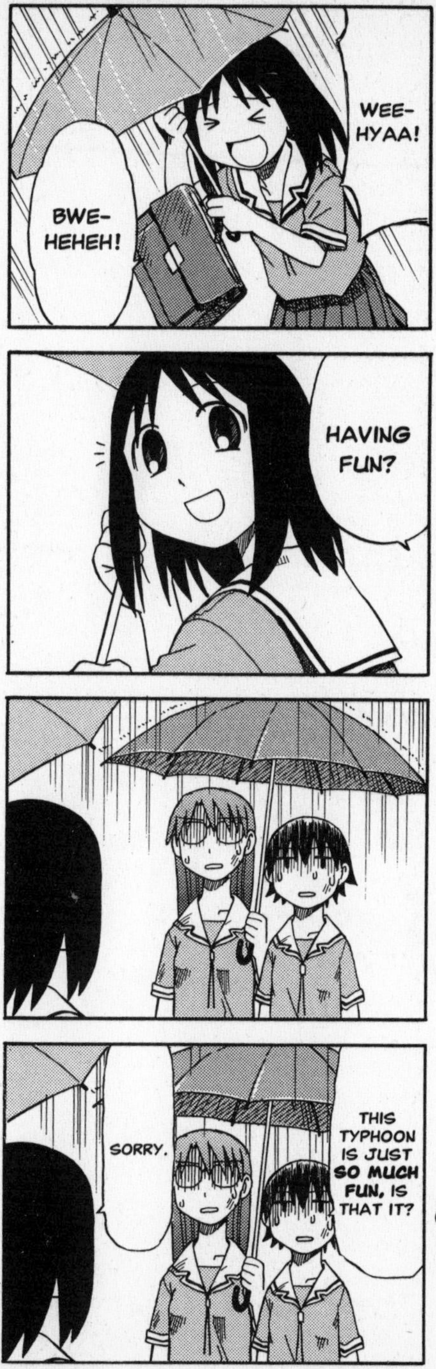
WEE-HYAA!
BWE-HEHEH!
HAVING FUN?
THIS TYPHOON IS JUST SO MUCH FUN, IS THAT IT?
SORRY.

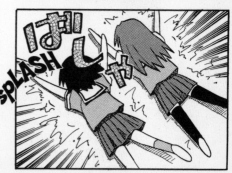

10 OCTOBER PART-1

AZU MANGA DAIOH

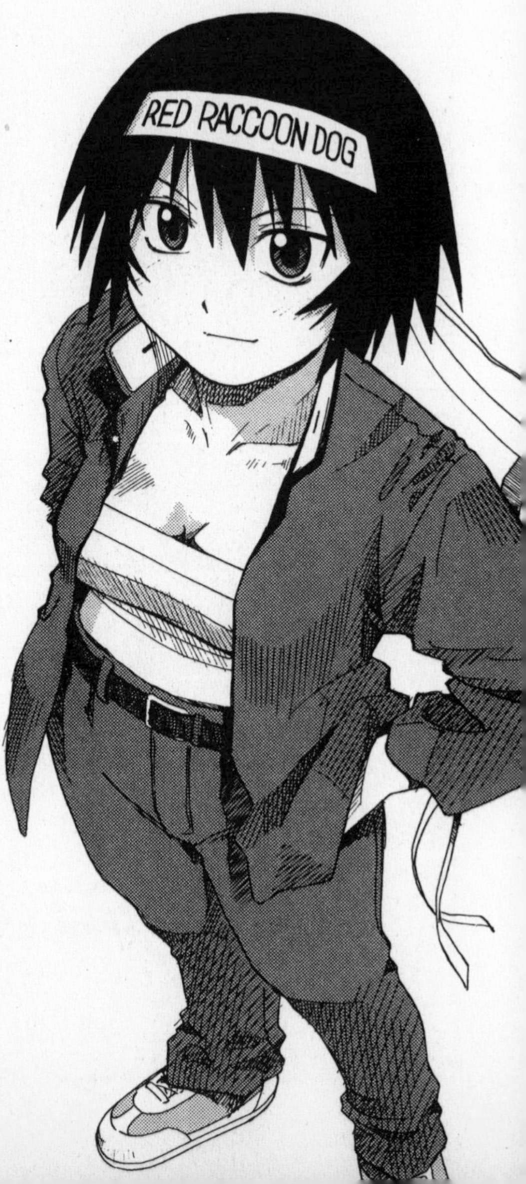
RED RACCOON DOG

THE FEELING

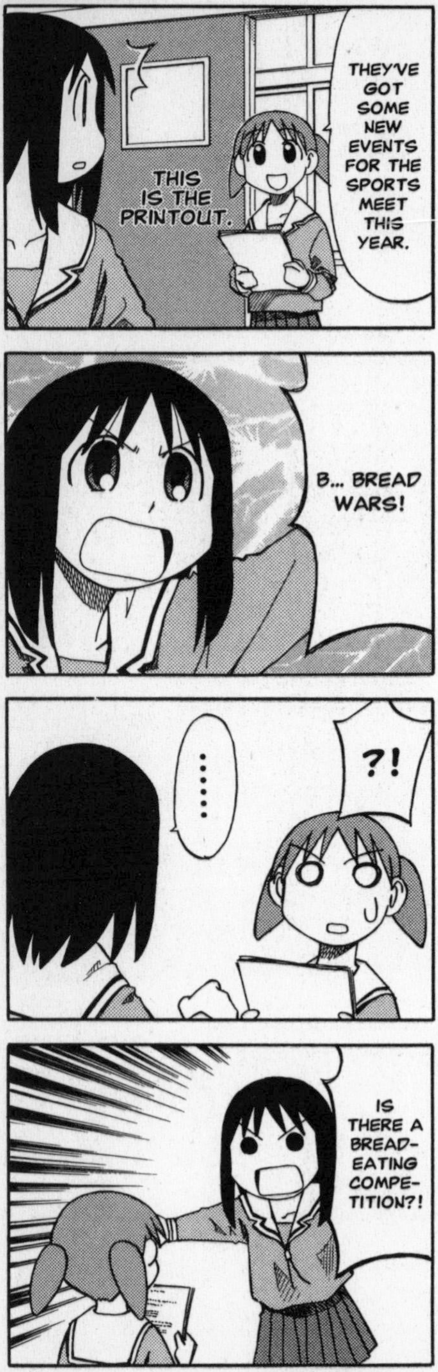
THEY'VE GOT SOME NEW EVENTS FOR THE SPORTS MEET THIS YEAR.
THIS IS THE PRINTOUT.
B... BREAD WARS!
?!
......
IS THERE A BREAD-EATING COMPETITION?!

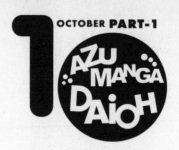

APTITUDE TEST

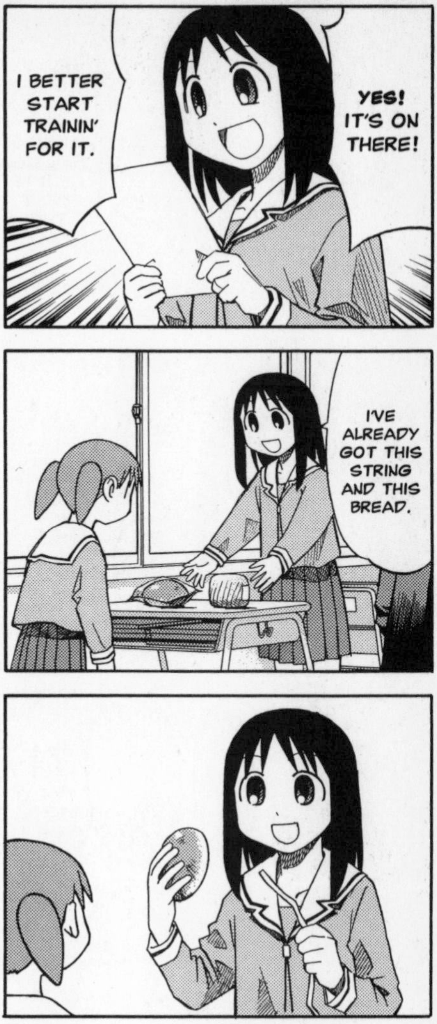
YES! IT'S ON THERE!
I BETTER START TRAININ' FOR IT.
I'VE ALREADY GOT THIS STRING AND THIS BREAD.
?

OUCH!

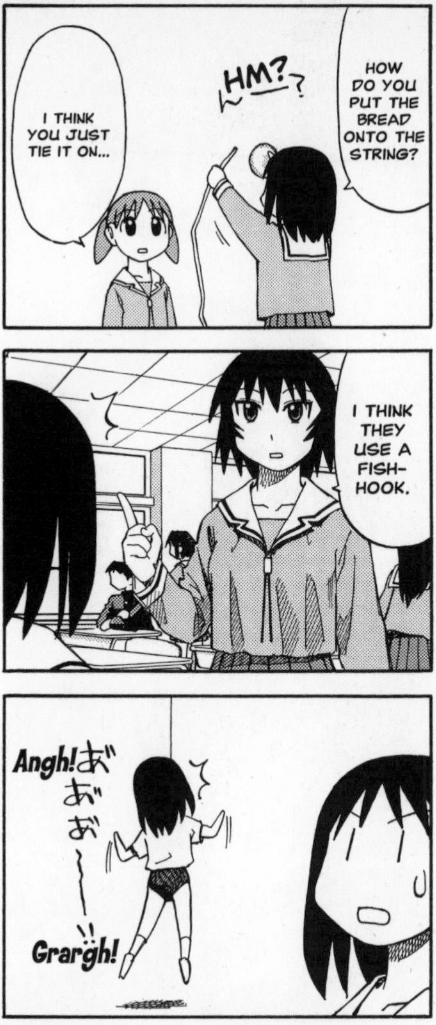
HOW DO YOU PUT THE BREAD ONTO THE STRING?
HM?
I THINK YOU JUST TIE IT ON...
I THINK THEY USE A FISH-HOOK.
Angh! あぁぁ〜〜
Grargh!
TH... THEY LET US DO SOMETHING THAT DANGER-OUS?!
OR MAYBE I'M WRONG.
shudder ブルブル

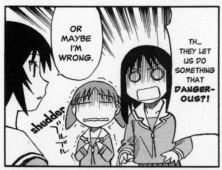

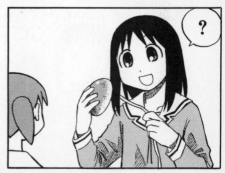

SMACKDOWN

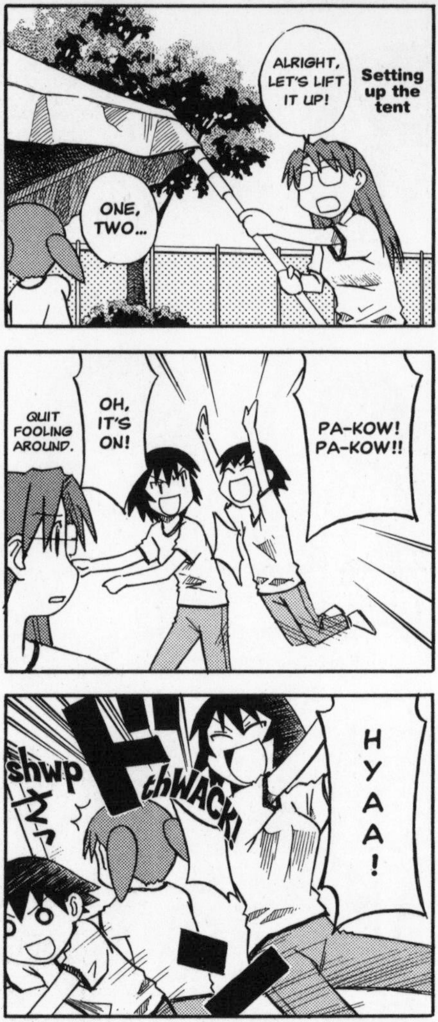
Setting up the tent
ALRIGHT, LET'S LIFT IT UP!
ONE, TWO...
PA-KOW! PA-KOW!!
OH, IT'S ON!
QUIT FOOLING AROUND.
HYAAA!
thWACK!
shwp
OH.
WAAAUGH!
ka-thmp

ALL IN VAIN

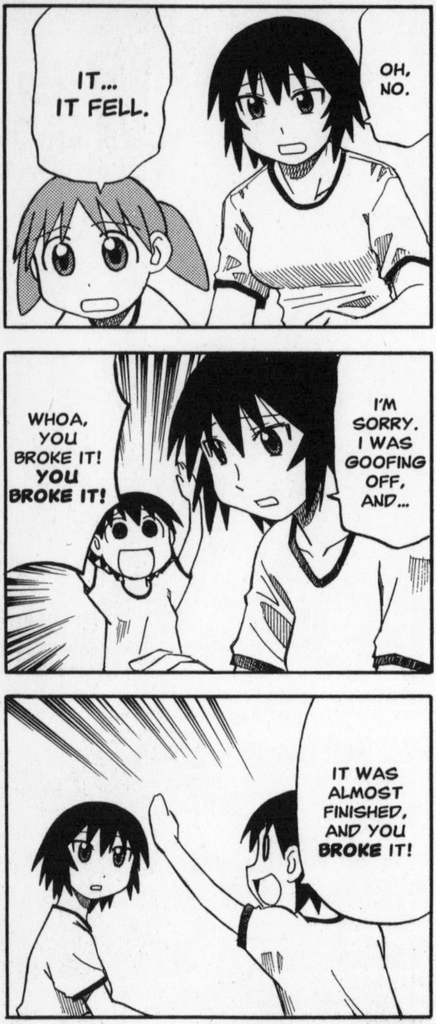
OH, NO.
IT... IT FELL.
I'M SORRY. I WAS GOOFING OFF, AND...
WHOA, YOU BROKE IT! YOU BROKE IT!
IT WAS ALMOST FINISHED, AND YOU BROKE IT!
teary-eyed
UM, UH...

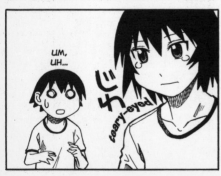

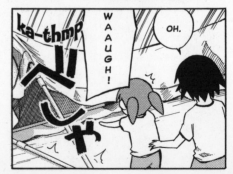

RESPONSIBILITY

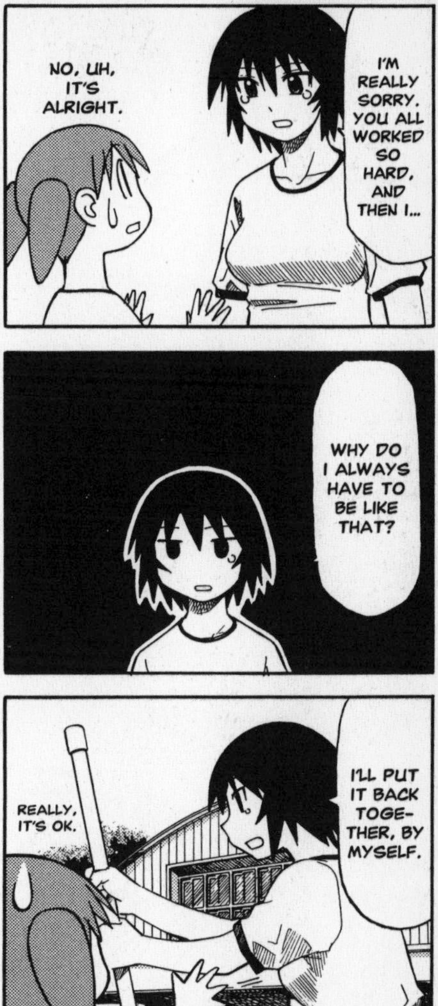
I'M REALLY SORRY. YOU ALL WORKED SO HARD, AND THEN I...
NO, UH, IT'S ALRIGHT.
WHY DO I ALWAYS HAVE TO BE LIKE THAT?
I'LL PUT IT BACK TOGE-THER, BY MYSELF.
REALLY, IT'S OK.
NO, NO, **NO!** THIS IS WHEN YOU'RE SUPPOSED TO GO, "IT WAS TOMO'S FAULT"! COME ON!
DON'T BE SO RESPONSIBLE ALL THE TIME!

THE MOOD MAKER

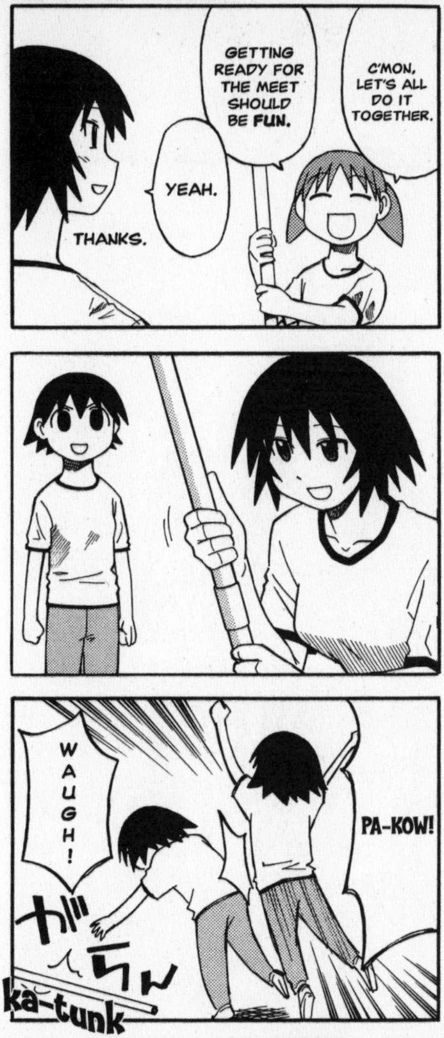
C'MON, LET'S ALL DO IT TOGETHER.
GETTING READY FOR THE MEET SHOULD BE **FUN.**
YEAH.
THANKS.
PA-KOW!
WAUGH!
がらん
ka-tunk
WHAT THE HECK ARE YOU DOIN'?!
THERE, **THAT'S** THE SPIRIT!
QUIT BEING AN IDIOT.

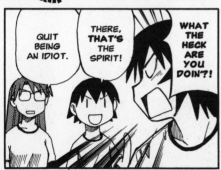

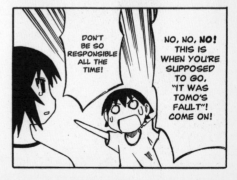

THE DIET

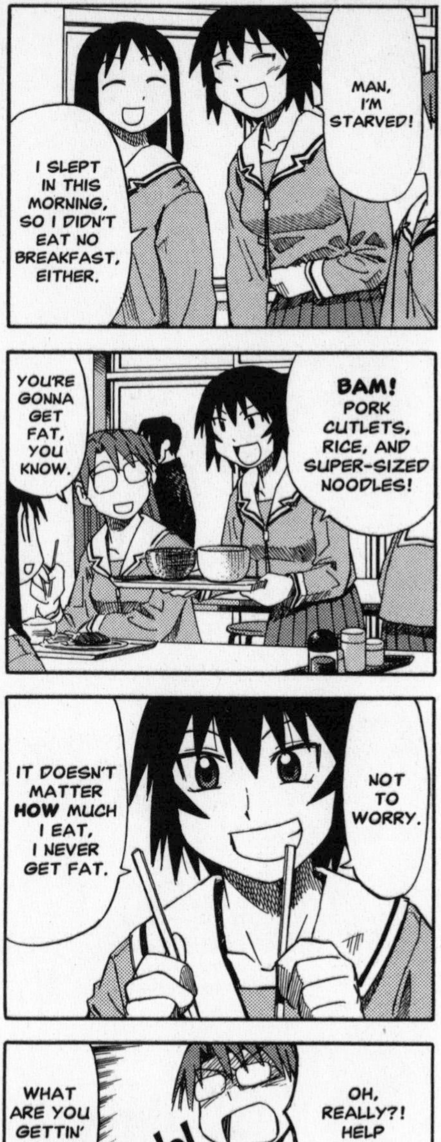
MAN, I'M STARVED!
I SLEPT IN THIS MORNING, SO I DIDN'T EAT NO BREAKFAST, EITHER.
BAM! PORK CUTLETS, RICE, AND SUPER-SIZED NOODLES!
YOU'RE GONNA GET FAT, YOU KNOW.
NOT TO WORRY.
IT DOESN'T MATTER HOW MUCH I EAT, I NEVER GET FAT.
OH, REALLY?! HELP YOURSELF TO THE CUTLETS, THEN! GO ON, EAT A HUNDRED OF 'EM!!
rattle!
WHAT ARE YOU GETTIN' ANGRY FOR?

LOW-CAL HAPPINESS

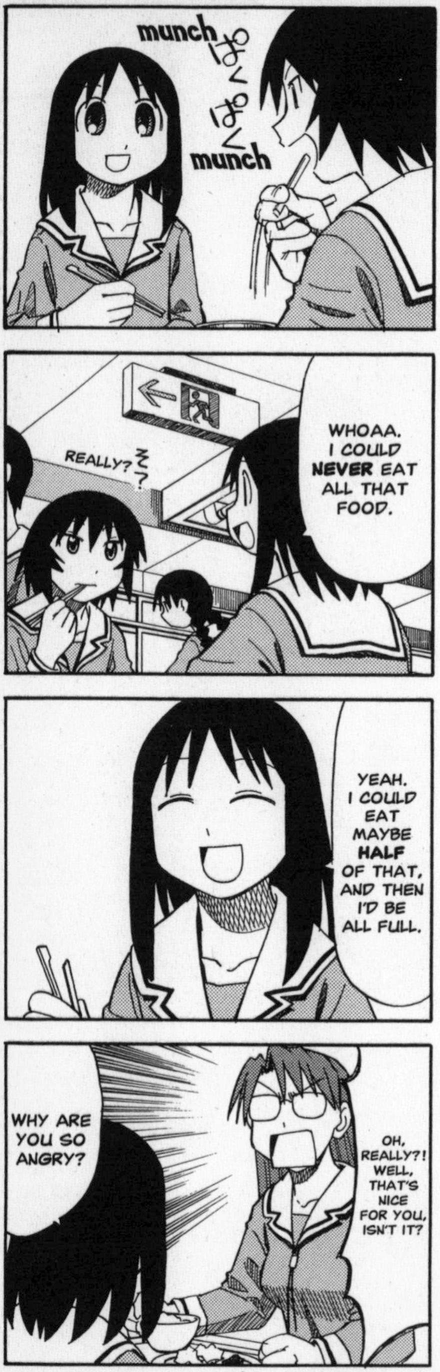
munch
ぱくぱく
munch
WHOAA. I COULD NEVER EAT ALL THAT FOOD.
REALLY?
YEAH. I COULD EAT MAYBE HALF OF THAT, AND THEN I'D BE ALL FULL.
OH, REALLY?! WELL, THAT'S NICE FOR YOU, ISN'T IT?
WHY ARE YOU SO ANGRY?

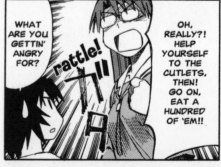

PRESIDENT OF THE GYM SHORTS ASSOCIATION

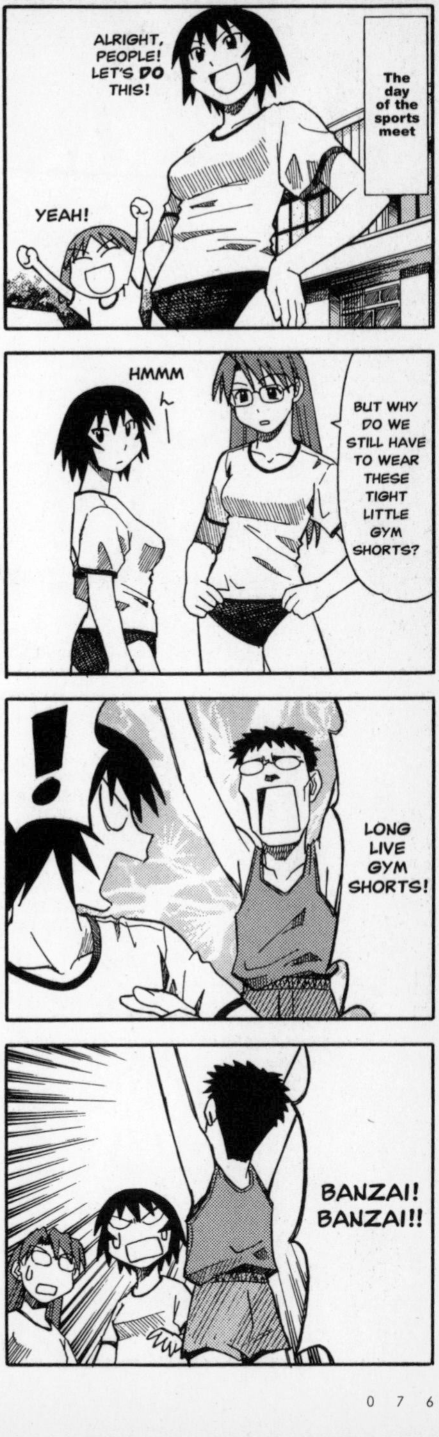
The day of the sports meet
ALRIGHT, PEOPLE! LET'S DO THIS!
YEAH!
BUT WHY DO WE STILL HAVE TO WEAR THESE TIGHT LITTLE GYM SHORTS?
HMMM
LONG LIVE GYM SHORTS!
!
BANZAI! BANZAI!!

THE CONFESSION

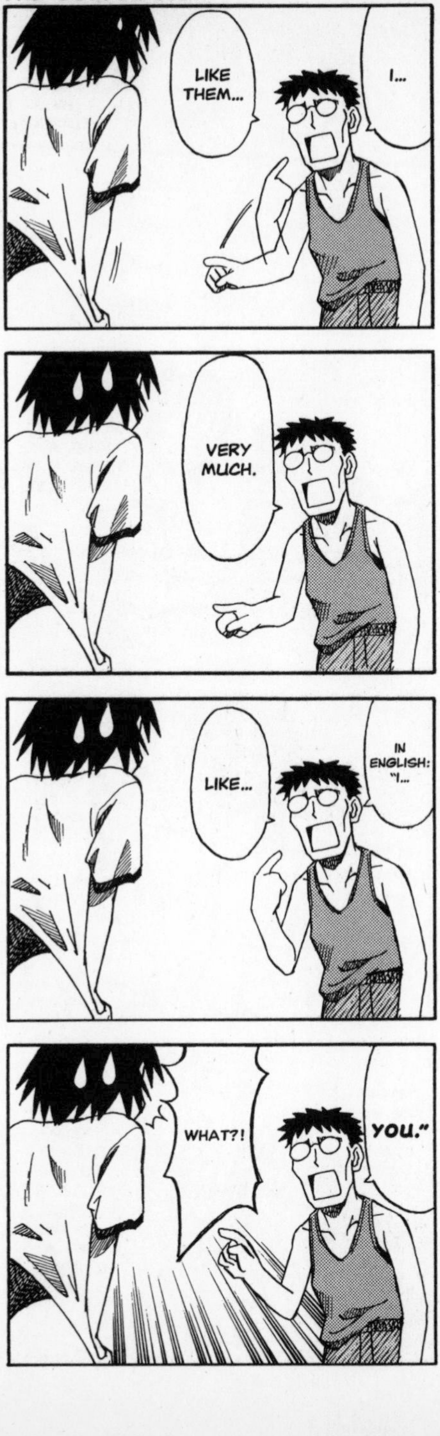
I...
LIKE THEM...
VERY MUCH.
IN ENGLISH: "I...
LIKE...
YOU."
WHAT?!

IN CUSTODY

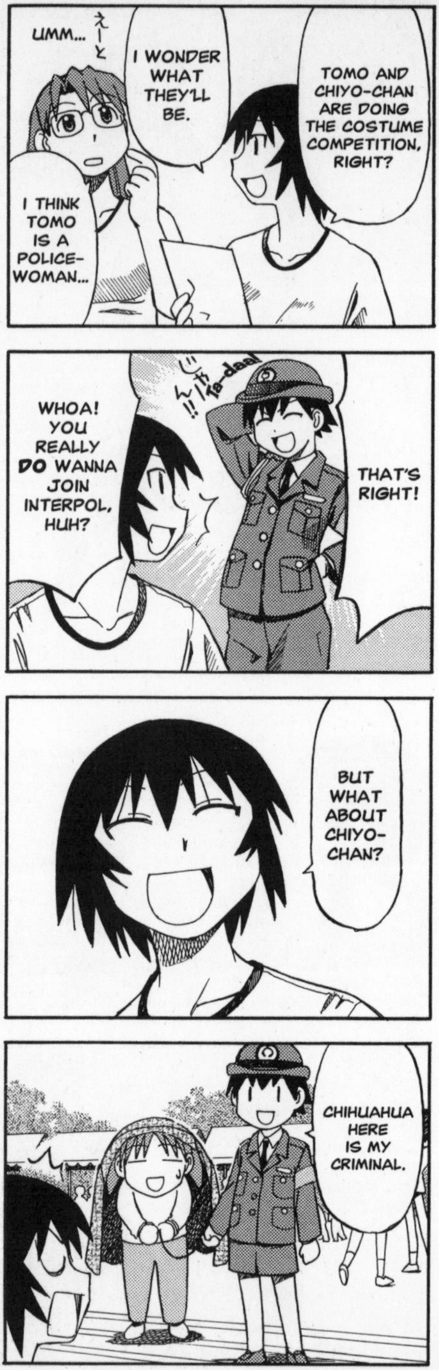
TOMO AND CHIYO-CHAN ARE DOING THE COSTUME COMPETITION, RIGHT?
I WONDER WHAT THEY'LL BE.
UMM... えーと
I THINK TOMO IS A POLICE-WOMAN...
THAT'S RIGHT!
じゃーん!! ta-daa!
WHOA! YOU REALLY DO WANNA JOIN INTERPOL, HUH?
BUT WHAT ABOUT CHIYO-CHAN?
CHIHUAHUA HERE IS MY CRIMINAL.

ESCORTING THE PRISONER

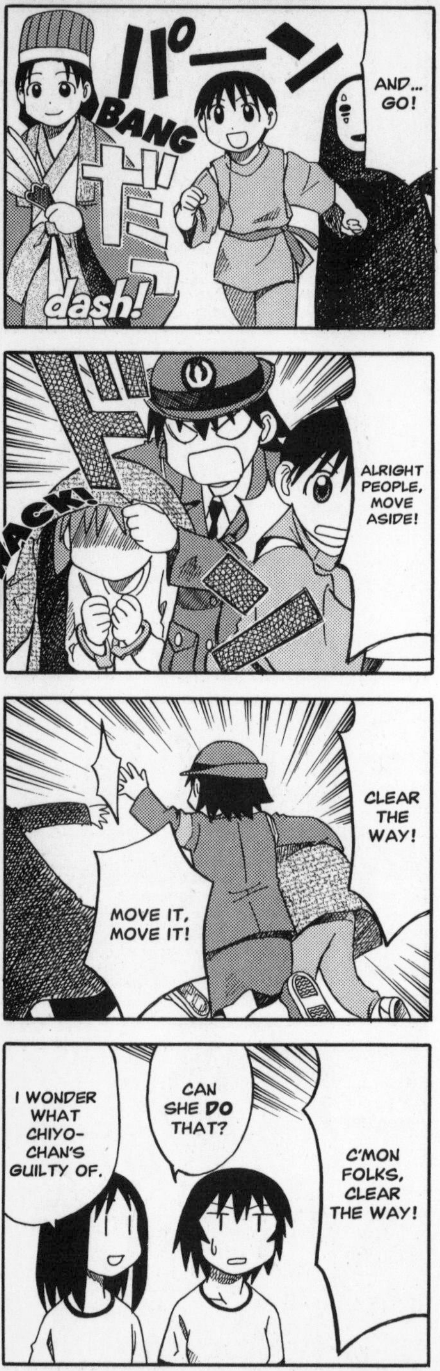
AND... GO!
パーン BANG
dash!
ALRIGHT PEOPLE, MOVE ASIDE!
BWACK!
CLEAR THE WAY!
MOVE IT, MOVE IT!
C'MON FOLKS, CLEAR THE WAY!
CAN SHE DO THAT?
I WONDER WHAT CHIYO-CHAN'S GUILTY OF.

LAWS OF THE ENTERTAINMENT DISTRICT

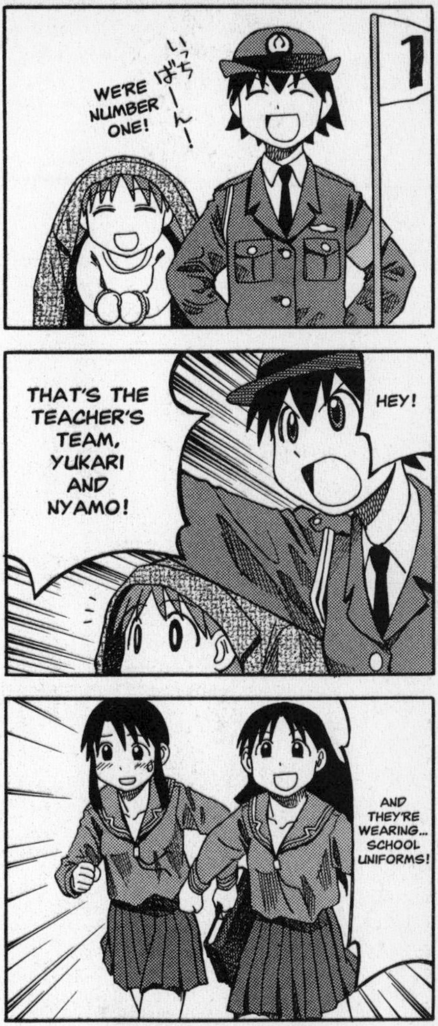
いっちばーーん!
WE'RE NUMBER ONE!
HEY!
THAT'S THE TEACHER'S TEAM, YUKARI AND NYAMO!
AND THEY'RE WEARING... SCHOOL UNIFORMS!
DOING A LITTLE DRESS UP FOR YOUR CLIENTS, EH? CRIMINALS! I ARREST YOU!
WHAT?!

THE STRAGGLER

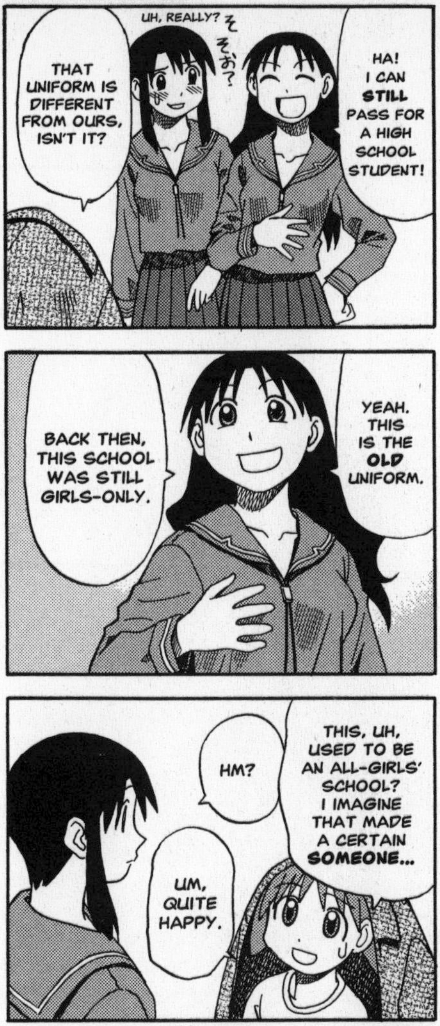
HA! I CAN STILL PASS FOR A HIGH SCHOOL STUDENT!
UH, REALLY?
そ そぉ?
THAT UNIFORM IS DIFFERENT FROM OURS, ISN'T IT?
YEAH. THIS IS THE OLD UNIFORM.
BACK THEN, THIS SCHOOL WAS STILL GIRLS-ONLY.
THIS, UH, USED TO BE AN ALL-GIRLS' SCHOOL? I IMAGINE THAT MADE A CERTAIN SOMEONE...
HM?
UM, QUITE HAPPY.
UPPER-CLASSMAN KUROSAWA? THIS IS FOR YOU.
WAUGH! WHAT ARE YOU DOING?! AND DON'T CALL ME "UPPER-CLASSMAN."

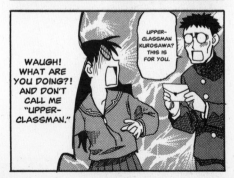

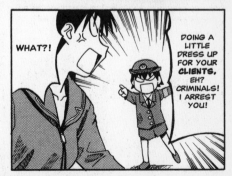

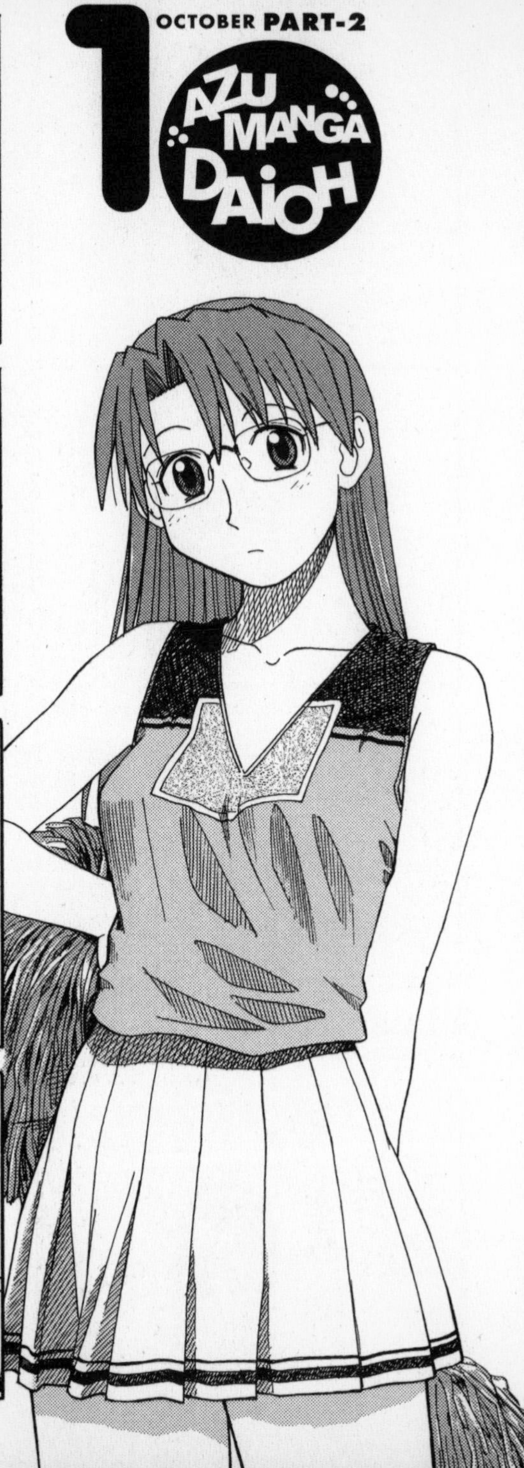
10
OCTOBER PART-2
AZUMANGA DAIOH

I DIDN'T THINK OF THAT

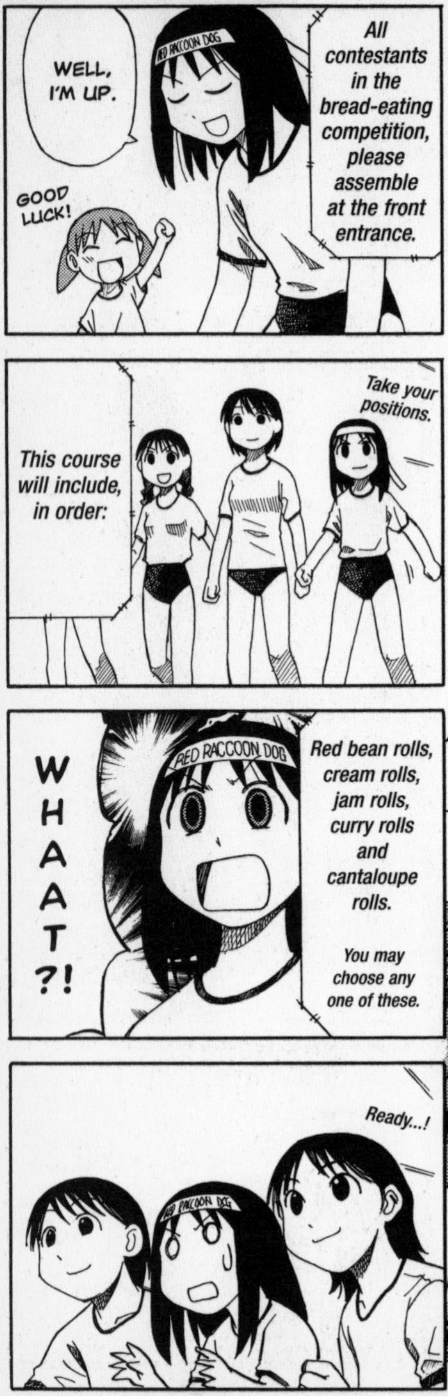
All contestants in the bread-eating competition, please assemble at the front entrance.
RED RACCOON DOG
WELL, I'M UP.
GOOD LUCK!
Take your positions.
This course will include, in order:
Red bean rolls, cream rolls, jam rolls, curry rolls and cantaloupe rolls.
You may choose any one of these.
RED RACCOON DOG
WHAAT?!
Ready...!
RED RACCOON DOG

UM...

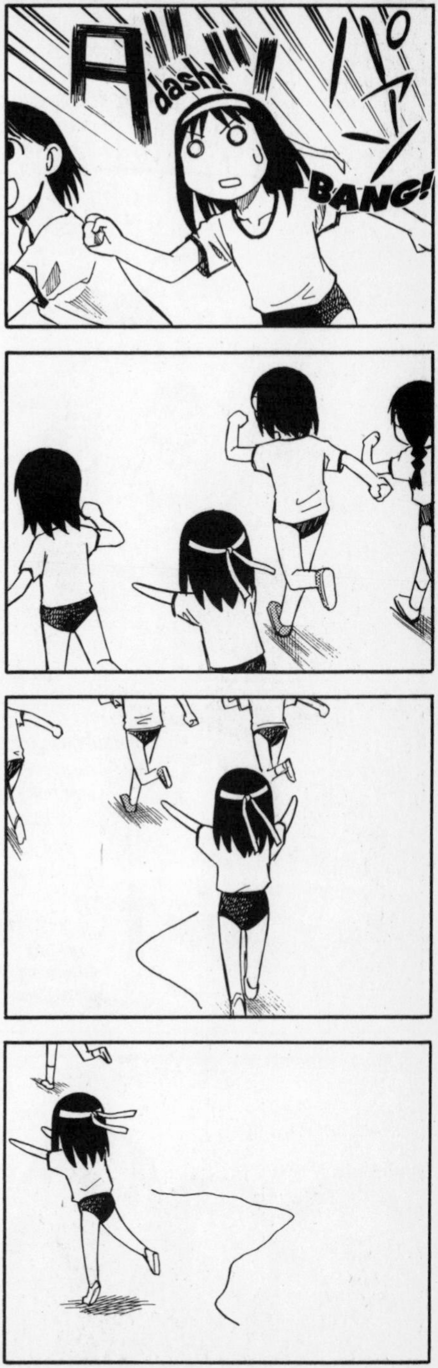
BANG!
dash!

CANTALOUPE ROLL

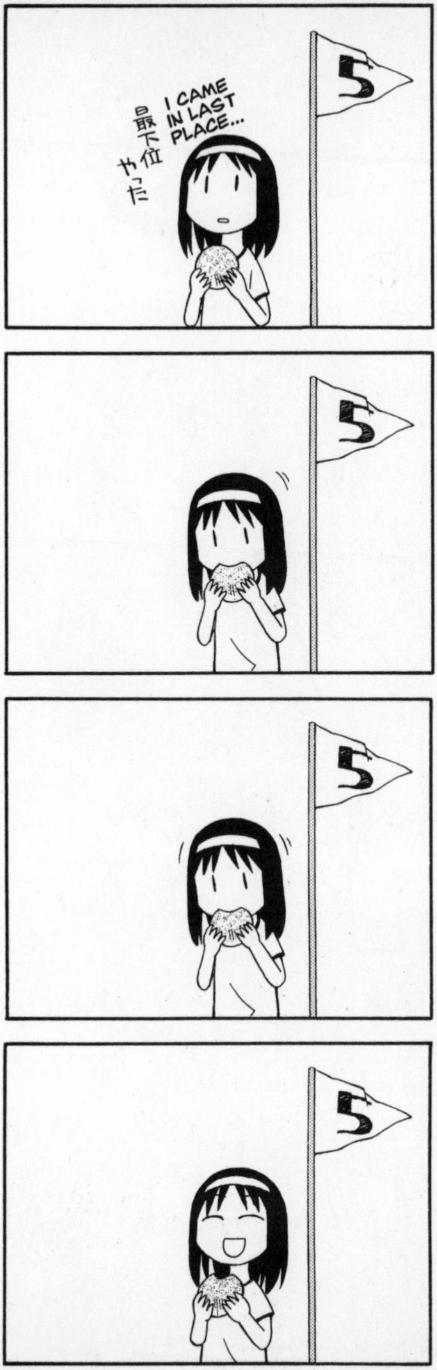
最下位やった
I CAME IN LAST PLACE...

THE CHEERLEADER

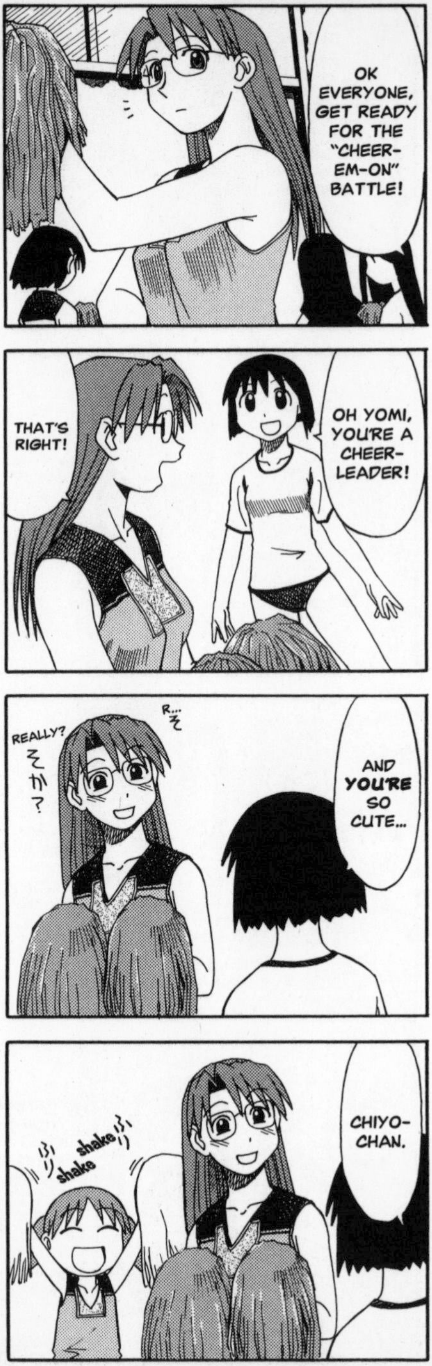
OK EVERYONE, GET READY FOR THE "CHEER-EM-ON" BATTLE!
OH YOMI, YOU'RE A CHEER-LEADER!
THAT'S RIGHT!
AND YOU'RE SO CUTE...
R... そ
REALLY? そか?
CHIYO-CHAN.
shake ふり
shake ふり

DRAG

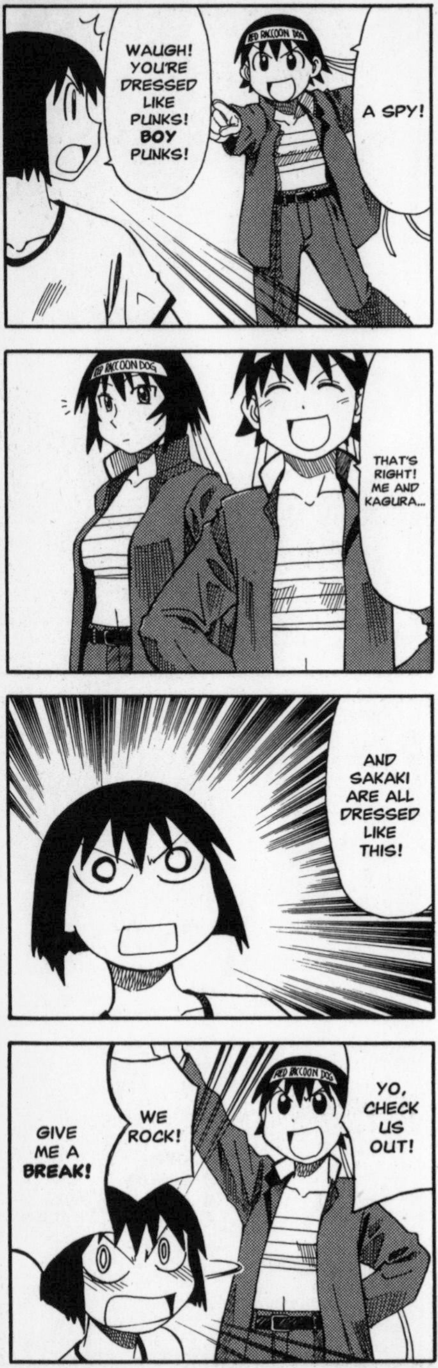
A SPY!
WAUGH! YOU'RE DRESSED LIKE PUNKS! BOY PUNKS!
THAT'S RIGHT! ME AND KAGURA...
AND SAKAKI ARE ALL DRESSED LIKE THIS!
YO, CHECK US OUT!
WE ROCK!
GIVE ME A BREAK!

THE STANDARD BEARER

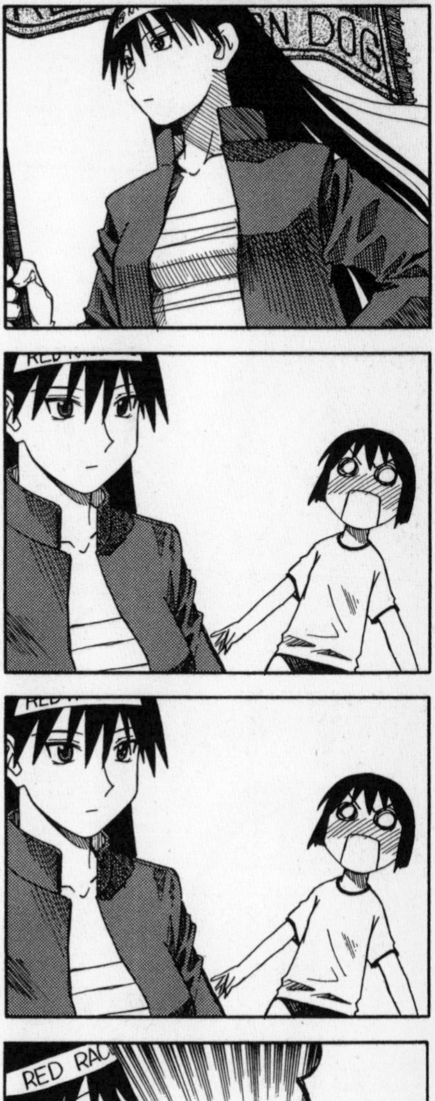
BANZAI, SAKAKI! BANZAI!

AND WE SHALL ALL RUN TOGETHER

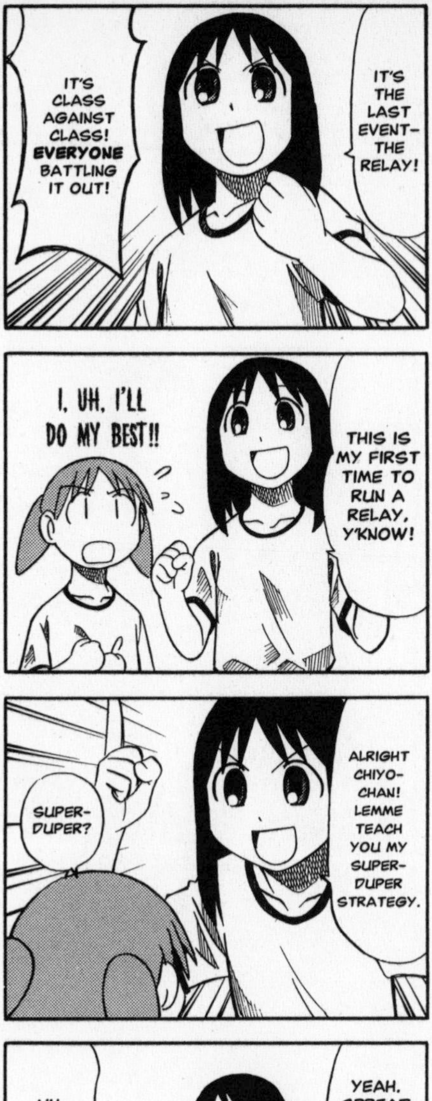
IT'S THE LAST EVENT— THE RELAY!
IT'S CLASS AGAINST CLASS! **EVERYONE** BATTLING IT OUT!
THIS IS MY FIRST TIME TO RUN A RELAY, Y'KNOW!
I, UH, I'LL DO MY BEST!!
ALRIGHT CHIYO-CHAN! LEMME TEACH YOU MY SUPER-DUPER STRATEGY.
SUPER-DUPER?
YEAH. SPREAD YOUR ARMS OUT LIKE **THIS**, AND IT'LL MAKE IT DIFFICULT FOR PEOPLE TO PASS YOU!
thp thp thp
UH, YOU THINK SO?

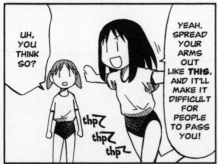

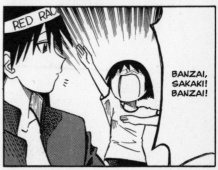

C'MON AND RUN!

HYAAAA!
Yayyy!
OSAKA!
thwack!
HERE GOES!
yayy!
Yayy!
Yayy!
THEY'RE PASSING YOU! THEY'RE PASSING YOU!

JUST A LITTLE FASTER

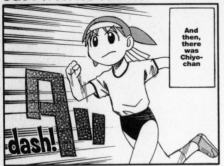

And then, there was Chiyo-chan
dash!
C'MON, CHIYO! THIS IS WHY YOU'VE BEEN RUNNING EVERY NIGHT!
VWOOSH!
Hngr!
Hnngr!
!!
I GET THE FEELING I'M DOING SOMETHING BAD...

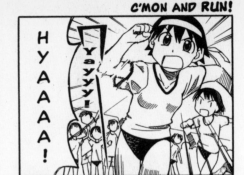

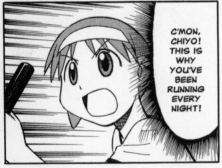

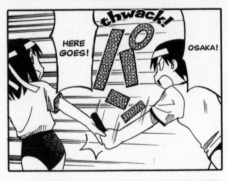

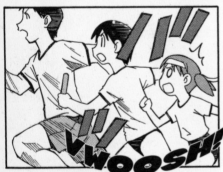

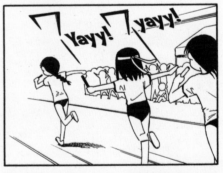

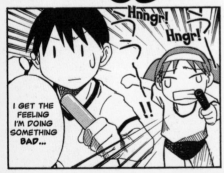

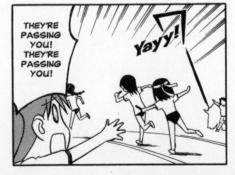

WATCH AND LEARN

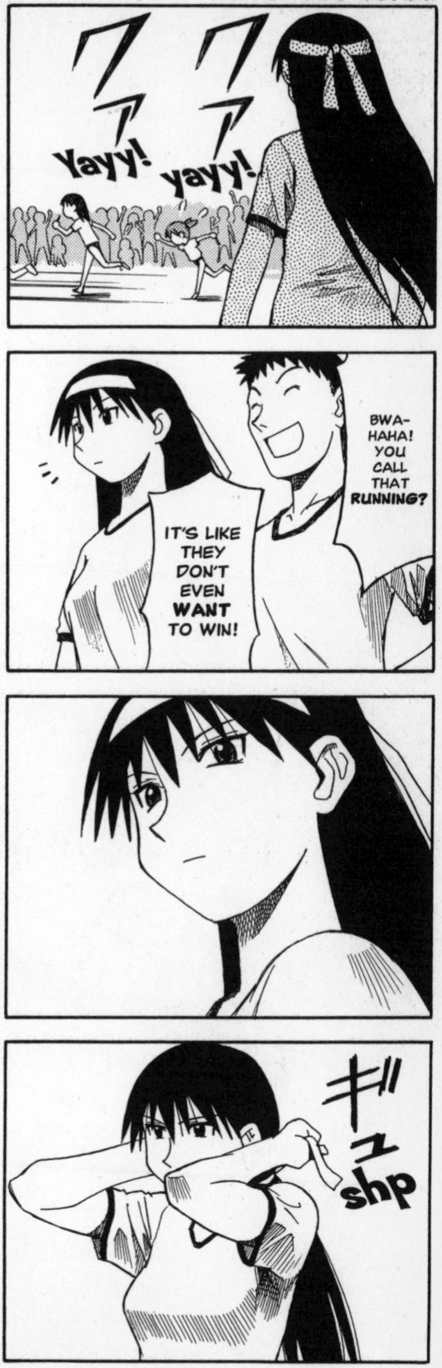
ワァ
yayy!
ワァ
Yayy!
BWA-HAHA! YOU CALL THAT RUNNING?
IT'S LIKE THEY DON'T EVEN WANT TO WIN!
ギュ
shp

BELIEVE

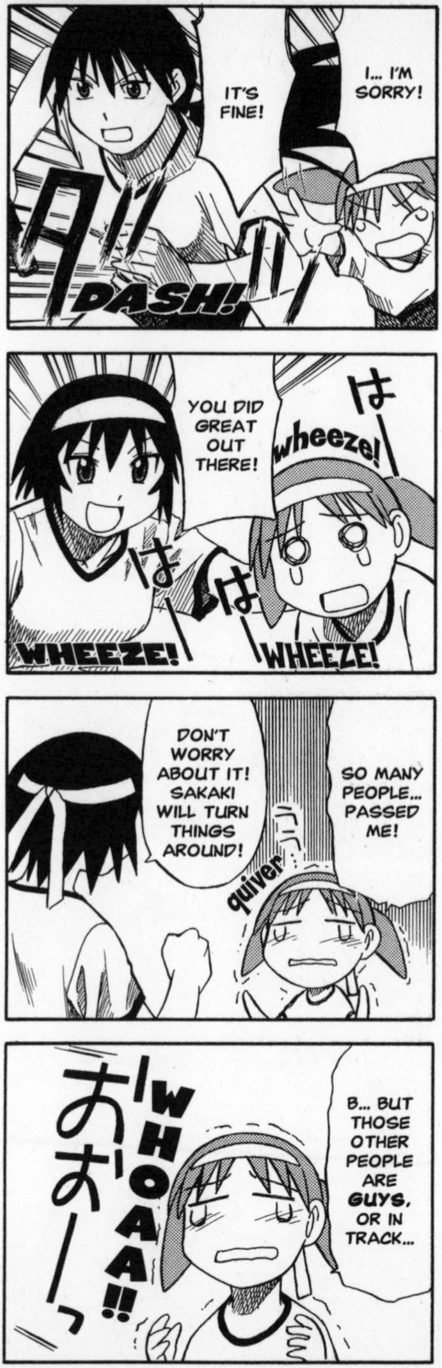
I... I'M SORRY!
IT'S FINE!
DASH!
は
wheeze!
YOU DID GREAT OUT THERE!
は
WHEEZE!
は
WHEEZE!
SO MANY PEOPLE... PASSED ME!
DON'T WORRY ABOUT IT! SAKAKI WILL TURN THINGS AROUND!
quiver
B... BUT THOSE OTHER PEOPLE ARE GUYS, OR IN TRACK...
おおーっ
WHOAA!!

IT COMES DOWN TO THIS

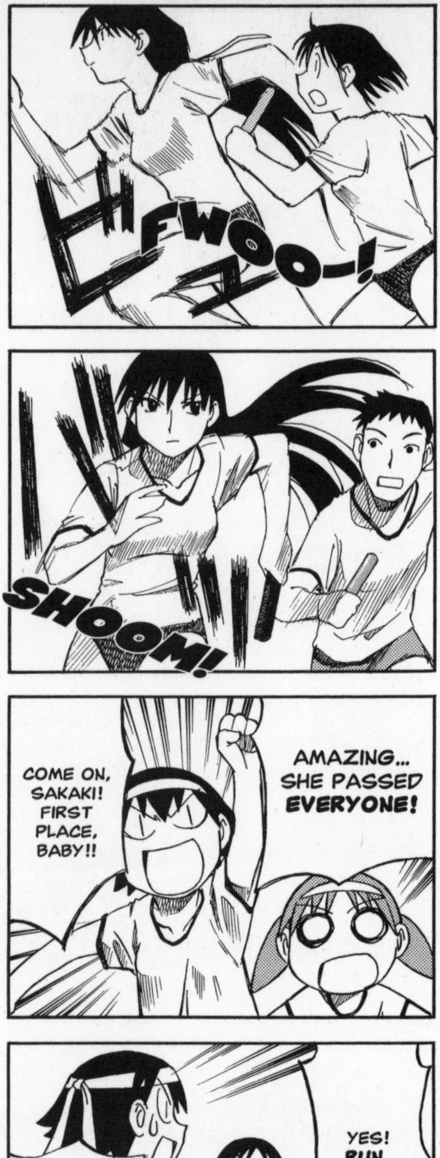
ヒュ
FWOO--!
SHOOM!
AMAZING... SHE PASSED EVERYONE!
COME ON, SAKAKI! FIRST PLACE, BABY!!
YES! RUN, SAKAKI, AND LEAVE THE REST UP TO ME!
OH, GREAT! THE LAST RUNNER'S OUR FRICKIN' HOMEROOM TEACHER!

THE SHOWDOWN

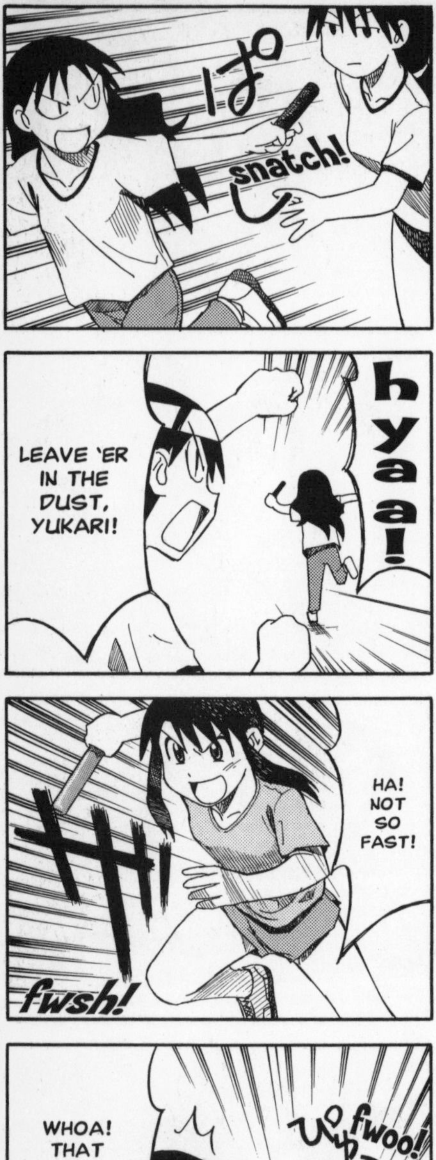
ぱし
snatch!
hyaa!
LEAVE 'ER IN THE DUST, YUKARI!
HA! NOT SO FAST!
fwsh!
ぴゅ
fwoo!
まて
WAIT!!
WHOA! THAT NYAMO IS FAST!

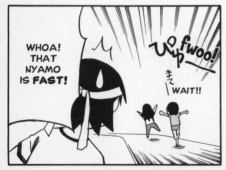

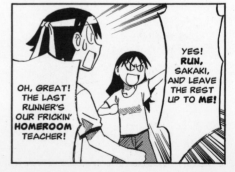

ALL OR NOTHING

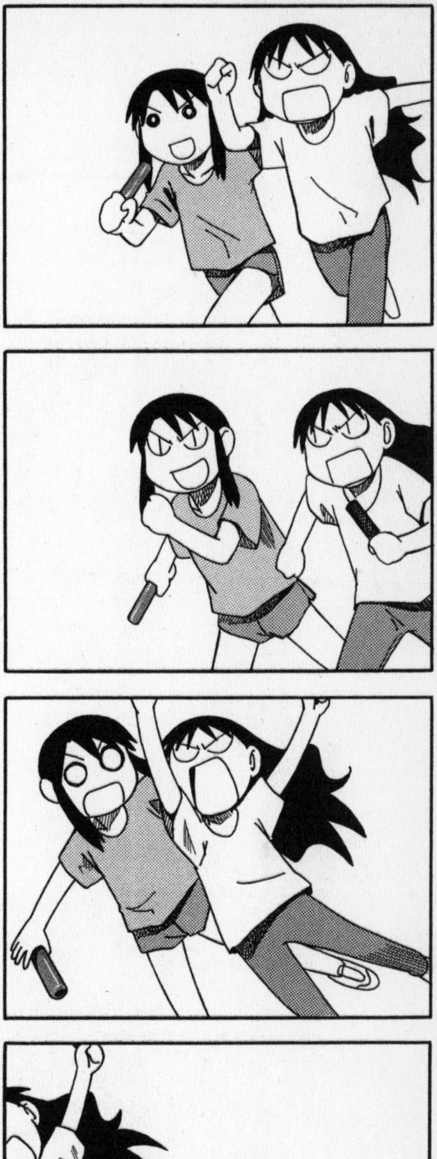

IN UNISON

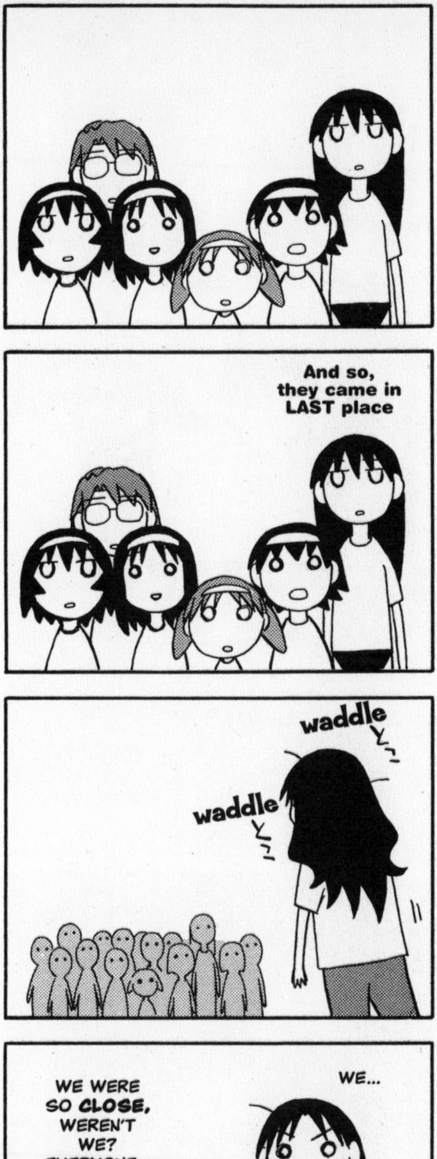
And so, they came in LAST place
waddle
waddle
WE...
WE WERE SO CLOSE, WEREN'T WE? EVERYONE...

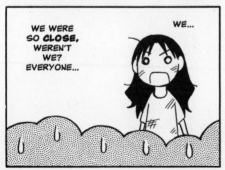

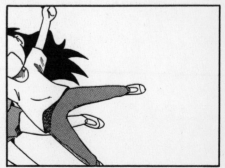

AZUMANGA DAIOH

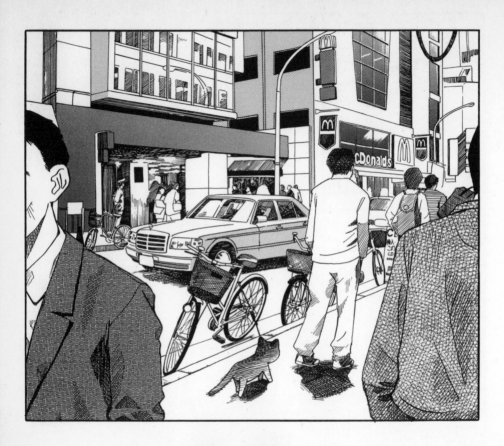

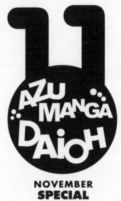

AZU MANGA DAIOH

NOVEMBER SPECIAL

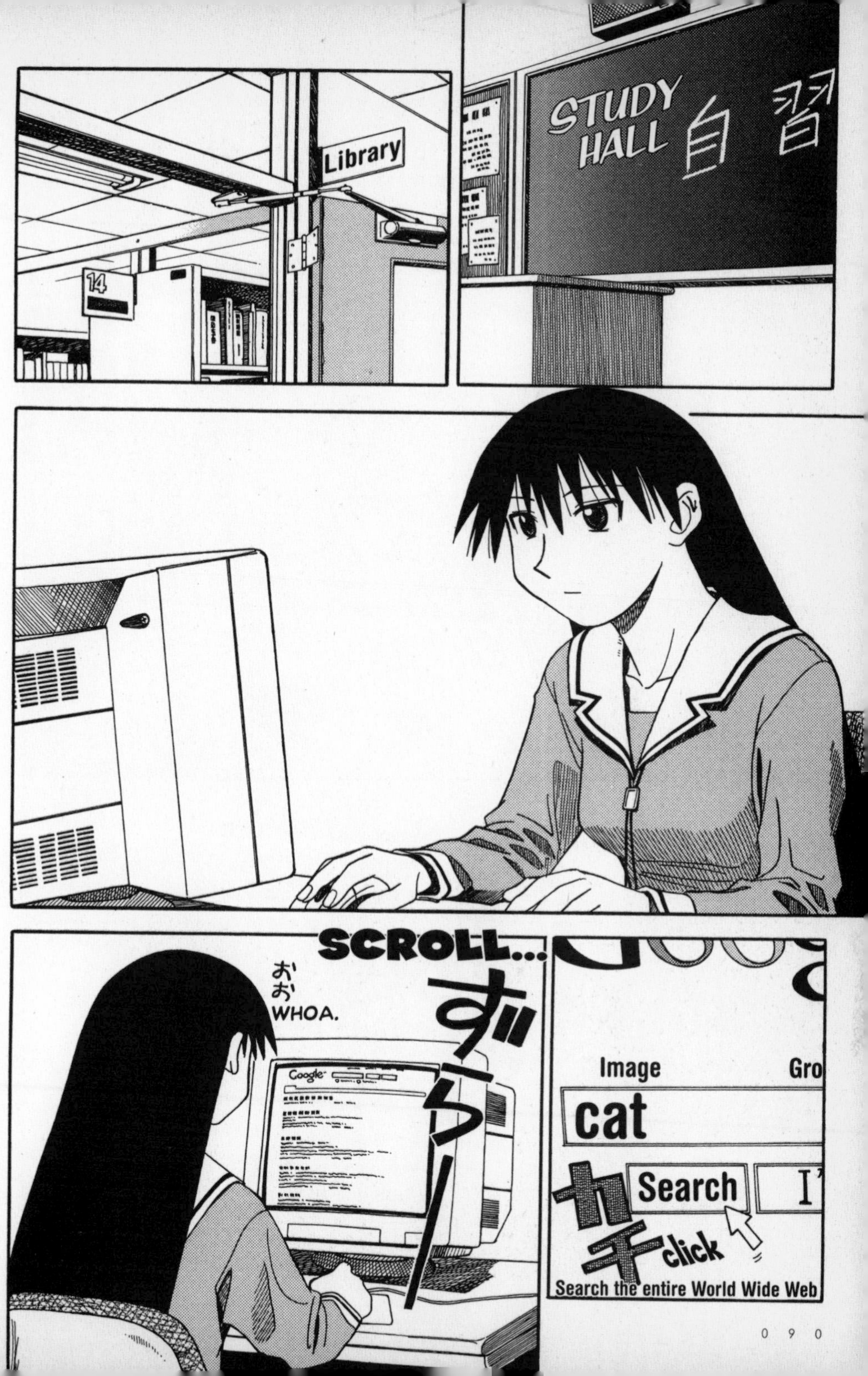
STUDY HALL 自習
Library
14
Image
Gro
cat
Search
I'
カチ click
Search the entire World Wide Web
SCROLL... ずらー
おお WHOA.
Google

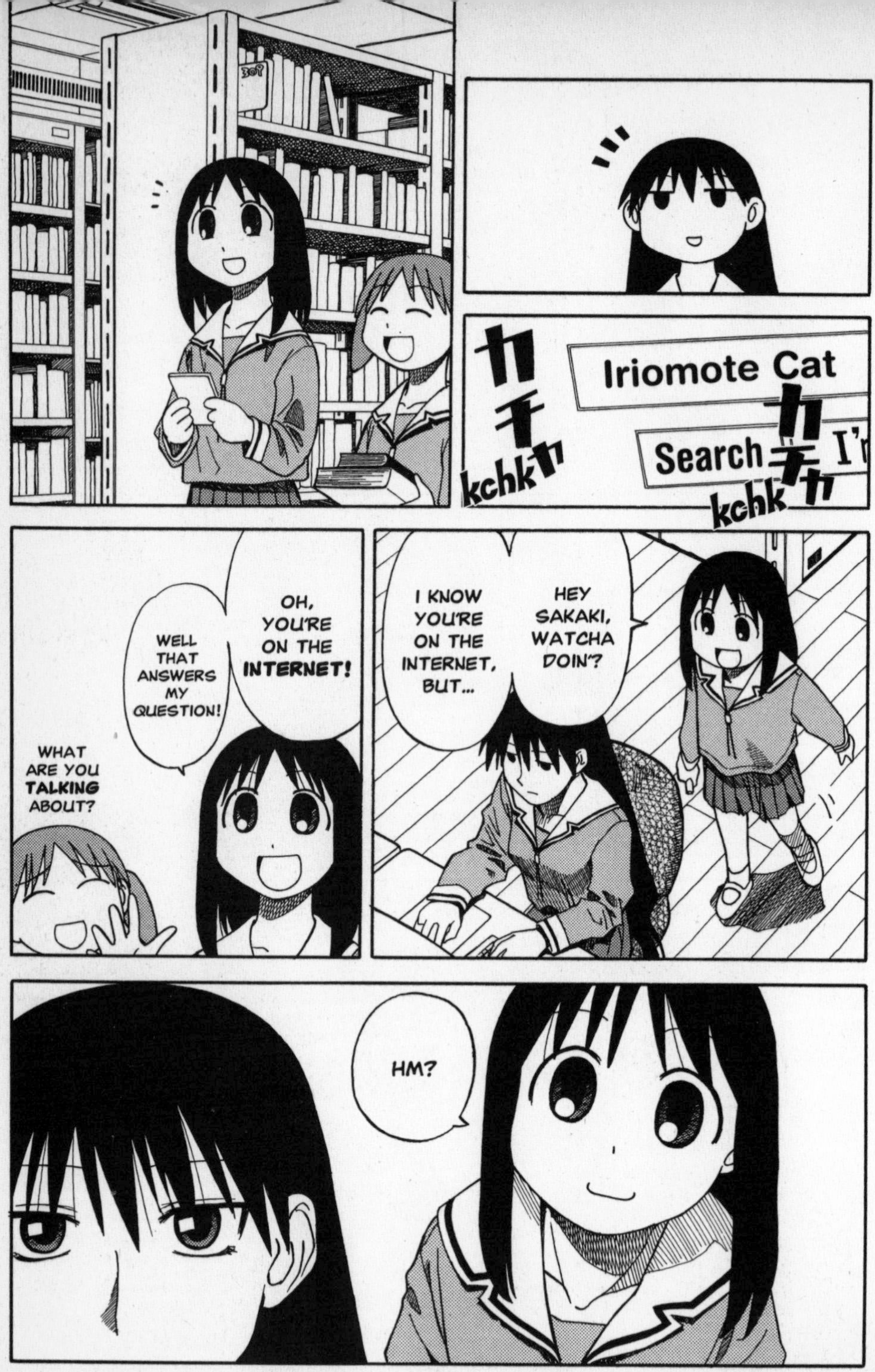

Iriomote Cat
Search
カチャ
kchk
カチャ
kchk
HEY SAKAKI, WATCHA DOIN'?
I KNOW YOU'RE ON THE INTERNET, BUT...
OH, YOU'RE ON THE **INTERNET!**
WELL THAT ANSWERS MY QUESTION!
WHAT ARE YOU **TALKING** ABOUT?
HM?

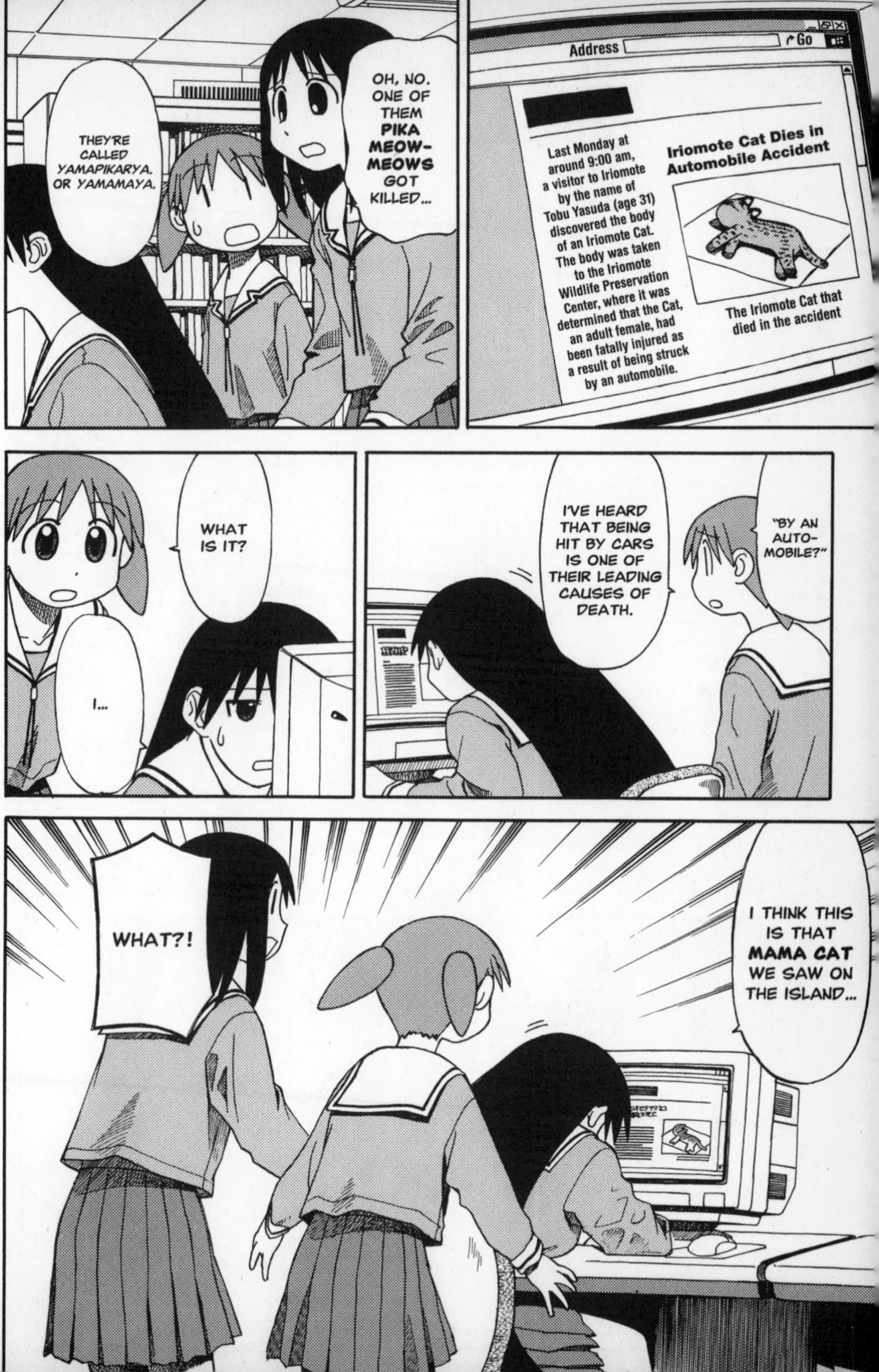
Address
Go
[redacted]
Iriomote Cat Dies in Automobile Accident
Last Monday at around 9:00 am, a visitor to Iriomote by the name of Tobu Yasuda (age 31) discovered the body of an Iriomote Cat. The body was taken to the Iriomote Wildlife Preservation Center, where it was determined that the Cat, an adult female, had been fatally injured as a result of being struck by an automobile.
The Iriomote Cat that died in the accident
OH, NO. ONE OF THEM PIKA MEOW-MEOWS GOT KILLED...
THEY'RE CALLED YAMAPIKARYA. OR YAMAMAYA.
"BY AN AUTO-MOBILE?"
I'VE HEARD THAT BEING HIT BY CARS IS ONE OF THEIR LEADING CAUSES OF DEATH.
WHAT IS IT?
I...
I THINK THIS IS THAT MAMA CAT WE SAW ON THE ISLAND...
WHAT?!

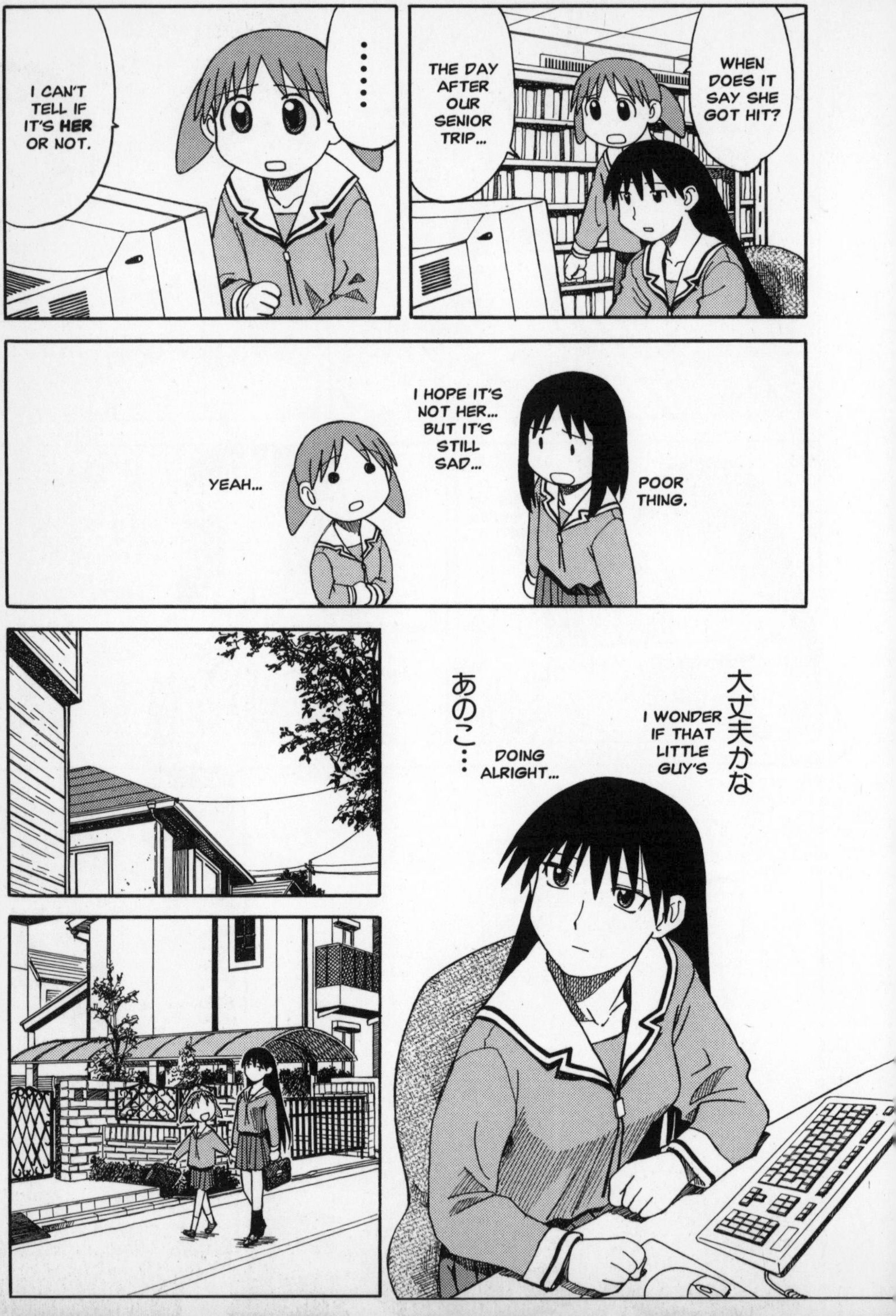
WHEN DOES IT SAY SHE GOT HIT?
THE DAY AFTER OUR SENIOR TRIP...
......
I CAN'T TELL IF IT'S **HER** OR NOT.
I HOPE IT'S NOT HER... BUT IT'S STILL SAD...
POOR THING.
YEAH...
大丈夫かな
I WONDER IF THAT LITTLE GUY'S
あのこ…
DOING ALRIGHT...

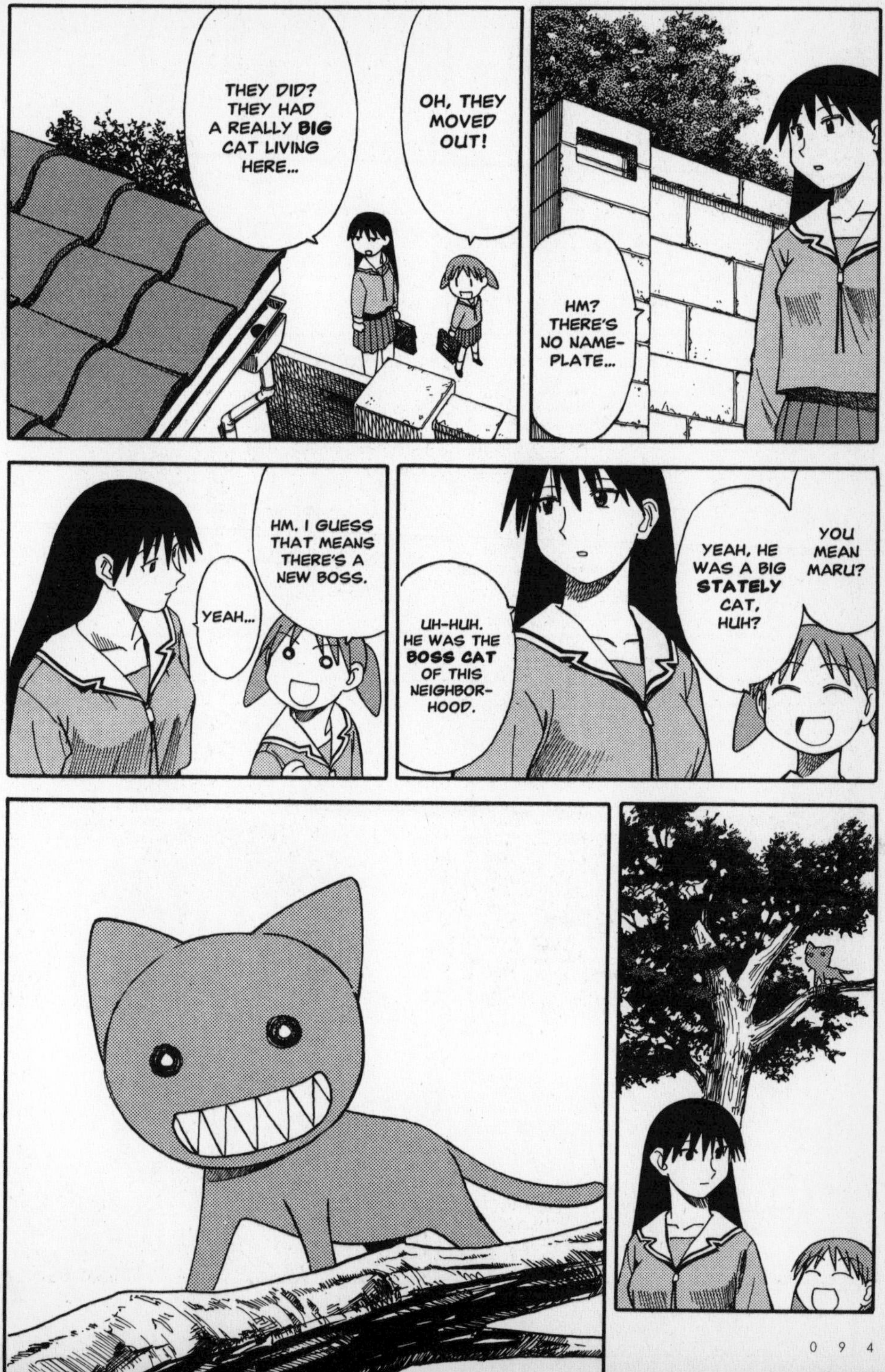
HM? THERE'S NO NAME-PLATE...
OH, THEY MOVED OUT!
THEY DID? THEY HAD A REALLY **BIG** CAT LIVING HERE...
YOU MEAN MARU?
YEAH, HE WAS A BIG **STATELY** CAT, HUH?
UH-HUH. HE WAS THE **BOSS CAT** OF THIS NEIGHBOR-HOOD.
HM. I GUESS THAT MEANS THERE'S A NEW BOSS.
YEAH...

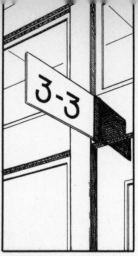

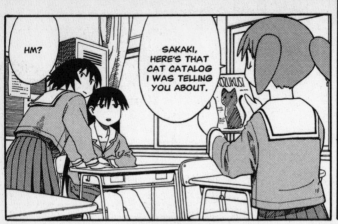

3-3
SAKAKI, HERE'S THAT CAT CATALOG I WAS TELLING YOU ABOUT.
KOZUKUSI
HM?
WHOA, WHAT'S UP? YOU THINKIN' ABOUT GETTING A CAT?
NEKOZUKUSI
NO, I CAN'T. MY MOM IS NO GOOD WITH CATS.
I'M JUST LOOKING...
YOU MEAN SHE **HATES** 'EM?
NO, NOT HATES...
SHE'S JUST VERY ALLERGIC.

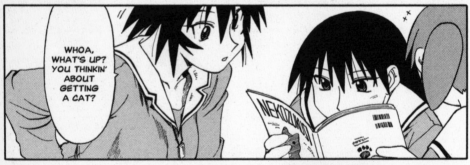

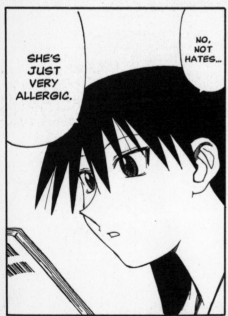

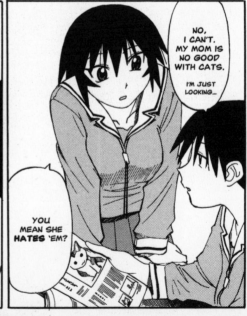

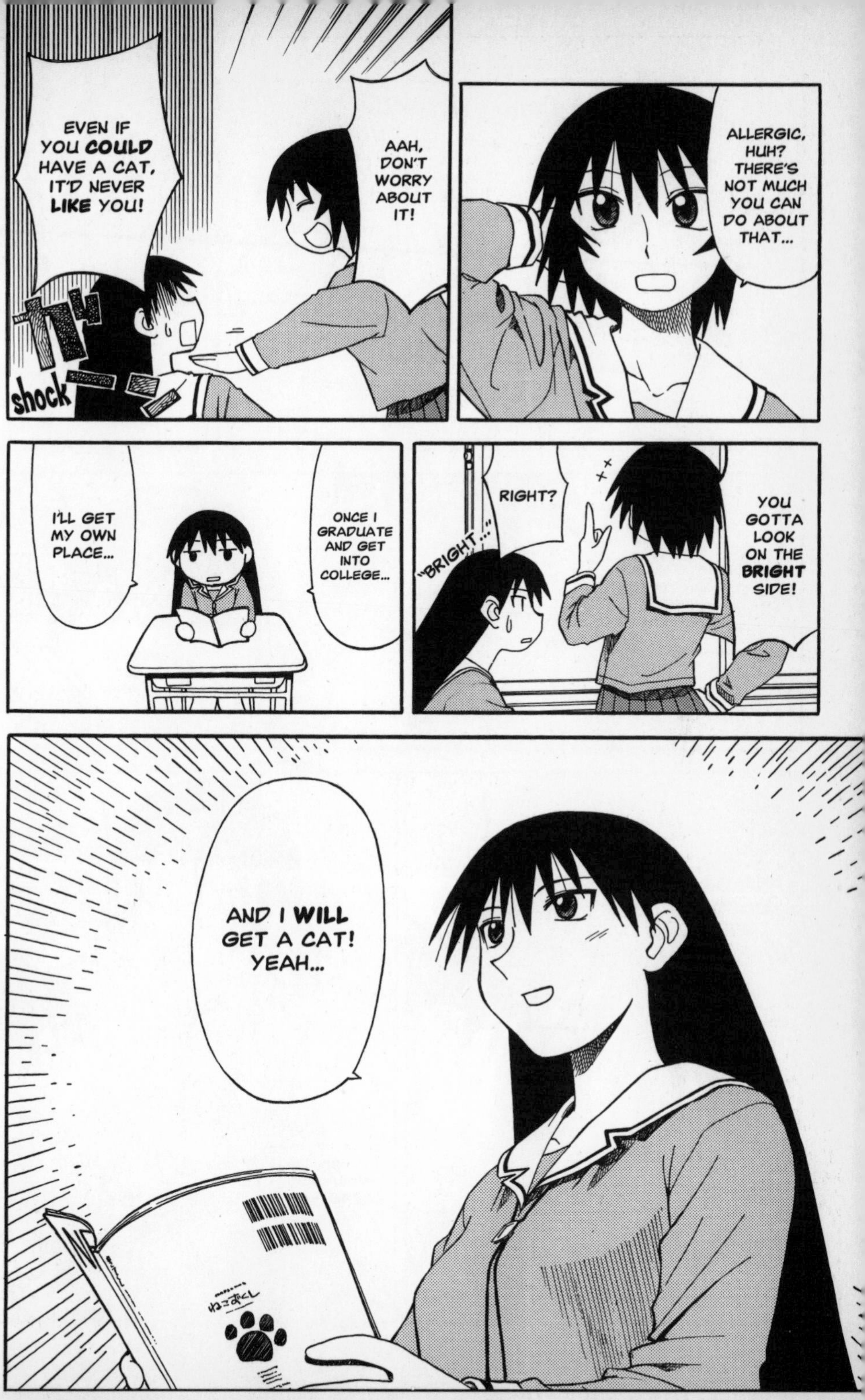
ALLERGIC, HUH? THERE'S NOT MUCH YOU CAN DO ABOUT THAT...
AAH, DON'T WORRY ABOUT IT!
EVEN IF YOU **COULD** HAVE A CAT, IT'D NEVER **LIKE** YOU!
shock
YOU GOTTA LOOK ON THE **BRIGHT** SIDE!
RIGHT?
"BRIGHT..."
ONCE I GRADUATE AND GET INTO COLLEGE...
I'LL GET MY OWN PLACE...
AND I **WILL** GET A CAT! YEAH...

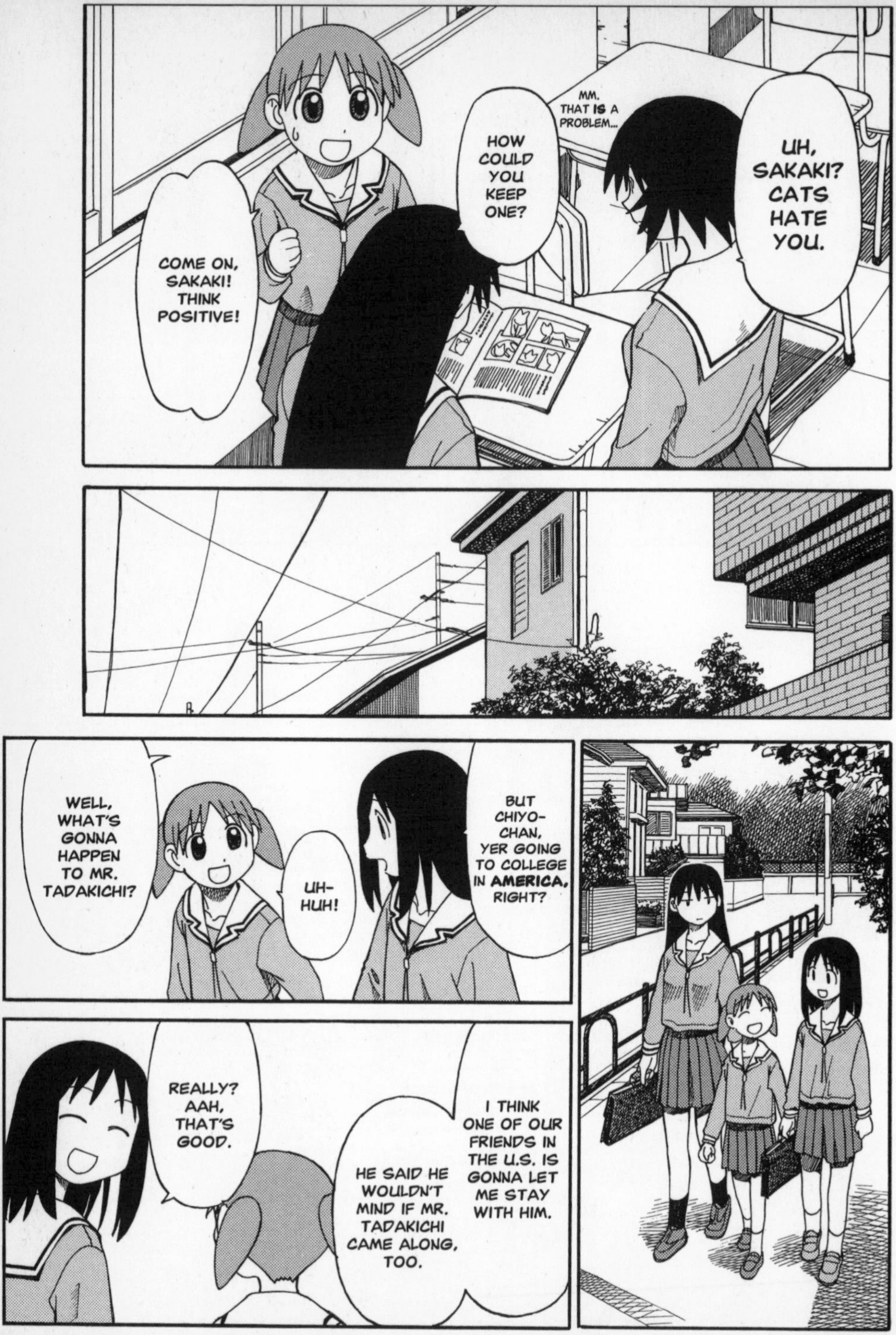
UH, SAKAKI? CATS HATE YOU.
MM. THAT IS A PROBLEM...
HOW COULD YOU KEEP ONE?
COME ON, SAKAKI! THINK POSITIVE!
BUT CHIYO-CHAN, YER GOING TO COLLEGE IN AMERICA, RIGHT?
UH-HUH!
WELL, WHAT'S GONNA HAPPEN TO MR. TADAKICHI?
I THINK ONE OF OUR FRIENDS IN THE U.S. IS GONNA LET ME STAY WITH HIM.
HE SAID HE WOULDN'T MIND IF MR. TADAKICHI CAME ALONG, TOO.
REALLY? AAH, THAT'S GOOD.

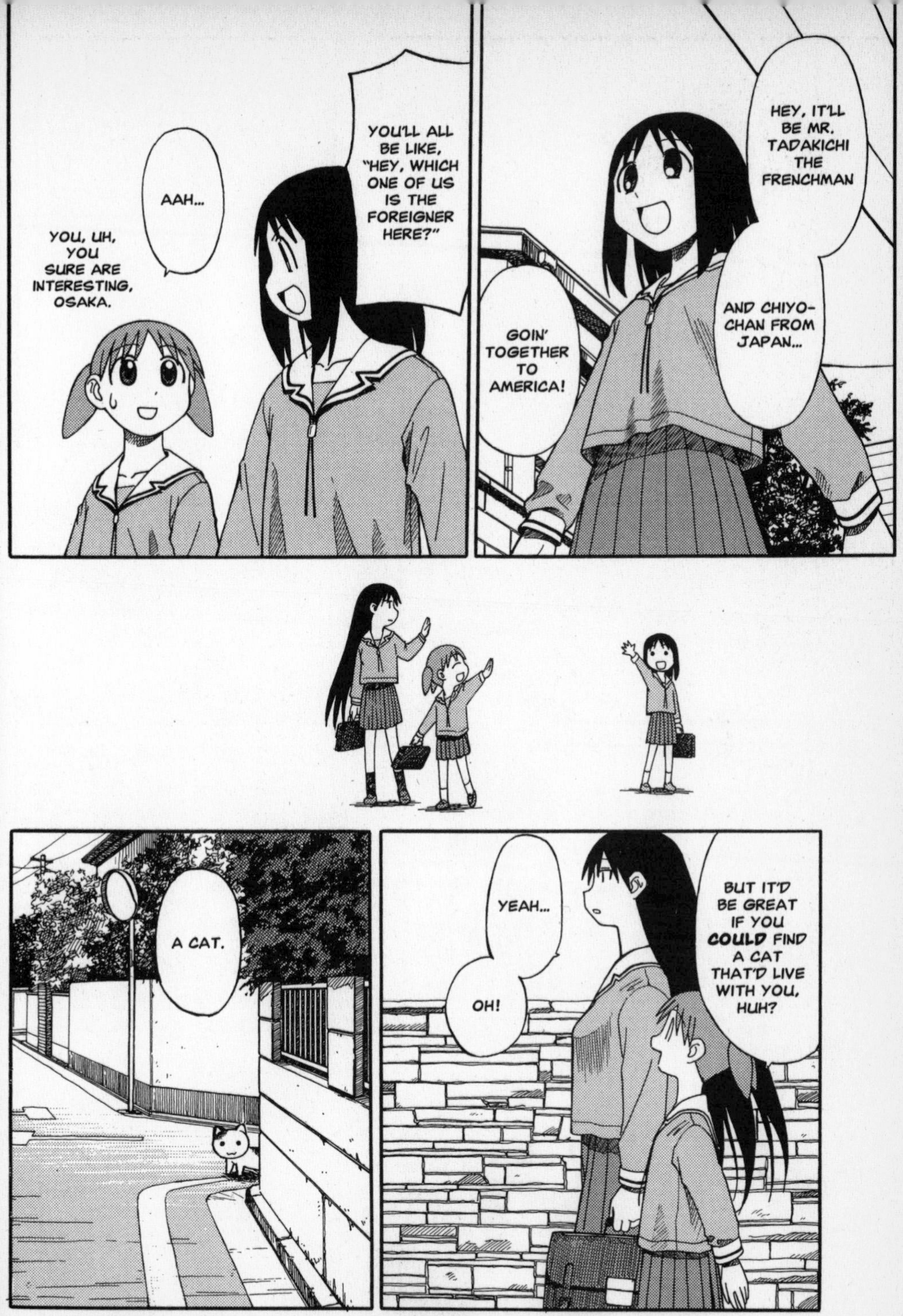
HEY, IT'LL BE MR. TADAKICHI THE FRENCHMAN
AND CHIYO-CHAN FROM JAPAN...
GOIN' TOGETHER TO AMERICA!
YOU'LL ALL BE LIKE, "HEY, WHICH ONE OF US IS THE FOREIGNER HERE?"
AAH...
YOU, UH, YOU SURE ARE INTERESTING, OSAKA.
BUT IT'D BE GREAT IF YOU **COULD** FIND A CAT THAT'D LIVE WITH YOU, HUH?
YEAH...
OH!
A CAT.

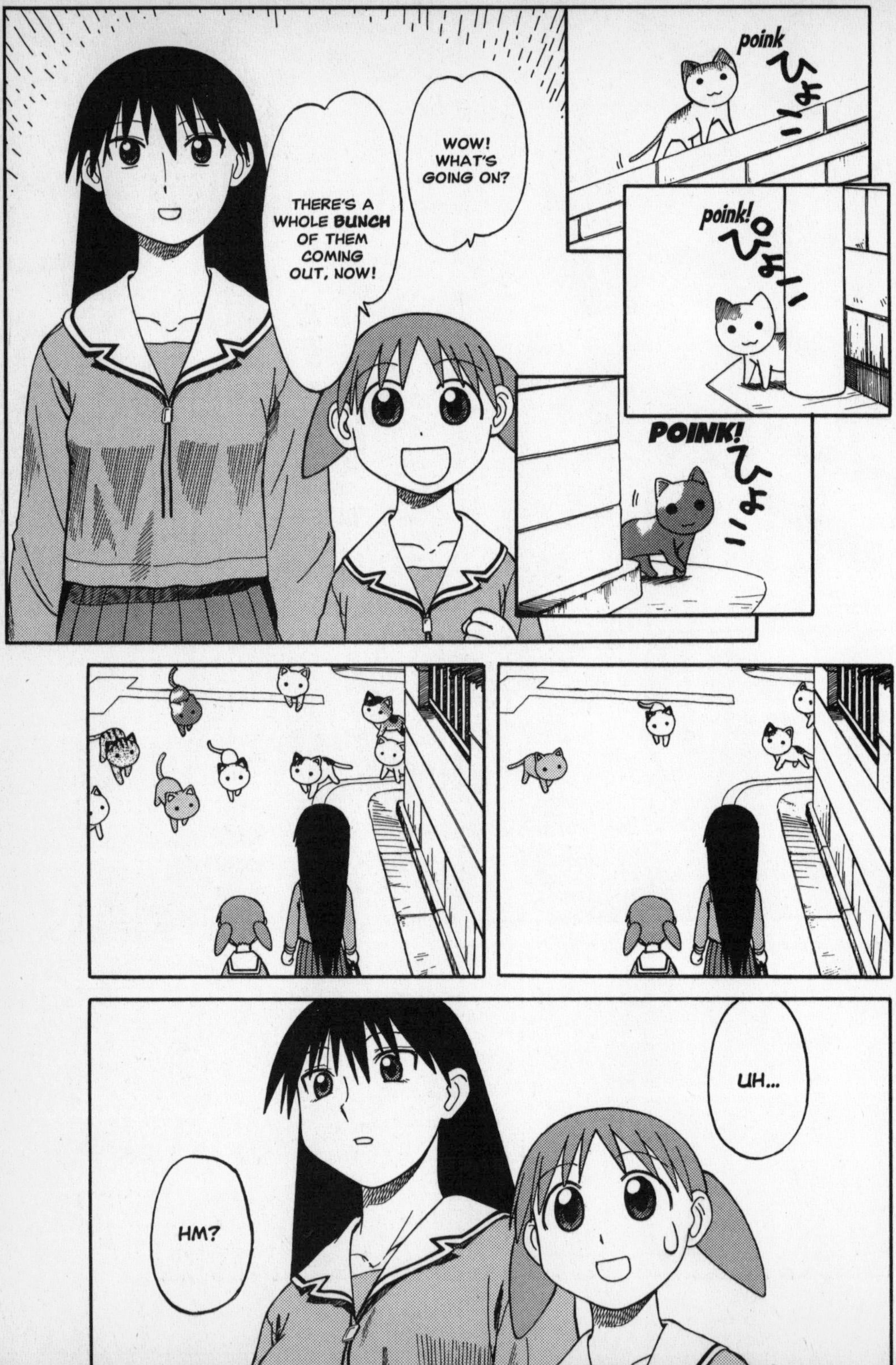
poink
ひょこ
poink!
ぴょこ
POINK!
ひょこ
WOW! WHAT'S GOING ON?
THERE'S A WHOLE BUNCH OF THEM COMING OUT, NOW!
UH...
HM?

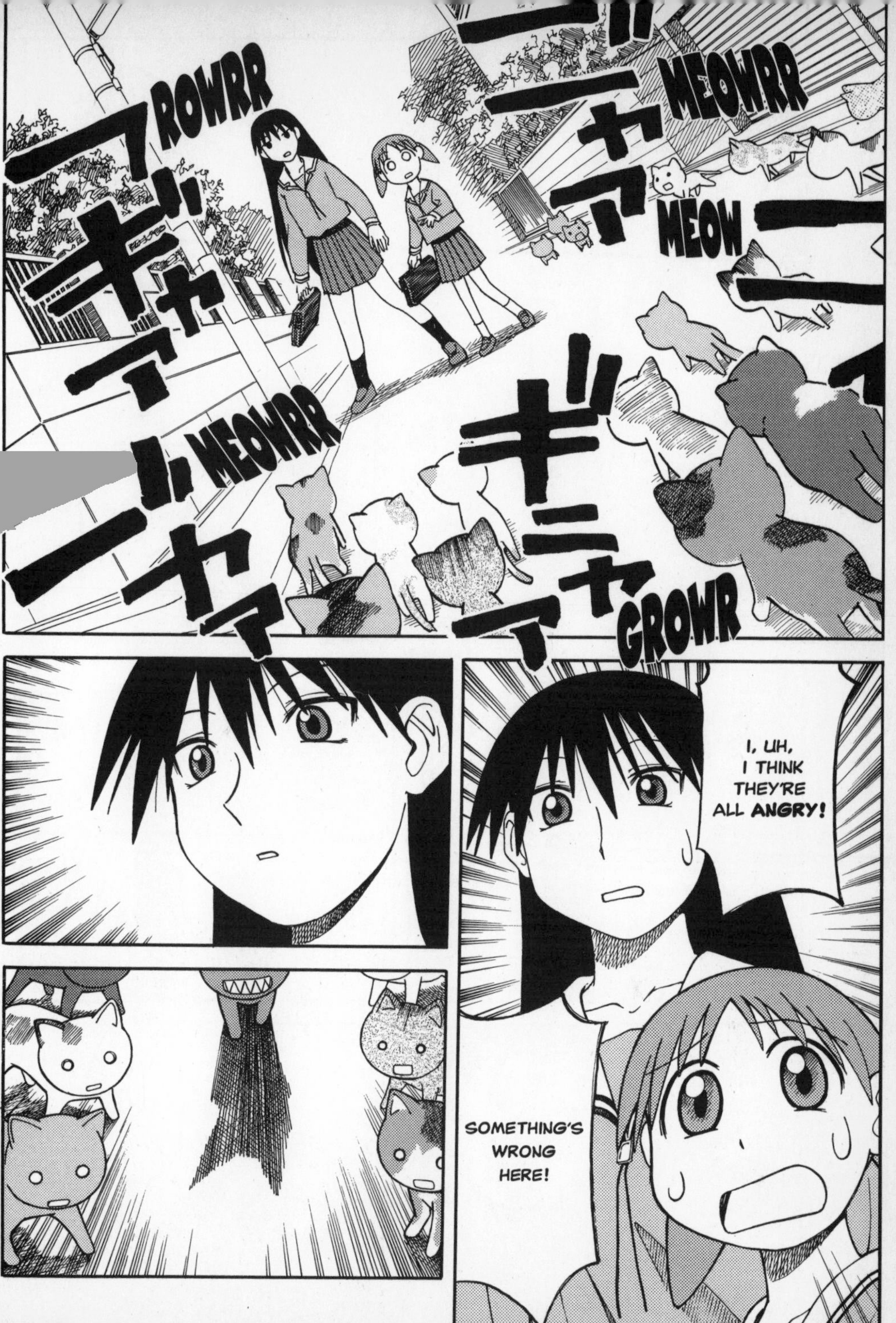
MEOWRR
MEOW
GROWR
ROWRR
MEOWRR
I, UH, I THINK THEY'RE ALL ANGRY!
SOMETHING'S WRONG HERE!

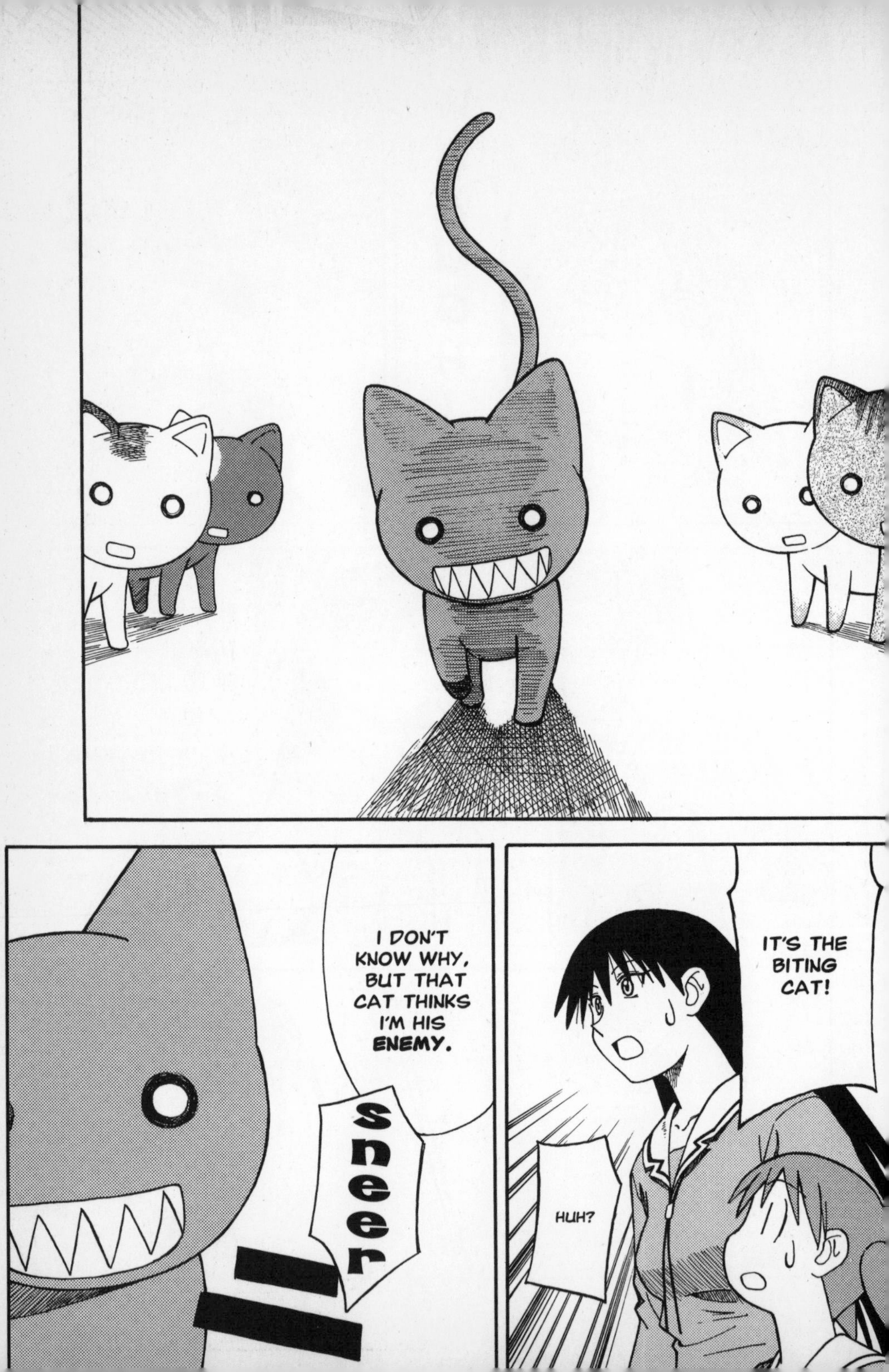
IT'S THE BITING CAT!
HUH?
I DON'T KNOW WHY, BUT THAT CAT THINKS I'M HIS ENEMY.
sneer

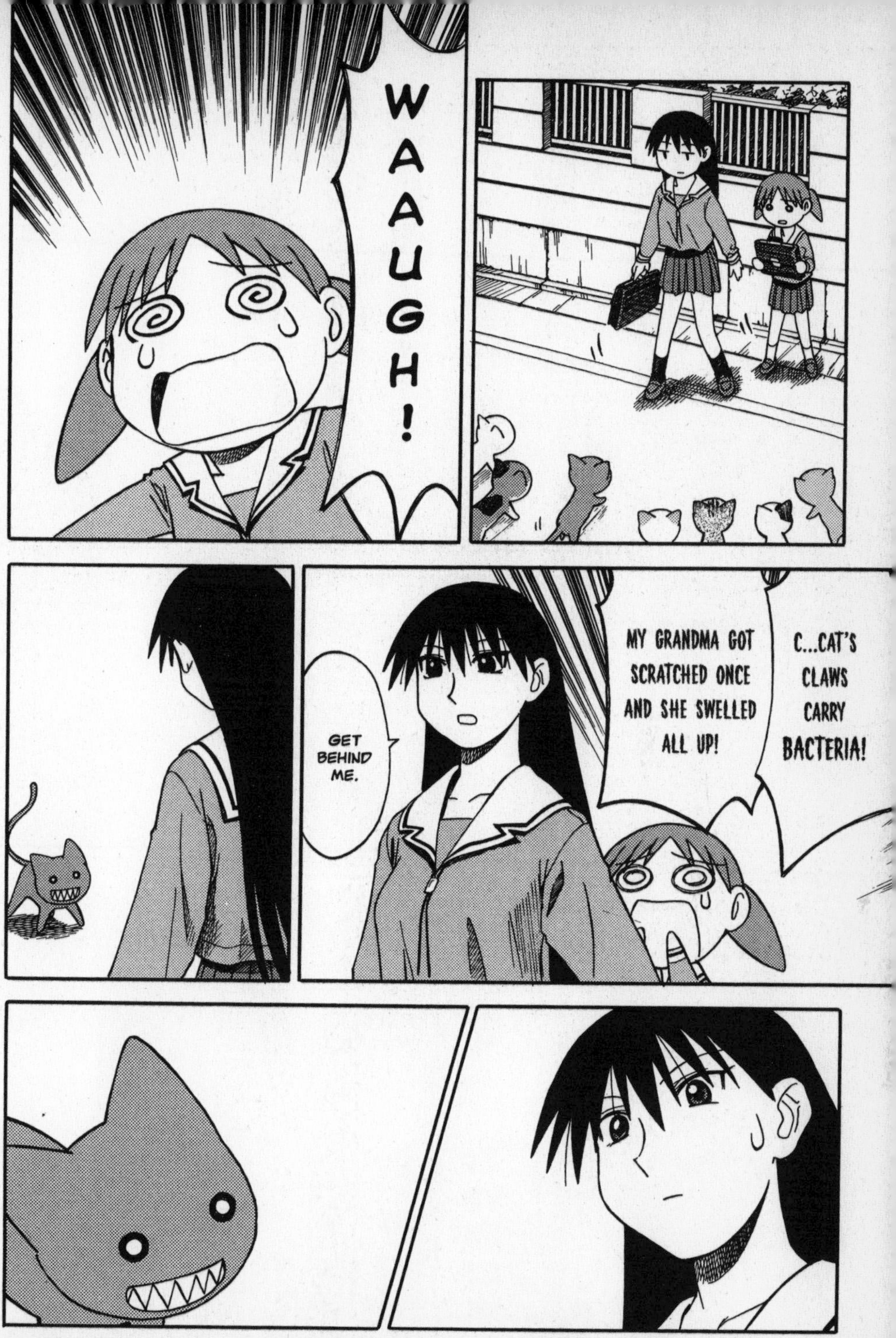
WAAUGH!
C...CAT'S CLAWS CARRY BACTERIA!
MY GRANDMA GOT SCRATCHED ONCE AND SHE SWELLED ALL UP!
GET BEHIND ME.

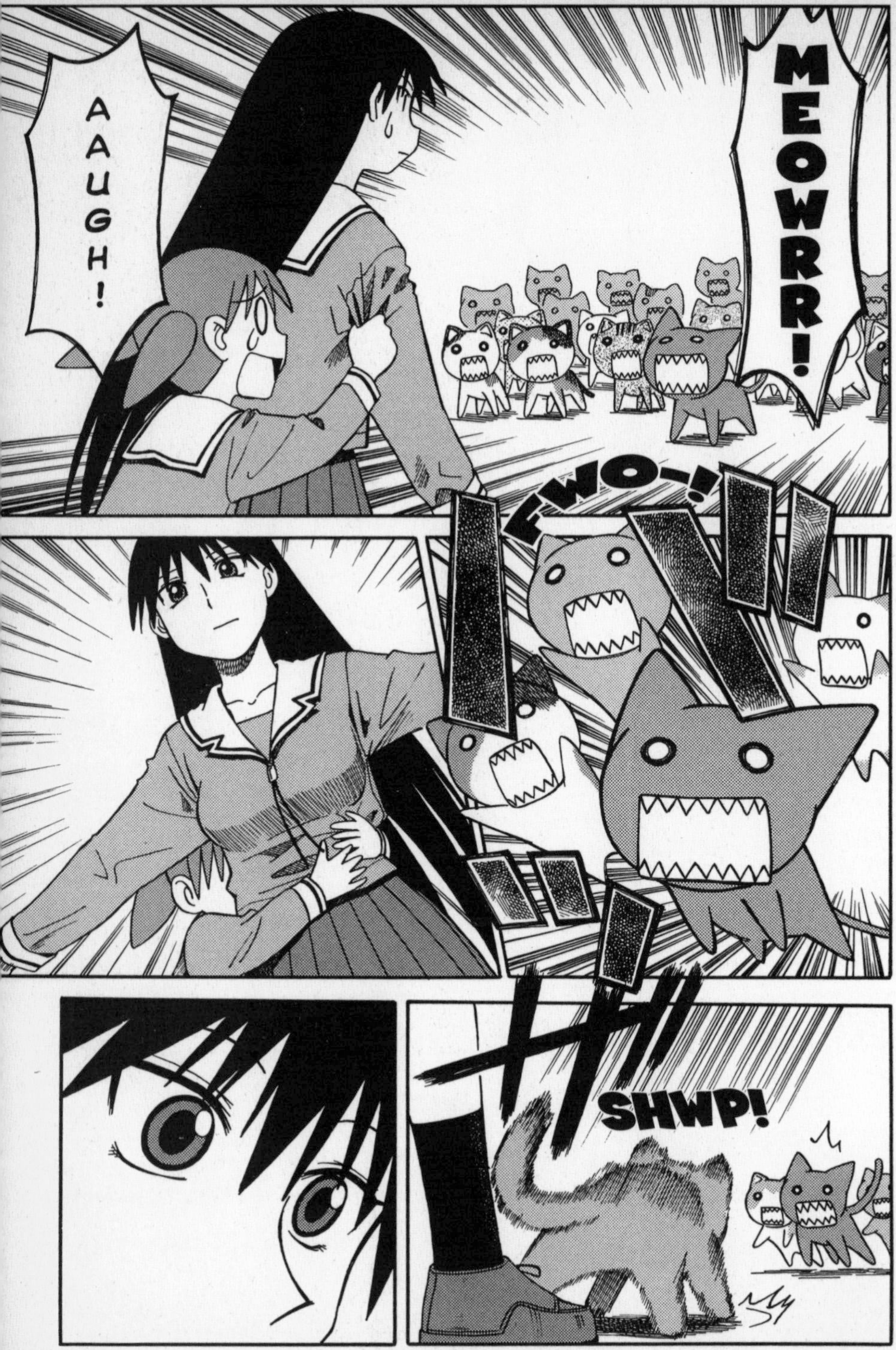
MEOWRR!
AAUGH!
FWO-!
SHWP!

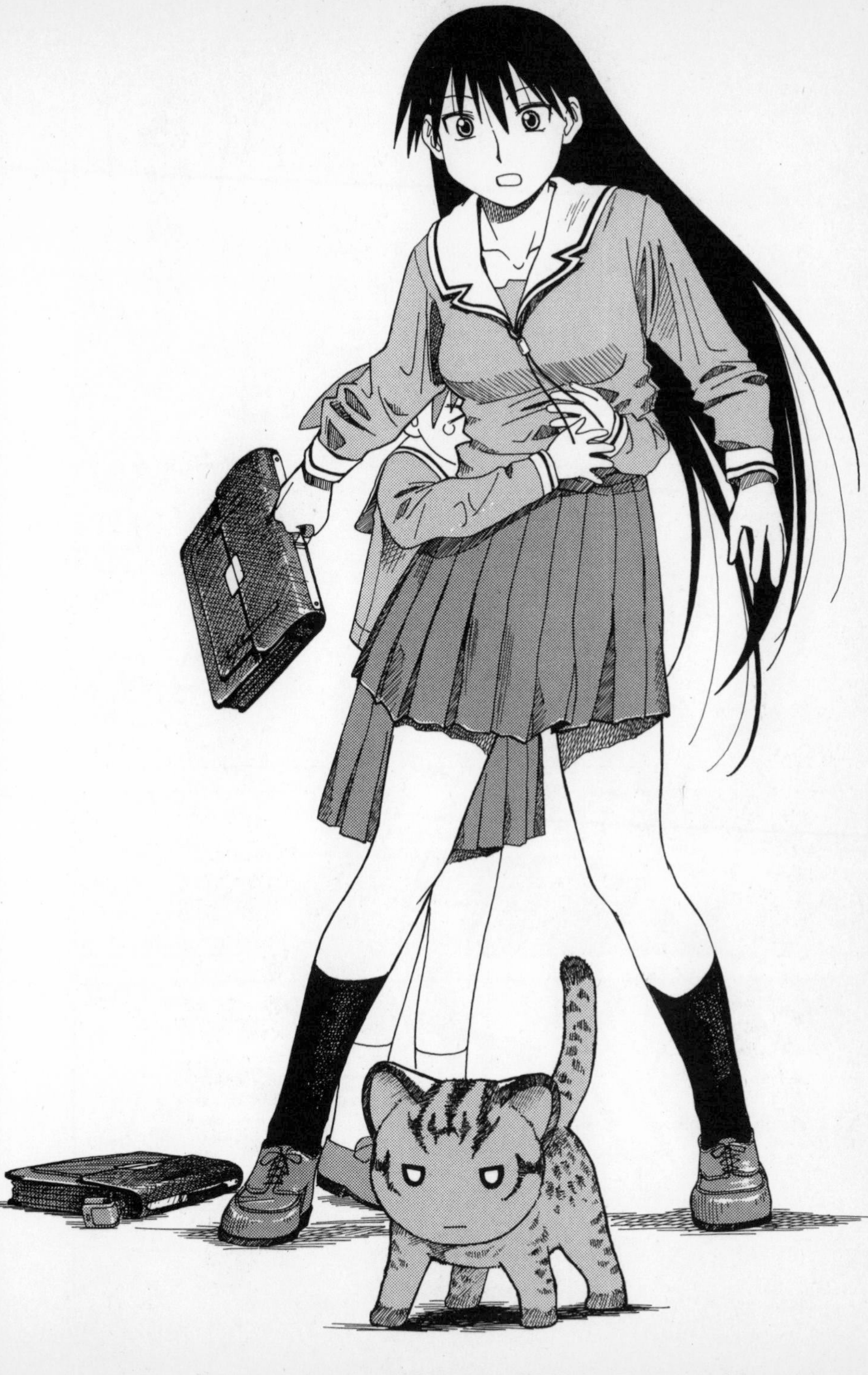

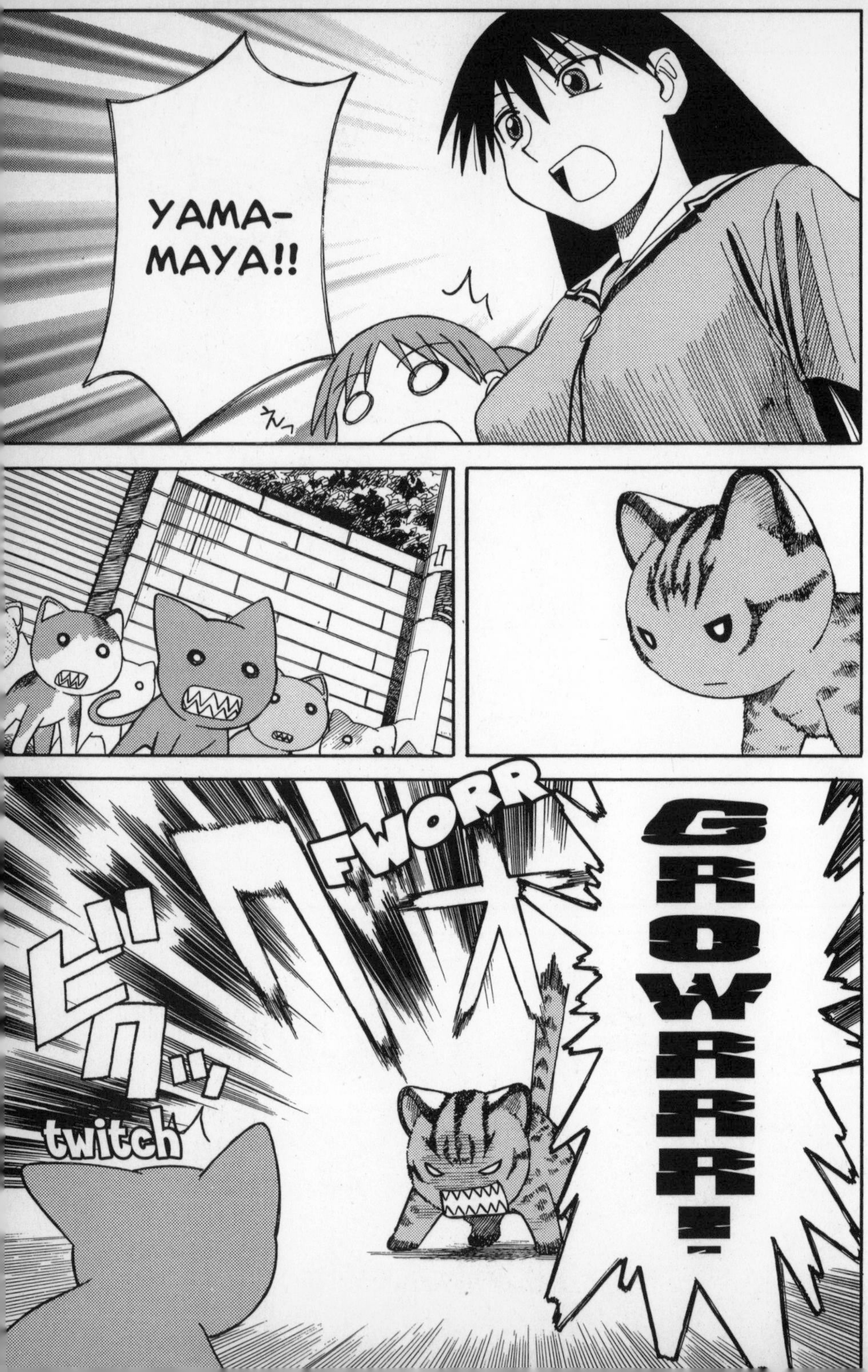
YAMA-
MAYA!!
GROWRRR!
FWORR
twitch

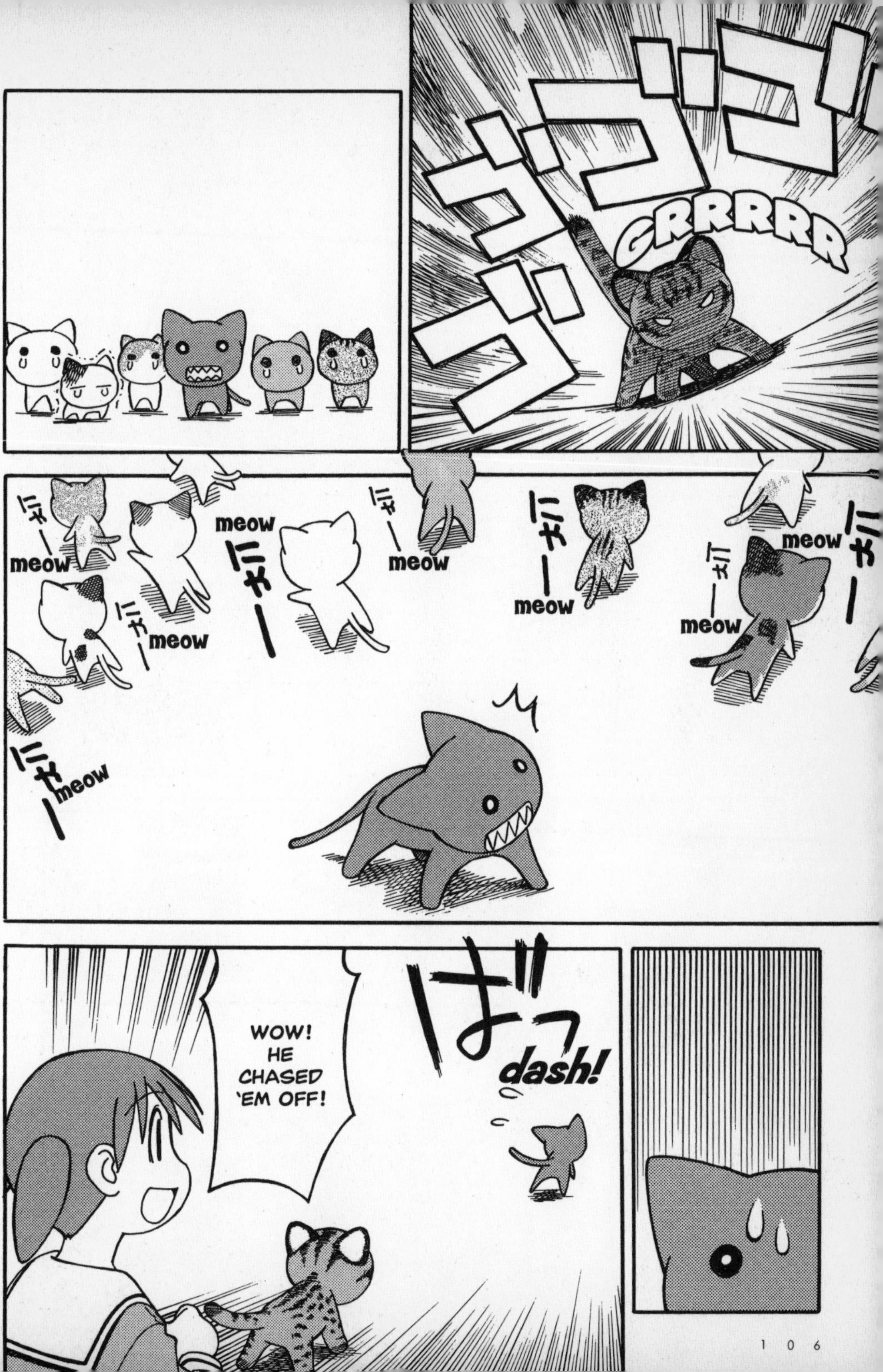
GRRRRR
meow
meow
meow
meow
meow
meow
meow
meow
meow
ばっ
dash!
WOW! HE CHASED 'EM OFF!

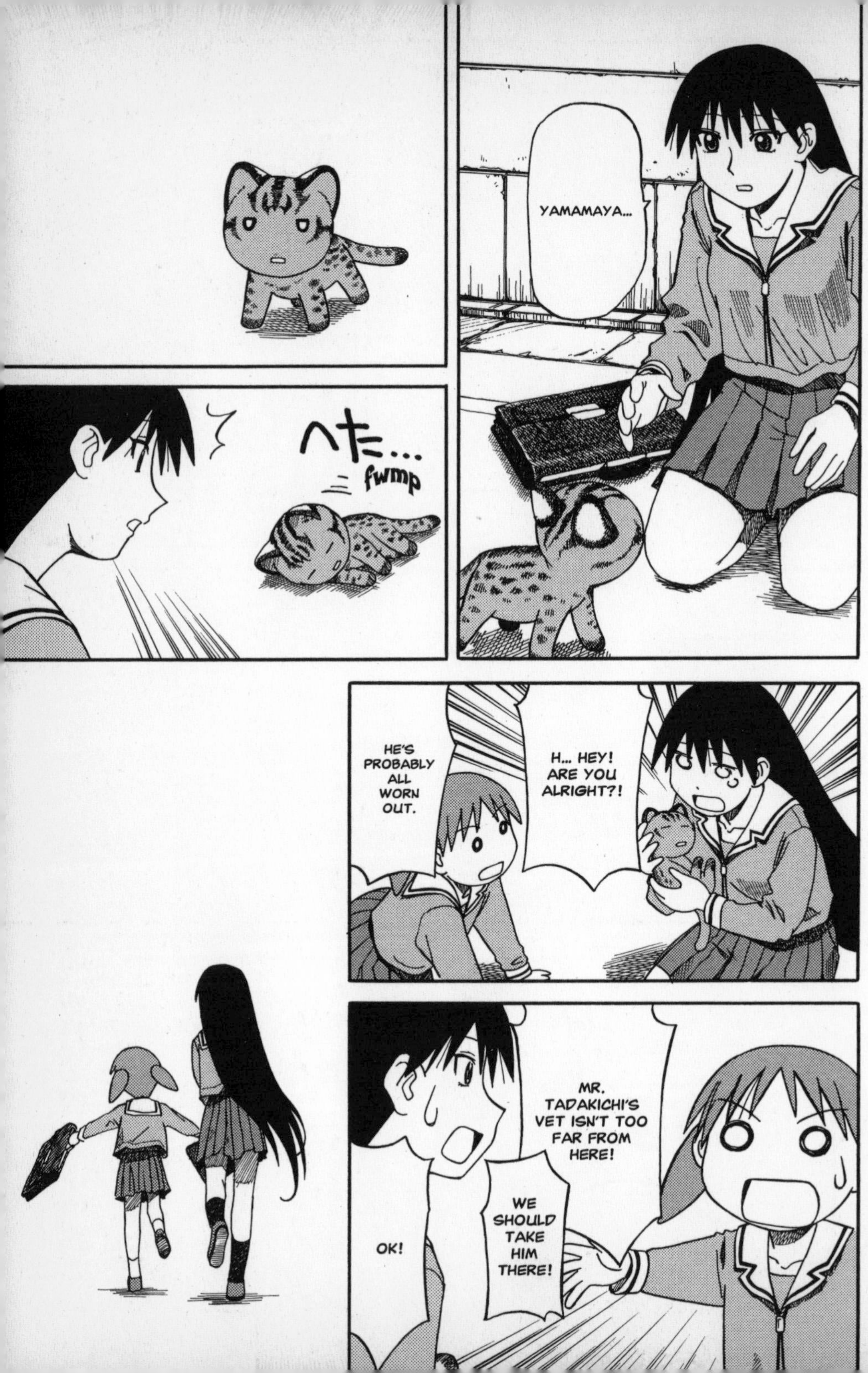
YAMAMAYA...
へた…
fwmp
H... HEY! ARE YOU ALRIGHT?!
HE'S PROBABLY ALL WORN OUT.
MR. TADAKICHI'S VET ISN'T TOO FAR FROM HERE!
WE SHOULD TAKE HIM THERE!
OK!

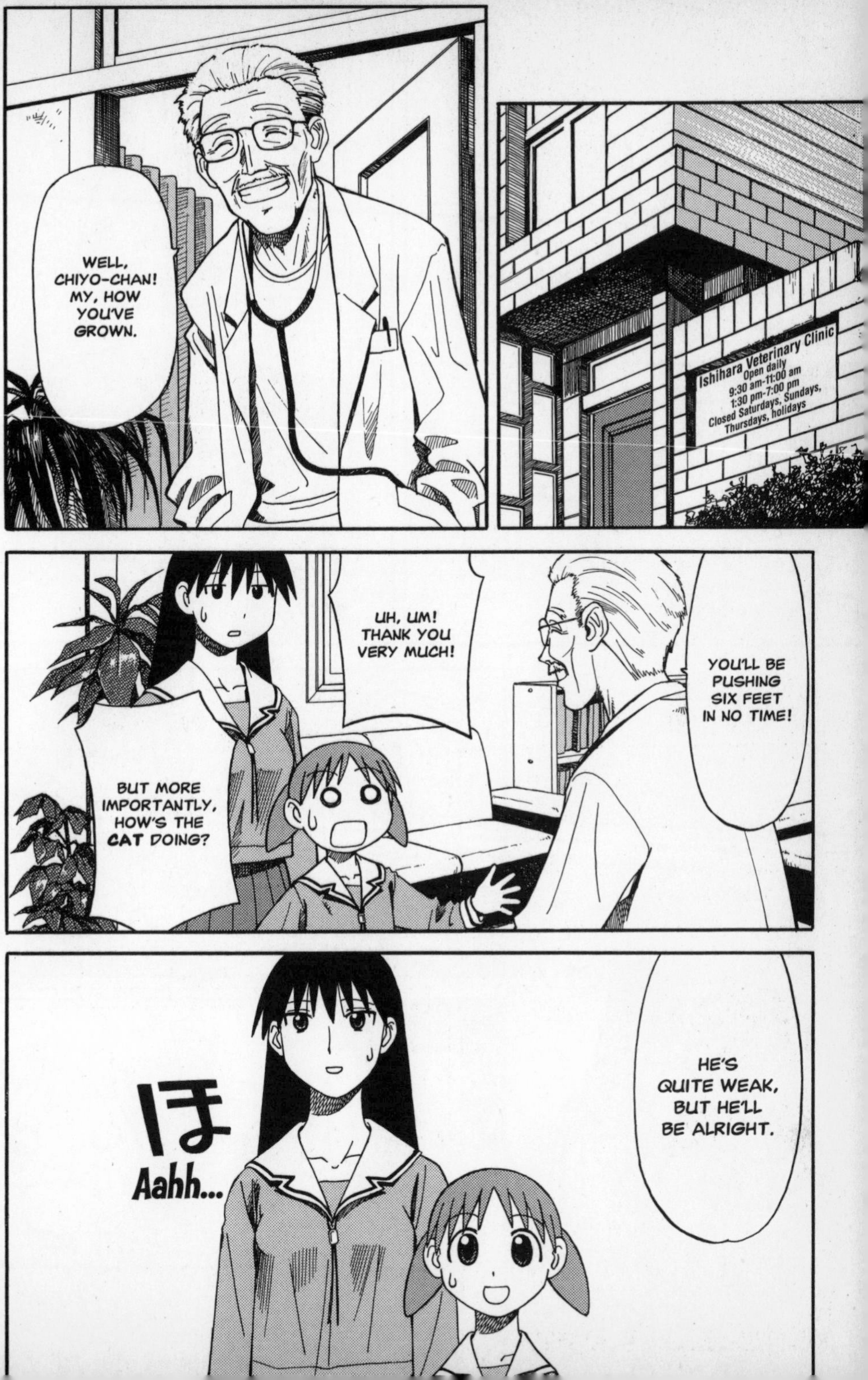
Ishihara Veterinary Clinic
Open daily
9:30 am-11:00 am
1:30 pm-7:00 pm
Closed Saturdays, Sundays, Thursdays, holidays
WELL, CHIYO-CHAN! MY, HOW YOU'VE GROWN.
YOU'LL BE PUSHING SIX FEET IN NO TIME!
UH, UM! THANK YOU VERY MUCH!
BUT MORE IMPORTANTLY, HOW'S THE CAT DOING?
HE'S QUITE WEAK, BUT HE'LL BE ALRIGHT.
ほ
Aahh...

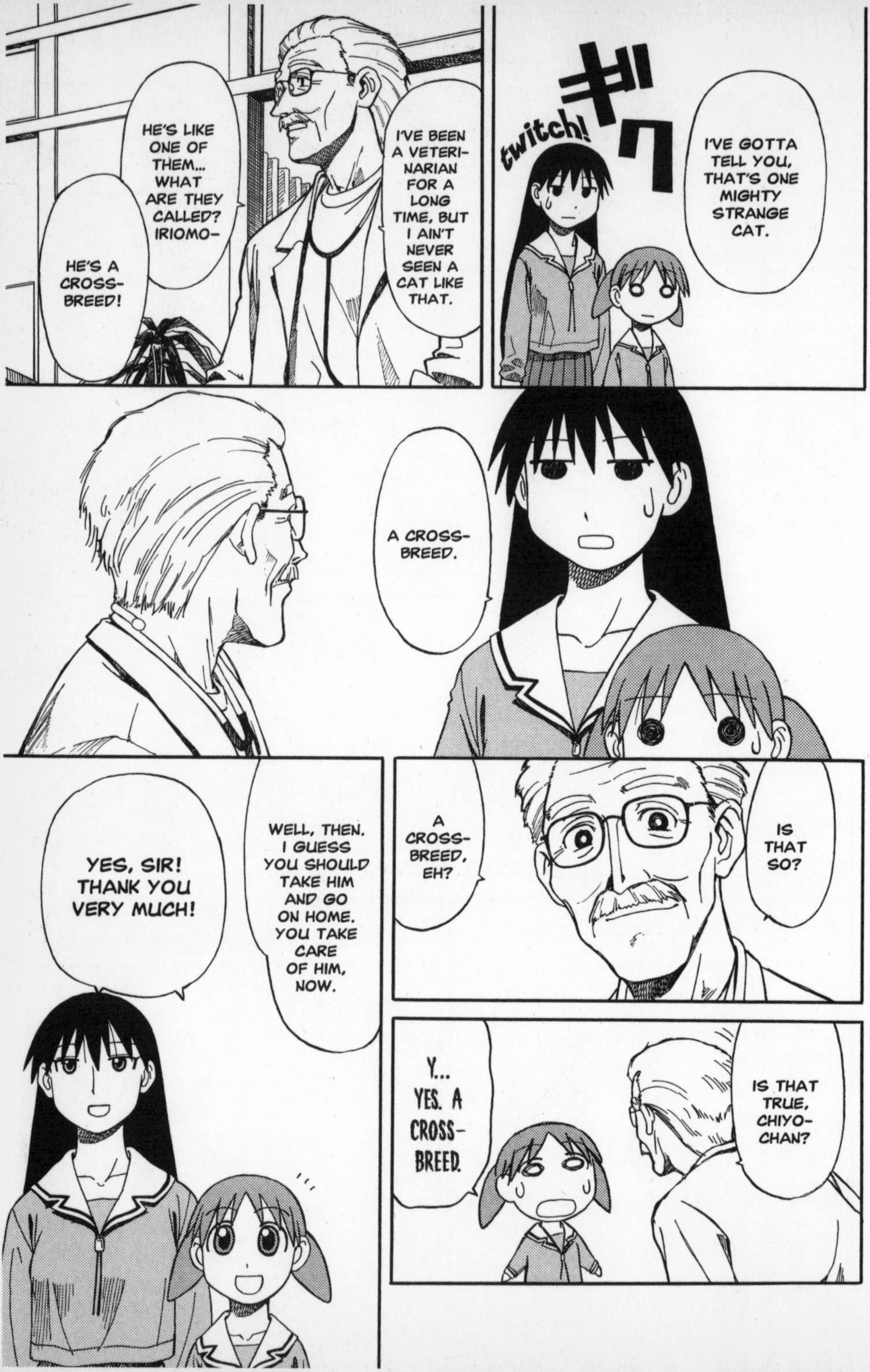
ギク
twitch!
I'VE GOTTA TELL YOU, THAT'S ONE MIGHTY STRANGE CAT.
I'VE BEEN A VETERINARIAN FOR A LONG TIME, BUT I AIN'T NEVER SEEN A CAT LIKE THAT.
HE'S LIKE ONE OF THEM... WHAT ARE THEY CALLED? IRIOMO-
HE'S A CROSS-BREED!
A CROSS-BREED.
IS THAT SO?
A CROSS-BREED, EH?
IS THAT TRUE, CHIYO-CHAN?
Y... YES. A CROSS-BREED.
WELL, THEN. I GUESS YOU SHOULD TAKE HIM AND GO ON HOME. YOU TAKE CARE OF HIM, NOW.
YES, SIR! THANK YOU VERY MUCH!

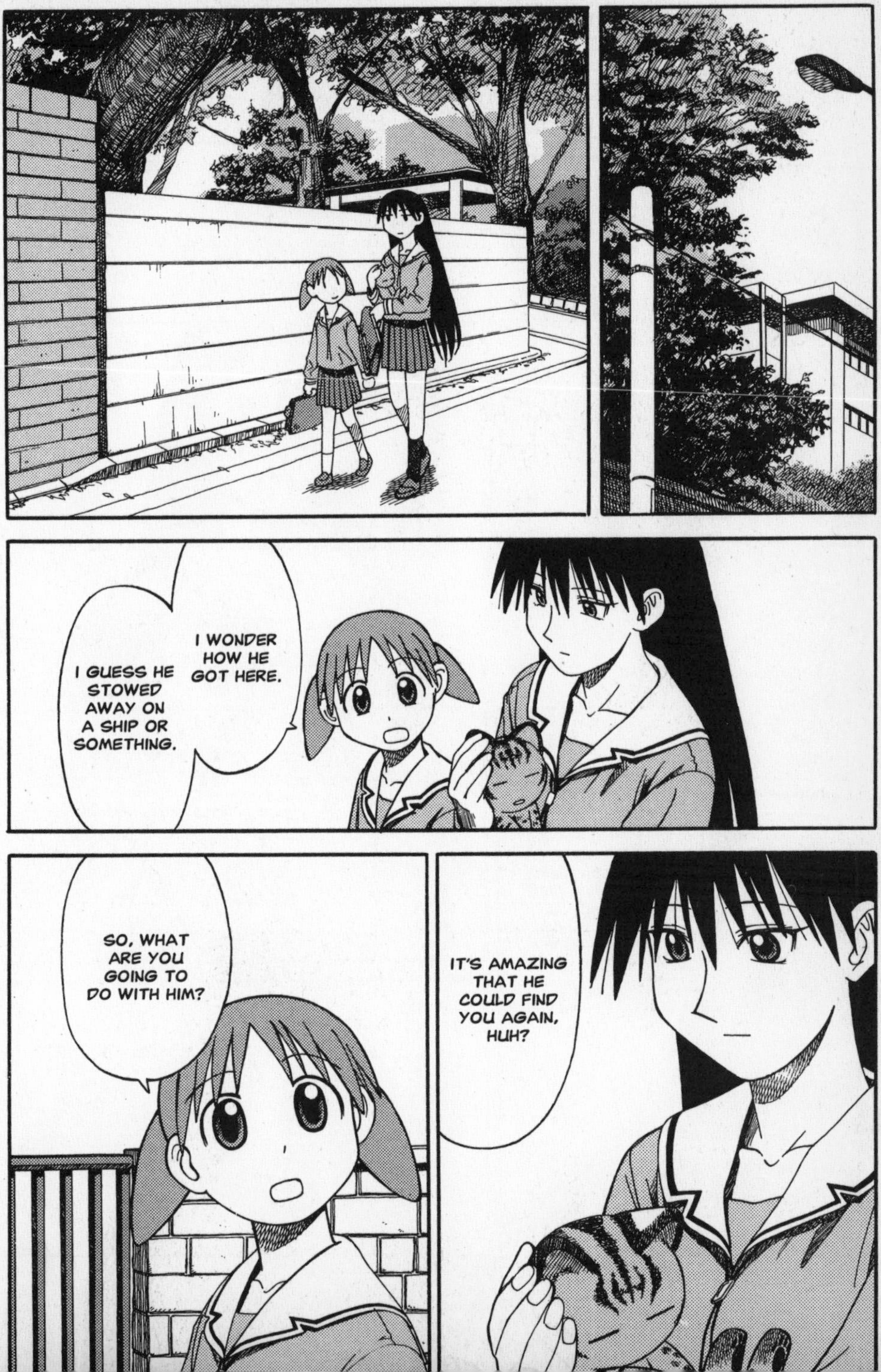
I WONDER HOW HE GOT HERE.
I GUESS HE STOWED AWAY ON A SHIP OR SOMETHING.
IT'S AMAZING THAT HE COULD FIND YOU AGAIN, HUH?
SO, WHAT ARE YOU GOING TO DO WITH HIM?

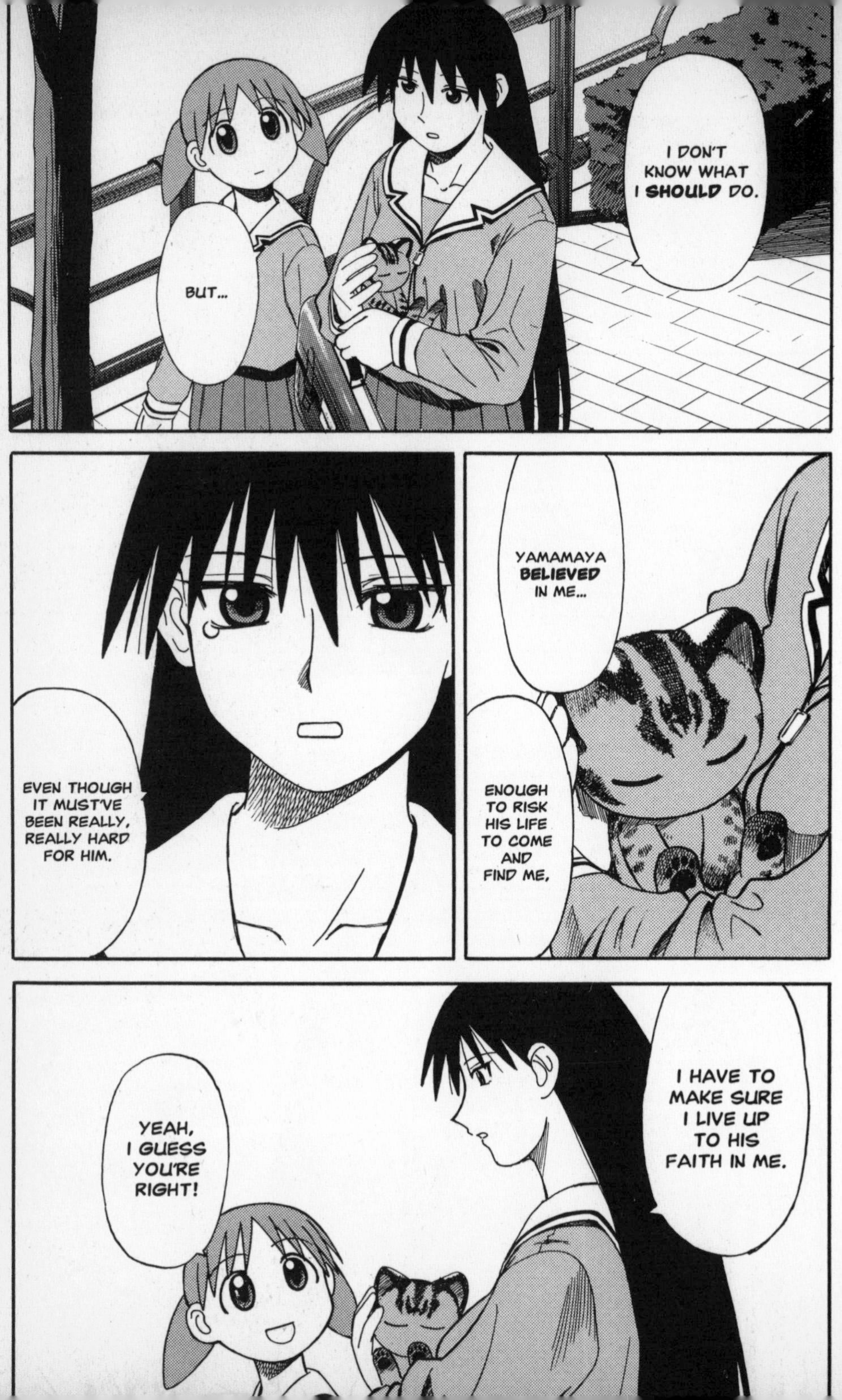
I DON'T KNOW WHAT I **SHOULD** DO.
BUT...
YAMAMAYA **BELIEVED** IN ME...
ENOUGH TO RISK HIS LIFE TO COME AND FIND ME,
EVEN THOUGH IT MUST'VE BEEN REALLY, REALLY HARD FOR HIM.
I HAVE TO MAKE SURE I LIVE UP TO HIS FAITH IN ME.
YEAH, I GUESS YOU'RE RIGHT!

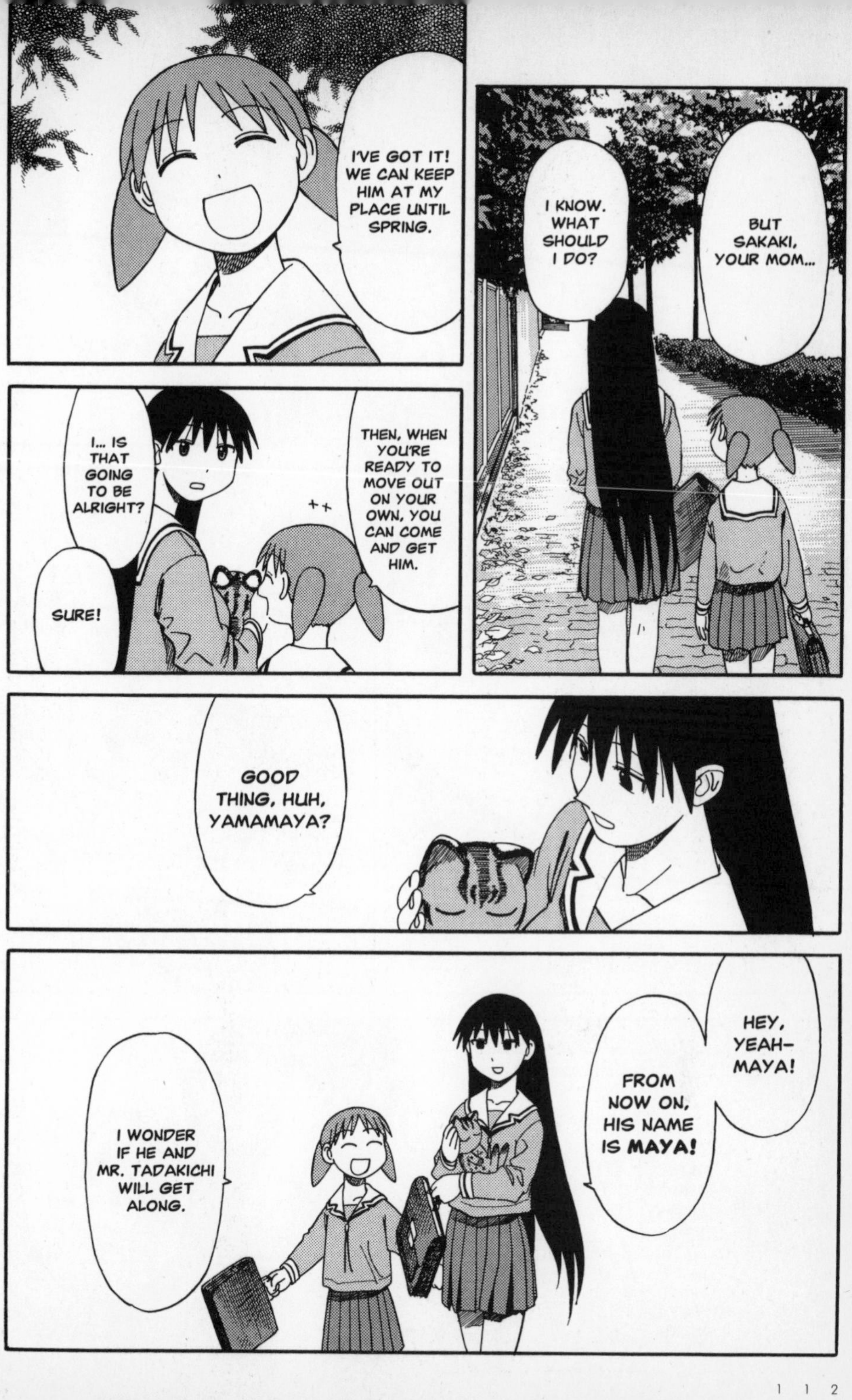
BUT SAKAKI, YOUR MOM...
I KNOW. WHAT SHOULD I DO?
I'VE GOT IT! WE CAN KEEP HIM AT MY PLACE UNTIL SPRING.
THEN, WHEN YOU'RE READY TO MOVE OUT ON YOUR OWN, YOU CAN COME AND GET HIM.
I... IS THAT GOING TO BE ALRIGHT?
SURE!
GOOD THING, HUH, YAMAMAYA?
HEY, YEAH-MAYA!
FROM NOW ON, HIS NAME IS **MAYA!**
I WONDER IF HE AND MR. TADAKICHI WILL GET ALONG.

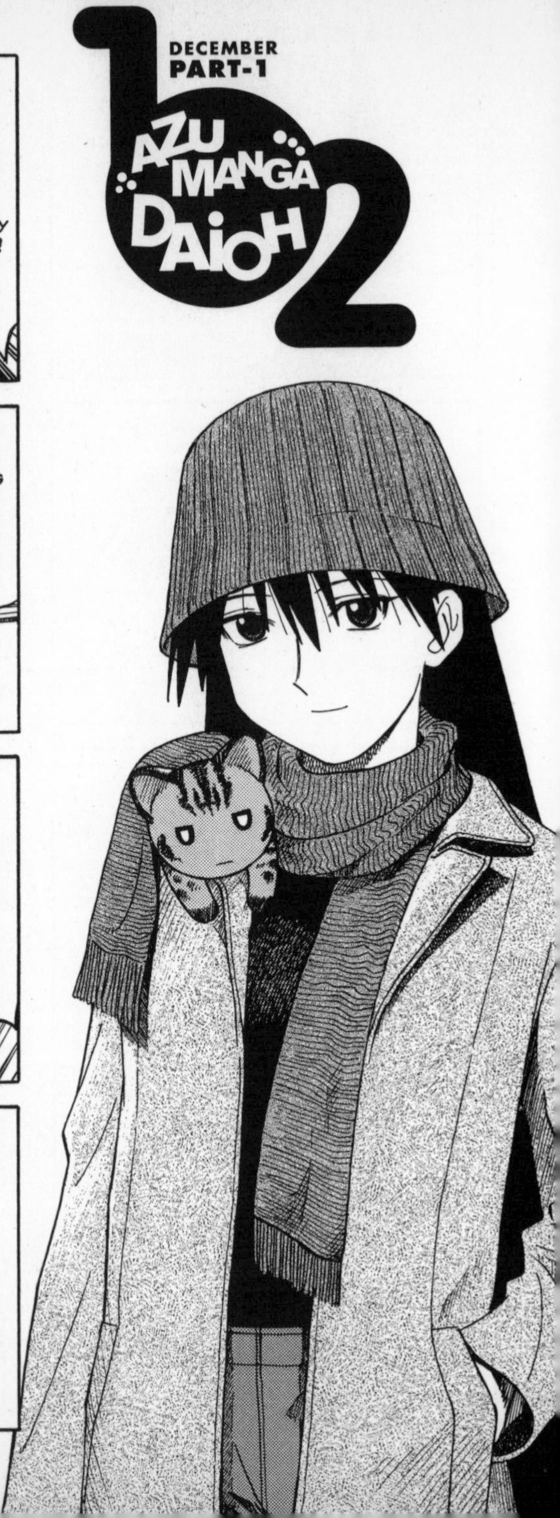
DECEMBER
PART-1
AZUMANGA DAIOH 2

C'MON, LET'S GO!

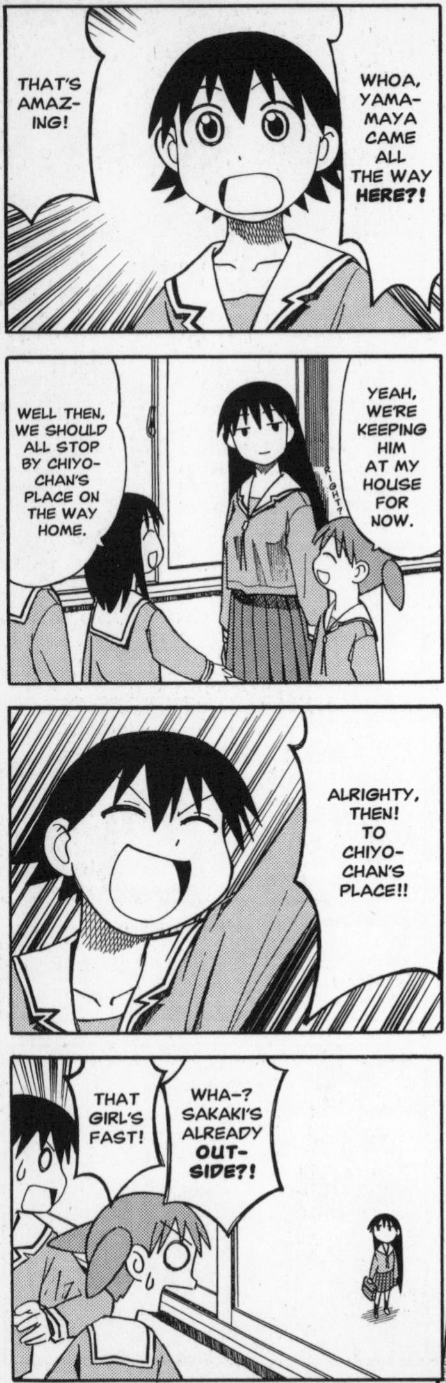
WHOA, YAMAMAYA CAME ALL THE WAY HERE?!
THAT'S AMAZING!
YEAH, WE'RE KEEPING HIM AT MY HOUSE FOR NOW.
RIGHT?
WELL THEN, WE SHOULD ALL STOP BY CHIYO-CHAN'S PLACE ON THE WAY HOME.
ALRIGHTY, THEN! TO CHIYO-CHAN'S PLACE!!
WHA-? SAKAKI'S ALREADY OUTSIDE?!
THAT GIRL'S FAST!

PIKA...

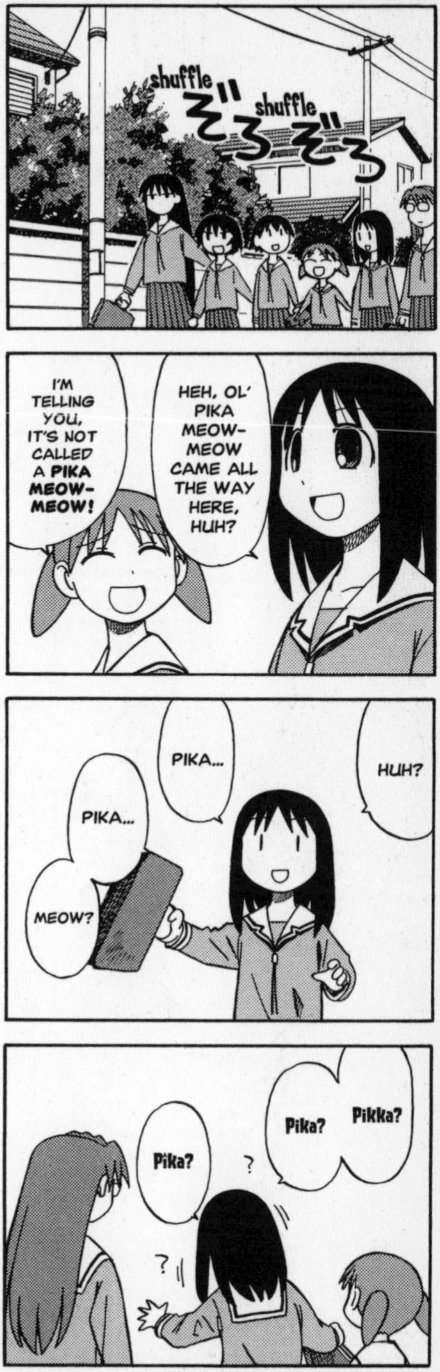
shuffle
ぞろぞろ
shuffle
HEH, OL' PIKA MEOW-MEOW CAME ALL THE WAY HERE, HUH?
I'M TELLING YOU, IT'S NOT CALLED A **PIKA MEOW-MEOW!**
HUH?
PIKA...
PIKA...
MEOW?
Pikka?
Pika?
Pika?

IRIOMOTE ISLAND

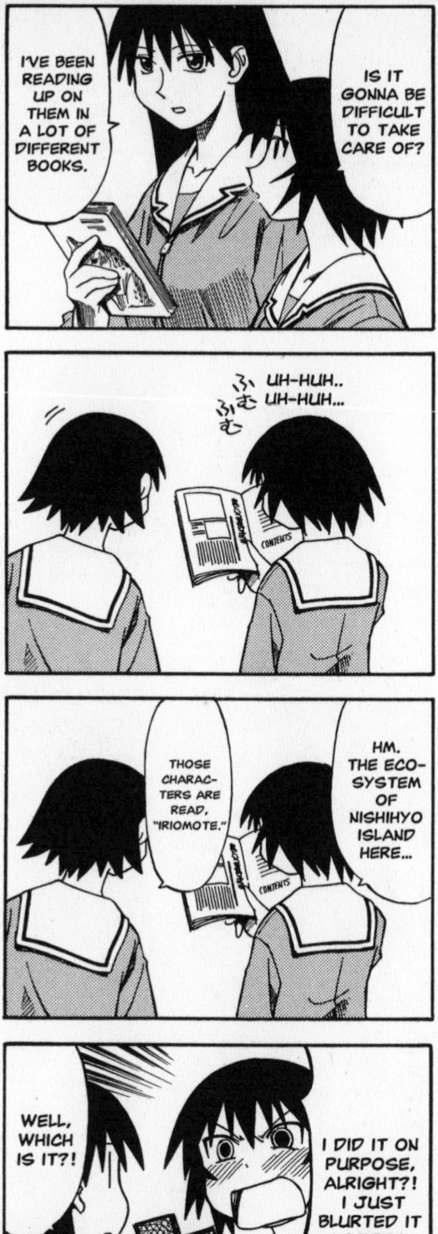
IS IT GONNA BE DIFFICULT TO TAKE CARE OF?
I'VE BEEN READING UP ON THEM IN A LOT OF DIFFERENT BOOKS.
ふむ ふむ
UH-HUH.. UH-HUH...
CONTENTS
HM. THE ECO-SYSTEM OF NISHIHYO ISLAND HERE...
THOSE CHARAC-TERS ARE READ, "IRIOMOTE."
CONTENTS
I DID IT ON PURPOSE, ALRIGHT?! I JUST BLURTED IT ACCIDEN-TALLY!
WELL, WHICH IS IT?!
RARR!

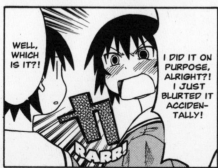

THEY'RE SO STRONG!

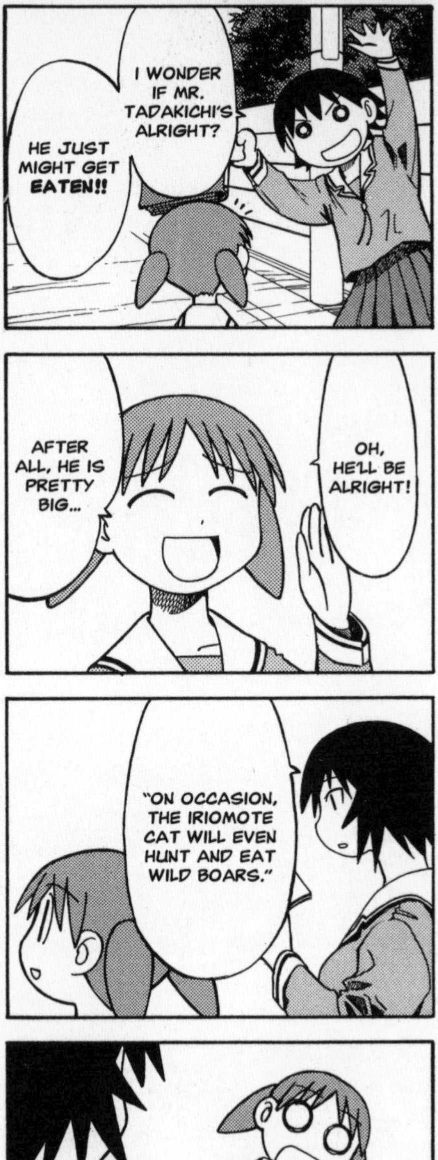
I WONDER IF MR. TADAKICHI'S ALRIGHT?
HE JUST MIGHT GET EATEN!!
OH, HE'LL BE ALRIGHT!
AFTER ALL, HE IS PRETTY BIG...
"ON OCCASION, THE IRIOMOTE CAT WILL EVEN HUNT AND EAT WILD BOARS."

WE HAVE TO HELP HIM!

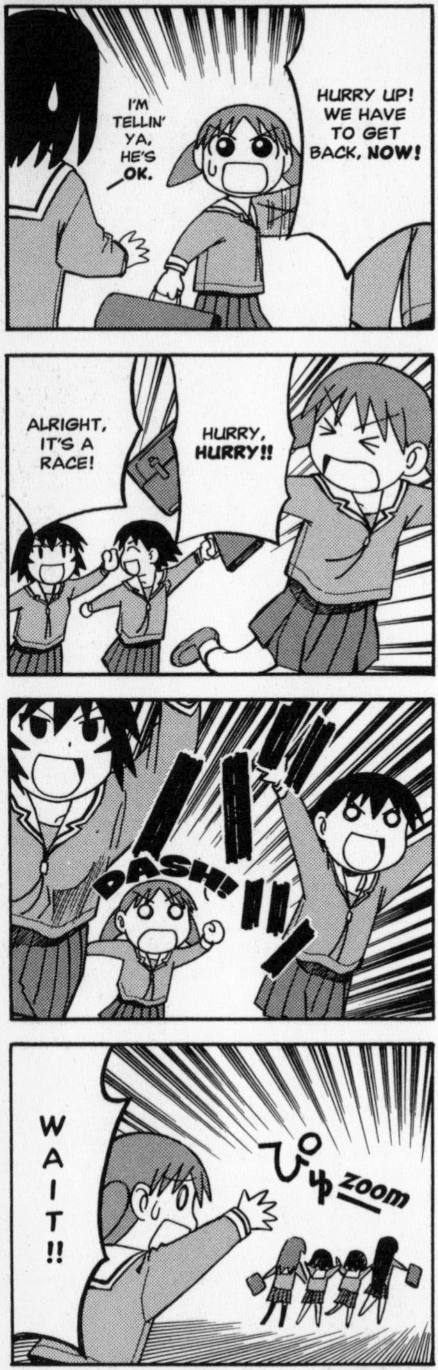
HURRY UP! WE HAVE TO GET BACK, NOW!
I'M TELLIN' YA, HE'S OK.
HURRY, HURRY!!
ALRIGHT, IT'S A RACE!
DASH!
ぴゅ
zoom
WAIT!!

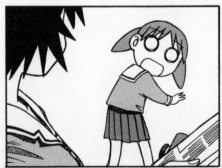

MR. TADAKICHI

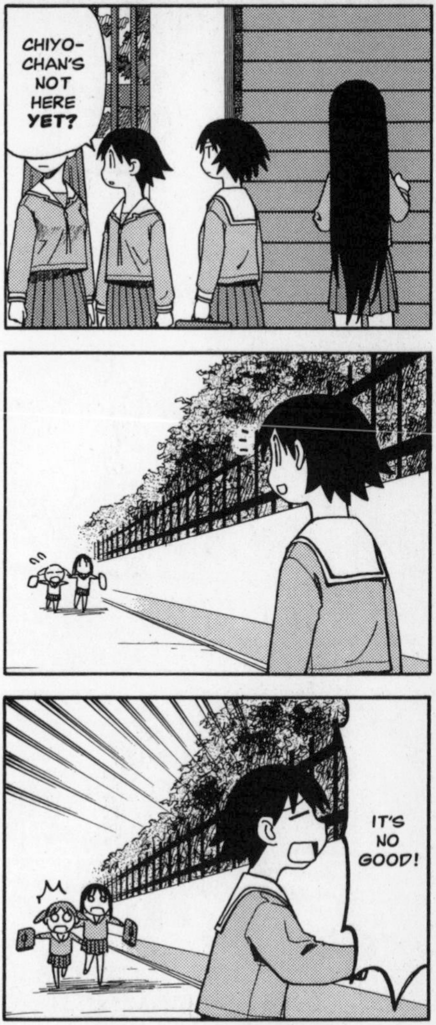
CHIYO-CHAN'S NOT HERE YET?
IT'S NO GOOD!
WE'RE TOO LATE.
WHAT?!

WE CAN DO THAT?

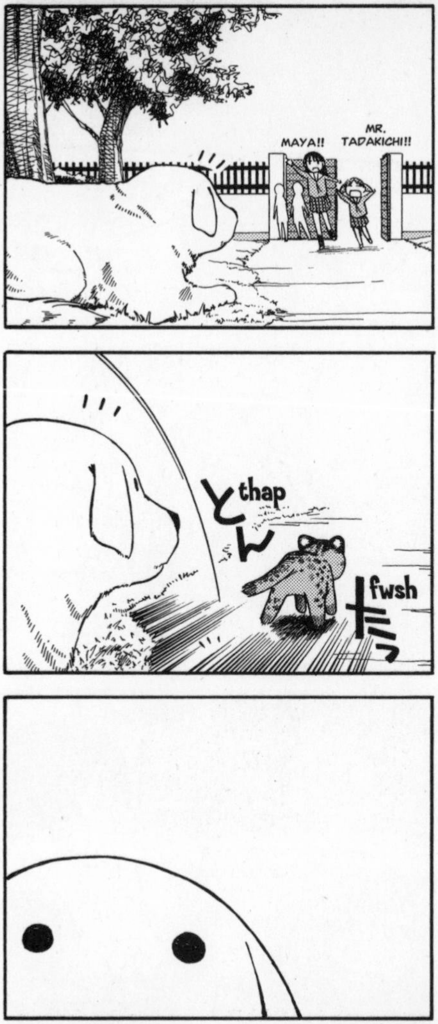
MR. TADAKICHI!!
MAYA!!
とん thap
たっ fwsh
ドドドド THWMP THWMP
♪
てててthp thp

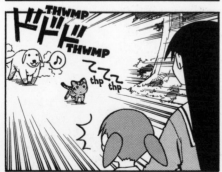

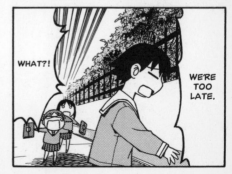

ME, TOO

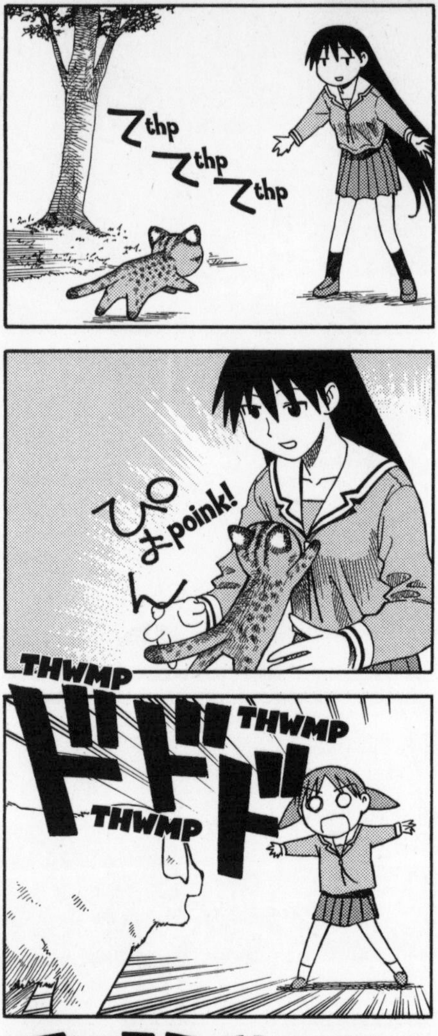

て thp て thp て thp
ぴょん poink!
THWMP
ドドド
THWMP
THWMP
ドド
BWOMP!

OVERWRITE: IMPOSSIBLE

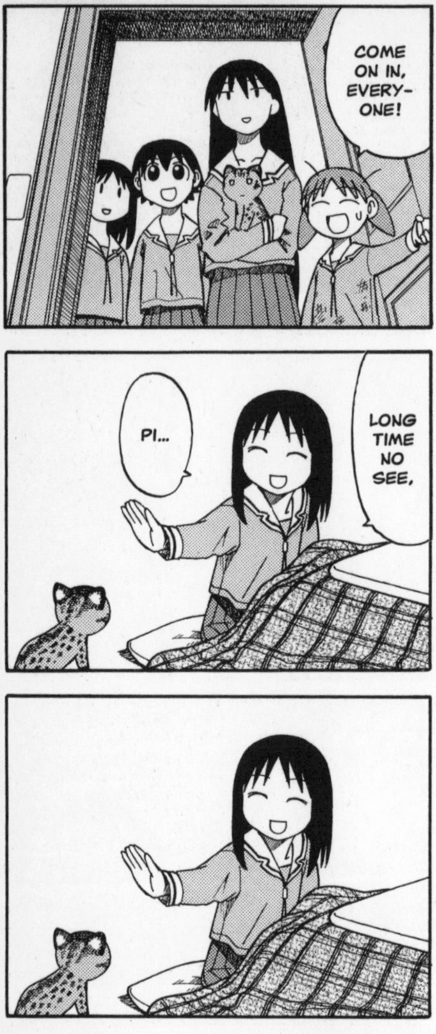

COME ON IN, EVERY-ONE!
LONG TIME NO SEE,
PI...
PIKA...
MEOW...
OH, FOR... JUST CALL HIM "PIKA MEOW-MEOW."

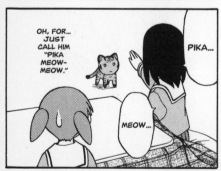

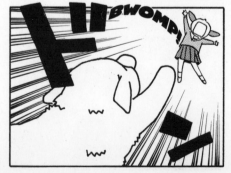

STOP IT!

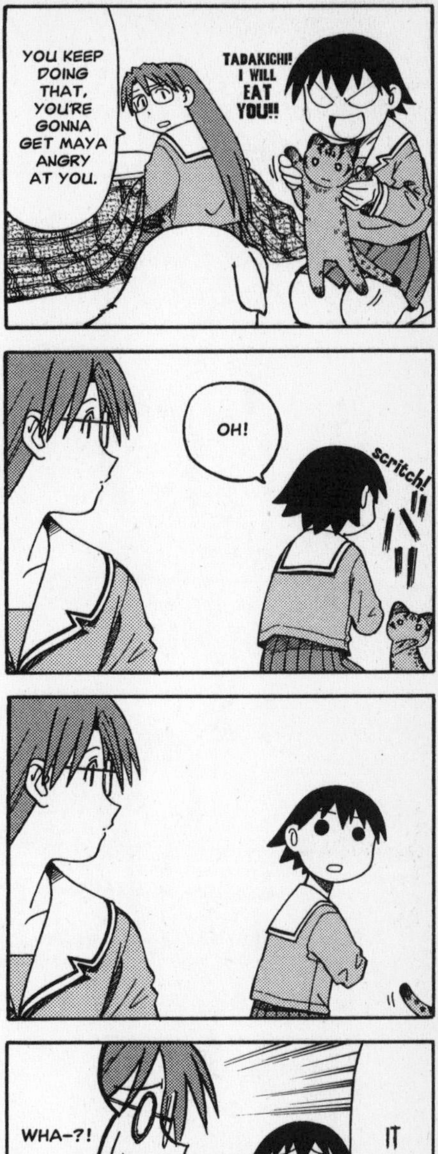
TADAKICHI!! I WILL EAT YOU!!
YOU KEEP DOING THAT, YOU'RE GONNA GET MAYA ANGRY AT YOU.
OH!
scritch!
IT HURTS...
WHA-?!
gush
だら～

EDUCATION

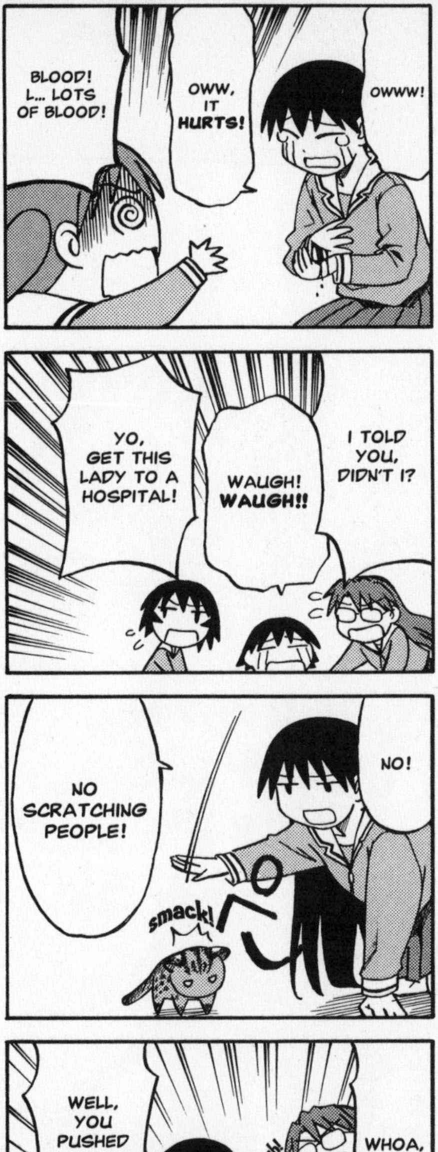
OWWW!
OWW, IT HURTS!
BLOOD! L... LOTS OF BLOOD!
I TOLD YOU, DIDN'T I?
WAUGH! WAUGH!!
YO, GET THIS LADY TO A HOSPITAL!
NO!
NO SCRATCHING PEOPLE!
smack!
WHOA, WELL DONE!
waugh!
えーん
えーん
waugh!
WELL, YOU PUSHED HIM TOO FAR!

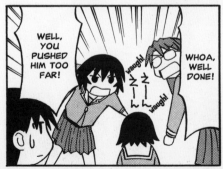

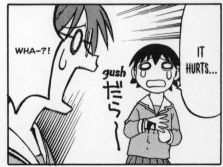

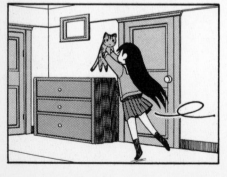

THE CENTER OF ATTENTION

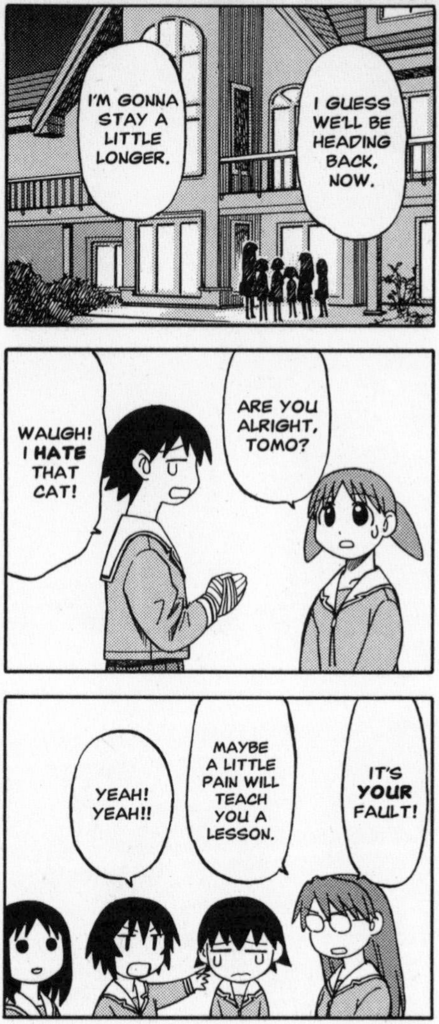
I GUESS WE'LL BE HEADING BACK, NOW.
I'M GONNA STAY A LITTLE LONGER.
ARE YOU ALRIGHT, TOMO?
WAUGH! I **HATE** THAT CAT!
IT'S **YOUR** FAULT!
MAYBE A LITTLE PAIN WILL TEACH YOU A LESSON.
YEAH! YEAH!!
ALRIGHT, SEE YA!
IDIOT! バーカ
IDIOT! バーカ
I CAN'T BELIEVE HOW MUCH ATTENTION SHE'S GETTING JUST FROM BEING HURT...

WITH MAYA

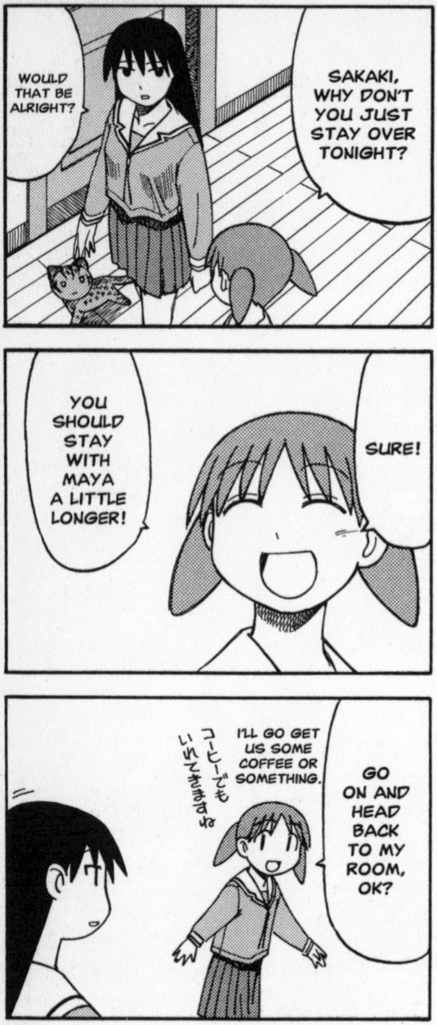
SAKAKI, WHY DON'T YOU JUST STAY OVER TONIGHT?
WOULD THAT BE ALRIGHT?
SURE!
YOU SHOULD STAY WITH MAYA A LITTLE LONGER!
GO ON AND HEAD BACK TO MY ROOM, OK?
I'LL GO GET US SOME COFFEE OR SOMETHING.
コーヒーでもいれてきますね

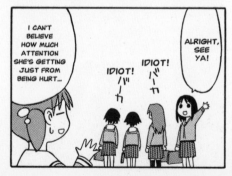

CAN'T STAND IT

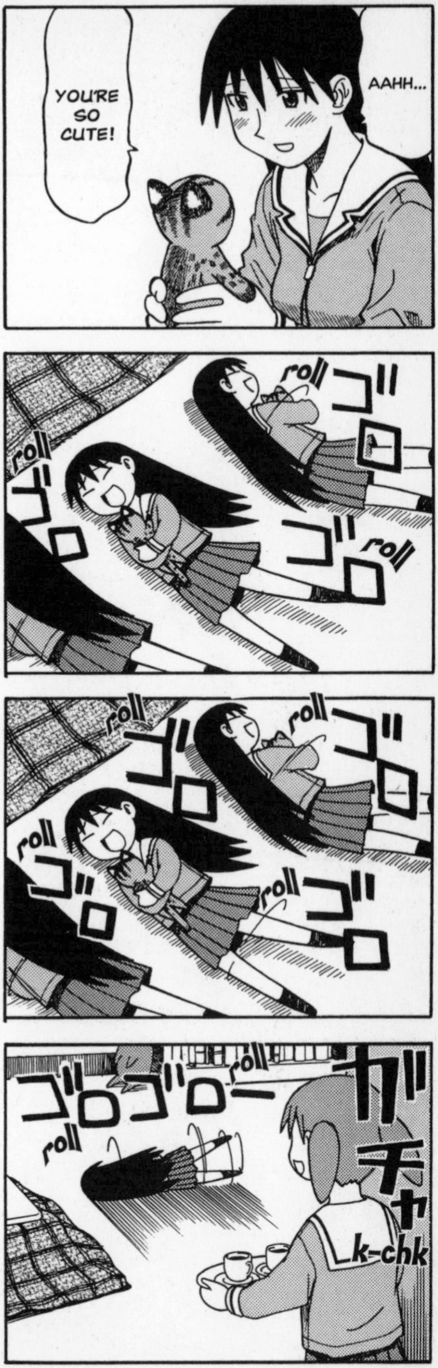
AAHH...
YOU'RE SO CUTE!
roll ゴロ
roll ゴロ
roll ゴロ
roll ゴロ
roll ゴロ
roll ゴロ
roll ゴロ
roll ゴロ
ガチャ
k-chk
roll ゴロゴロー
roll

NOTHING. NOTHING AT ALL...

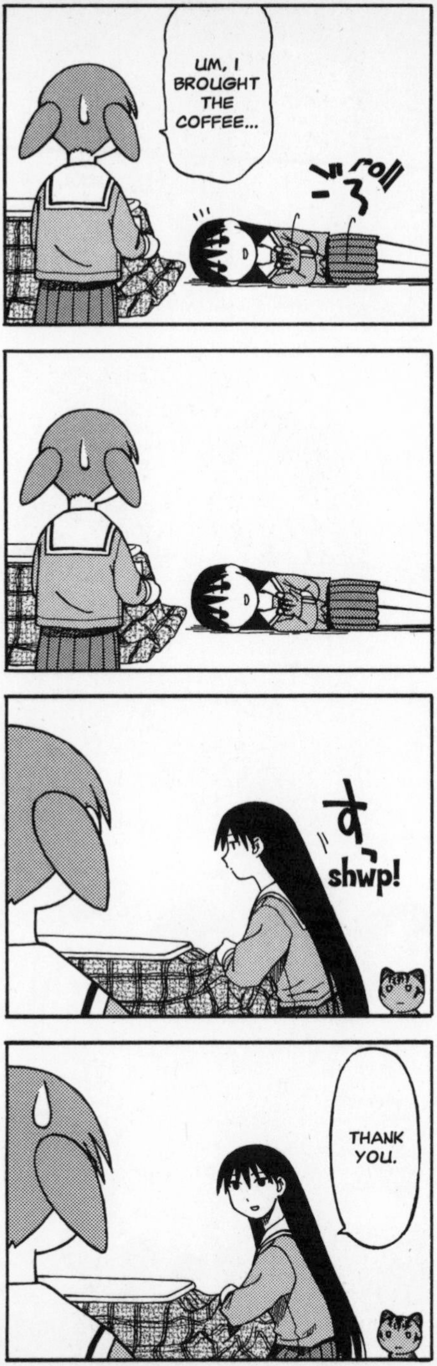
UM, I BROUGHT THE COFFEE...
roll ごろ
す
shwp!
THANK YOU.

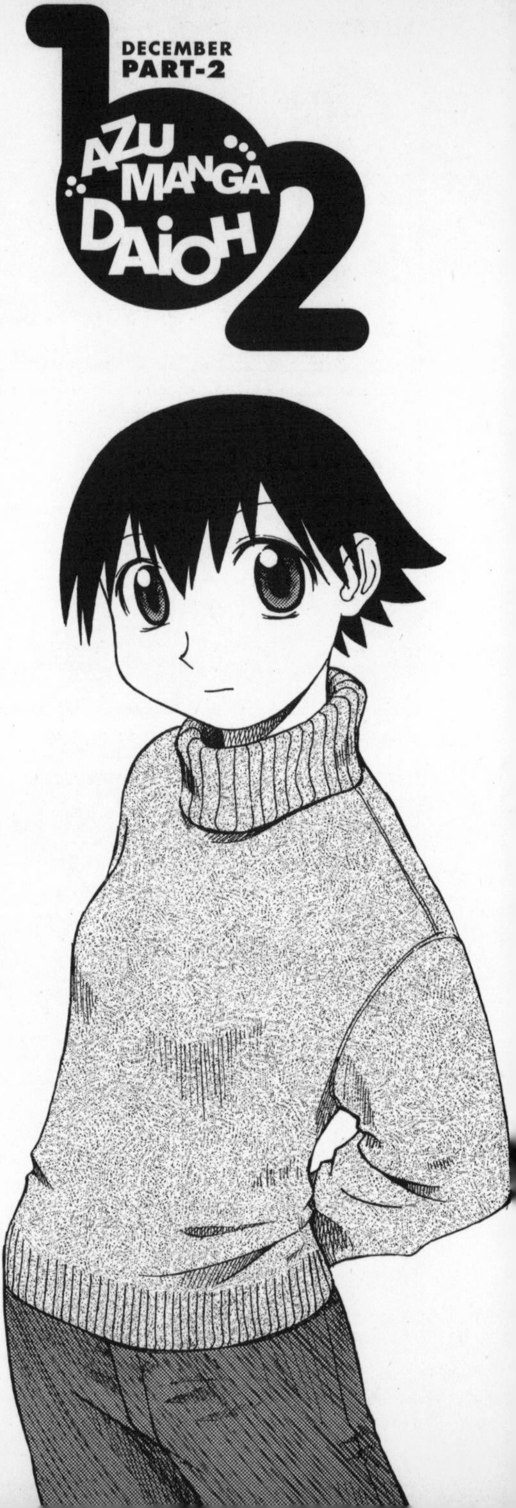
DECEMBER PART-2
AZU MANGA DAIOH 2

WILD

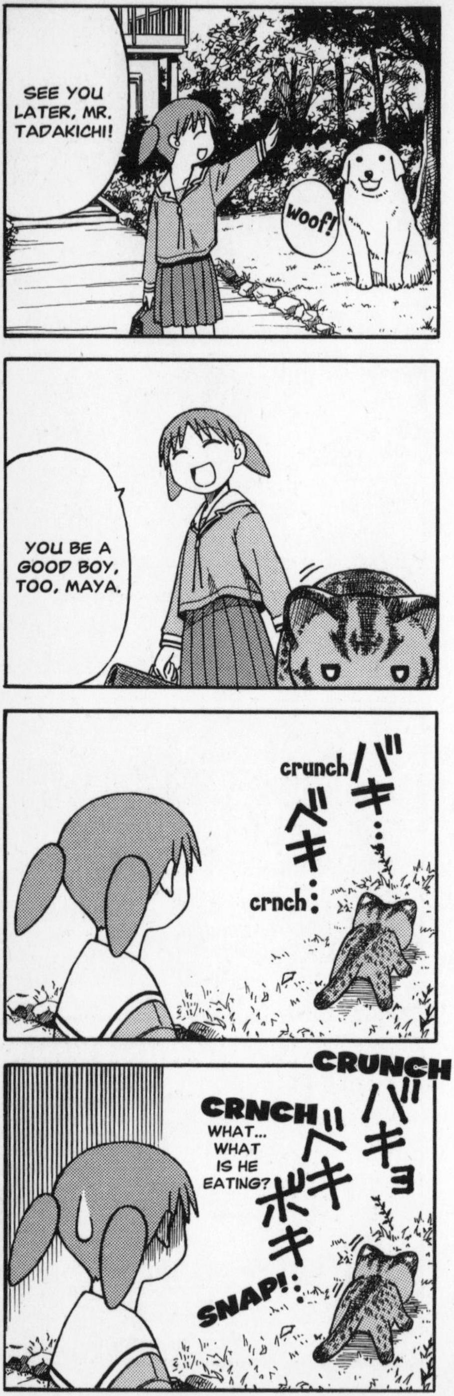
SEE YOU LATER, MR. TADAKICHI!
woof!
YOU BE A GOOD BOY, TOO, MAYA.
バキ… crunch
ベキ… crnch
バキョ CRUNCH
ベキ CRNCH
WHAT... WHAT IS HE EATING?
ボキ… SNAP!

EVASION

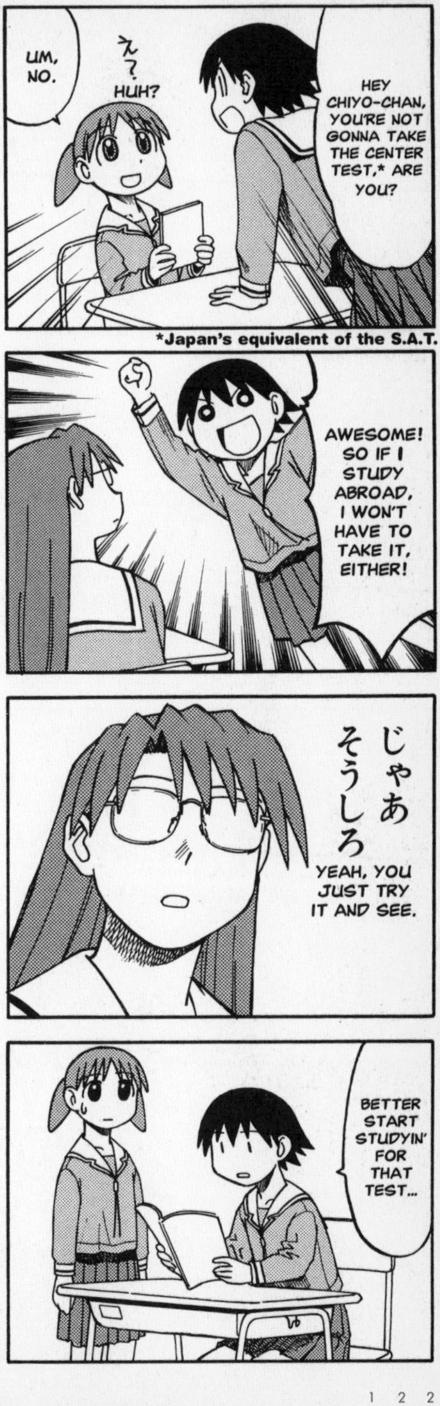
HEY CHIYO-CHAN, YOU'RE NOT GONNA TAKE THE CENTER TEST,* ARE YOU?
え？
HUH?
UM, NO.
AWESOME! SO IF I STUDY ABROAD, I WON'T HAVE TO TAKE IT, EITHER!
じゃあそうしろ
YEAH, YOU JUST TRY IT AND SEE.
BETTER START STUDYIN' FOR THAT TEST...

*Japan's equivalent of the S.A.T.

QUESTION #1

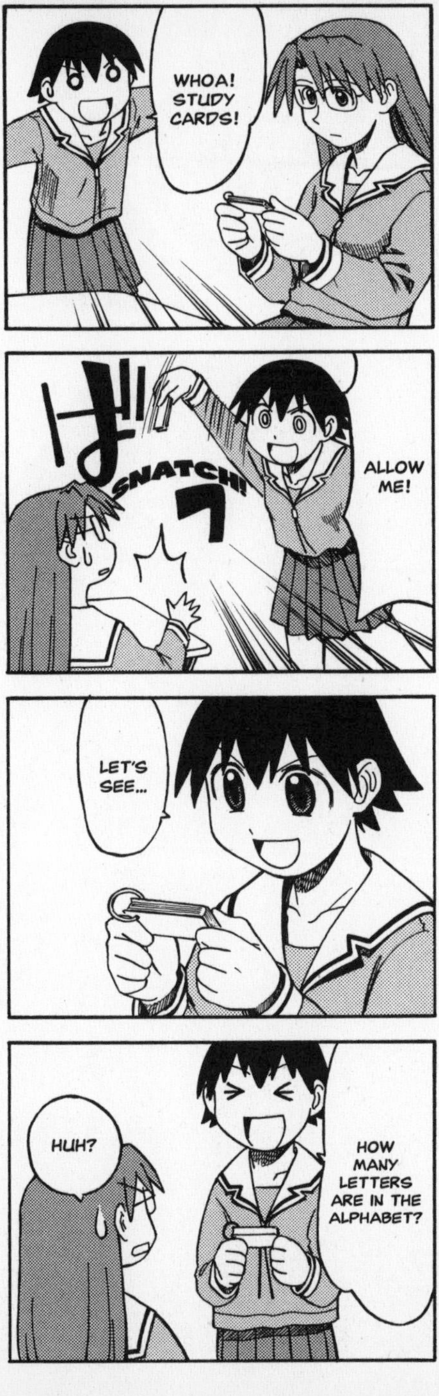
WHOA! STUDY CARDS!
ばっ
SNATCH!
ALLOW ME!
LET'S SEE...
HOW MANY LETTERS ARE IN THE ALPHABET?
HUH?

OH, I GET IT!

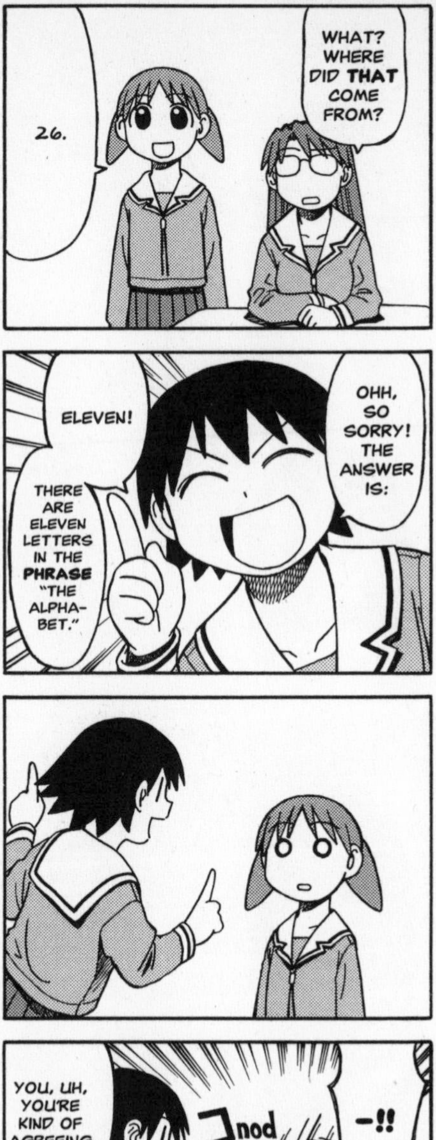
WHAT? WHERE DID **THAT** COME FROM?
26.
OHH, SO SORRY! THE ANSWER IS:
ELEVEN!
THERE ARE ELEVEN LETTERS IN THE **PHRASE** "THE ALPHABET."
-!!
nod
YOU, UH, YOU'RE KIND OF AGREEING WITH ME **TOO** MUCH THERE.
nod

SHE'S RIGHT!

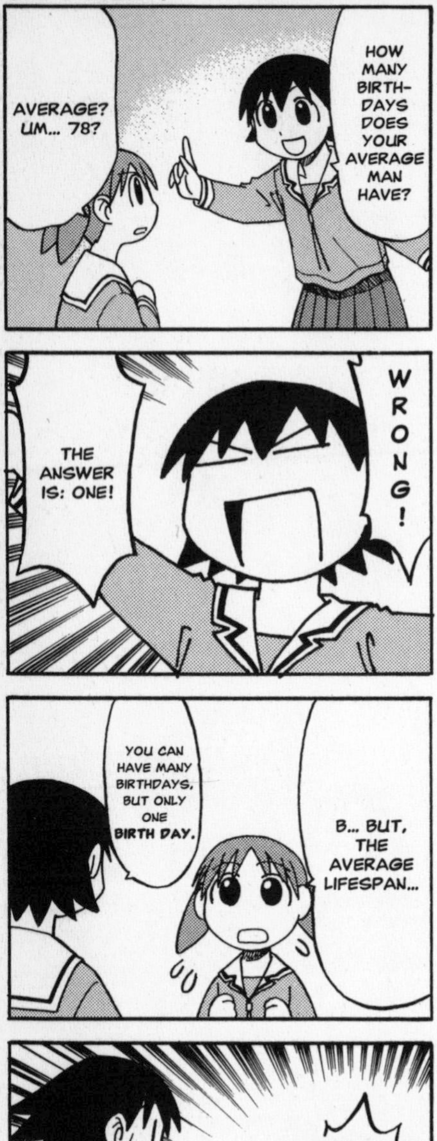
HOW MANY BIRTHDAYS DOES YOUR AVERAGE MAN HAVE?
AVERAGE? UM... 78?
WRONG!
THE ANSWER IS: ONE!
B... BUT, THE AVERAGE LIFESPAN...
YOU CAN HAVE MANY BIRTHDAYS, BUT ONLY ONE **BIRTH DAY**.
HEH. THIS IS FUN.

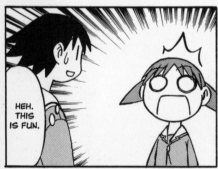

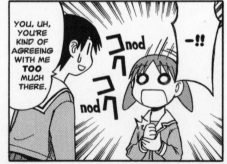

AN INNATE ABILITY?

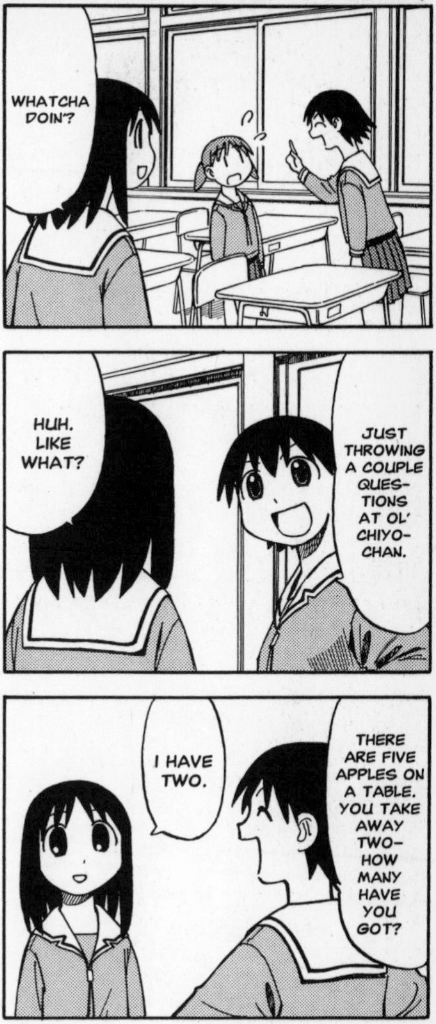
WHATCHA DOIN'?
JUST THROWING A COUPLE QUESTIONS AT OL' CHIYO-CHAN.
HUH. LIKE WHAT?
THERE ARE FIVE APPLES ON A TABLE. YOU TAKE AWAY TWO— HOW MANY HAVE YOU GOT?
I HAVE TWO.
WHOA! SHE KNEW THE ANSWER RIGHT AWAY!
THAT'S AMAZ-ING!
WHAT? REALLY?

IN FULL FORCE

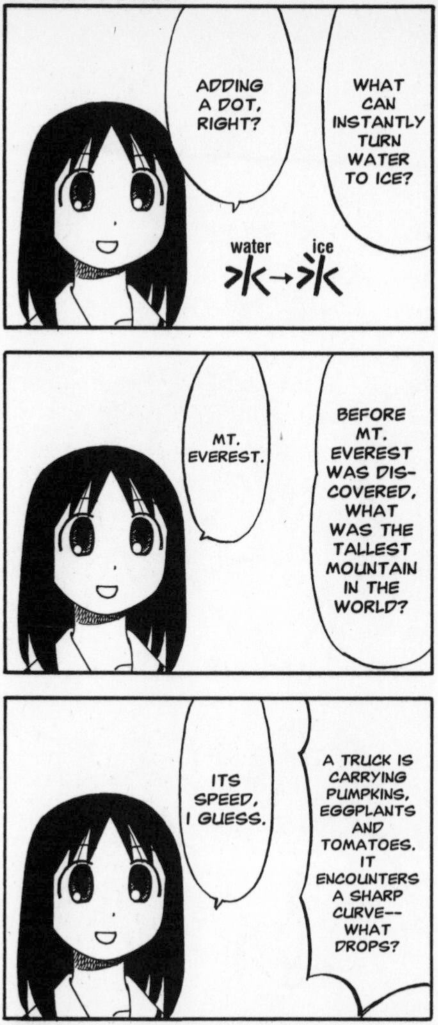
WHAT CAN INSTANTLY TURN WATER TO ICE?
ADDING A DOT, RIGHT?
water 水 → ice 氷
BEFORE MT. EVEREST WAS DIS-COVERED, WHAT WAS THE TALLEST MOUNTAIN IN THE WORLD?
MT. EVEREST.
A TRUCK IS CARRYING PUMPKINS, EGGPLANTS AND TOMATOES. IT ENCOUNTERS A SHARP CURVE-- WHAT DROPS?
ITS SPEED, I GUESS.
TH... THAT'S INCREDI-BLE!
WHAT ARE YOU?!
ぱち clap ぱち clap ぱち ぱち clap
WHAT, DID I GET 'EM RIGHT?

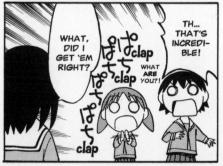

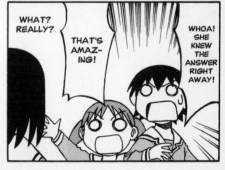

CAREER ADVICE

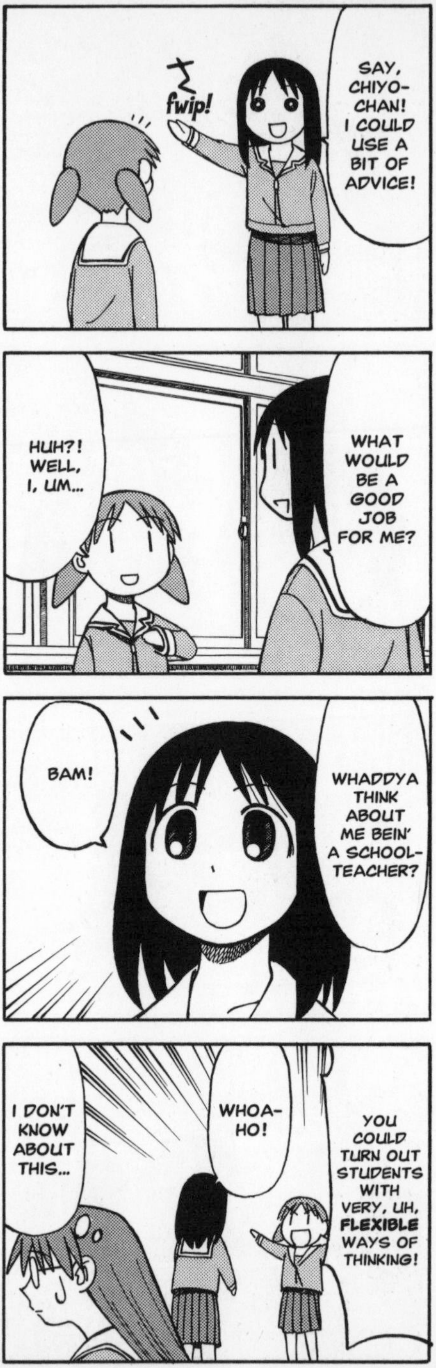
SAY, CHIYO-CHAN! I COULD USE A BIT OF ADVICE!
fwip!
WHAT WOULD BE A GOOD JOB FOR ME?
HUH?! WELL, I, UM...
WHADDYA THINK ABOUT ME BEIN' A SCHOOL-TEACHER?
BAM!
YOU COULD TURN OUT STUDENTS WITH VERY, UH, **FLEXIBLE** WAYS OF THINKING!
WHOA-HO!
I DON'T KNOW ABOUT THIS...

DON'T MOCK ME!

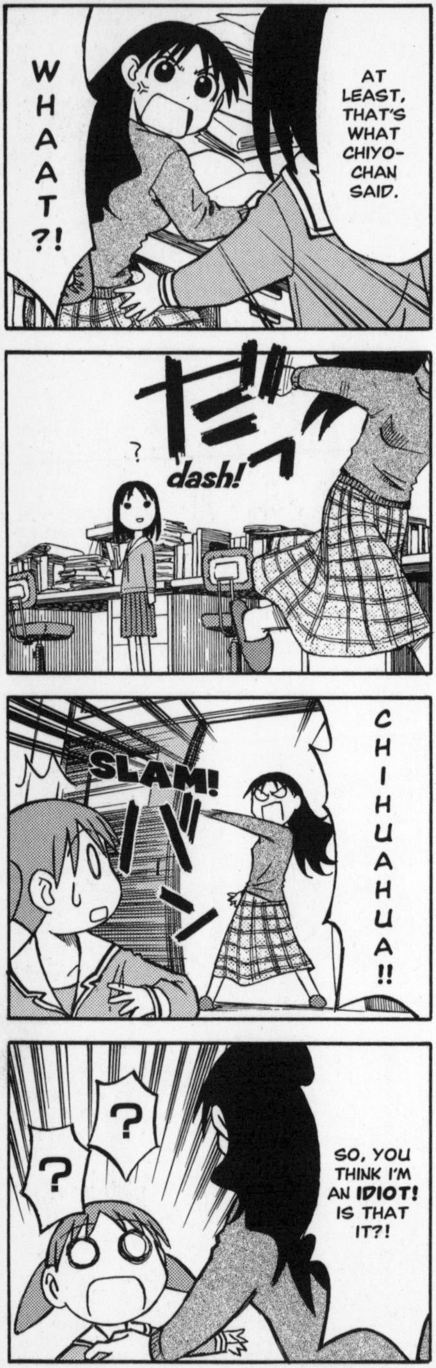
AT LEAST, THAT'S WHAT CHIYO-CHAN SAID.
WHAAT?!
dash!
?
CHIHUAHUA!!
SLAM!
SO, YOU THINK I'M AN **IDIOT!** IS THAT IT?!
?
?

THE DREAM

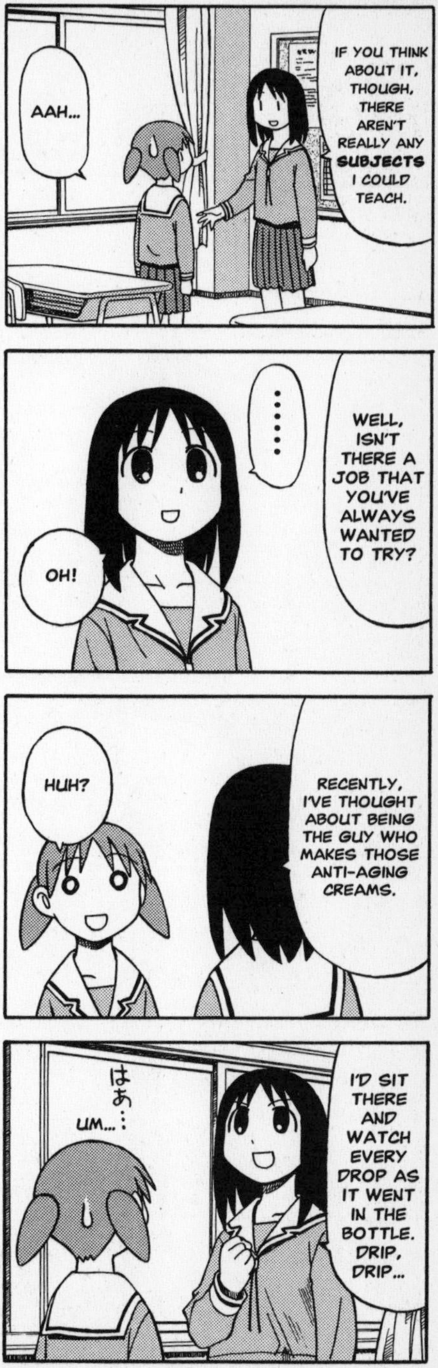
IF YOU THINK ABOUT IT, THOUGH, THERE AREN'T REALLY ANY SUBJECTS I COULD TEACH.
AAH...
WELL, ISN'T THERE A JOB THAT YOU'VE ALWAYS WANTED TO TRY?
......
OH!
RECENTLY, I'VE THOUGHT ABOUT BEING THE GUY WHO MAKES THOSE ANTI-AGING CREAMS.
HUH?
I'D SIT THERE AND WATCH EVERY DROP AS IT WENT IN THE BOTTLE. DRIP, DRIP...
はぁ…
UM...

GUIDANCE

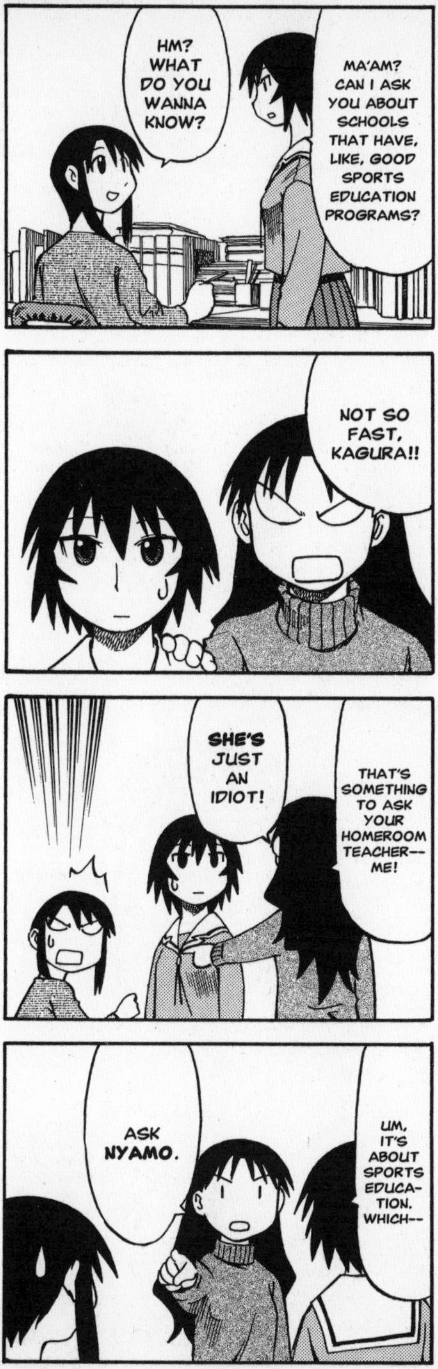
MA'AM? CAN I ASK YOU ABOUT SCHOOLS THAT HAVE, LIKE, GOOD SPORTS EDUCATION PROGRAMS?
HM? WHAT DO YOU WANNA KNOW?
NOT SO FAST, KAGURA!!
THAT'S SOMETHING TO ASK YOUR HOMEROOM TEACHER-- ME!
SHE'S JUST AN IDIOT!
UM, IT'S ABOUT SPORTS EDUCA-TION. WHICH--
ASK NYAMO.

FORTUNE TELLING

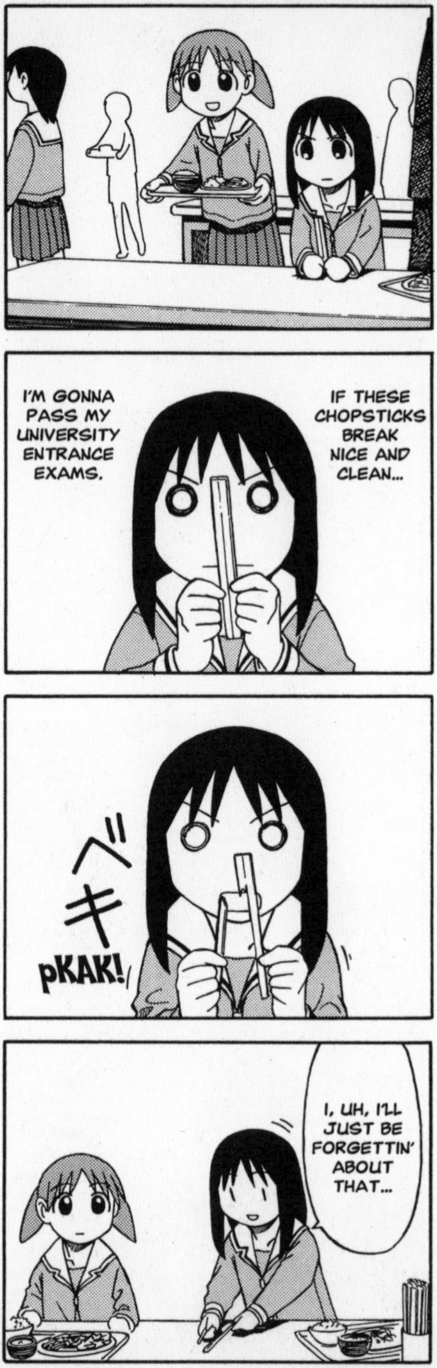
IF THESE CHOPSTICKS BREAK NICE AND CLEAN...
I'M GONNA PASS MY UNIVERSITY ENTRANCE EXAMS.
ベキ
pKAK!
I, UH, I'LL JUST BE FORGETTIN' ABOUT THAT...

INSTRUCTION

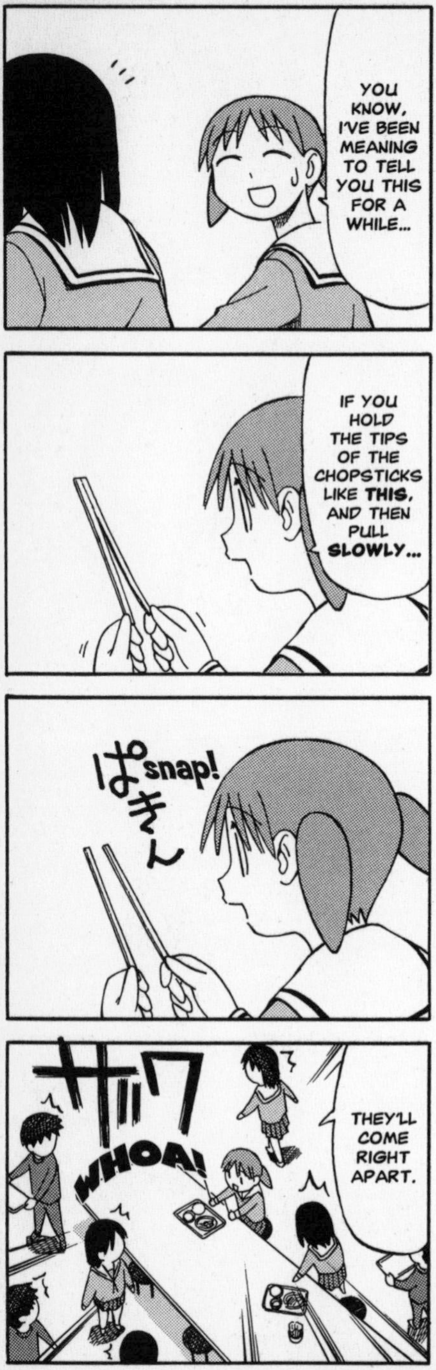
YOU KNOW, I'VE BEEN MEANING TO TELL YOU THIS FOR A WHILE...
IF YOU HOLD THE TIPS OF THE CHOPSTICKS LIKE **THIS**, AND THEN PULL **SLOWLY**...
ぱきん
snap!
ザワ
WHOA!
THEY'LL COME RIGHT APART.

THE SECRET WAY INTO SCHOOL

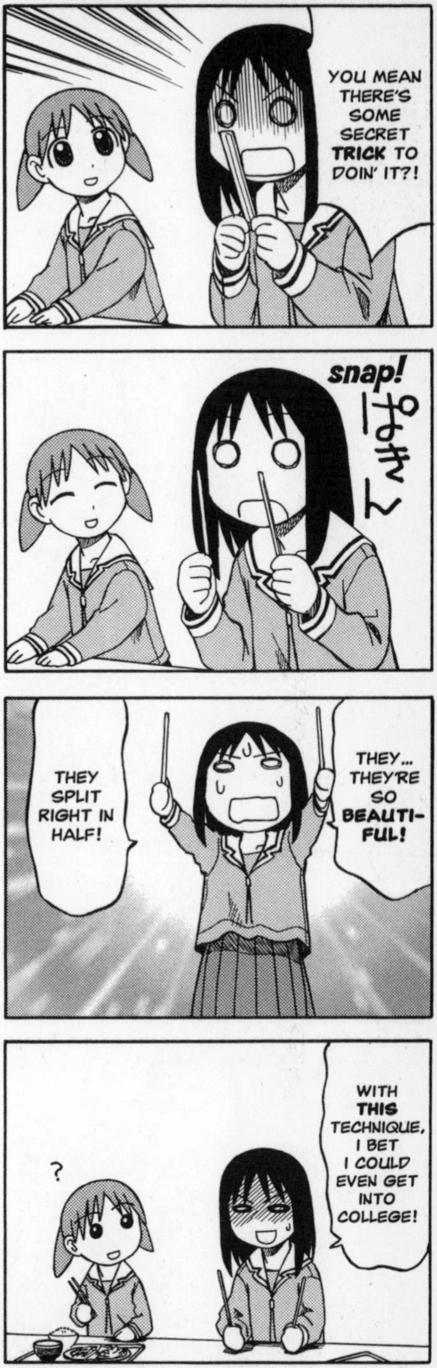
YOU MEAN THERE'S SOME SECRET **TRICK** TO DOIN' IT?!
snap! ぱきん
THEY... THEY'RE SO **BEAUTIFUL!**
THEY SPLIT RIGHT IN HALF!
WITH **THIS** TECHNIQUE, I BET I COULD EVEN GET INTO COLLEGE!
?

THE RITUAL

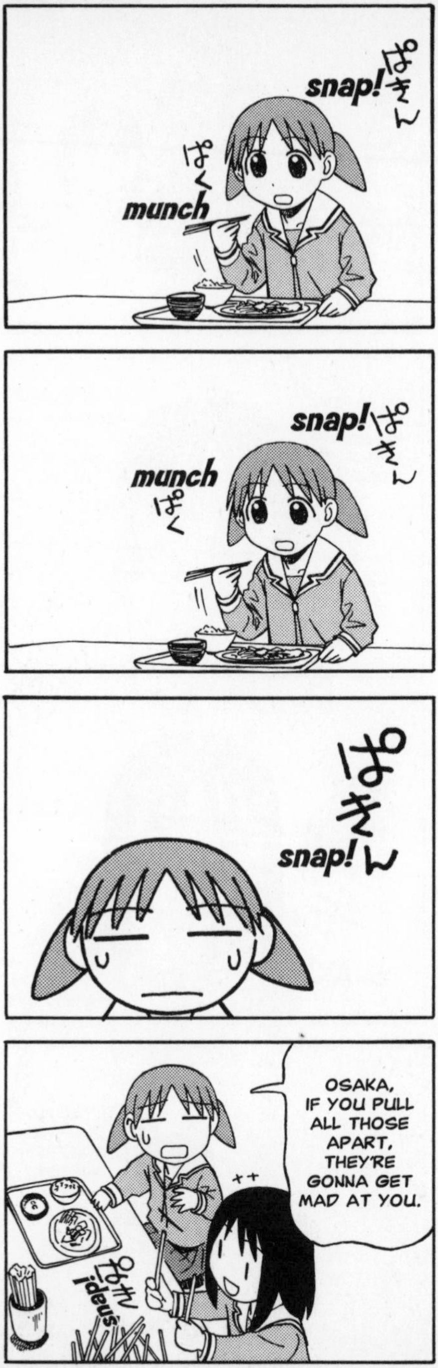
ぱきん snap!
ぱく munch
snap! ぱきん
munch ぱく
ぱきん snap!
OSAKA, IF YOU PULL ALL THOSE APART, THEY'RE GONNA GET MAD AT YOU.
ぱきん snap!

AZU MANGA DAIOH

JANUARY
PART-1

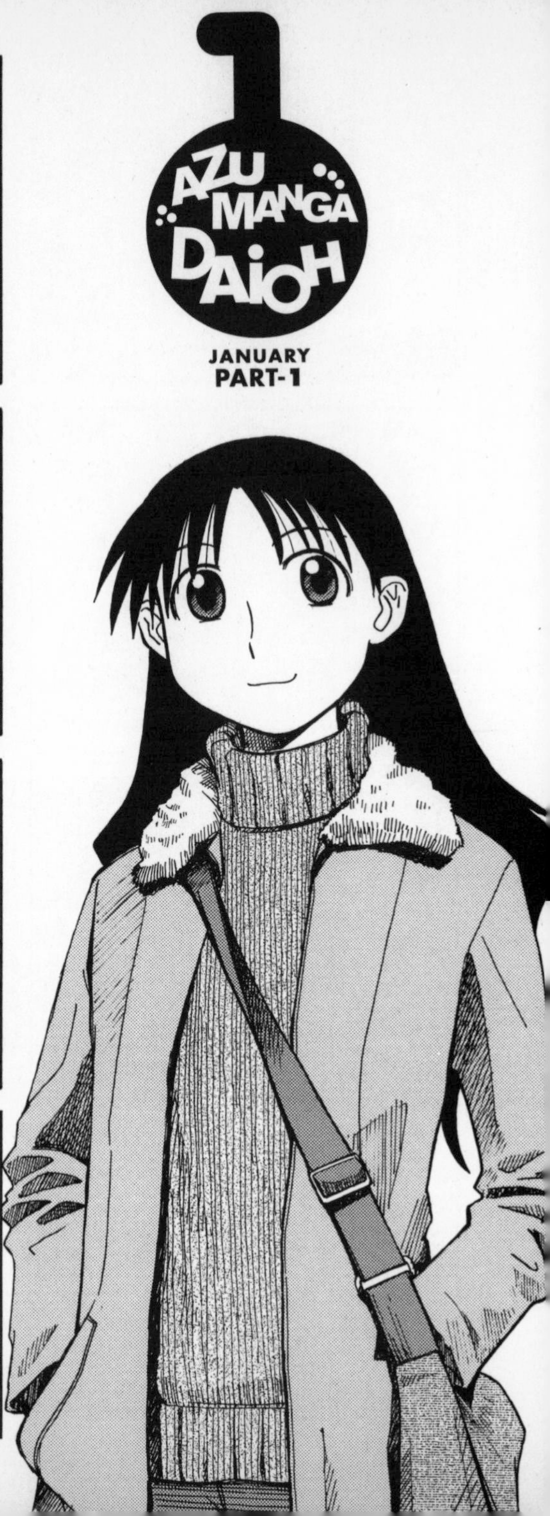

THE LANDMARK

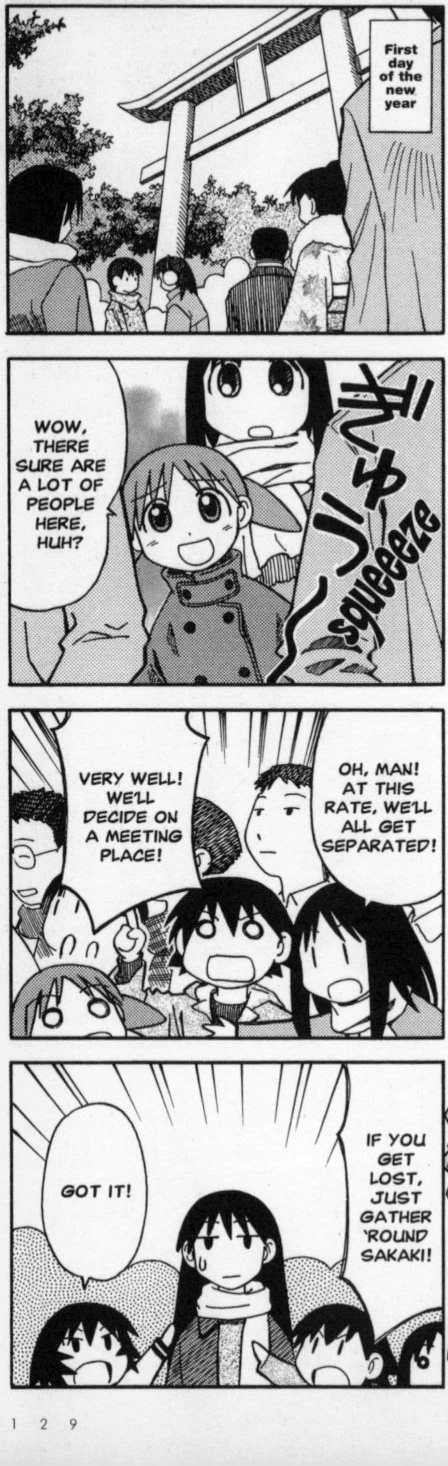
First day of the new year
squeeeze
WOW, THERE SURE ARE A LOT OF PEOPLE HERE, HUH?
OH, MAN! AT THIS RATE, WE'LL ALL GET SEPARATED!
VERY WELL! WE'LL DECIDE ON A MEETING PLACE!
IF YOU GET LOST, JUST GATHER 'ROUND SAKAKI!
GOT IT!

AN UNEXPECTED CHOICE

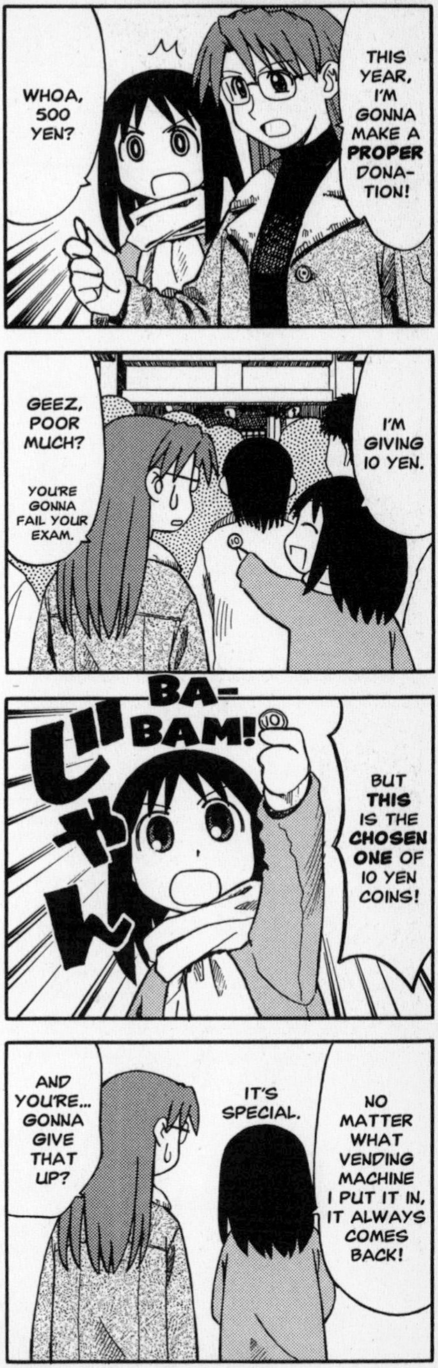
THIS YEAR, I'M GONNA MAKE A PROPER DONATION!
WHOA, 500 YEN?
I'M GIVING 10 YEN.
GEEZ, POOR MUCH?
YOU'RE GONNA FAIL YOUR EXAM.
BUT THIS IS THE CHOSEN ONE OF 10 YEN COINS!
BA-BAM!
じゃん
NO MATTER WHAT VENDING MACHINE I PUT IT IN, IT ALWAYS COMES BACK!
IT'S SPECIAL.
AND YOU'RE... GONNA GIVE THAT UP?

THIS IS FUN

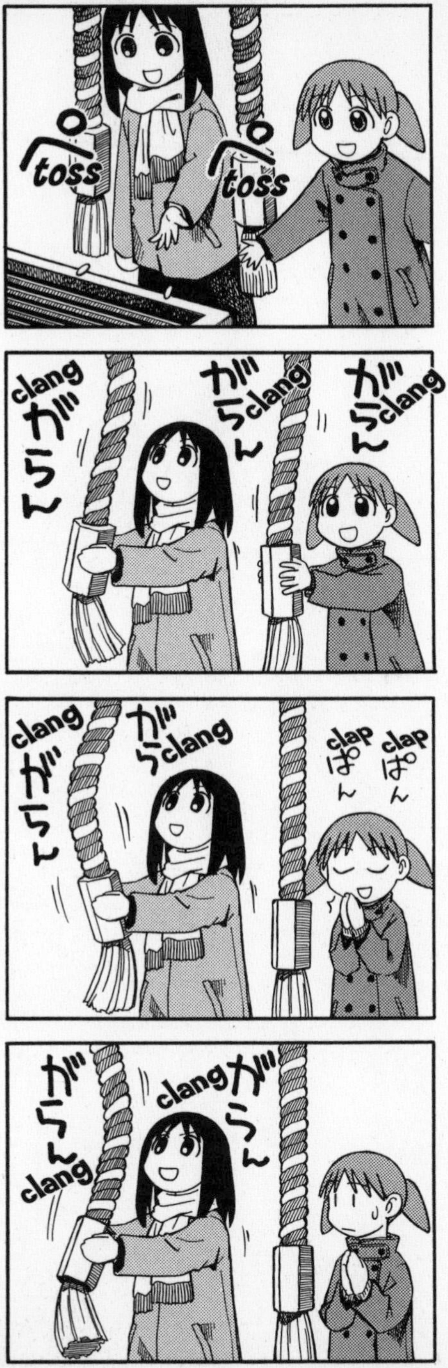
toss
toss
がらん clang
がらん clang
clang がらん
がらん clang
clang がらん
ぱん clap
ぱん clap
がらん clang
clang がらん

THE POWER OF MONEY

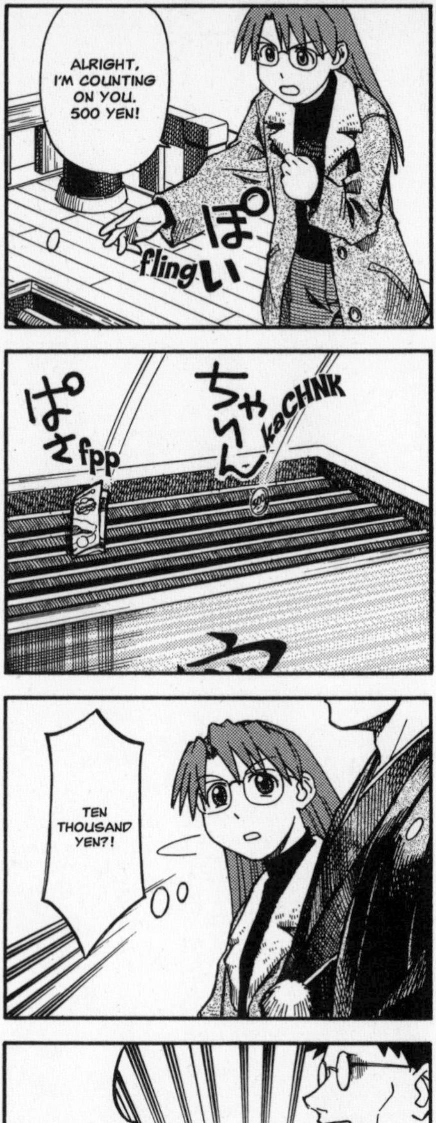
ALRIGHT, I'M COUNTING ON YOU. 500 YEN!
ぽい
fling
ぱさ
fpp
ちゃりん
kaCHNK
TEN THOUSAND YEN?!
WAAUGH!

THE WISH

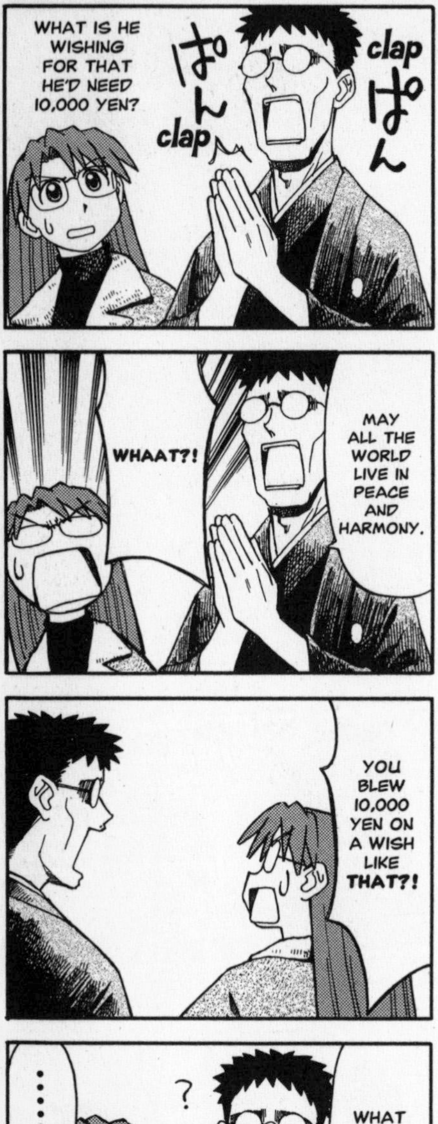
ぱん
clap
ぱん
clap
WHAT IS HE WISHING FOR THAT HE'D NEED 10,000 YEN?
MAY ALL THE WORLD LIVE IN PEACE AND HARMONY.
WHAAT?!
YOU BLEW 10,000 YEN ON A WISH LIKE THAT?!
WHAT COULD BE A GREATER WISH THAN WORLD PEACE?
?
......

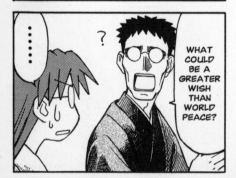

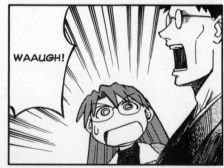

FOOD

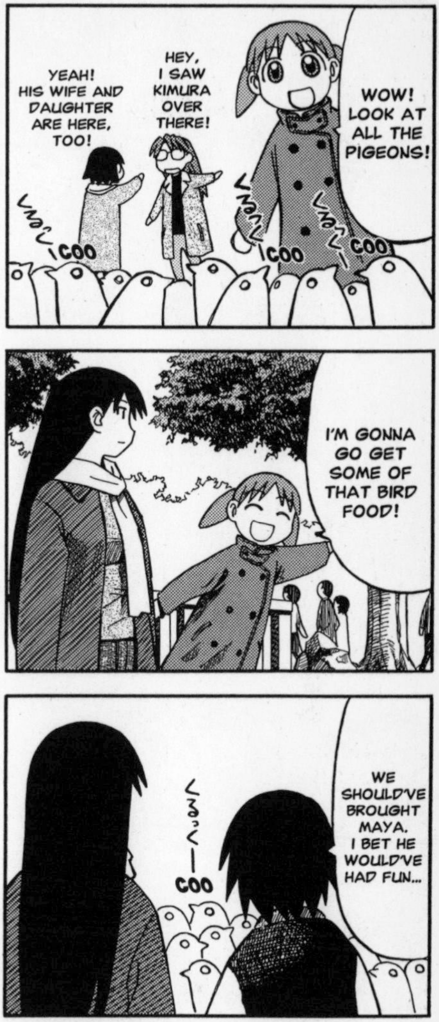
WOW! LOOK AT ALL THE PIGEONS!
HEY, I SAW KIMURA OVER THERE!
YEAH! HIS WIFE AND DAUGHTER ARE HERE, TOO!
くるっくー COO
くるっくー COO
くるっくー COO
I'M GONNA GO GET SOME OF THAT BIRD FOOD!
WE SHOULD'VE BROUGHT MAYA. I BET HE WOULD'VE HAD FUN...
くるっくー COO
THESE PIGEONS ARE SO DUMB, THEY WOULDN'T EVEN KNOW WHAT HIT 'EM!
くるっく COO!
くるっく COO!

THE SWARM

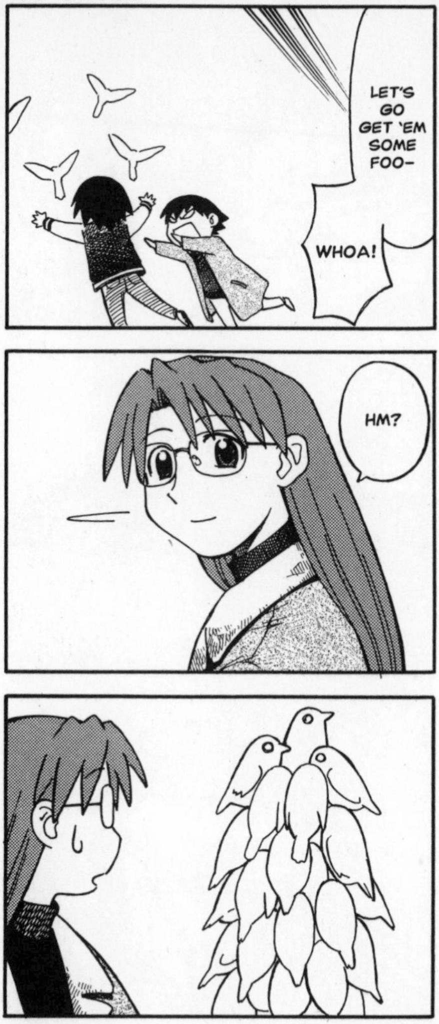
LET'S GO GET 'EM SOME FOO-
WHOA!
HM?
AAGH...
CHIYO-CHAN!!

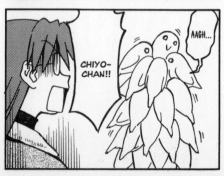

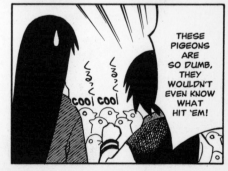

BATTLE OF THE FORTUNES

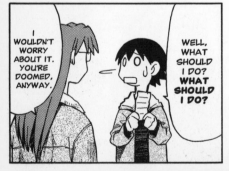

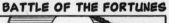

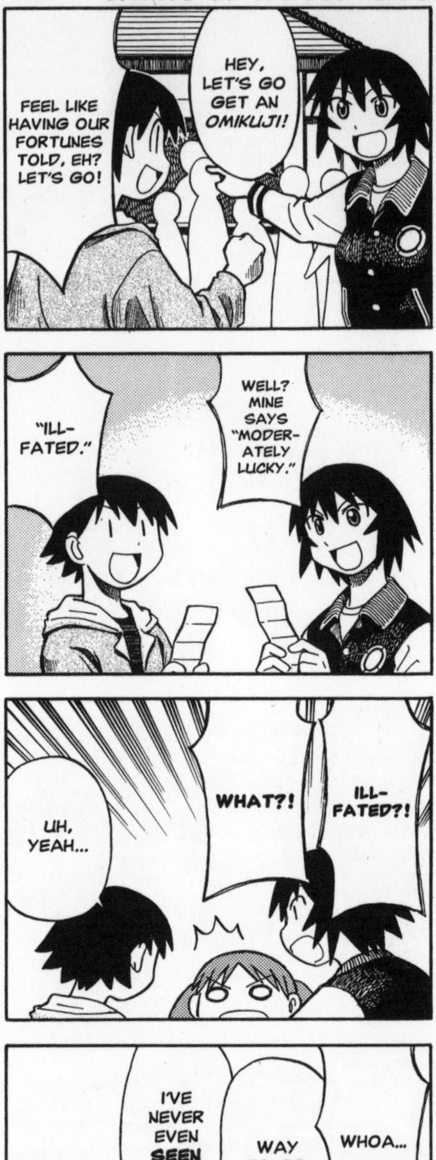
HEY, LET'S GO GET AN *OMIKUJI*!
FEEL LIKE HAVING OUR FORTUNES TOLD, EH? LET'S GO!
WELL? MINE SAYS "MODERATELY LUCKY."
"ILL-FATED."
ILL-FATED?!
WHAT?!
UH, YEAH...
WHOA...
WAY TO GO, TOMO!
I'VE NEVER EVEN **SEEN** ONE OF THESE...
Ill-fated...

WHAT SHOULD I DO?

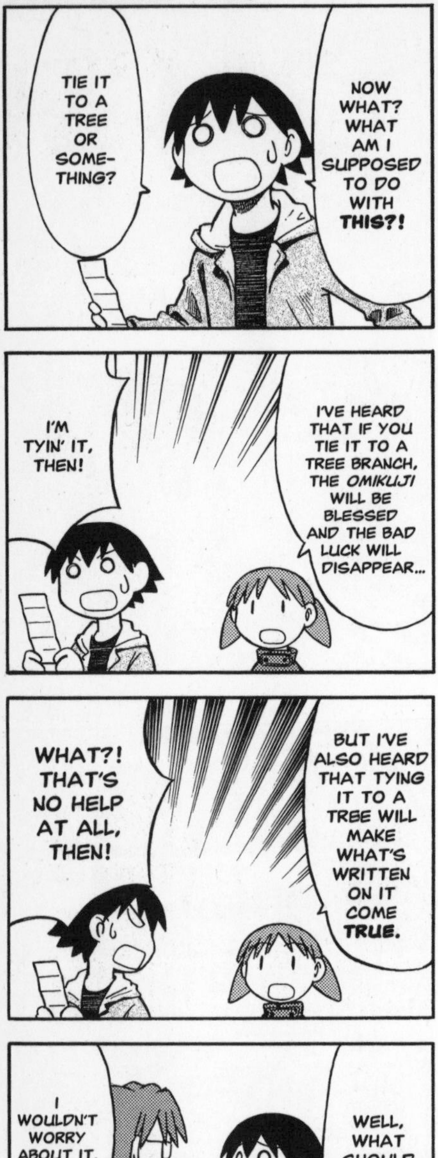
NOW WHAT? WHAT AM I SUPPOSED TO DO WITH **THIS?!**
TIE IT TO A TREE OR SOMETHING?
I'VE HEARD THAT IF YOU TIE IT TO A TREE BRANCH, THE *OMIKUJI* WILL BE BLESSED AND THE BAD LUCK WILL DISAPPEAR...
I'M TYIN' IT, THEN!
BUT I'VE ALSO HEARD THAT TYING IT TO A TREE WILL MAKE WHAT'S WRITTEN ON IT COME **TRUE.**
WHAT?! THAT'S NO HELP AT ALL, THEN!
WELL, WHAT SHOULD I DO? **WHAT SHOULD I DO?**
I WOULDN'T WORRY ABOUT IT. YOU'RE DOOMED, ANYWAY.

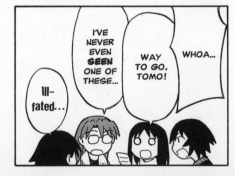

THE CHANCE

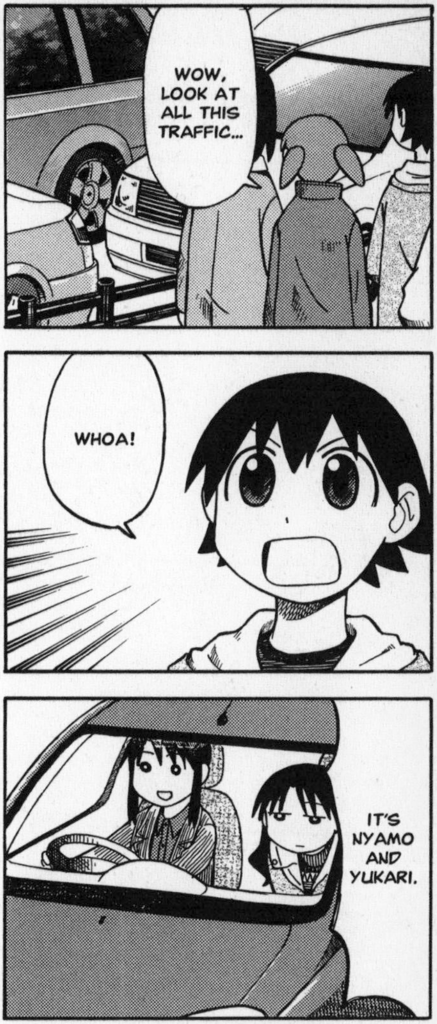
WOW, LOOK AT ALL THIS TRAFFIC...
WHOA!
IT'S NYAMO AND YUKARI.
Whoa, hey!
THEY'RE TRAPPED, GIRLS. LET'S GET 'EM!

INVASION OF THE NUMBNUTS

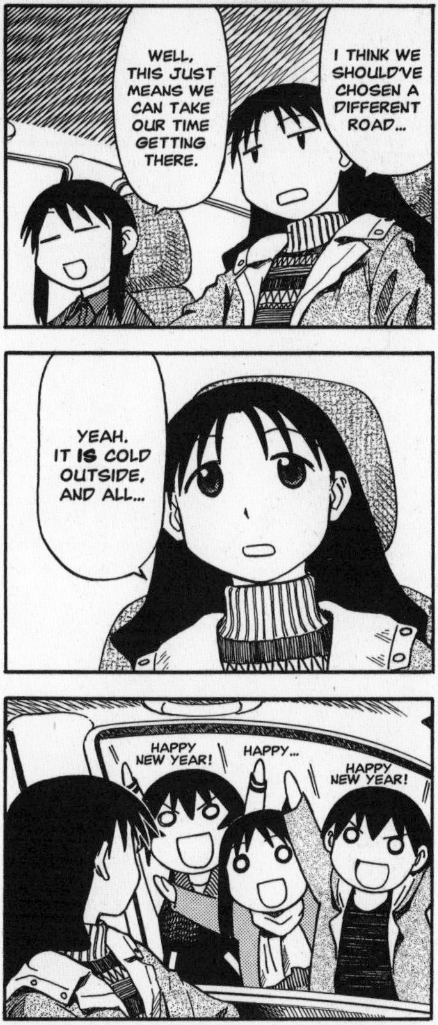
I THINK WE SHOULD'VE CHOSEN A DIFFERENT ROAD...
WELL, THIS JUST MEANS WE CAN TAKE OUR TIME GETTING THERE.
YEAH. IT **IS** COLD OUTSIDE, AND ALL...
HAPPY NEW YEAR!
HAPPY...
HAPPY NEW YEAR!
HAPPY...
..PY NEW YEAR!
HAPPY NEW YEAR!

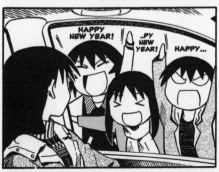

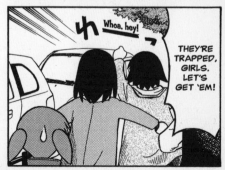

C'MON, TEACH!

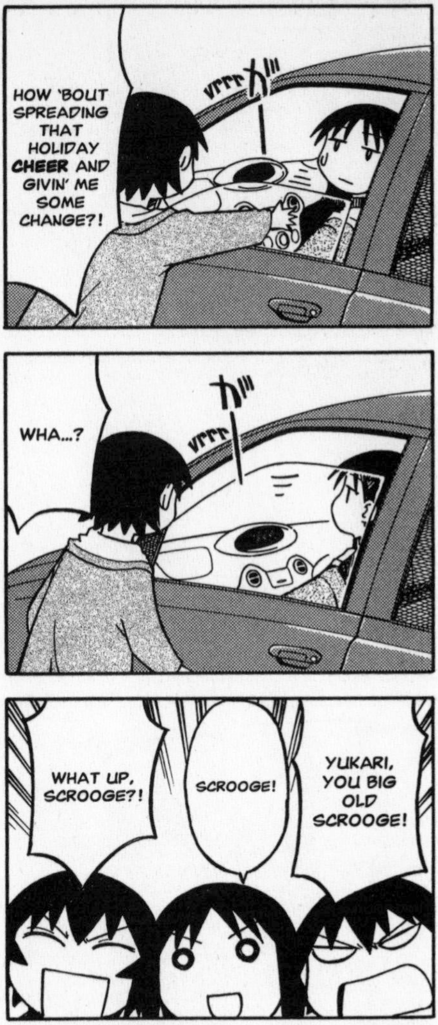
HOW 'BOUT SPREADING THAT HOLIDAY **CHEER** AND GIVIN' ME SOME CHANGE?!
vrrr
WHA...?
vrrr
YUKARI, YOU BIG OLD SCROOGE!
SCROOGE!
WHAT UP, SCROOGE?!
RUN!
dash!

NOT TOO BRIGHT

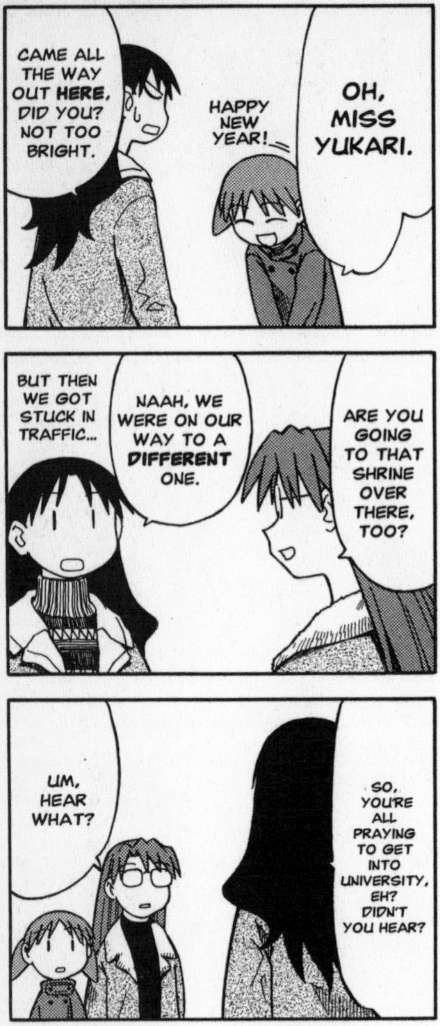
OH, MISS YUKARI.
HAPPY NEW YEAR!
CAME ALL THE WAY OUT **HERE**, DID YOU? NOT TOO BRIGHT.
ARE YOU GOING TO THAT SHRINE OVER THERE, TOO?
NAAH, WE WERE ON OUR WAY TO A **DIFFERENT** ONE.
BUT THEN WE GOT STUCK IN TRAFFIC...
SO, YOU'RE ALL PRAYING TO GET INTO UNIVERSITY, EH? DIDN'T YOU HEAR?
UM, HEAR WHAT?
THE SHRINE OWNER'S OWN **SON** FAILED HIS ENTRANCE EXAM.
IT DON'T WORK!
WHAT?!

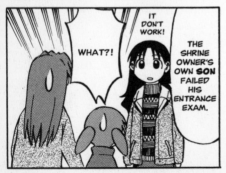

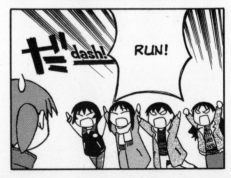

PRAYING TO PASS

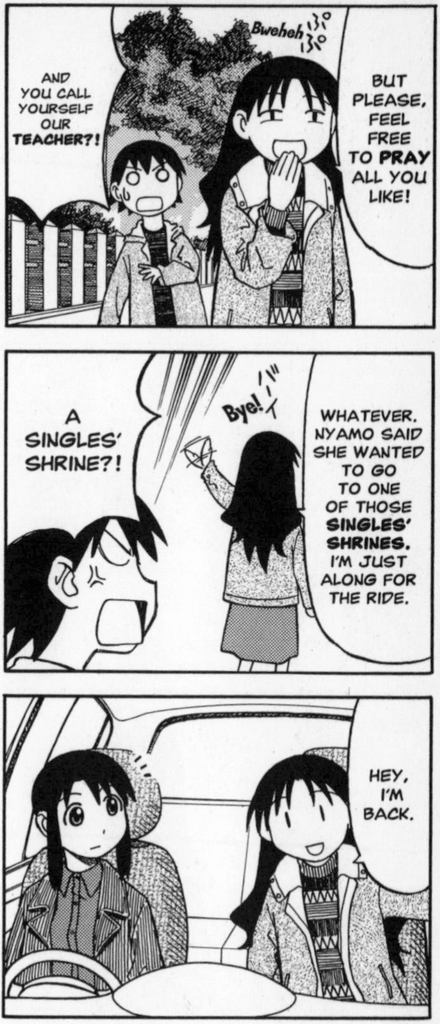
BUT PLEASE, FEEL FREE TO **PRAY** ALL YOU LIKE!
Bweheh
AND YOU CALL YOURSELF OUR **TEACHER?!**
WHATEVER. NYAMO SAID SHE WANTED TO GO TO ONE OF THOSE **SINGLES' SHRINES.** I'M JUST ALONG FOR THE RIDE.
Bye!
A SINGLES' SHRINE?!
HEY, I'M BACK.
NYAMO, YOU BIG **PERVERT!**
THAT'S COLD, NYAMO! **COLD!!**
YOU SHOULD BE PRAYIN' FOR US TO PASS!
WH... WHAT?!

FOR YOU

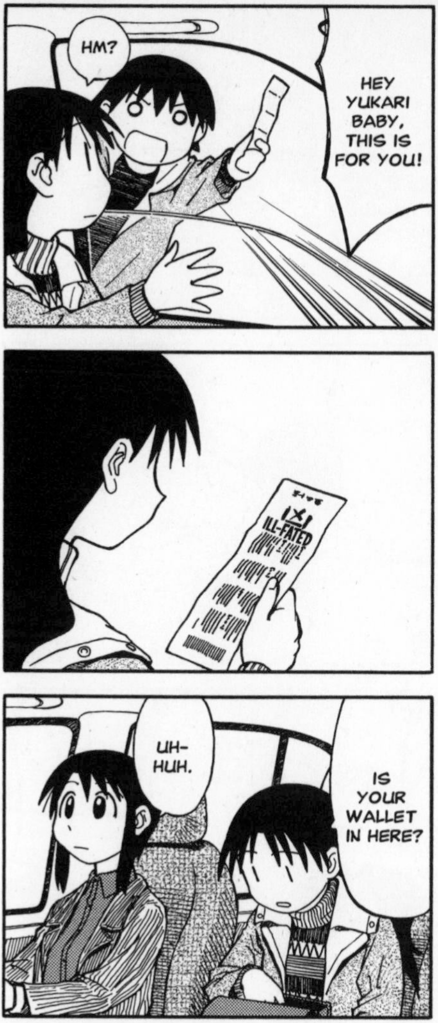
HEY YUKARI BABY, THIS IS FOR YOU!
HM?
ILL-FATED
IS YOUR WALLET IN HERE?
UH-HUH.
HEY! DON'T GO TAKING ANY OF MY MONEY!
RELAX, I'M NOT TAKING YOUR MONEY.
I'LL JUST BE PUTTING THIS IN HERE...

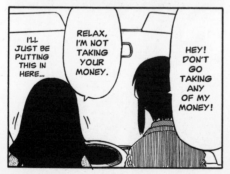

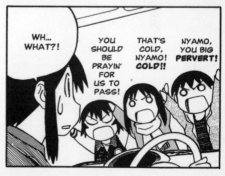

AZU MANGA DAIOH

JANUARY PART-2

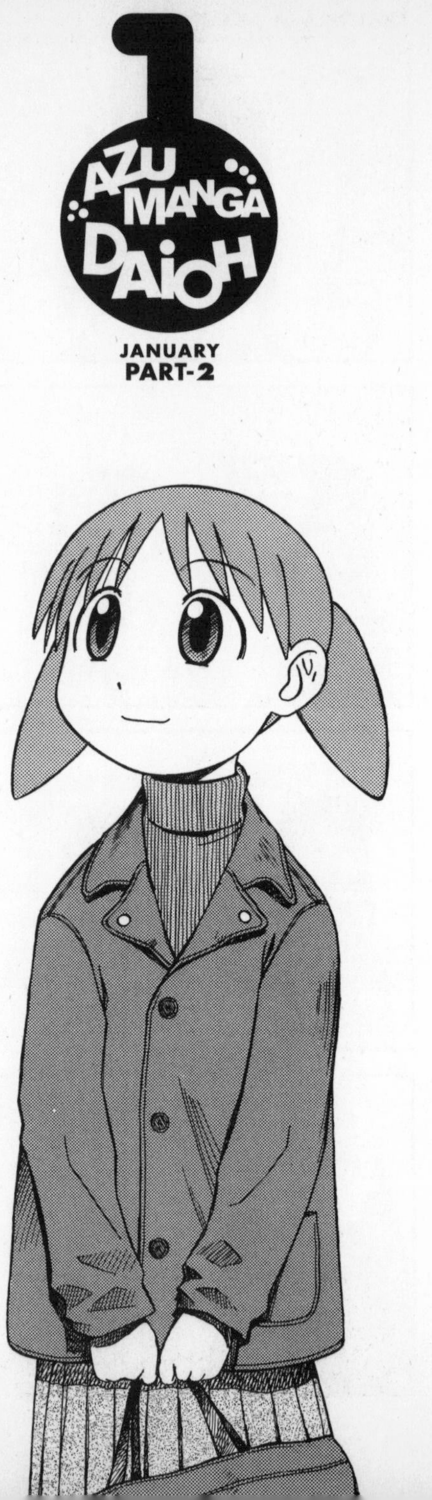

LET'S DO IT!

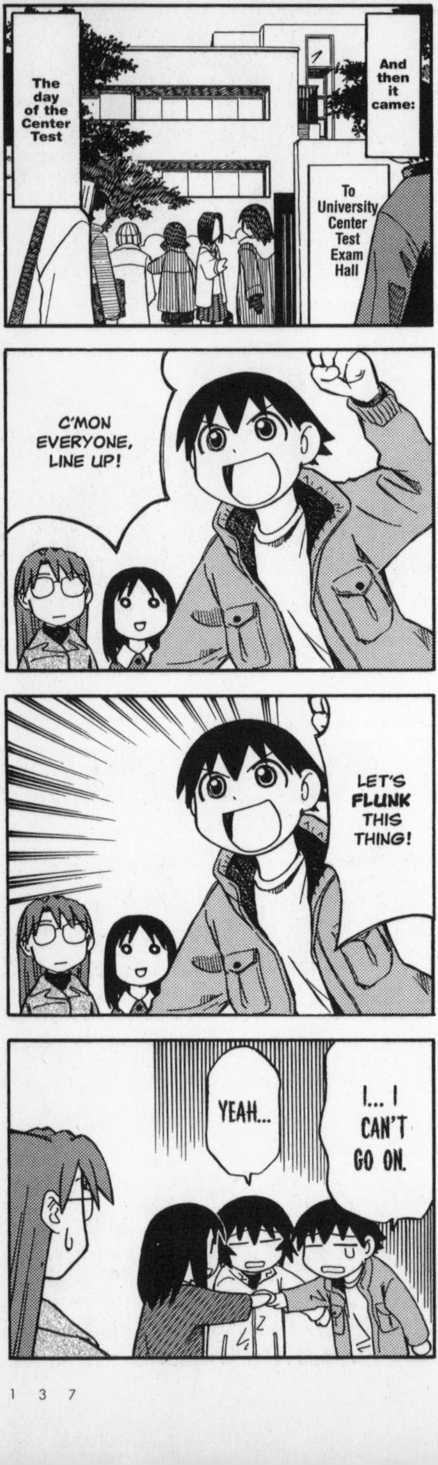
And then it came:
The day of the Center Test
To University Center Test Exam Hall
C'MON EVERYONE, LINE UP!
LET'S FLUNK THIS THING!
I... I CAN'T GO ON.
YEAH...

WE WILL PASS

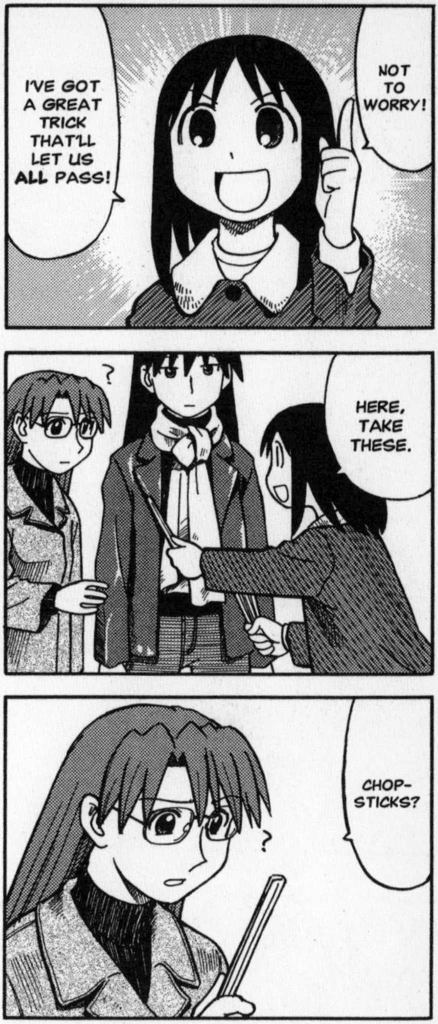
NOT TO WORRY!
I'VE GOT A GREAT TRICK THAT'LL LET US **ALL** PASS!
HERE, TAKE THESE.
CHOP-STICKS?
AHEM. PLEASE LISTEN CAREFULLY!
OH LORD, NOW WHAT?

THE OSAKA APPROACH

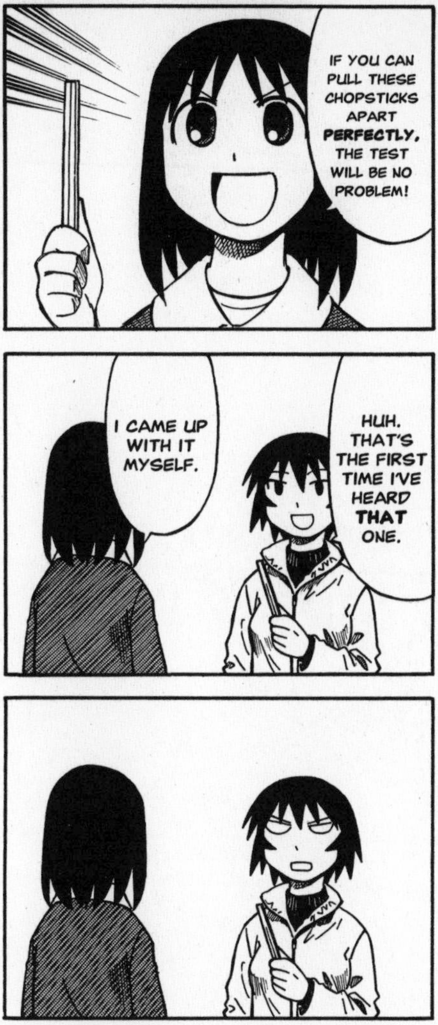
IF YOU CAN PULL THESE CHOPSTICKS APART **PERFECTLY**, THE TEST WILL BE NO PROBLEM!
HUH. THAT'S THE FIRST TIME I'VE HEARD **THAT** ONE.
I CAME UP WITH IT MYSELF.
DON'T WORRY, IT'LL WORK!
YOU CAN'T JUST **MAKE** SOMETHING LIKE THAT UP!

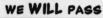

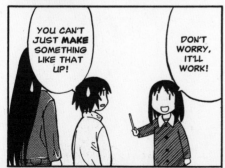

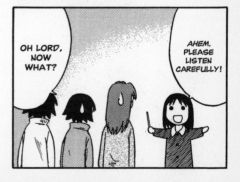

DEFEAT

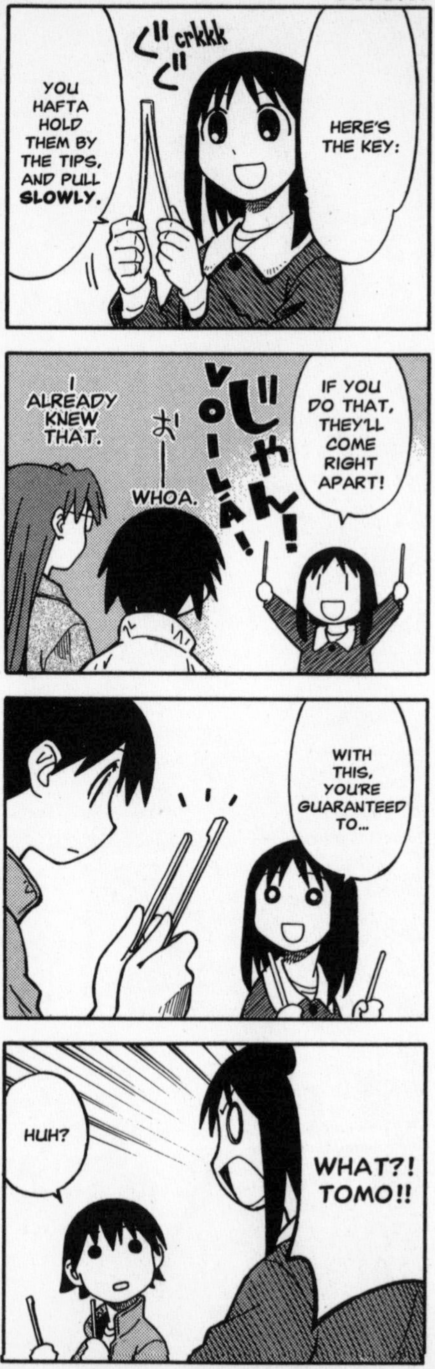
HERE'S THE KEY:
くぃ crkkk くぃ
YOU HAFTA HOLD THEM BY THE TIPS, AND PULL **SLOWLY**.
IF YOU DO THAT, THEY'LL COME RIGHT APART!
じゃん! VOILÀ!
おー WHOA.
I ALREADY KNEW THAT.
WITH THIS, YOU'RE GUARANTEED TO...
WHAT?! TOMO!!
HUH?

WHAT HAVE YOU DONE?!

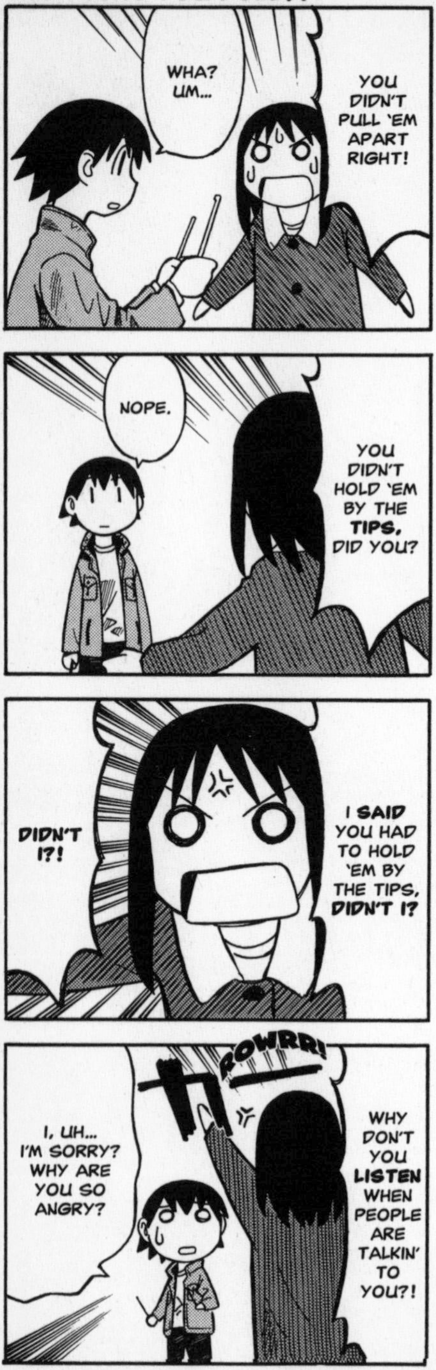
YOU DIDN'T PULL 'EM APART RIGHT!
WHA? UM...
YOU DIDN'T HOLD 'EM BY THE **TIPS,** DID YOU?
NOPE.
I **SAID** YOU HAD TO HOLD 'EM BY THE TIPS, **DIDN'T I?**
DIDN'T I?!
ROWRR!
WHY DON'T YOU **LISTEN** WHEN PEOPLE ARE TALKIN' TO YOU?!
I, UH... I'M SORRY? WHY ARE YOU SO ANGRY?

THE CHIYO CHARM

THERE'S NO HOPE FOR YOU, TOMO. NONE AT ALL.
N... NO! IT CAN'T BE!
DON'T WORRY, OSAKA.
UM... えーと
I BROUGHT SOME **CHARMS**.
PASS!
I WANTED TO BUY SOME WHEN WE WERE AT THAT SHRINE, BUT I ENDED UP JUST MAKING THEM MYSELF.
みんな1個ずつ
EVERYONE GETS ONE.
おー
OH!
おー
WHOA...
YEAH... NOW **THIS** LOOKS LIKE IT'LL WORK!
HEY, WHAT?!
なんやー?

THE MOMENT OF TRUTH

WELL, I GUESS IT'S TIME TO GO IN.
L... LET'S DO IT!
I'LL BE KEEPING MY FINGERS CROSSED FOR YOU.
GOOD LUCK, EVERYONE!
ビッ
shwip!

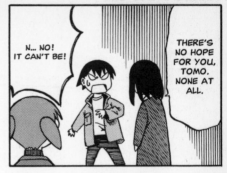

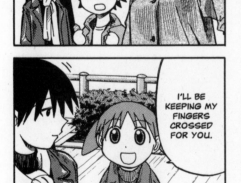

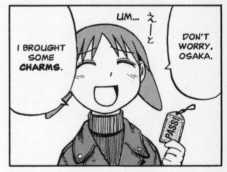

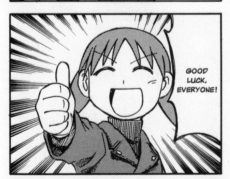

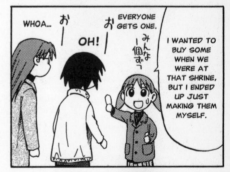

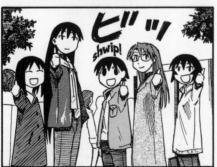

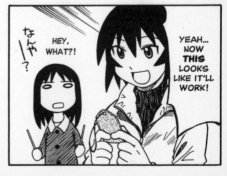

DONE

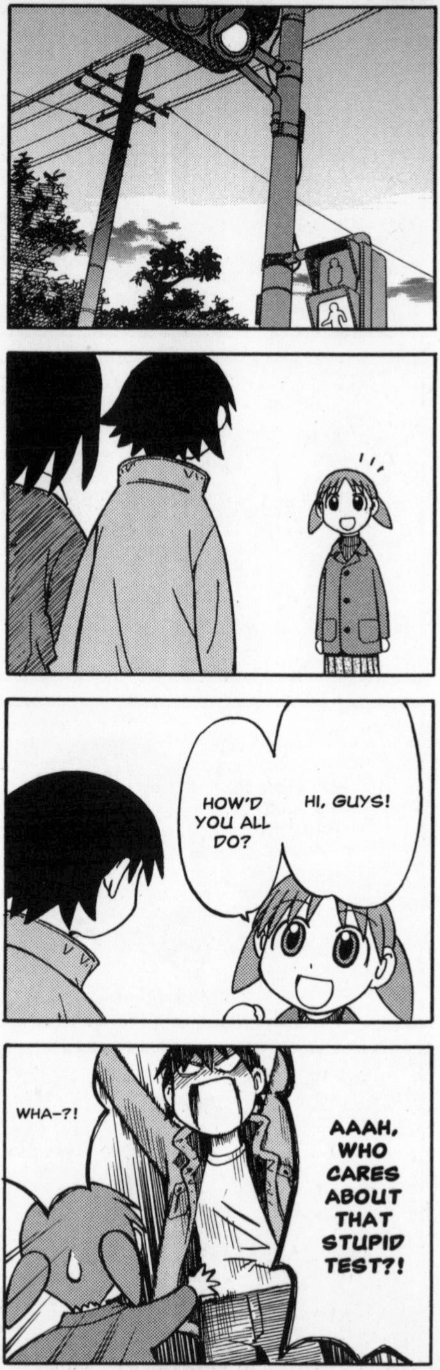
HI, GUYS!
HOW'D YOU ALL DO?
AAAH, WHO CARES ABOUT THAT STUPID TEST?!
WHA-?!

THE GAP

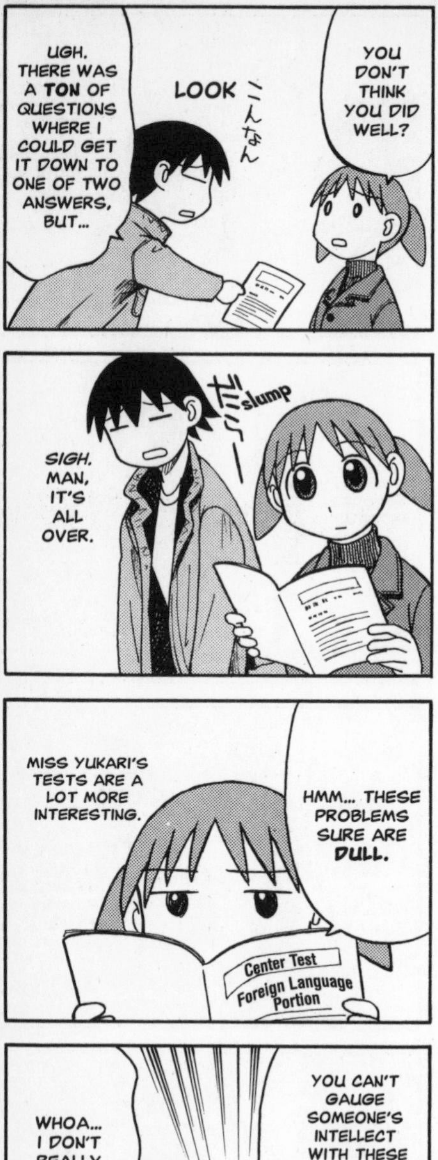
YOU DON'T THINK YOU DID WELL?
LOOK こんなん
UGH. THERE WAS A **TON** OF QUESTIONS WHERE I COULD GET IT DOWN TO ONE OF TWO ANSWERS, BUT...
slump
SIGH. MAN, IT'S ALL OVER.
HMM... THESE PROBLEMS SURE ARE **DULL.**
MISS YUKARI'S TESTS ARE A LOT MORE INTERESTING.
Center Test
Foreign Language Portion
YOU CAN'T GAUGE SOMEONE'S INTELLECT WITH THESE KINDS OF QUESTIONS! IT'S NOT YOUR FAULT— IT'S THE TEST'S!
WHOA... I DON'T REALLY GET THAT, BUT IT WORKS FOR ME!

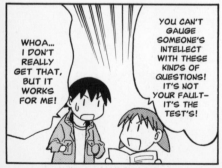

DON'T GET 'EM

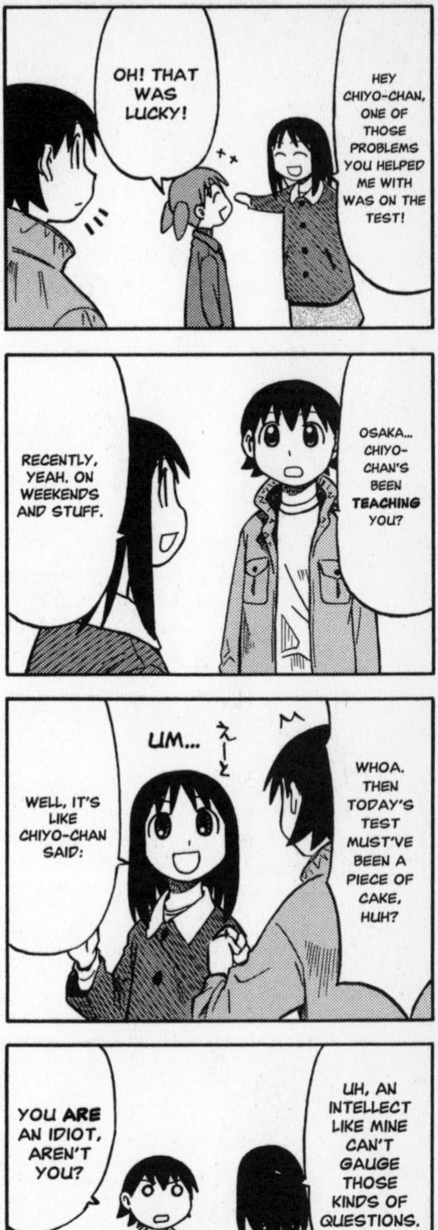
HEY CHIYO-CHAN, ONE OF THOSE PROBLEMS YOU HELPED ME WITH WAS ON THE TEST!
OH! THAT WAS LUCKY!
OSAKA... CHIYO-CHAN'S BEEN **TEACHING** YOU?
RECENTLY, YEAH. ON WEEKENDS AND STUFF.
WHOA. THEN TODAY'S TEST MUST'VE BEEN A PIECE OF CAKE, HUH?
えーと
UM...
WELL, IT'S LIKE CHIYO-CHAN SAID:
UH, AN INTELLECT LIKE MINE CAN'T GAUGE THOSE KINDS OF QUESTIONS.
YOU **ARE** AN IDIOT, AREN'T YOU?

THE TEACHER, THE DOG AND THE CAT

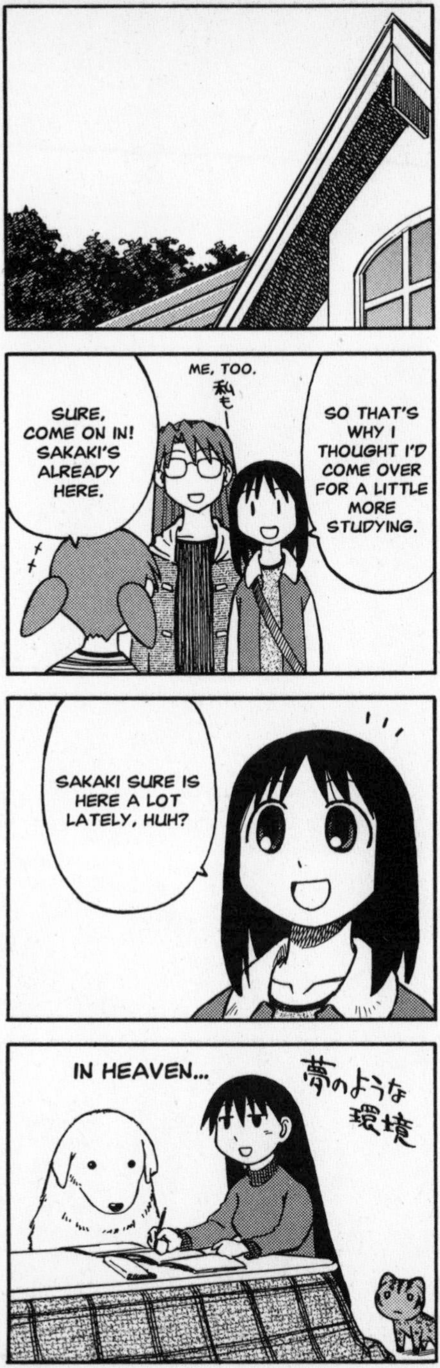
SO THAT'S WHY I THOUGHT I'D COME OVER FOR A LITTLE MORE STUDYING.
ME, TOO.
私も
SURE, COME ON IN! SAKAKI'S ALREADY HERE.
SAKAKI SURE IS HERE A LOT LATELY, HUH?
夢のような環境
IN HEAVEN...

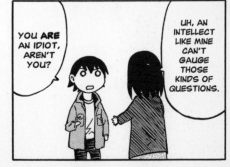

FOR A GOOD CAUSE

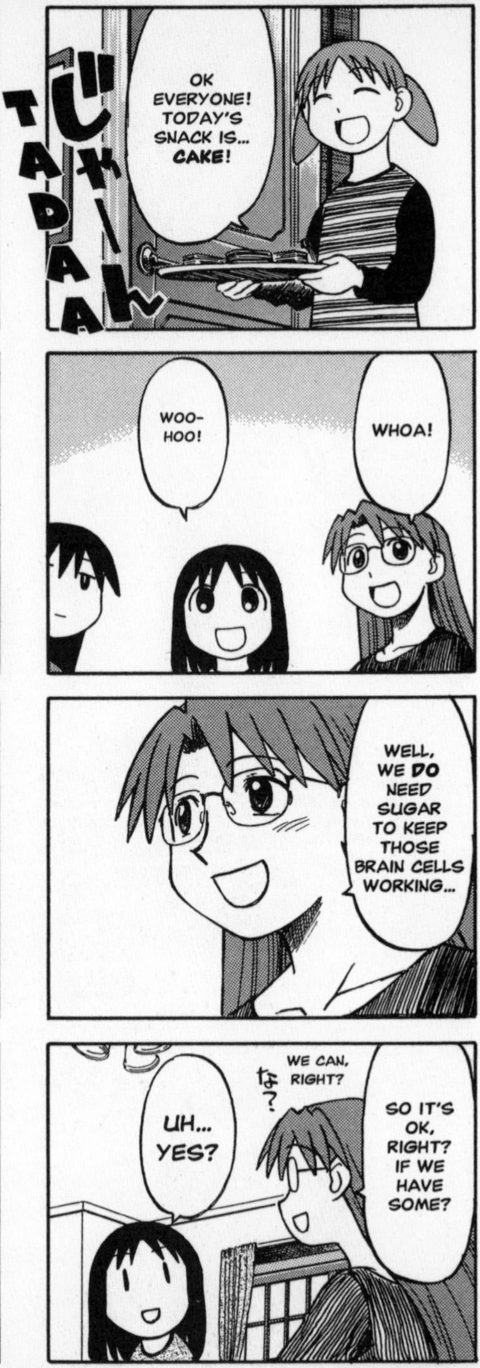
TADAA
じゃーん
OK EVERYONE! TODAY'S SNACK IS... **CAKE**!
WHOA!
WOO-HOO!
WELL, WE **DO** NEED SUGAR TO KEEP THOSE BRAIN CELLS WORKING...
SO IT'S OK, RIGHT? IF WE HAVE SOME?
WE CAN, RIGHT?
な？
UH... YES?

JUST A LITTLE, MISS SAKAKI

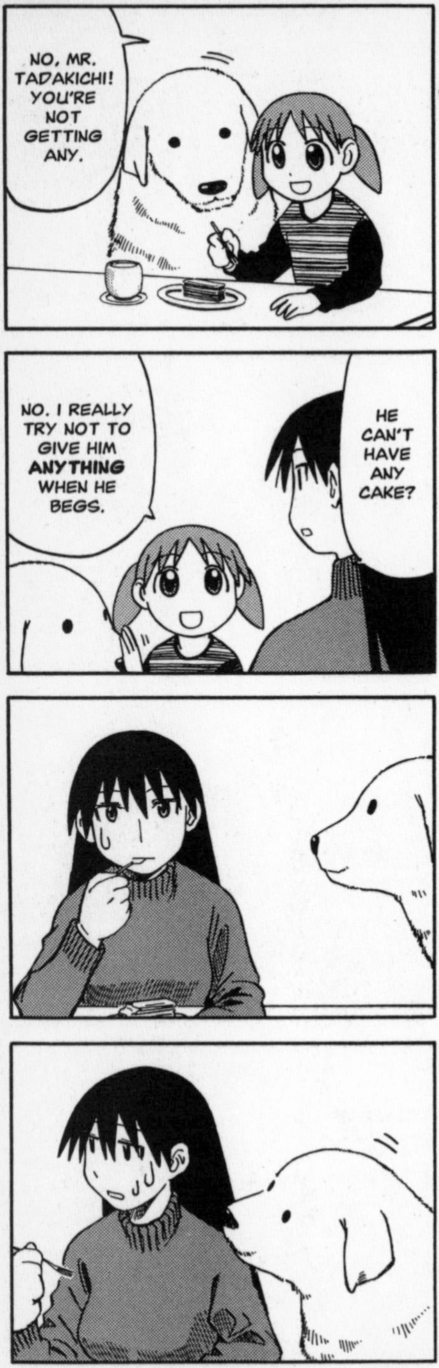
NO, MR. TADAKICHI! YOU'RE NOT GETTING ANY.
HE CAN'T HAVE ANY CAKE?
NO. I REALLY TRY NOT TO GIVE HIM **ANYTHING** WHEN HE BEGS.

G'NIGHT

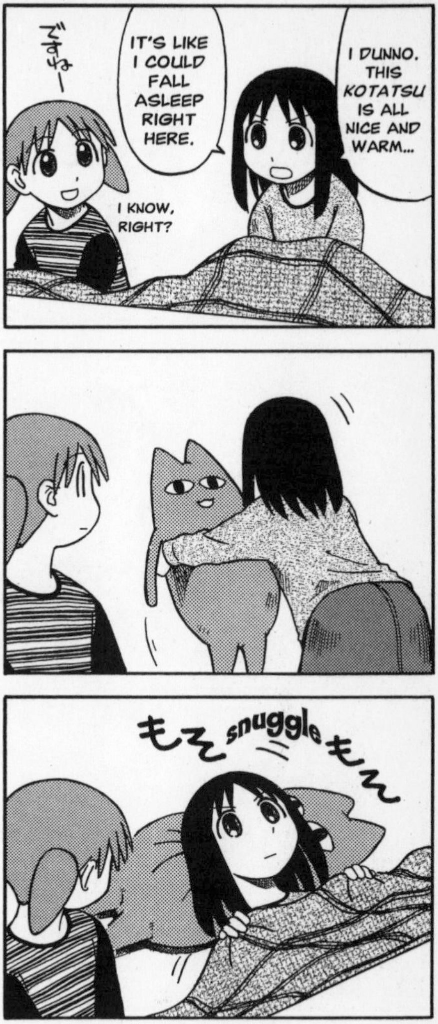
I DUNNO. THIS KOTATSU IS ALL NICE AND WARM...
IT'S LIKE I COULD FALL ASLEEP RIGHT HERE.
ですねー
I KNOW, RIGHT?
snuggle
SHE... SHE DID FALL ASLEEP!
なんかじゃなくて…

HUNTING

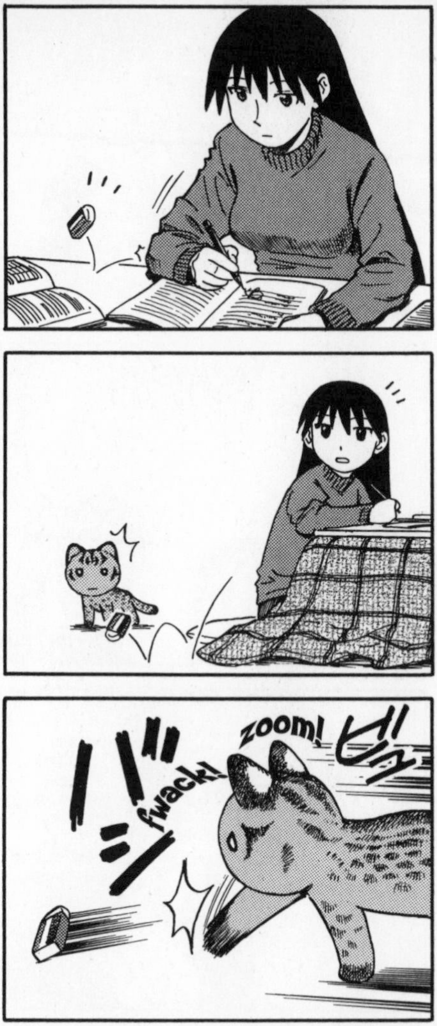
zoom!
fwack!
thBONK!

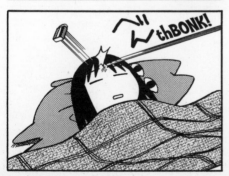

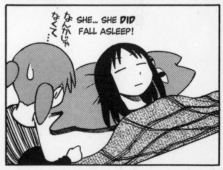

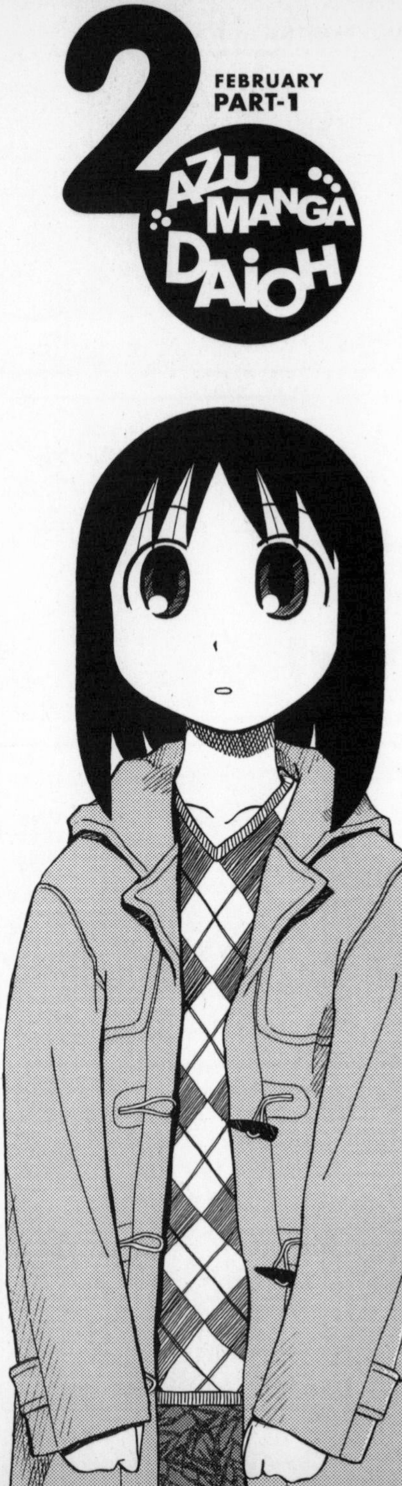
2
FEBRUARY
PART-1
AZU MANGA DAIOH

THE STUDY GROUP

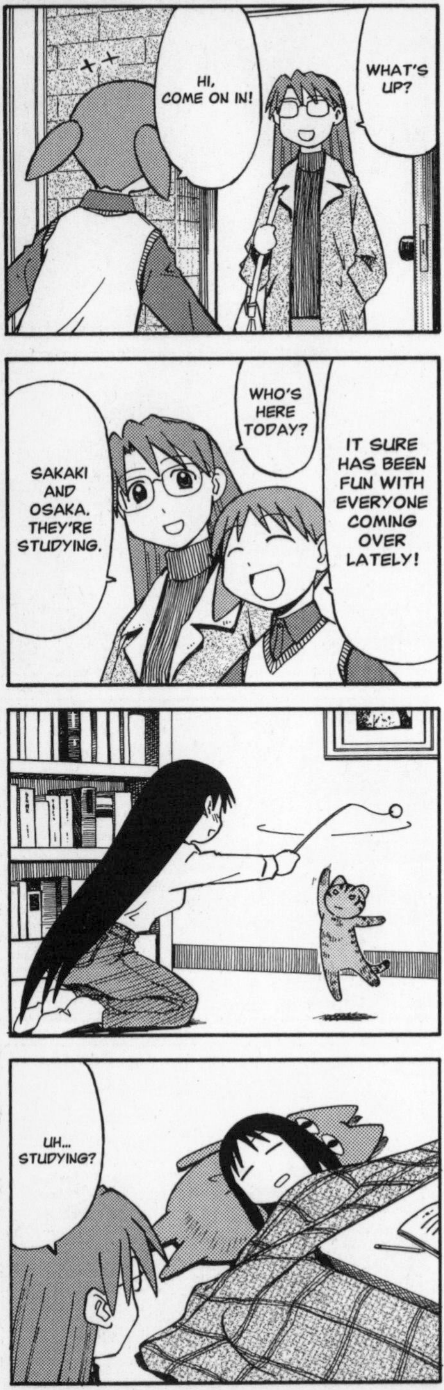
WHAT'S UP?
HI, COME ON IN!
IT SURE HAS BEEN FUN WITH EVERYONE COMING OVER LATELY!
WHO'S HERE TODAY?
SAKAKI AND OSAKA. THEY'RE STUDYING.
UH... STUDYING?

THE ARRIVAL

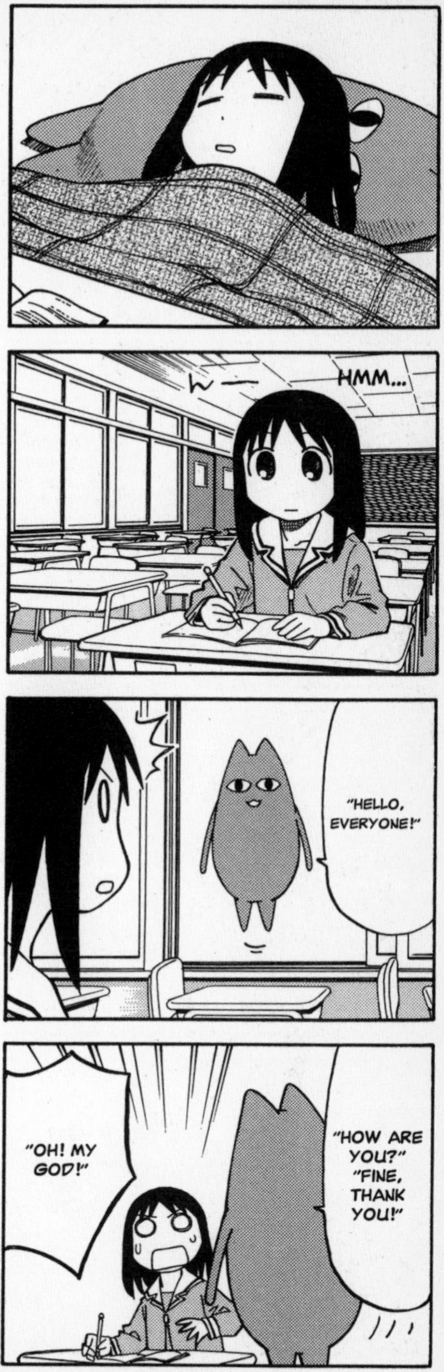
HMM...
"HELLO, EVERYONE!"
"HOW ARE YOU?" "FINE, THANK YOU!"
"OH! MY GOD!"

CHIYO-CHAN'S DAD

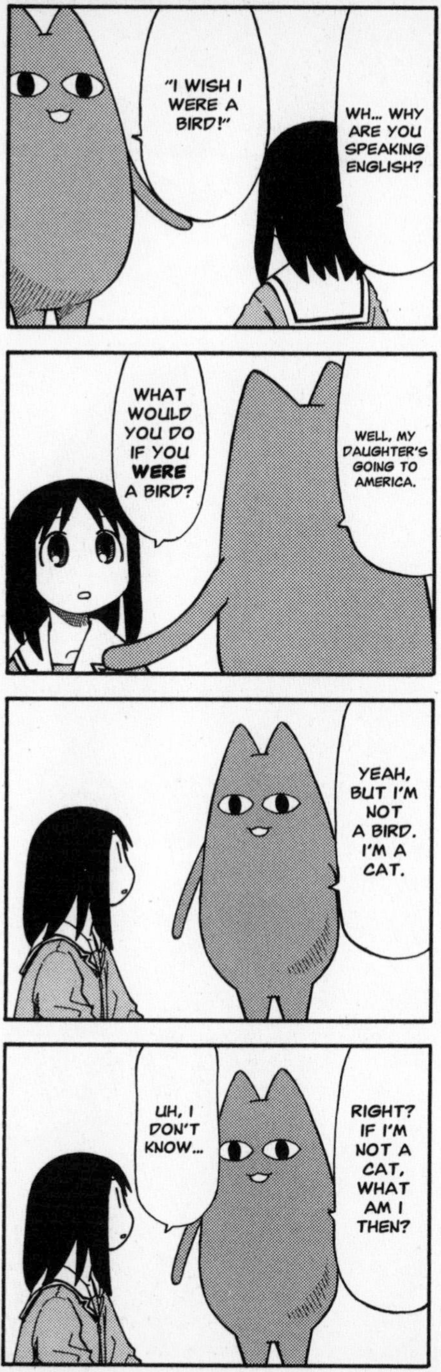
WH... WHY ARE YOU SPEAKING ENGLISH?
"I WISH I WERE A BIRD!"
WELL, MY DAUGHTER'S GOING TO AMERICA.
WHAT WOULD YOU DO IF YOU WERE A BIRD?
YEAH, BUT I'M NOT A BIRD. I'M A CAT.
RIGHT? IF I'M NOT A CAT, WHAT AM I THEN?
UH, I DON'T KNOW...

I'M SORRY

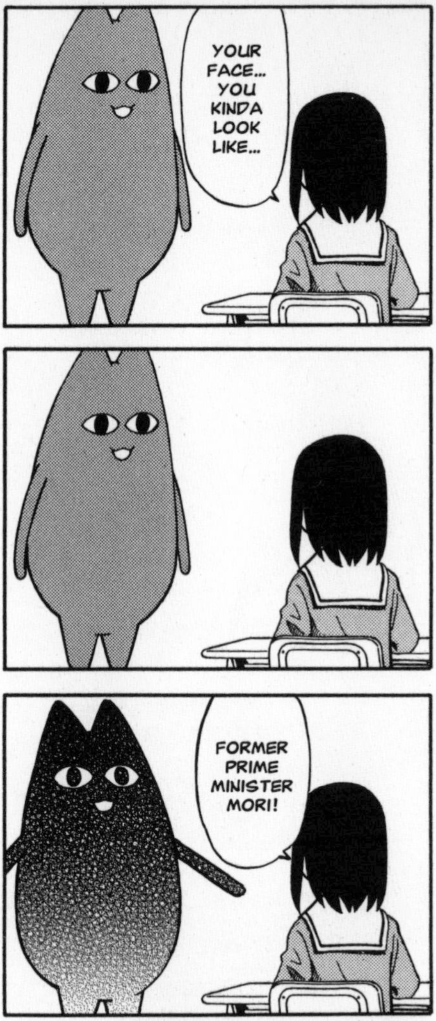
YOUR FACE... YOU KINDA LOOK LIKE...
FORMER PRIME MINISTER MORI!
"I'M SORRY!"
GWORRR

THE CAT

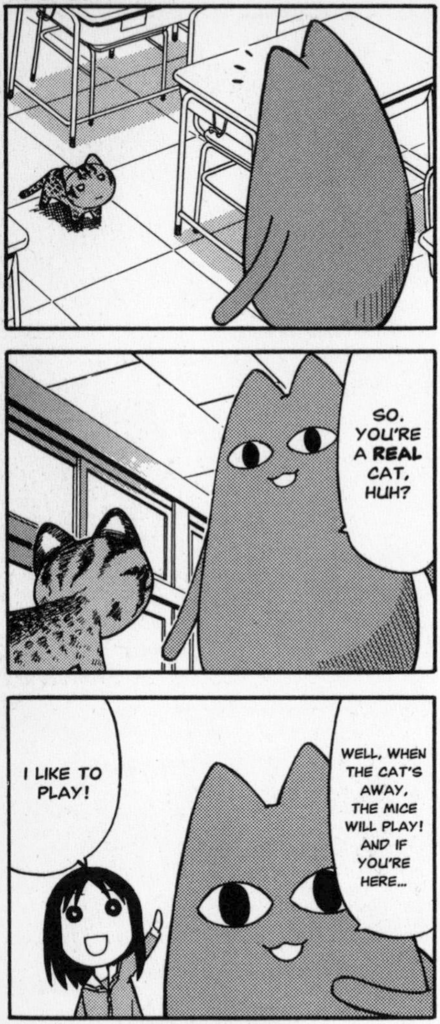
SO. YOU'RE A REAL CAT, HUH?
WELL, WHEN THE CAT'S AWAY, THE MICE WILL PLAY! AND IF YOU'RE HERE...
I LIKE TO PLAY!
WHO FRICKIN' ASKED YOU?!
WHA-?!

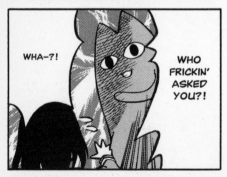

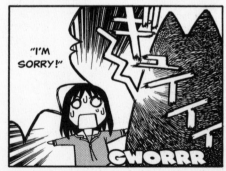

AWAKE

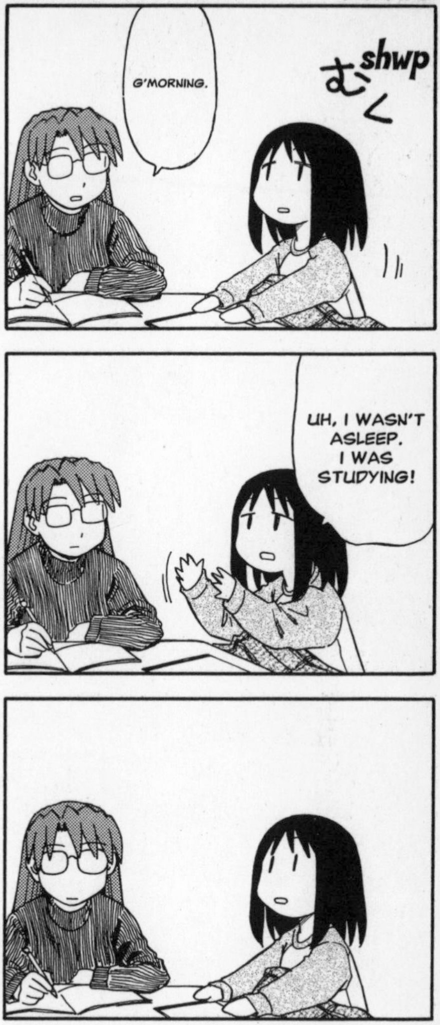

むく shwp
G'MORNING.
UH, I WASN'T ASLEEP. I WAS STUDYING!
OH. THIS IS CHIYO-CHAN'S PLACE.
YUP. RISE AND SHINE.

FREEZE!

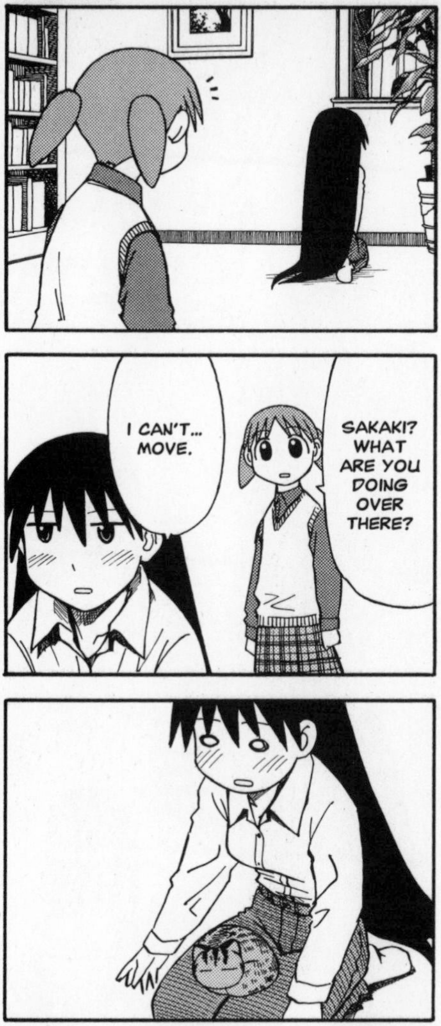

SAKAKI? WHAT ARE YOU DOING OVER THERE?
I CAN'T... MOVE.

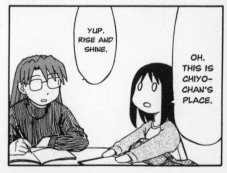

TRUE IDENTITY

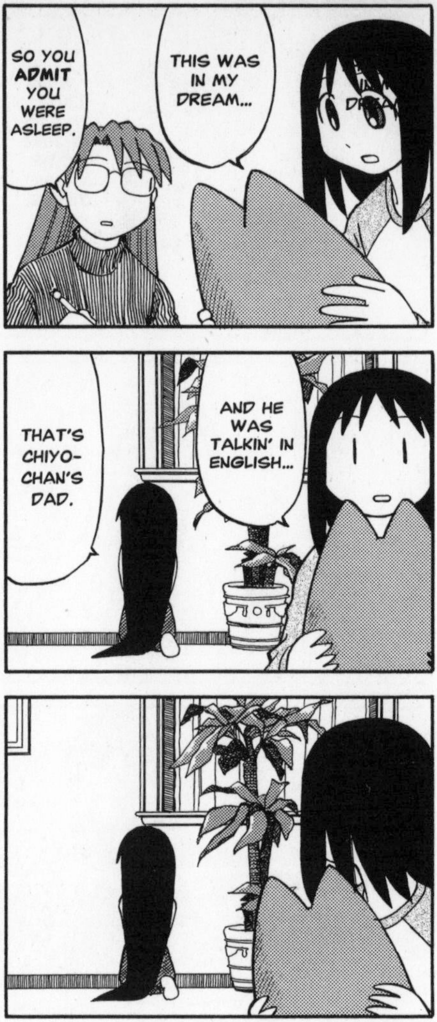
THIS WAS IN MY DREAM...
SO YOU **ADMIT** YOU WERE ASLEEP.
AND HE WAS TALKIN' IN ENGLISH...
THAT'S CHIYO-CHAN'S DAD.
OHH. THAT MAKES SENSE.
WHEN HE SAID, "MY DAUGHTER."
WHY WOULD **THAT** MAKE SENSE?

HEADS TOGETHER

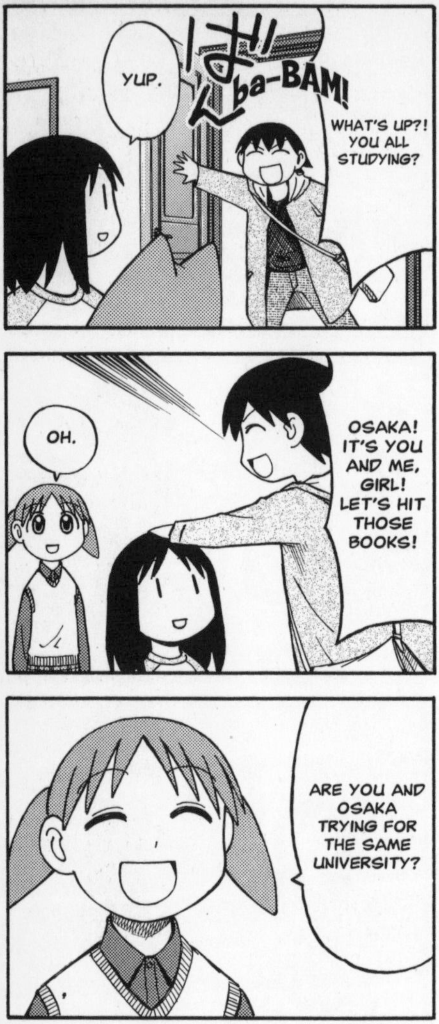
ばん ba-BAM!
WHAT'S UP?! YOU ALL STUDYING?
YUP.
OSAKA! IT'S YOU AND ME, GIRL! LET'S HIT THOSE BOOKS!
OH.
ARE YOU AND OSAKA TRYING FOR THE SAME UNIVERSITY?
YUP. TOKYO U.
WHAT?!
GOTCHA.

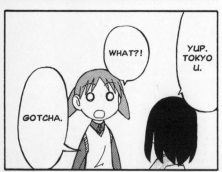

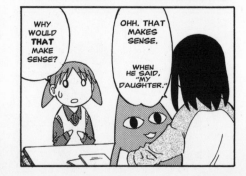

A REFLEX ACTION

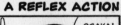

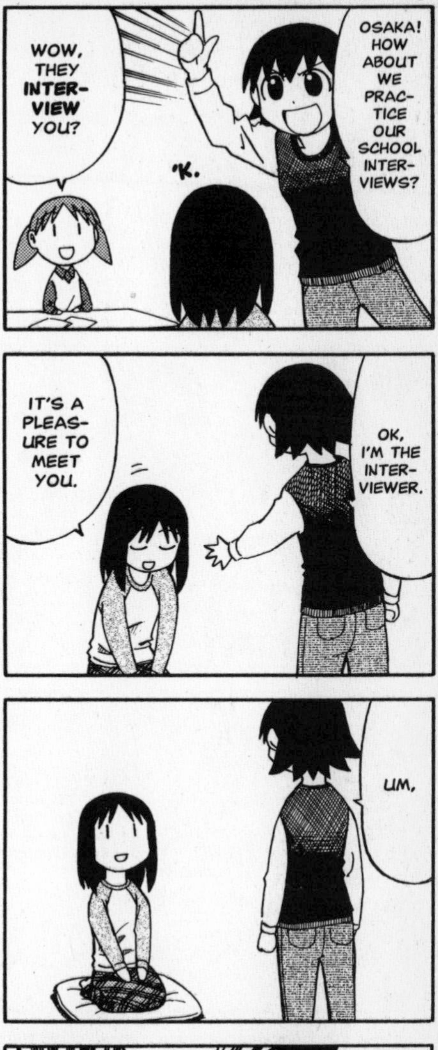
OSAKA! HOW ABOUT WE PRACTICE OUR SCHOOL INTERVIEWS?
WOW, THEY **INTERVIEW** YOU?
'K.
OK, I'M THE INTERVIEWER.
IT'S A PLEASURE TO MEET YOU.
UM,
SO, WHAT WAS THE ONE THING REALLY DRIVEN HOME BY YOUR HIGH SCHOOL EXPERIENCE?
DRIVEN HOME? UH, I POUNDED IN A **WEDGE**, ONCE!

NOTHING GAINED

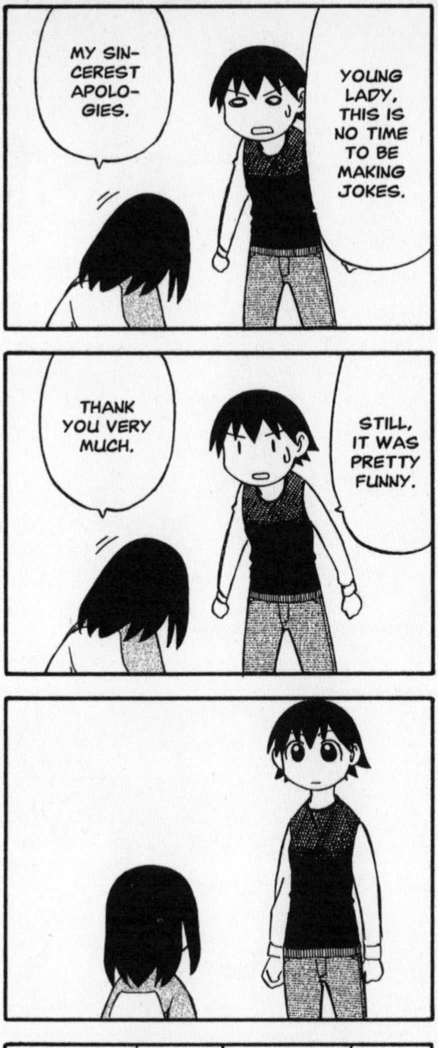
YOUNG LADY, THIS IS NO TIME TO BE MAKING JOKES.
MY SINCEREST APOLOGIES.
STILL, IT WAS PRETTY FUNNY.
THANK YOU VERY MUCH.
HEY, WHAT'S A "WEDGE" AGAIN?
I'M AFRAID I CANNOT RECALL.

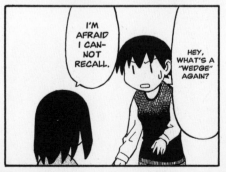

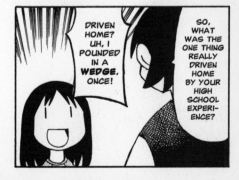

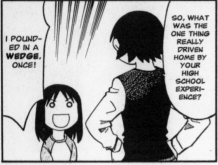

WEDGE

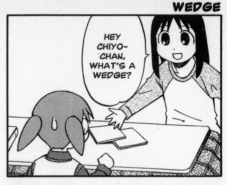

HEY CHIYO-CHAN, WHAT'S A WEDGE?
YOU DRIVE IT INTO A CREVICE, ON A TREE OR SOMETHING, LIKE THIS. IT'S USED FOR TIGHTENING OR SECURING.
YOU CAN FIND THEM ON SHRINE GATES, TOO.
SOMETIMES THEY AREN'T REALLY NECESSARY, THEY'RE JUST THERE FOR DESIGN.
LET'S DO IT!
GOT IT! TOMO, ONE MORE TIME!

PERFECT!

SO, WHAT WAS THE ONE THING REALLY DRIVEN HOME BY YOUR HIGH SCHOOL EXPERIENCE?
I POUNDED IN A **WEDGE**, ONCE!
BY THE WAY, SIR, A WEDGE IS SOMETHING YOU **DRIVE** INTO A SPACE TO TIGHTEN OR SECURE IT!
IT'S USED ON SHRINE GATES, BUT SOMETIMES IT'S JUST THERE FOR DESIGN!
GOOD! YOU PASS!
THANK YOU VERY MUCH.

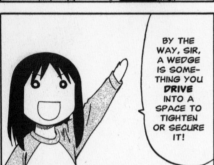

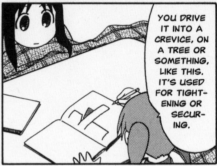

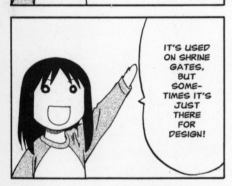

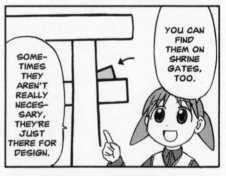

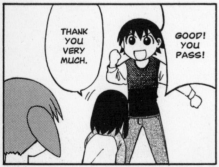

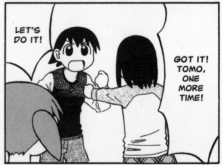

THE ONLY THING

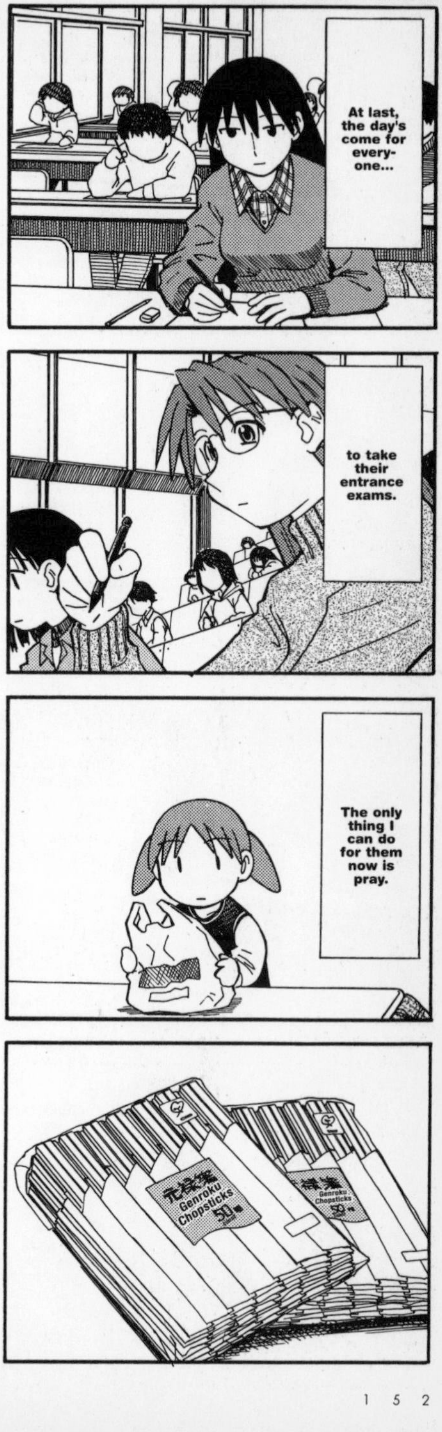

At last, the day's come for every-one...
to take their entrance exams.
The only thing I can do for them now is pray.
元禄箸
Genroku Chopsticks
50膳

A THOUSAND CHOPSTICKS

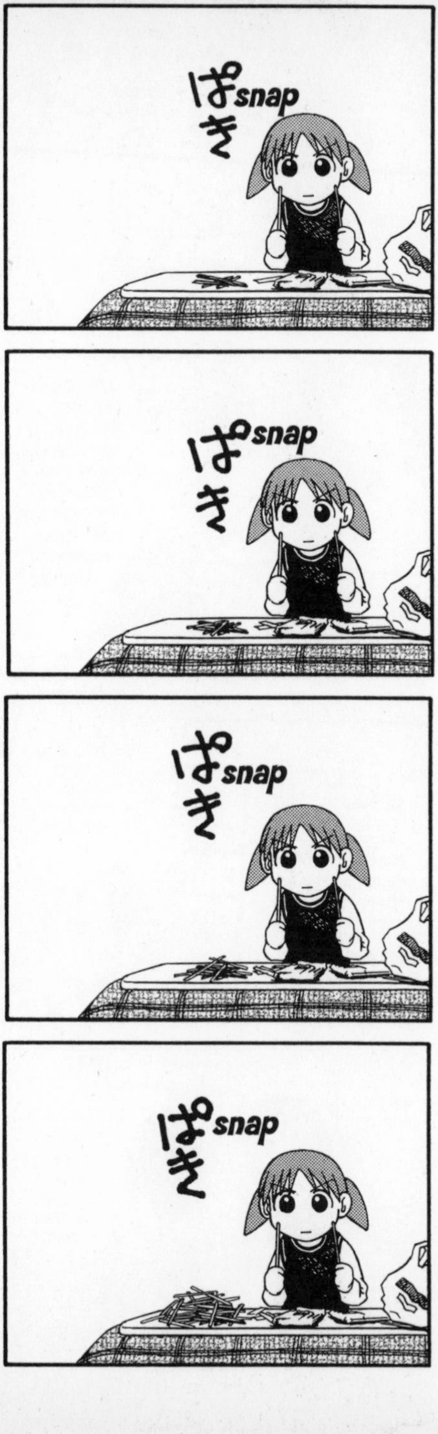

ぱき snap
ぱき snap
ぱき snap
ぱき snap

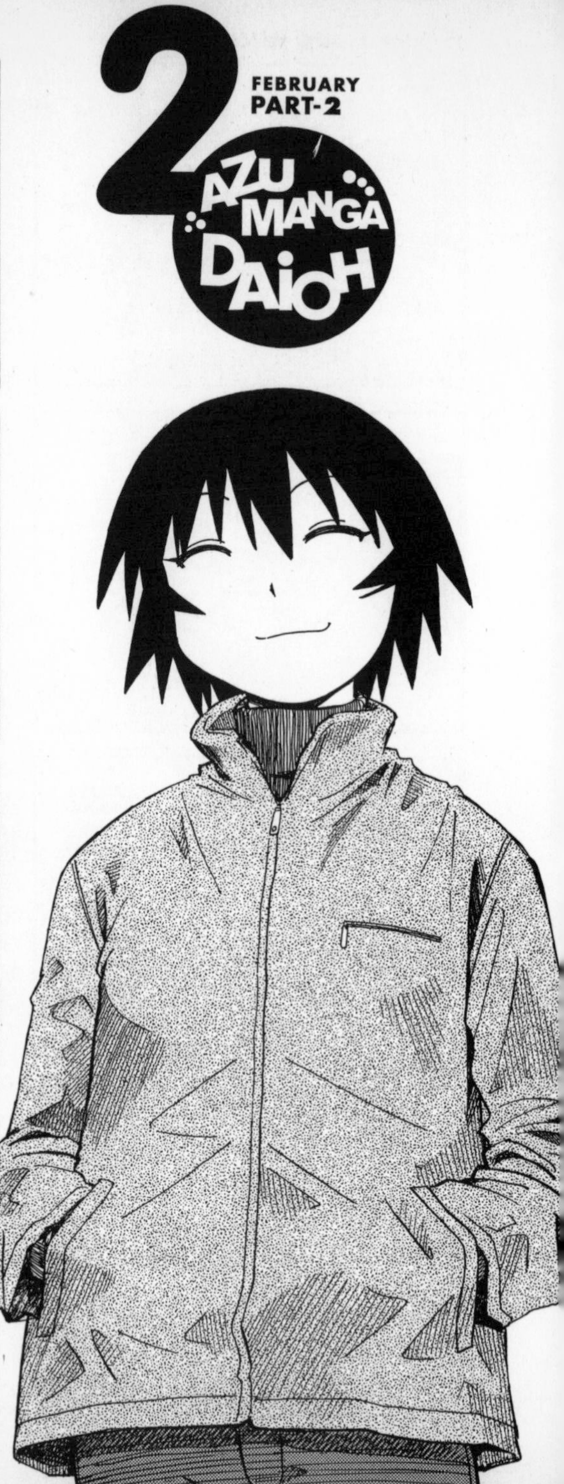
2
FEBRUARY PART-2
AZUMANGA DAIOH

UNIVERSITY

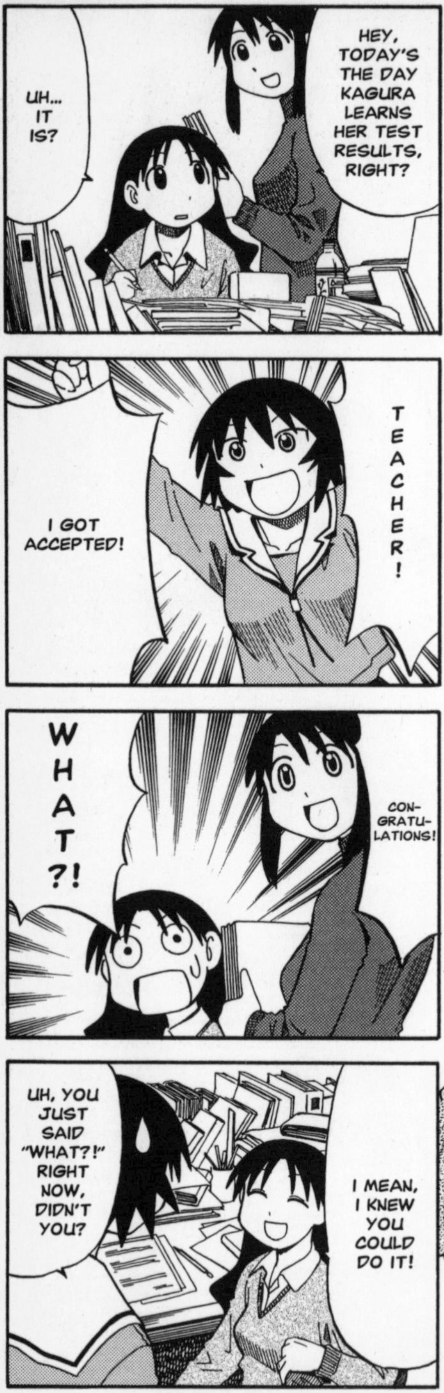
HEY, TODAY'S THE DAY KAGURA LEARNS HER TEST RESULTS, RIGHT?
UH... IT IS?
TEACHER!
I GOT ACCEPTED!
CONGRATULATIONS!
WHAT?!
I MEAN, I KNEW YOU COULD DO IT!
UH, YOU JUST SAID "WHAT?!" RIGHT NOW, DIDN'T YOU?

GLOWING

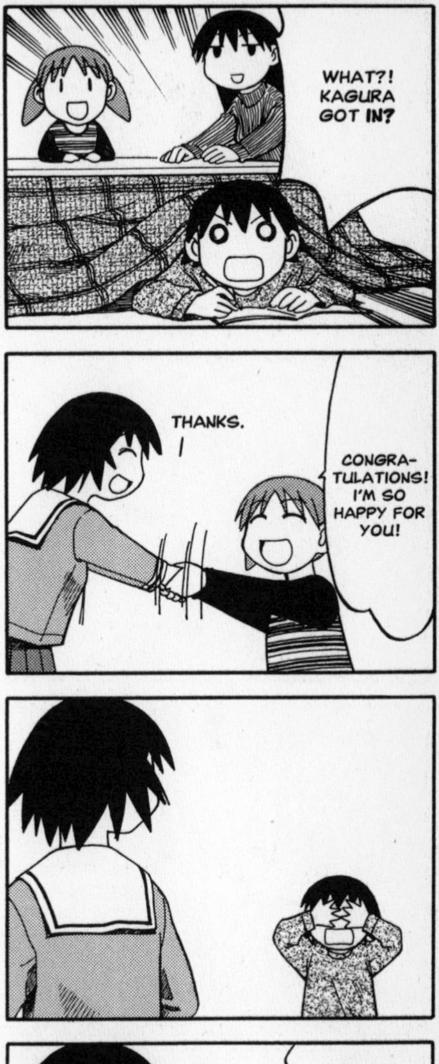

WHAT?! KAGURA GOT **IN?**
CONGRA-TULATIONS! I'M SO HAPPY FOR YOU!
THANKS.
AARGH! KAGURA'S POSITIVELY **GLOWING!** IT'S LIKE STARING INTO THE SUN!!

DIDN'T MAKE IT

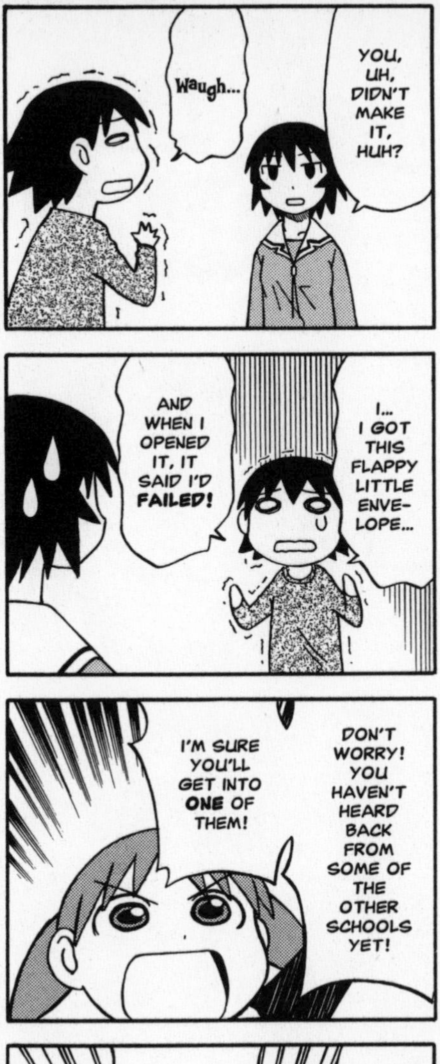

YOU, UH, DIDN'T MAKE IT, HUH?
Waugh...
I... I GOT THIS FLAPPY LITTLE ENVE-LOPE...
AND WHEN I OPENED IT, IT SAID I'D **FAILED!**
DON'T WORRY! YOU HAVEN'T HEARD BACK FROM SOME OF THE OTHER SCHOOLS YET!
I'M SURE YOU'LL GET INTO **ONE** OF THEM!
YOU SWEAR? YOU SWEAR ON YOUR **LIFE?**
I **SWEAR!!**

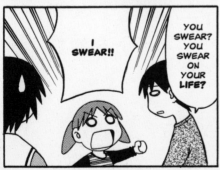

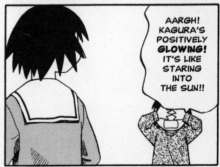

DON'T OPEN IT!

HEY, GUYS!
EVERYONE'S HERE, HUH?
OH, OSAKA!
I GOT MY RESULTS IN THE MAIL...
BUT I HAVEN'T LOOKED AT 'EM YET.
SEEING AS HOW YOU HELPED ME STUDY AND ALL...
I THOUGHT WE COULD LOOK AT IT TOGETHER.
I WONDER WHAT IT SAYS...
AUGH! A FLAPPY LITTLE ENVELOPE!

OH...

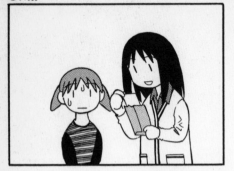

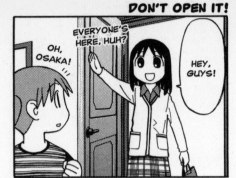

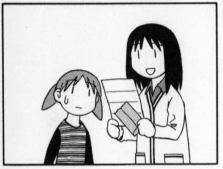

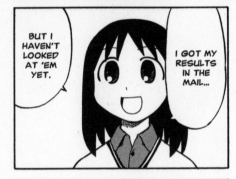

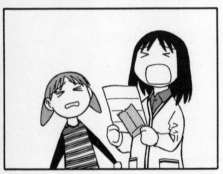

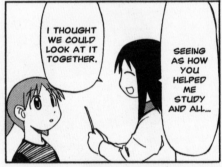

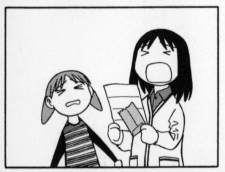

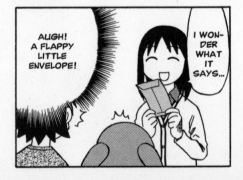

FELL TOO FAR

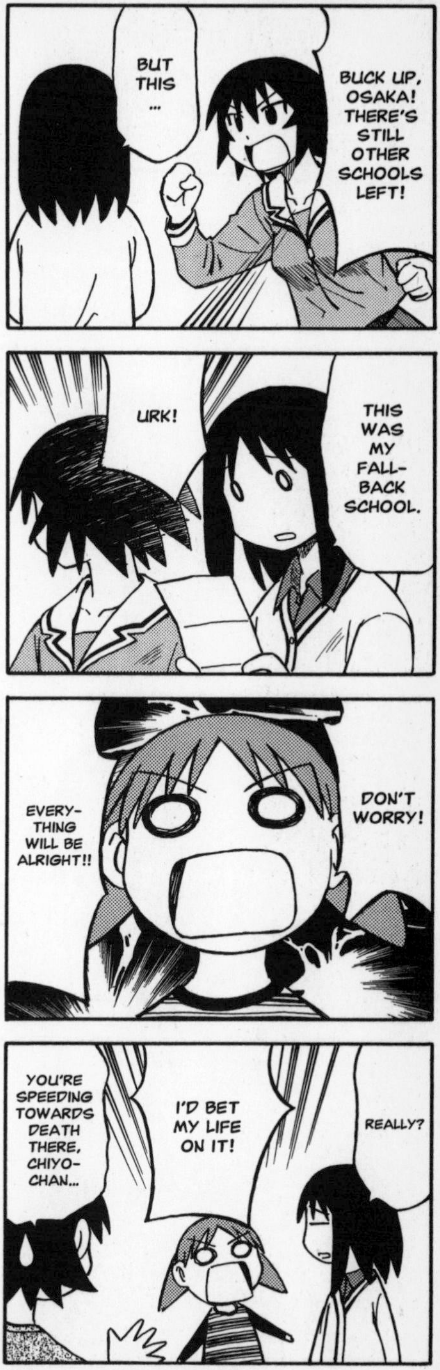
BUCK UP, OSAKA! THERE'S STILL OTHER SCHOOLS LEFT!
BUT THIS ...
THIS WAS MY FALL-BACK SCHOOL.
URK!
DON'T WORRY!
EVERYTHING WILL BE ALRIGHT!!
REALLY?
I'D BET MY LIFE ON IT!
YOU'RE SPEEDING TOWARDS DEATH THERE, CHIYO-CHAN...

IF THEY'RE INJURED

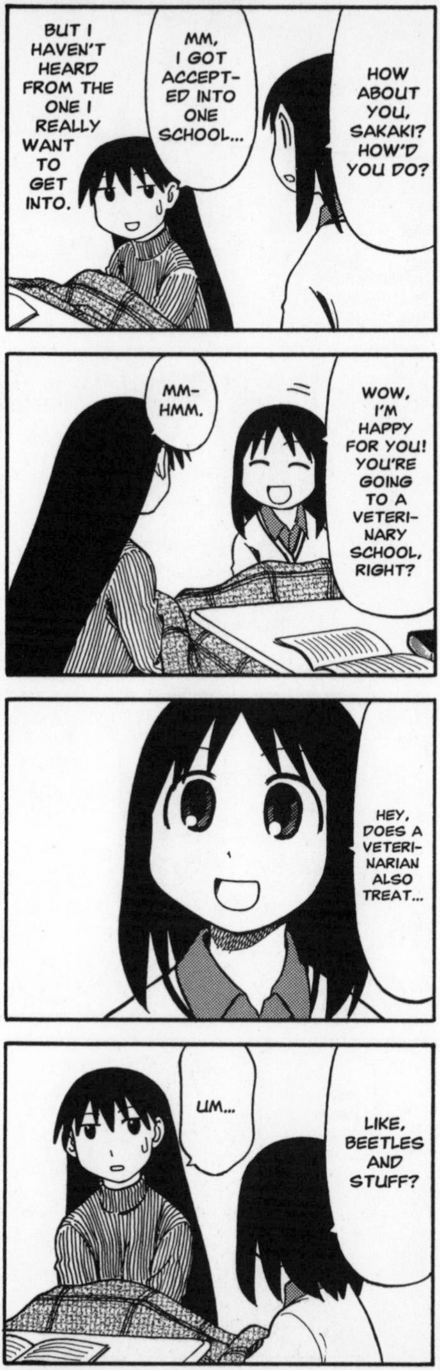
HOW ABOUT YOU, SAKAKI? HOW'D YOU DO?
MM, I GOT ACCEPTED INTO ONE SCHOOL...
BUT I HAVEN'T HEARD FROM THE ONE I REALLY WANT TO GET INTO.
WOW, I'M HAPPY FOR YOU! YOU'RE GOING TO A VETERINARY SCHOOL, RIGHT?
MM-HMM.
HEY, DOES A VETERINARIAN ALSO TREAT...
LIKE, BEETLES AND STUFF?
UM...

TOMO AND OSAKA'S FATEFUL DAY

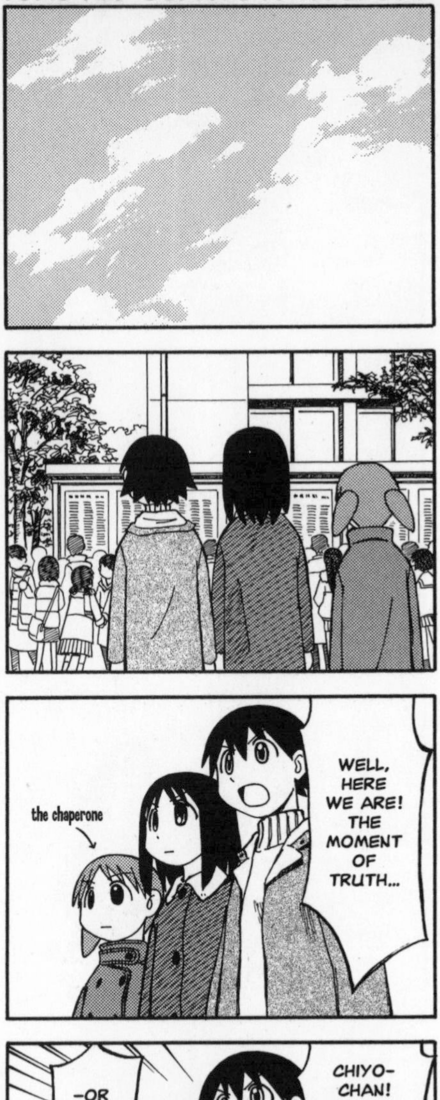

WELL, HERE WE ARE! THE MOMENT OF TRUTH...
the chaperone
CHIYO-CHAN! TODAY, WILL YOU LIVE OR DIE?!
-OR DIE?!

THE POWER OF GENIUS

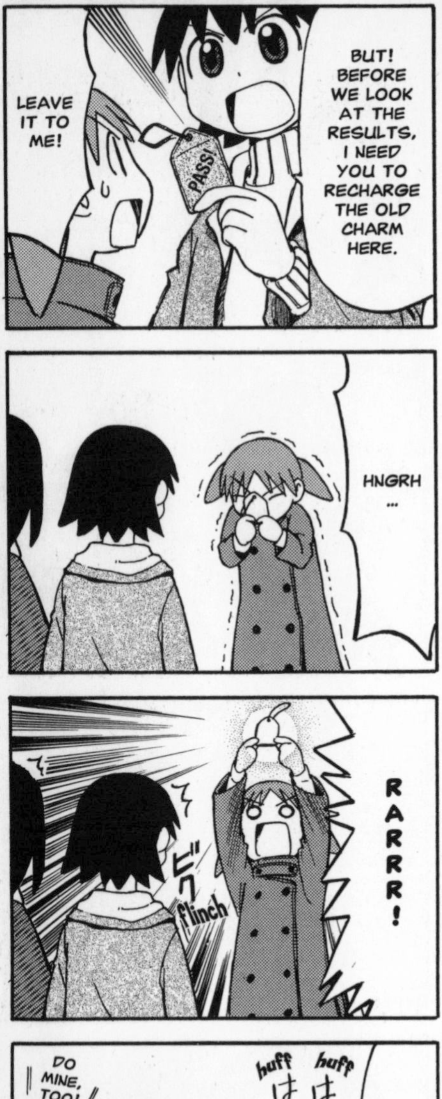

BUT! BEFORE WE LOOK AT THE RESULTS, I NEED YOU TO RECHARGE THE OLD CHARM HERE.
PASS!
LEAVE IT TO ME!
HNGRH ...
RARRRR!
ビク
flinch
huff
はー
huff
はー
HERE! THERE'LL BE NO PROBLEM, NOW.
DO MINE, TOO!

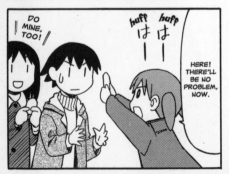

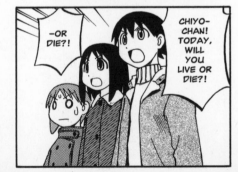

OH.

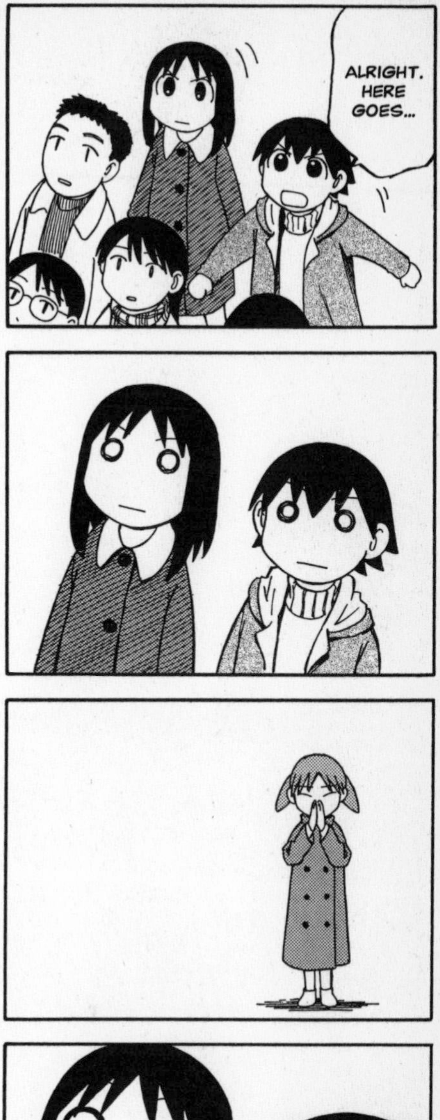
ALRIGHT. HERE GOES...

LIFE!

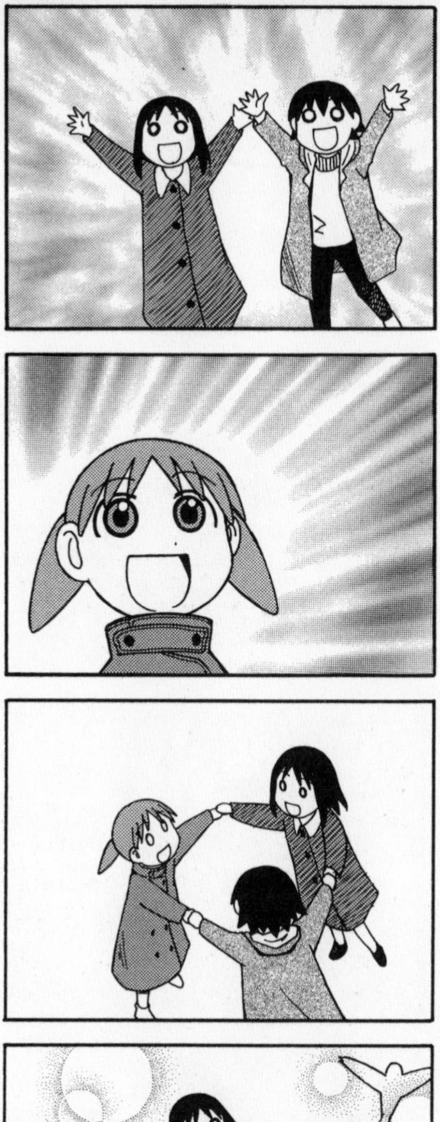

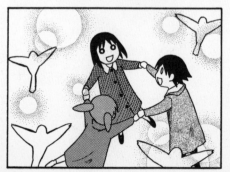

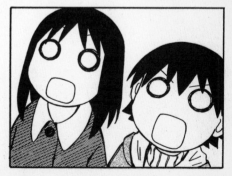

FAILURE

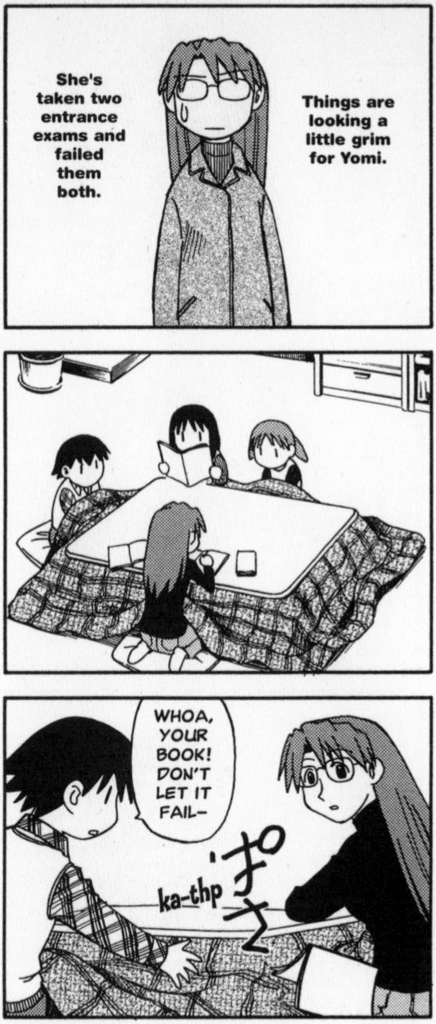
Things are looking a little grim for Yomi.
She's taken two entrance exams and failed them both.
WHOA, YOUR BOOK! DON'T LET IT FAIL–
ぽき
ka-thp
UH, FALL.
......

ENCOURAGEMENT

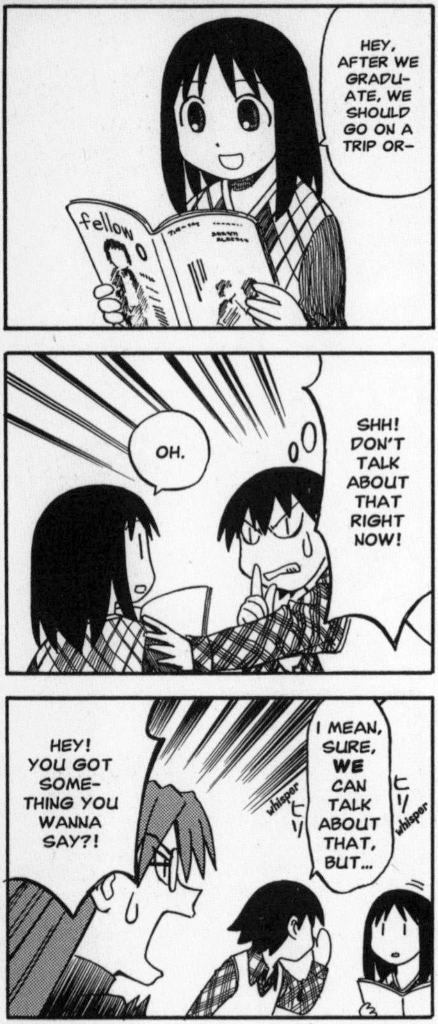
HEY, AFTER WE GRADUATE, WE SHOULD GO ON A TRIP OR–
fellow
SHH! DON'T TALK ABOUT THAT RIGHT NOW!
OH.
ヒソ whisper
I MEAN, SURE, WE CAN TALK ABOUT THAT, BUT...
ヒソ whisper
HEY! YOU GOT SOMETHING YOU WANNA SAY?!
DON'T WORRY! UH, I'M SURE YOU'LL PASS THE NEXT ONE!
DON'T SAY IT LIKE YOU'RE FEELING SORRY FOR ME!!

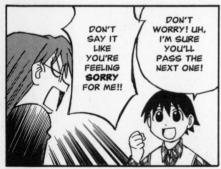

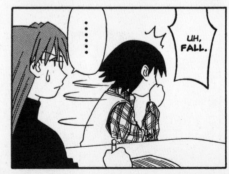

TOGETHER!

DAMMIT, I WILL **DEFINITELY** PASS THIS NEXT EXAM!
AND WHEN I DO, WE WILL **ALL** GO ON A TRIP SOMEWHERE! TOGETHER!
THAT SOUNDS GREAT! WE CAN CELEBRATE GETTING INTO UNIVERSITY!
YEAH. THAT IS, I **HOPE** WE CAN ALL CELEBRATE GETTING INTO UNIVERSITY.
YOU KNOW, HEARIN' THAT FROM YOU REALLY **TICKS ME OFF!**

THE TRIALS OF TEST-TAKING

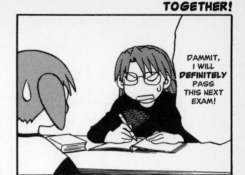

HMM. TOMO, OSAKA AND KAGURA HAVE ALL GOTTEN INTO UNIVERSITY.
ず
slrp
HA HA HA!
WEIRD.

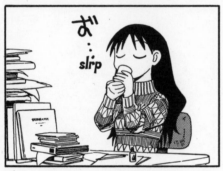

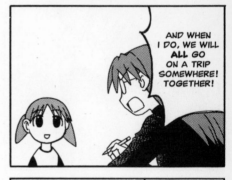

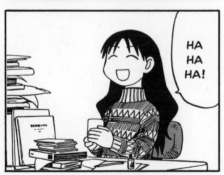

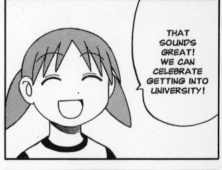

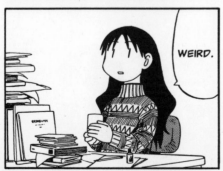

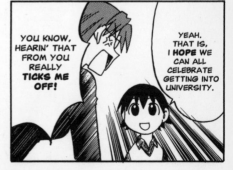

AZUMANGA DAIOH

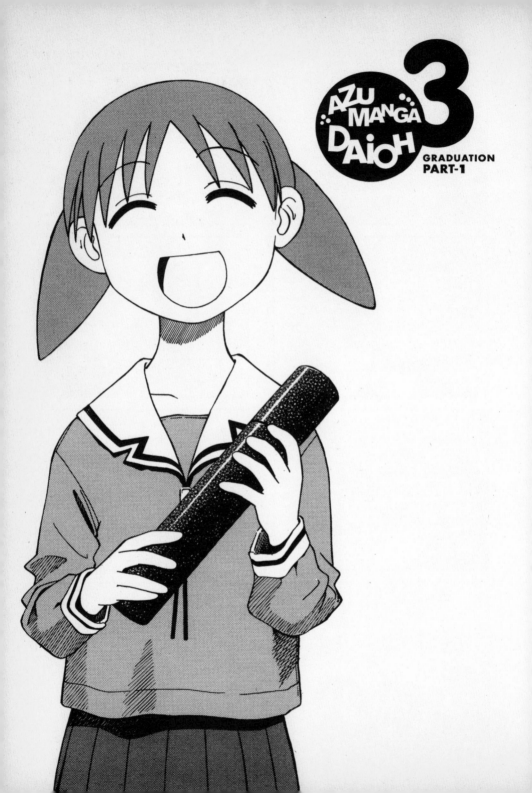

AZUMANGA DAIOH 3

GRADUATION PART-1

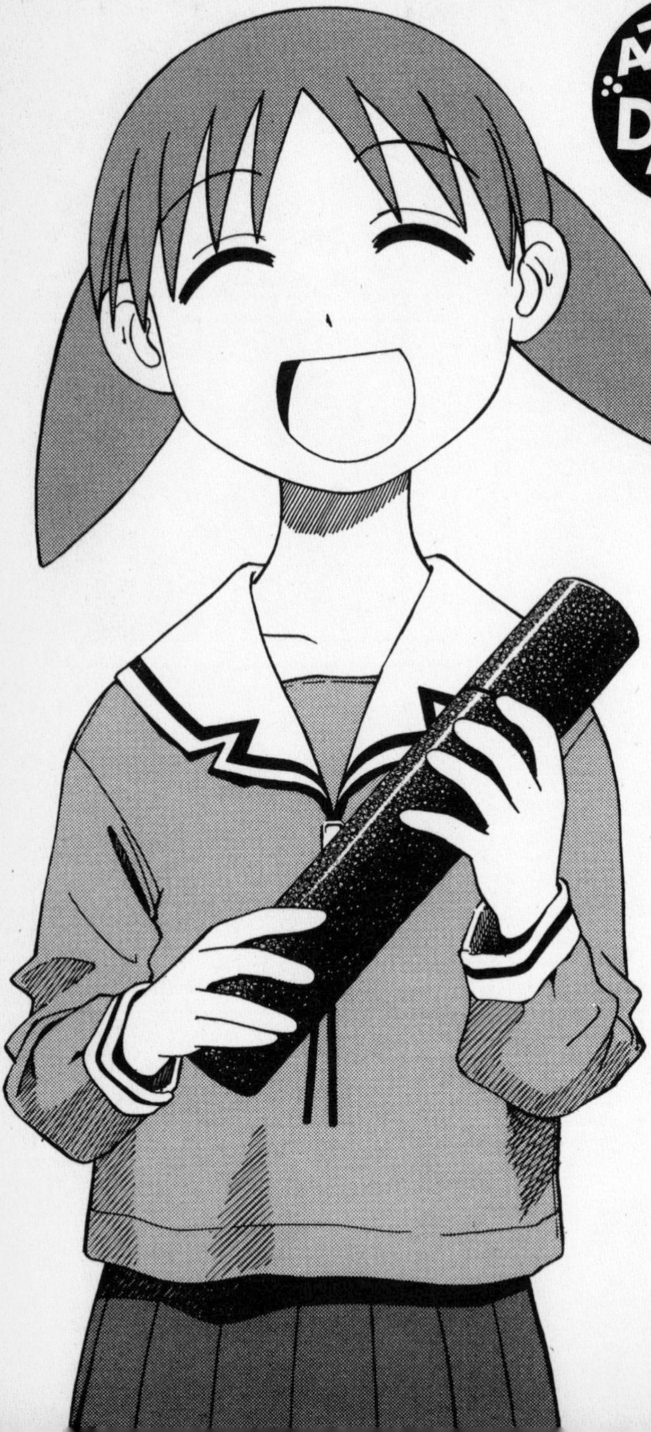

MALNOURISHED

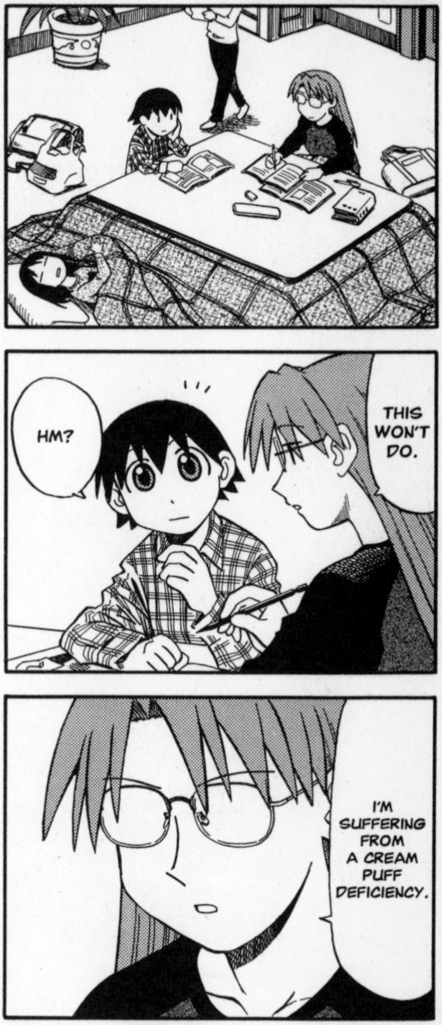
THIS WON'T DO.
HM?
I'M SUFFERING FROM A CREAM PUFF DEFICIENCY.
A CREAM PUFF...?
YES. A CREAM PUFF DEFICIENCY.

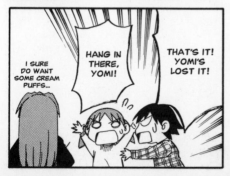

THE NEW THEORY

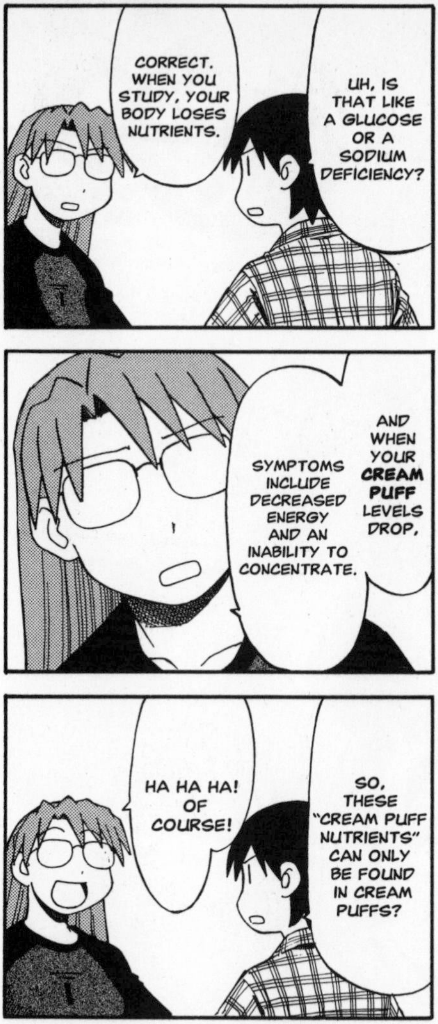
UH, IS THAT LIKE A GLUCOSE OR A SODIUM DEFICIENCY?
CORRECT. WHEN YOU STUDY, YOUR BODY LOSES NUTRIENTS.
AND WHEN YOUR **CREAM PUFF** LEVELS DROP,
SYMPTOMS INCLUDE DECREASED ENERGY AND AN INABILITY TO CONCENTRATE.
SO, THESE "CREAM PUFF NUTRIENTS" CAN ONLY BE FOUND IN CREAM PUFFS?
HA HA HA! OF COURSE!
THAT'S IT! YOMI'S LOST IT!
HANG IN THERE, YOMI!
I SURE DO WANT SOME CREAM PUFFS...

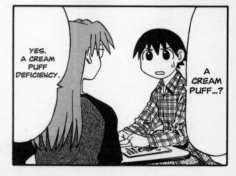

WAUGH! WAUGH!

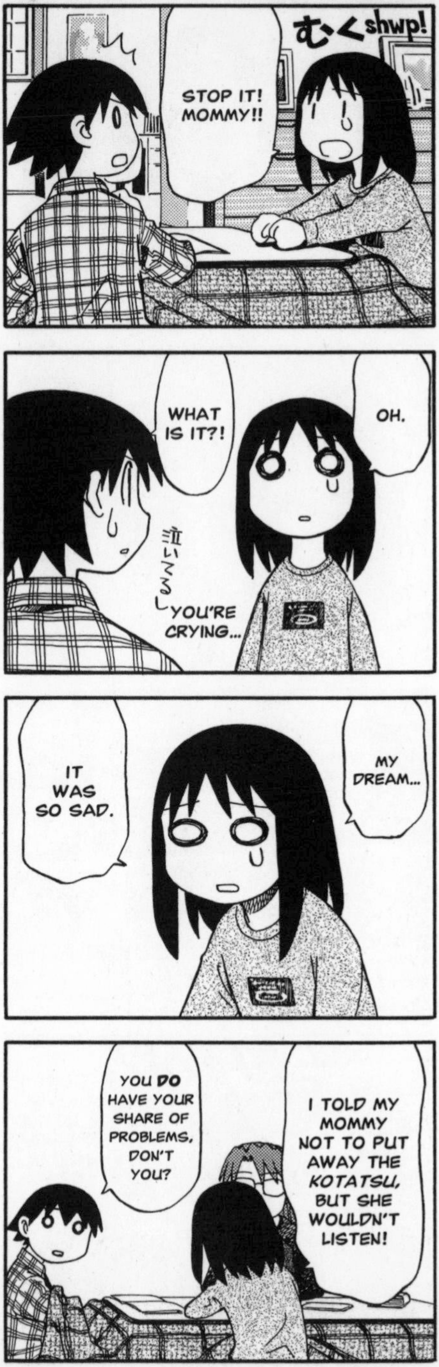
むく shwp!
STOP IT! MOMMY!!
OH.
WHAT IS IT?!
泣いてるし
YOU'RE CRYING...
MY DREAM...
IT WAS SO SAD.
I TOLD MY MOMMY NOT TO PUT AWAY THE KOTATSU, BUT SHE WOULDN'T LISTEN!
YOU DO HAVE YOUR SHARE OF PROBLEMS, DON'T YOU?

YOU'VE GROWN

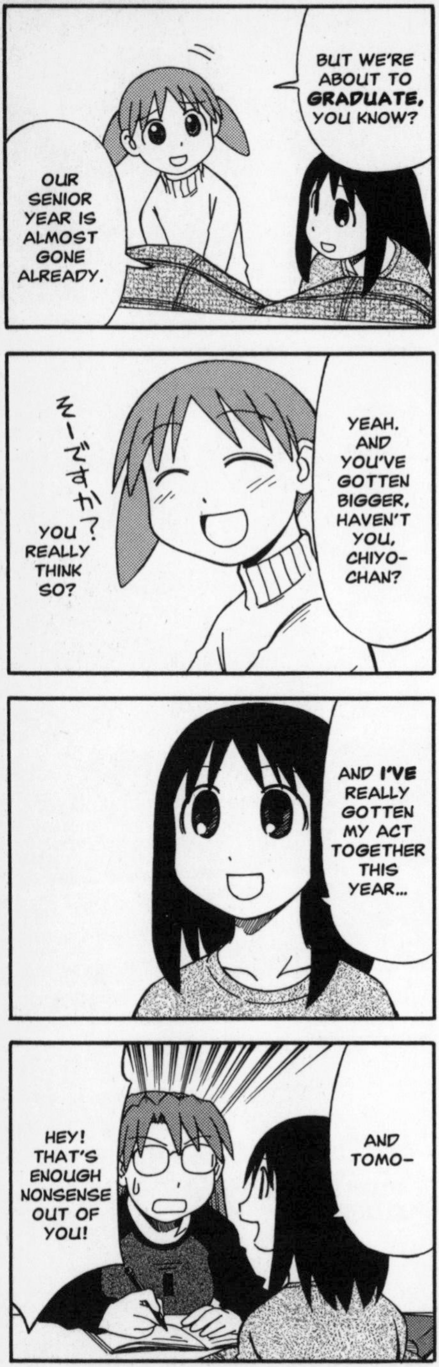
BUT WE'RE ABOUT TO GRADUATE, YOU KNOW?
OUR SENIOR YEAR IS ALMOST GONE ALREADY.
YEAH. AND YOU'VE GOTTEN BIGGER, HAVEN'T YOU, CHIYO-CHAN?
そーですか？
YOU REALLY THINK SO?
AND I'VE REALLY GOTTEN MY ACT TOGETHER THIS YEAR...
AND TOMO-
HEY! THAT'S ENOUGH NONSENSE OUT OF YOU!

LET'S GO TO AN AMUSEMENT PARK

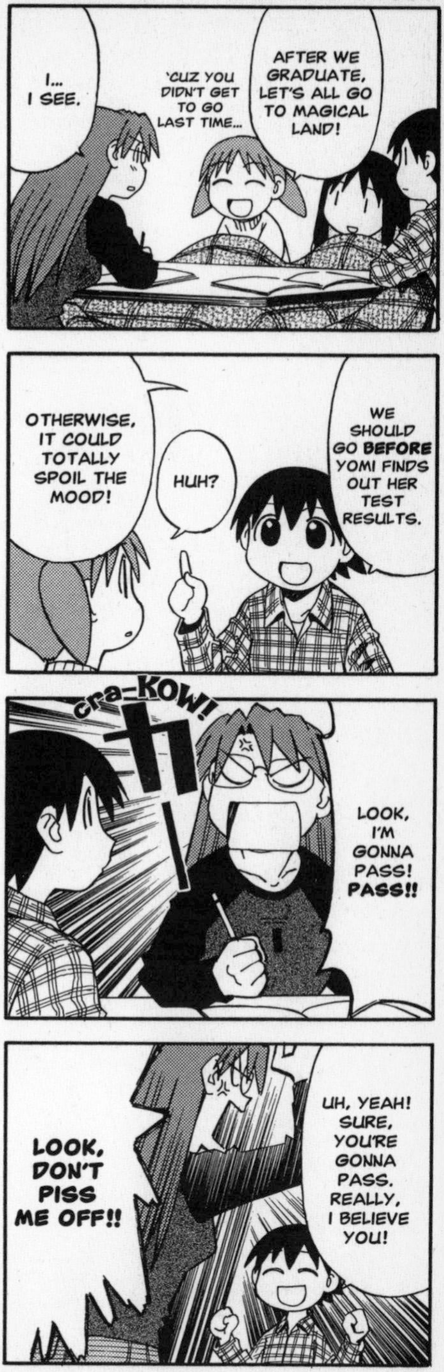
AFTER WE GRADUATE, LET'S ALL GO TO MAGICAL LAND!
'CUZ YOU DIDN'T GET TO GO LAST TIME...
I... I SEE.
WE SHOULD GO **BEFORE** YOMI FINDS OUT HER TEST RESULTS.
HUH?
OTHERWISE, IT COULD TOTALLY SPOIL THE MOOD!
cra-KOW!
LOOK, I'M GONNA PASS! **PASS!!**
UH, YEAH! SURE, YOU'RE GONNA PASS. REALLY, I BELIEVE YOU!
LOOK, DON'T PISS ME OFF!!

CHIYO'S POWER BECOMES NOTHING

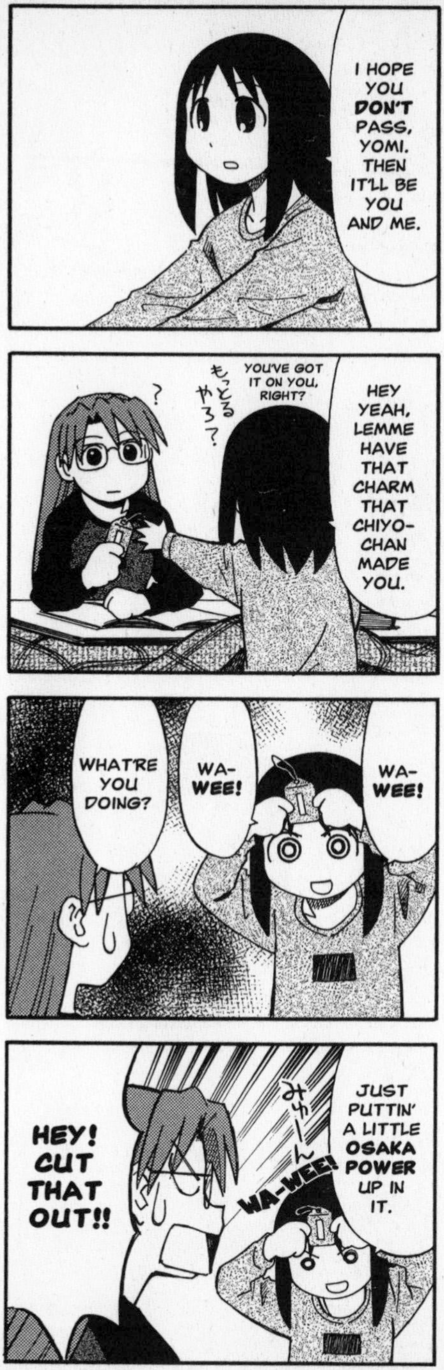
I HOPE YOU **DON'T** PASS, YOMI. THEN IT'LL BE YOU AND ME.
HEY YEAH, LEMME HAVE THAT CHARM THAT CHIYO-CHAN MADE YOU.
YOU'VE GOT IT ON YOU, RIGHT?
もっとるやろ？
?
WA-**WEE!**
WA-**WEE!**
WHAT'RE YOU DOING?
JUST PUTTIN' A LITTLE **OSAKA POWER** UP IN IT.
みゅーん
WA-WEE!
HEY! CUT THAT OUT!!

MY FIRST GRADUATION

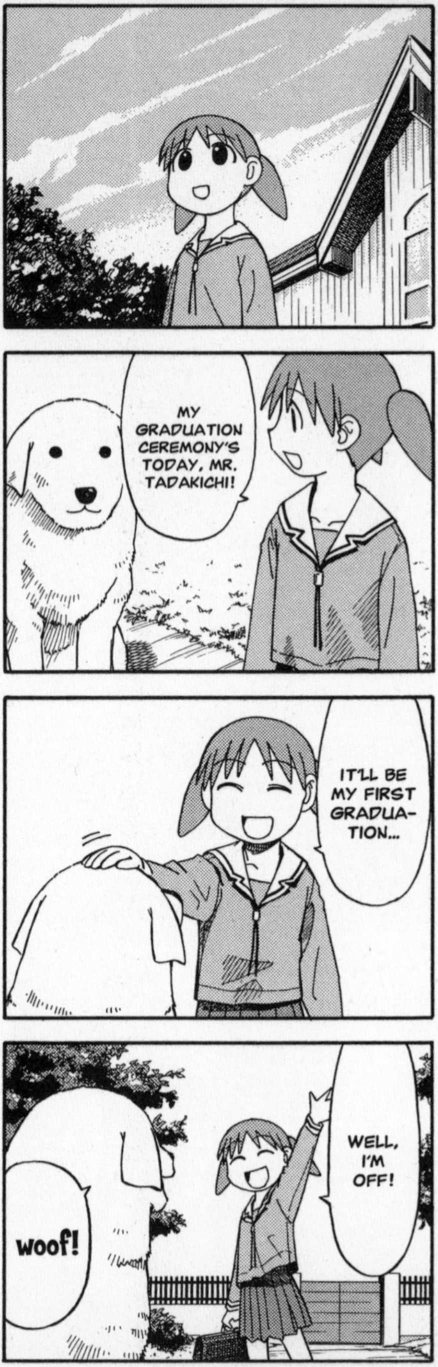
MY GRADUATION CEREMONY'S TODAY, MR. TADAKICHI!
IT'LL BE MY FIRST GRADUA-TION...
WELL, I'M OFF!
woof!

TODAY... NAAH, I WON'T KILL YA

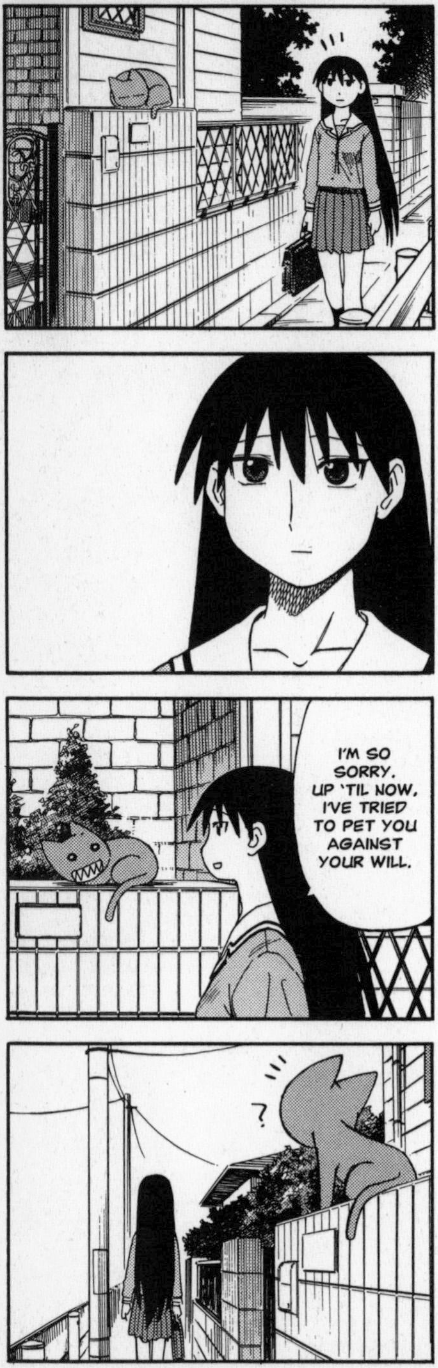
I'M SO SORRY. UP 'TIL NOW, I'VE TRIED TO PET YOU AGAINST YOUR WILL.
?

THE BITING CAT

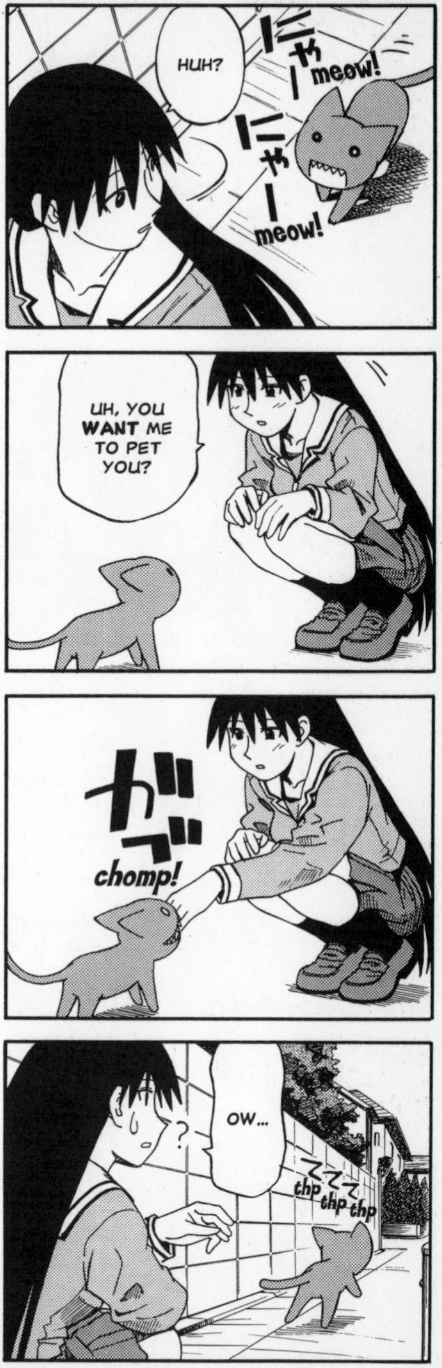
にゃー
meow!
にゃー
meow!
HUH?
UH, YOU **WANT** ME TO PET YOU?
がぶ
chomp!
OW...
?
ててて
thp thp thp

LOOK WHAT I BROUGHT

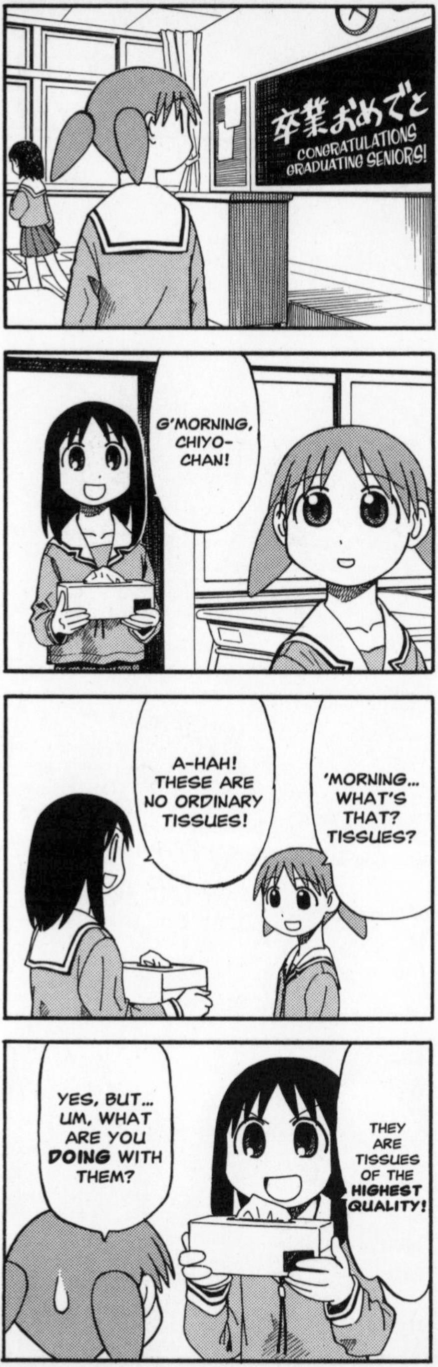
卒業おめでと
CONGRATULATIONS GRADUATING SENIORS!
G'MORNING, CHIYO-CHAN!
'MORNING... WHAT'S THAT? TISSUES?
A-HAH! THESE ARE NO ORDINARY TISSUES!
THEY ARE TISSUES OF THE **HIGHEST QUALITY!**
YES, BUT... UM, WHAT ARE YOU **DOING** WITH THEM?

THE SECRET REVEALED

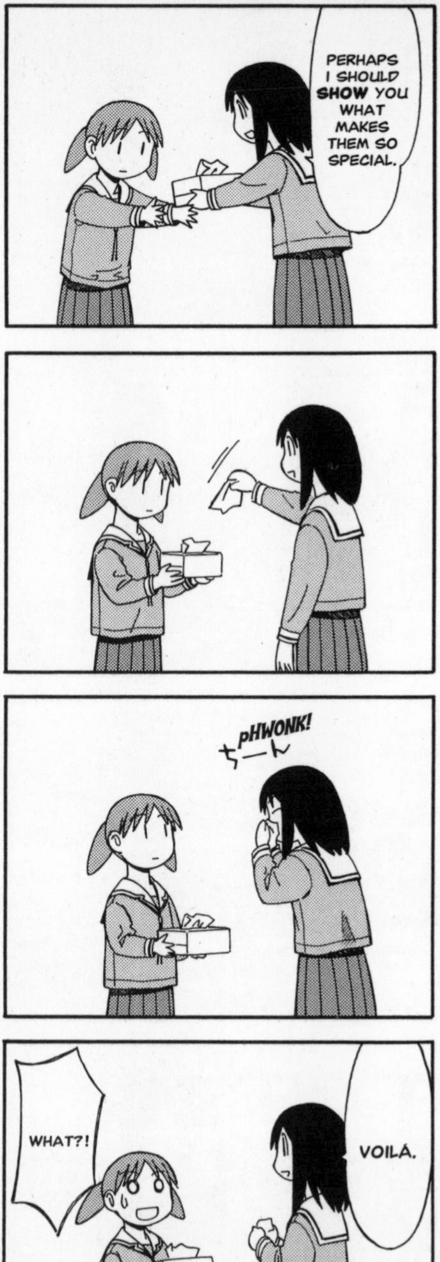
PERHAPS I SHOULD **SHOW** YOU WHAT MAKES THEM SO SPECIAL.
pHWONK!
ちーん
VOILÁ.
WHAT?!

DIFFICULT

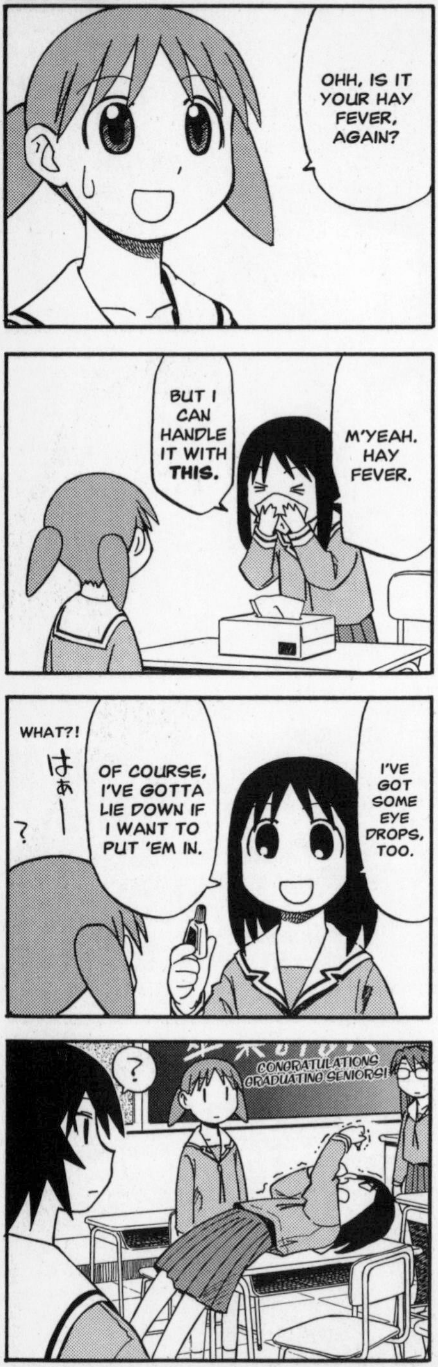
OHH, IS IT YOUR HAY FEVER, AGAIN?
M'YEAH. HAY FEVER.
BUT I CAN HANDLE IT WITH **THIS.**
I'VE GOT SOME EYE DROPS, TOO.
OF COURSE, I'VE GOTTA LIE DOWN IF I WANT TO PUT 'EM IN.
WHAT?!
はぁー
?
?
CONGRATULATIONS GRADUATING SENIORS!!

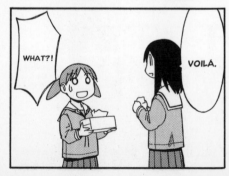

THE GRAND ENTRANCE

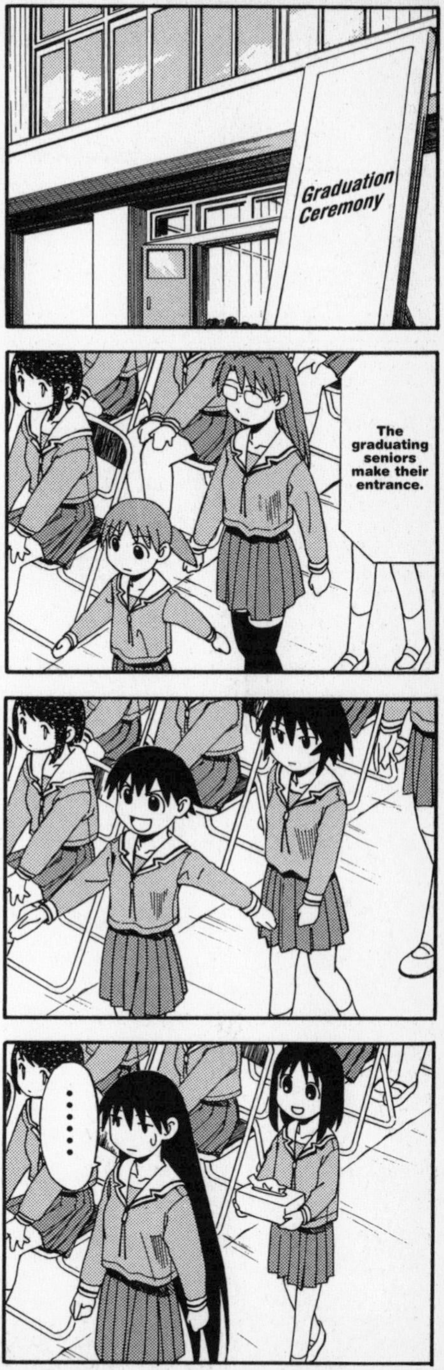
Graduation Ceremony
The graduating seniors make their entrance.
......

OSAKA'S SPEECH

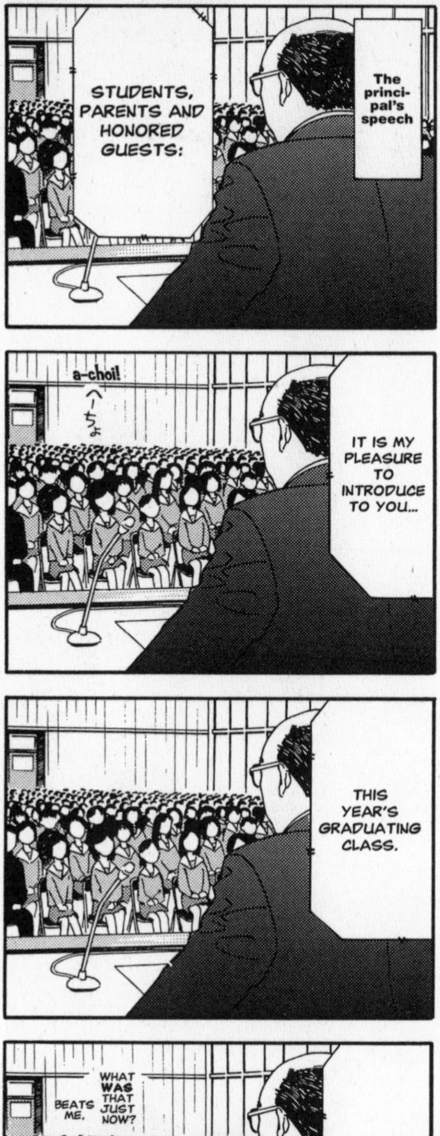
The principal's speech
STUDENTS, PARENTS AND HONORED GUESTS:
IT IS MY PLEASURE TO INTRODUCE TO YOU...
a-choi!
へーちょ
THIS YEAR'S GRADUATING CLASS.
GRADUATION MARKS A NEW DAY IN...
WHAT WAS THAT JUST NOW?
BEATS ME.

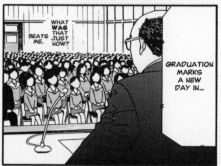

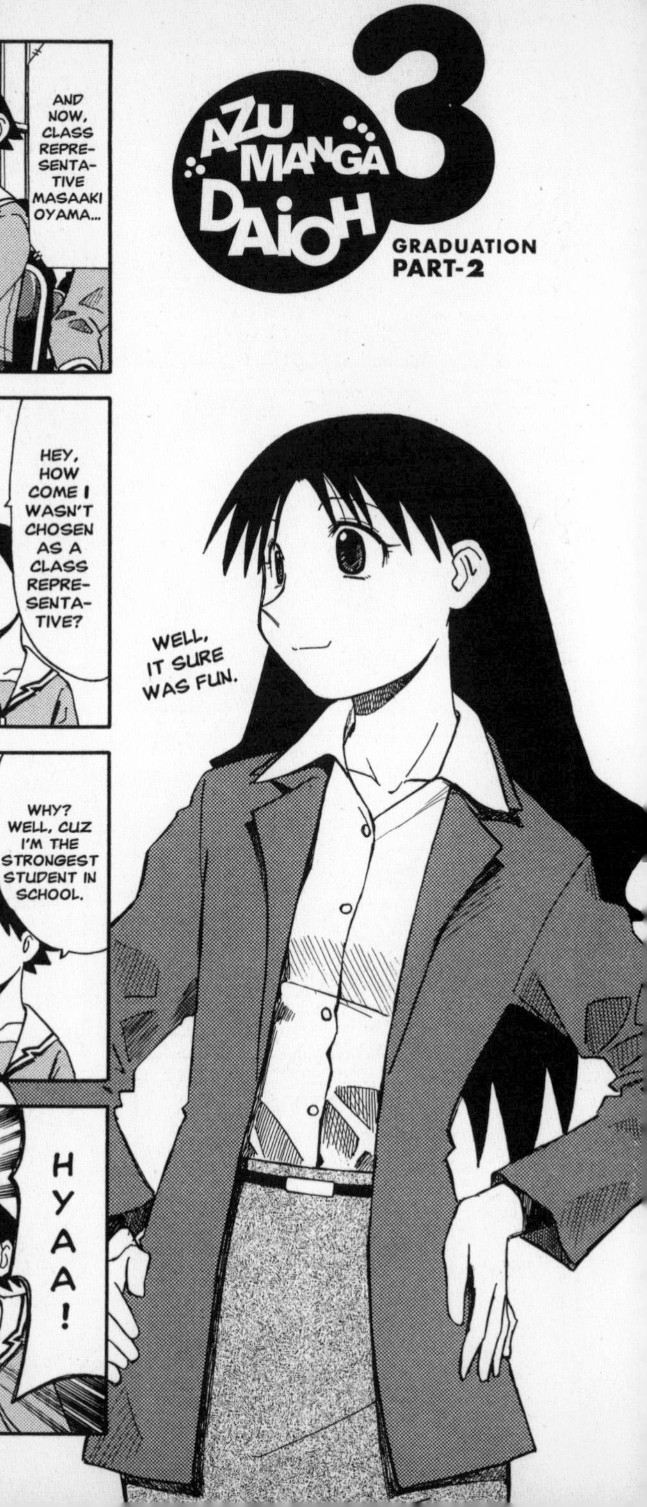
AZU MANGA DAIOH 3
GRADUATION PART-2
WELL, IT SURE WAS FUN.

THE STRONGEST STUDENT

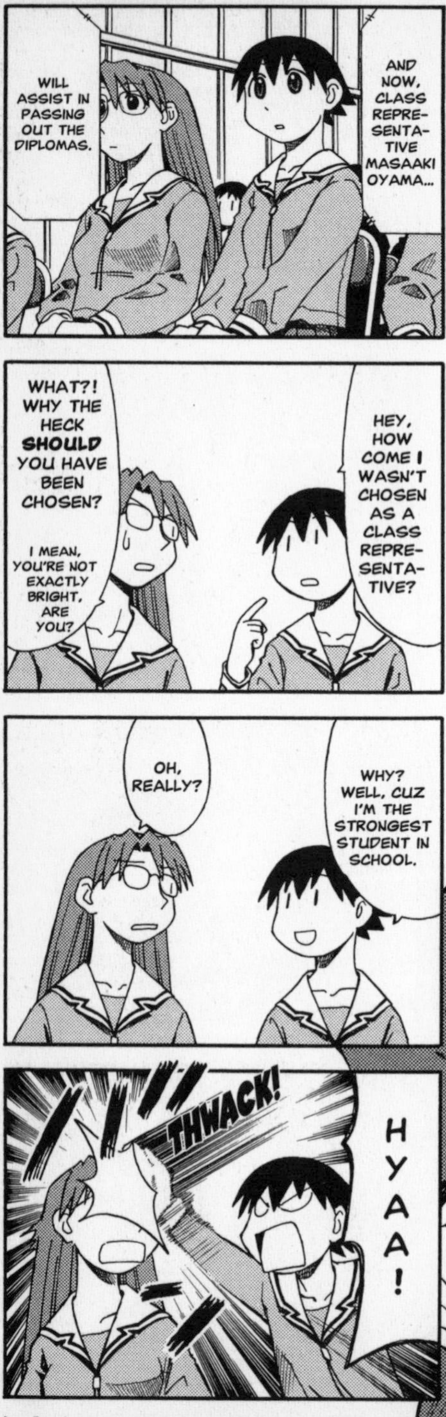
AND NOW, CLASS REPRESENTATIVE MASAAKI OYAMA...
WILL ASSIST IN PASSING OUT THE DIPLOMAS.
HEY, HOW COME I WASN'T CHOSEN AS A CLASS REPRESENTATIVE?
WHAT?! WHY THE HECK SHOULD YOU HAVE BEEN CHOSEN?
I MEAN, YOU'RE NOT EXACTLY BRIGHT, ARE YOU?
WHY? WELL, CUZ I'M THE STRONGEST STUDENT IN SCHOOL.
OH, REALLY?
HYAA!
THWACK!

CHOP! CHOP! CHOP!

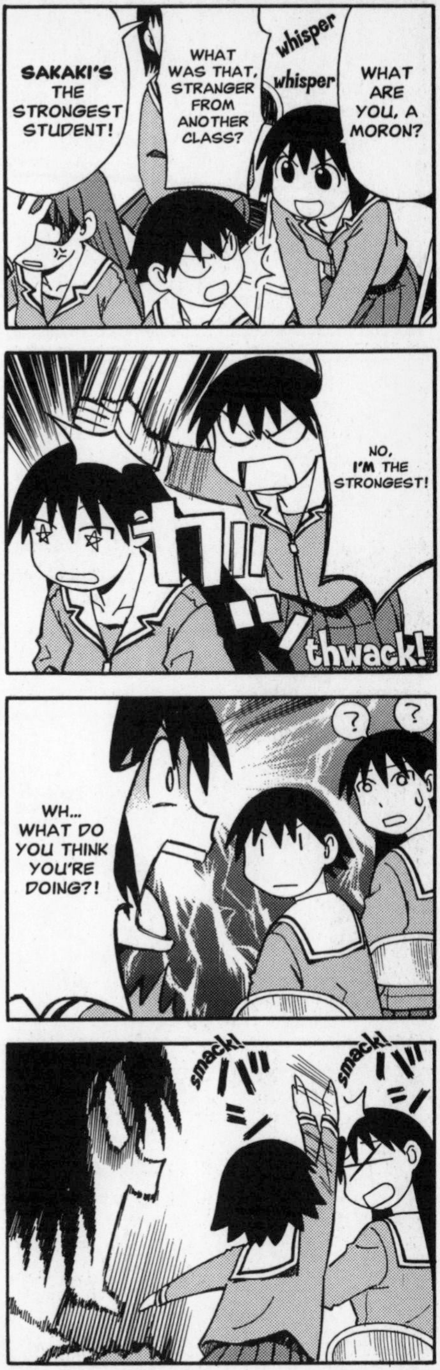
WHAT ARE YOU, A MORON?
whisper
whisper
WHAT WAS THAT, STRANGER FROM ANOTHER CLASS?
SAKAKI'S THE STRONGEST STUDENT!
NO, I'M THE STRONGEST!
thwack!
WH... WHAT DO YOU THINK YOU'RE DOING?!
smack!
smack!

IT'S ME!

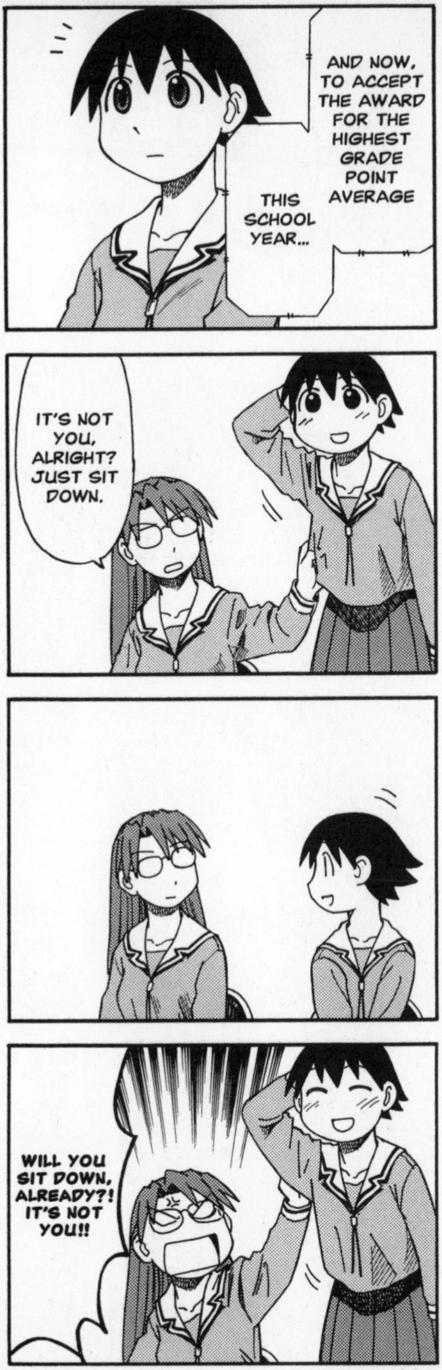
AND NOW, TO ACCEPT THE AWARD FOR THE HIGHEST GRADE POINT AVERAGE
THIS SCHOOL YEAR...
IT'S NOT YOU, ALRIGHT? JUST SIT DOWN.
WILL YOU SIT DOWN, ALREADY?! IT'S NOT YOU!!

THE *REAL* STRONGEST STUDENT

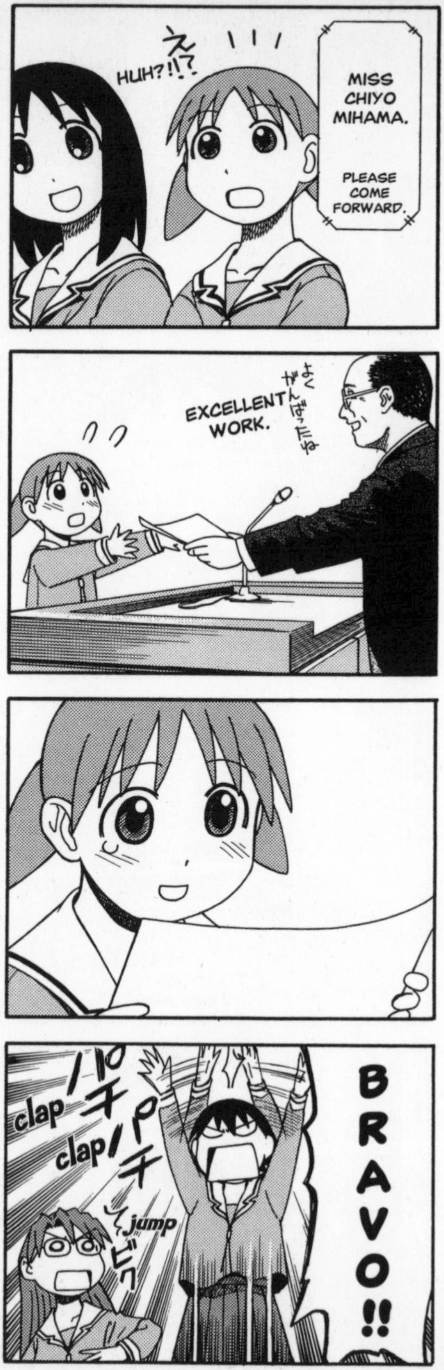
MISS CHIYO MIHAMA.
PLEASE COME FORWARD.
え
HUH?!!?
よくがんばったね
EXCELLENT WORK.
BRAVO!!
パチパチ
clap clap
ビクッ
jump

CONGRATULATIONS!

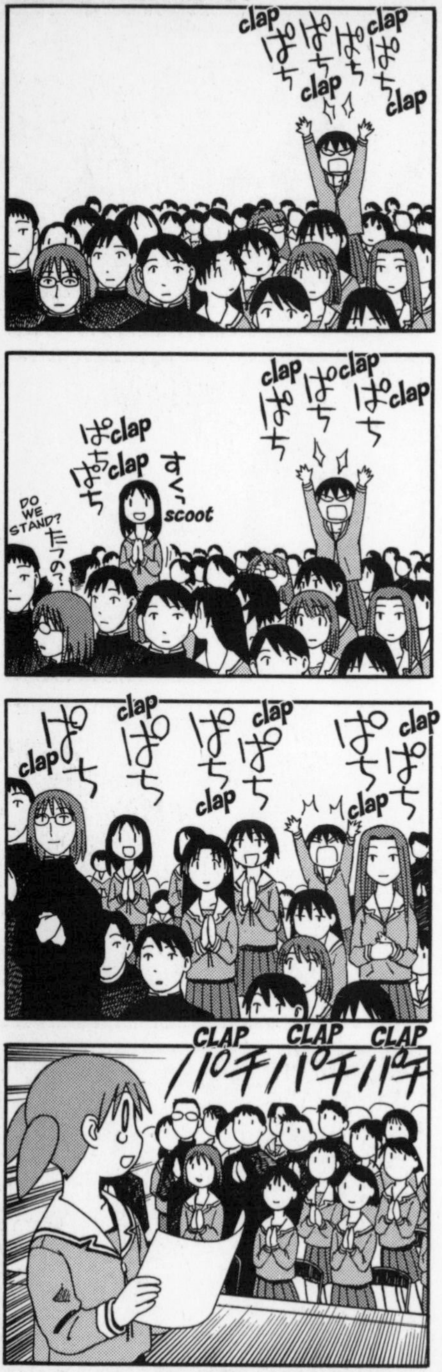
ぱちぱちぱちぱち
clap clap clap clap
ぱちぱちぱちぱち
clap clap clap
すくっ
scoot
ぱちぱち
clap clap
たつの?
DO WE STAND?
ぱちぱちぱちぱちぱちぱち
clap clap clap clap clap
パチパチパチ
CLAP CLAP CLAP

MIXED EMOTIONS

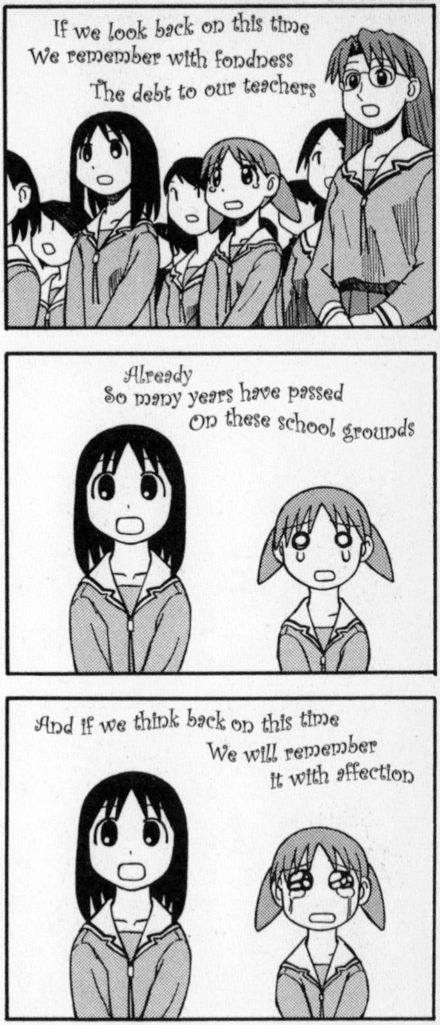
If we look back on this time
We remember with fondness
The debt to our teachers
Already
So many years have passed
On these school grounds
And if we think back on this time
We will remember
it with affection
But now it is time
For us to part

SADNESS

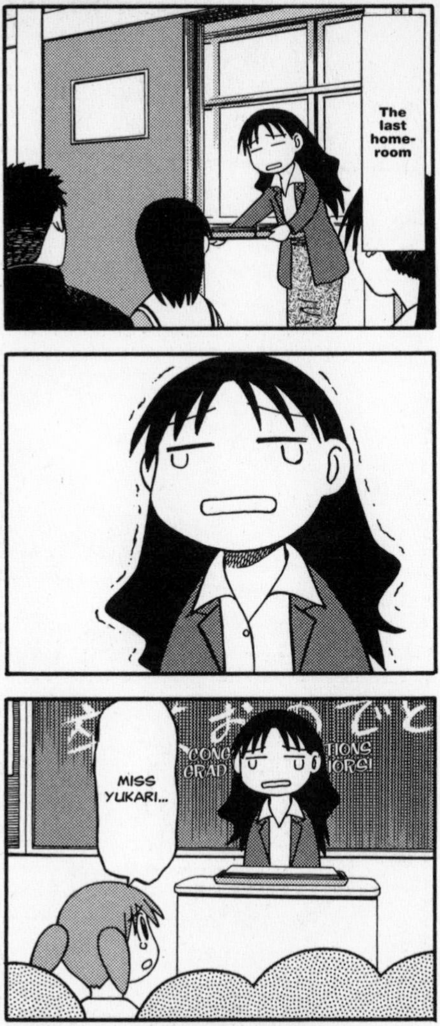
The last home-room
MISS YUKARI...
WHAT?!
I... I LOST MY WALLET.

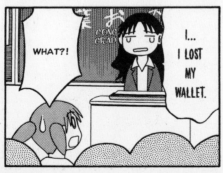

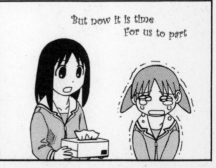

USE THIS

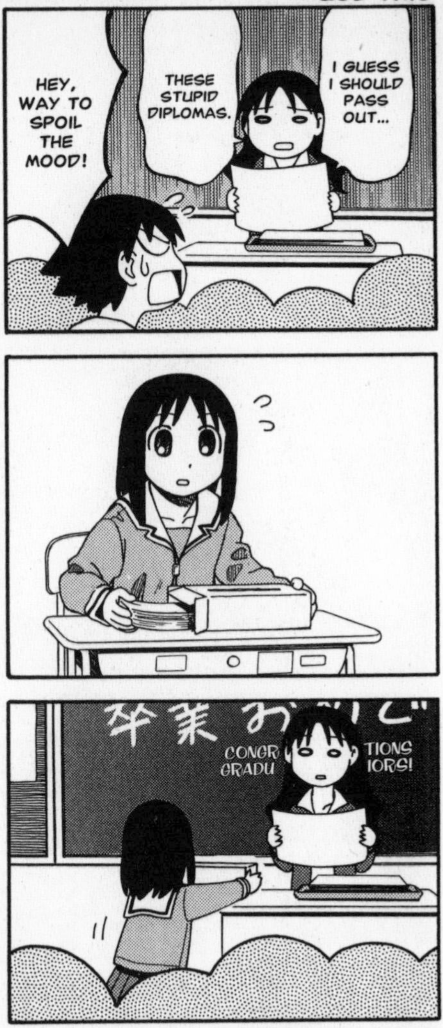
I GUESS I SHOULD PASS OUT...
THESE STUPID DIPLOMAS.
HEY, WAY TO SPOIL THE MOOD!
TIONS
IORS!
CONGR
GRADU
donations

SUB-PAR

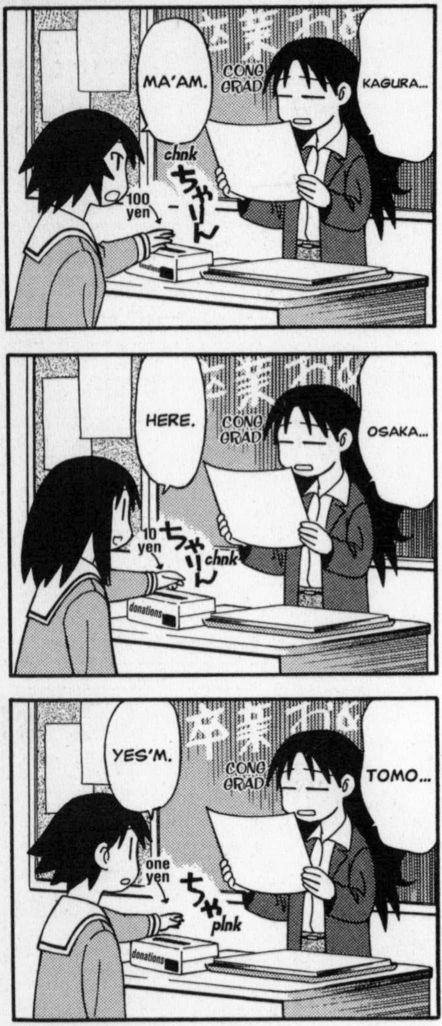
KAGURA...
CONG
GRAD
MA'AM.
chnk
ちゃりん
100 yen
OSAKA...
CONG
GRAD
HERE.
10 yen
ちゃりん
chnk
donations
TOMO...
CONG
GRAD
YES'M.
one yen
ちゃ
plnk
donations
THAT'S IT! I DON'T NEED YOUR CHUMP CHANGE!!
BWACK!
WHA-?! WHAT A WENCH!

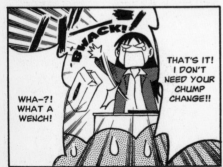

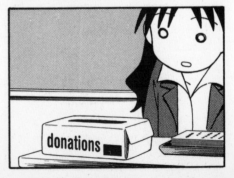

CONGRATULATIONS

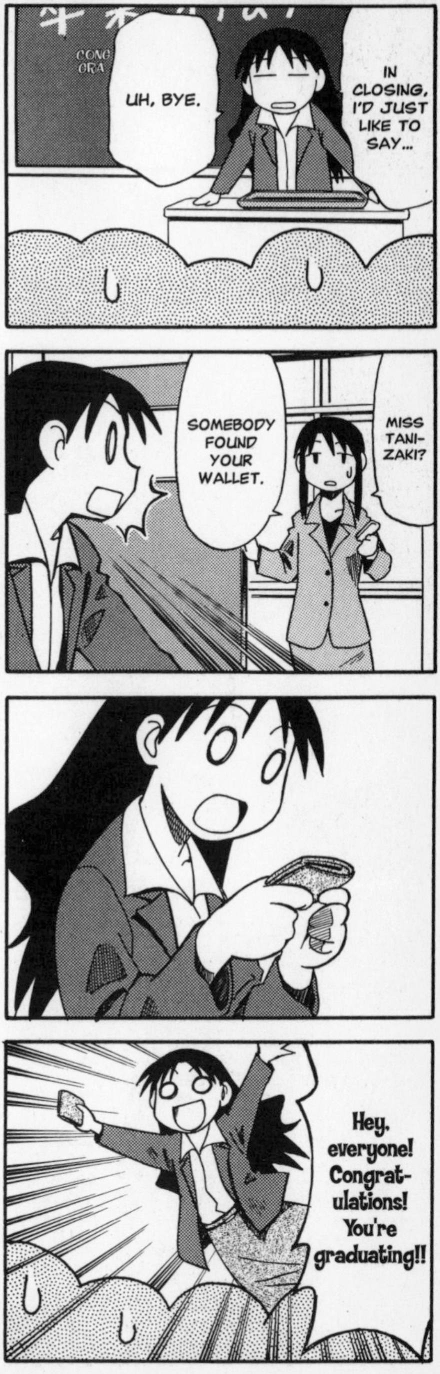
IN CLOSING, I'D JUST LIKE TO SAY...
UH, BYE.
MISS TANI-ZAKI?
SOMEBODY FOUND YOUR WALLET.
Hey, everyone! Congrat-ulations! You're graduating!!

FLOWERS

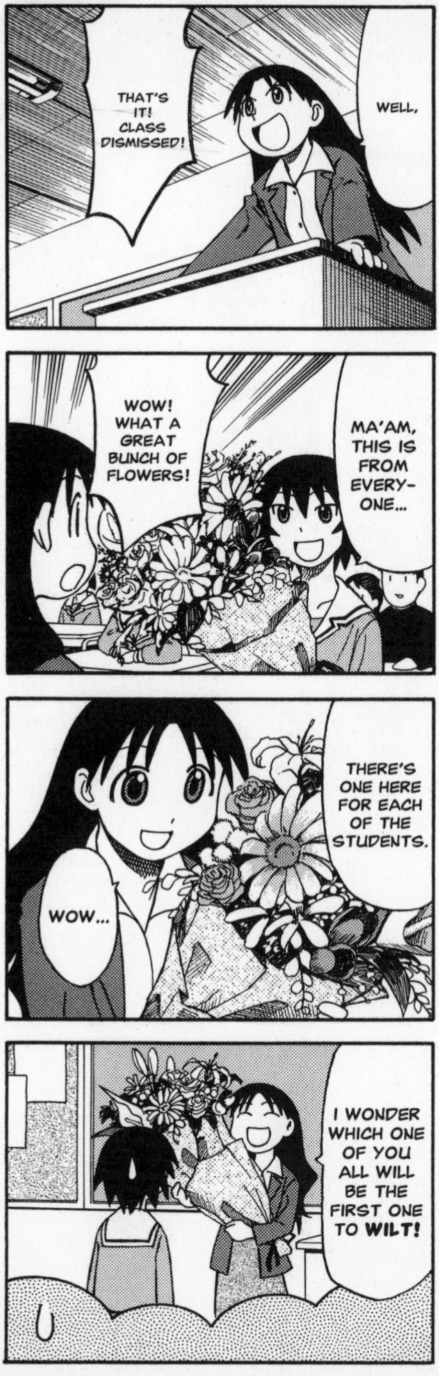
WELL,
THAT'S IT! CLASS DISMISSED!
MA'AM, THIS IS FROM EVERY-ONE...
WOW! WHAT A GREAT BUNCH OF FLOWERS!
THERE'S ONE HERE FOR EACH OF THE STUDENTS.
WOW...
I WONDER WHICH ONE OF YOU ALL WILL BE THE FIRST ONE TO **WILT**!

SPUR OF THE MOMENT

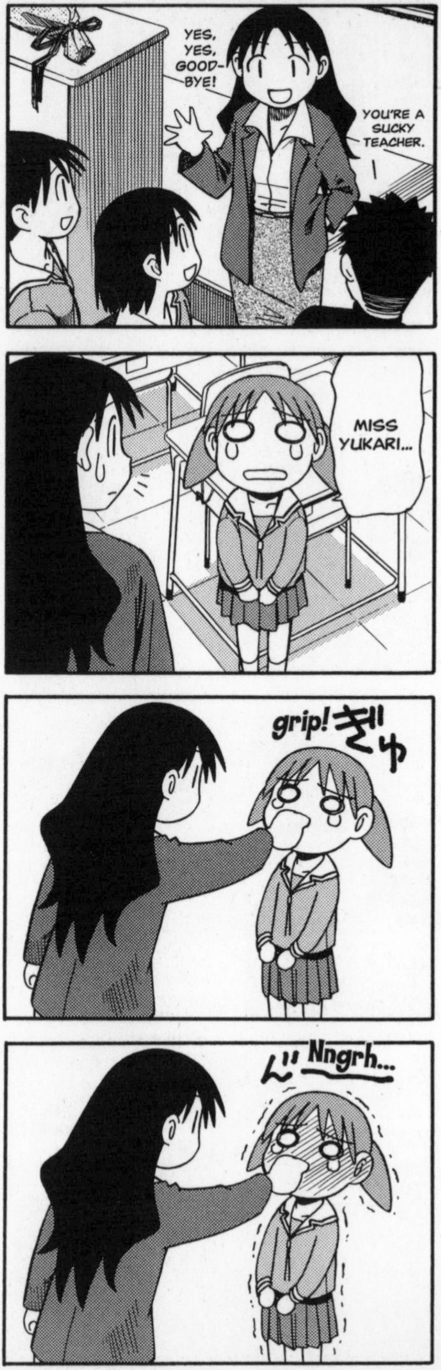
YES, YES, GOOD-BYE!
YOU'RE A SUCKY TEACHER.
MISS YUKARI...
grip! ぎゅ
ん" Nngrh...

TOGETHER

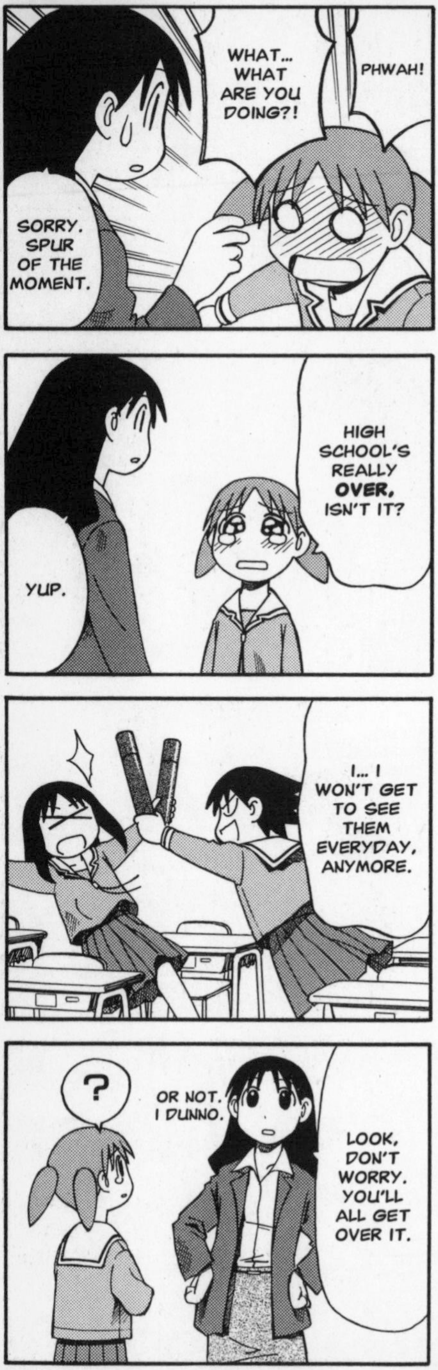
PHWAH!
WHAT... WHAT ARE YOU DOING?!
SORRY. SPUR OF THE MOMENT.
HIGH SCHOOL'S REALLY **OVER,** ISN'T IT?
YUP.
I... I WON'T GET TO SEE THEM EVERYDAY, ANYMORE.
LOOK, DON'T WORRY. YOU'LL ALL GET OVER IT.
OR NOT. I DUNNO.
?

THE ONLY WAY

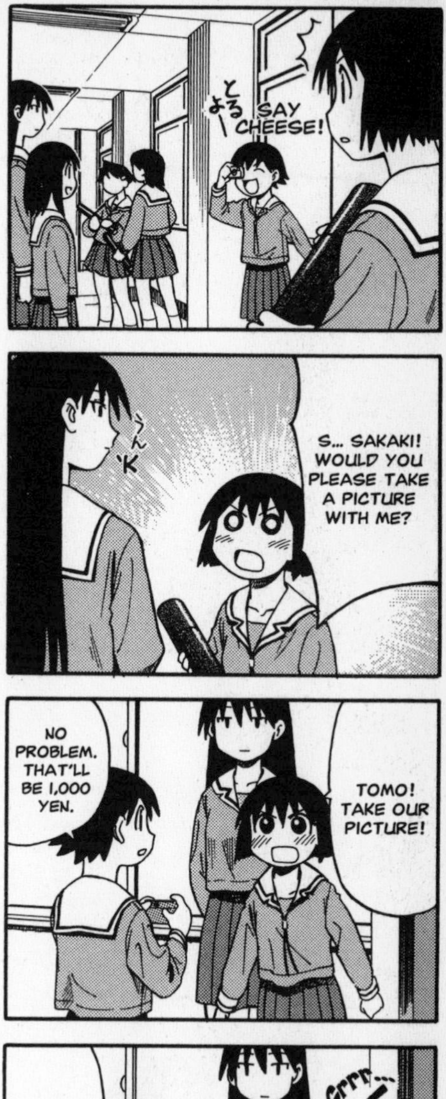
とるよ
SAY CHEESE!
うん
K
S... SAKAKI! WOULD YOU PLEASE TAKE A PICTURE WITH ME?
TOMO! TAKE OUR PICTURE!
NO PROBLEM. THAT'LL BE 1,000 YEN.
Grrr...
く...
I, UH, I WAS KIDDING.

OFF WITH THEIR HEADS!

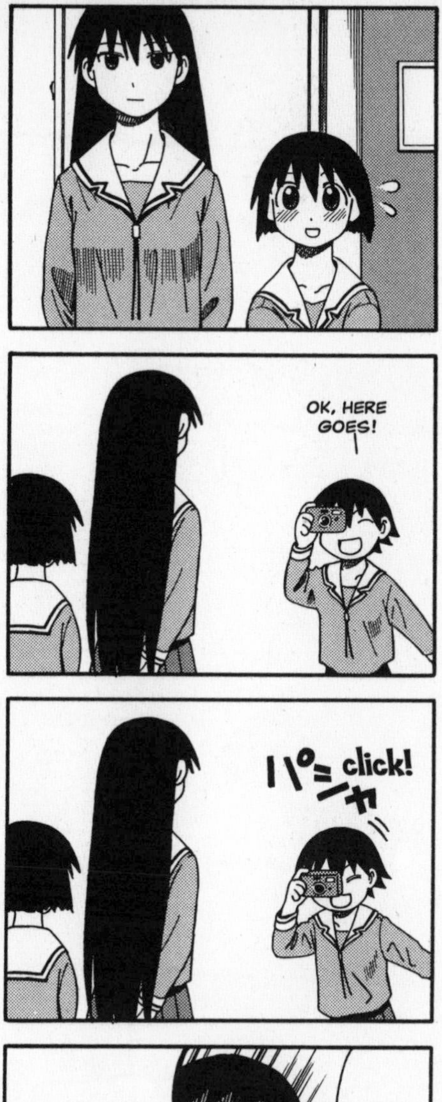
OK, HERE GOES!
パシャ
click!
ALL DONE!
HEY! YOU WERE POINTING THAT THING AT THE **GROUND!!**

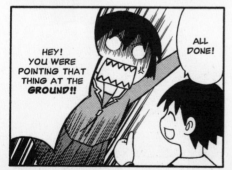

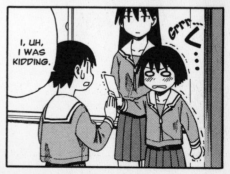

MY PRECIOUS

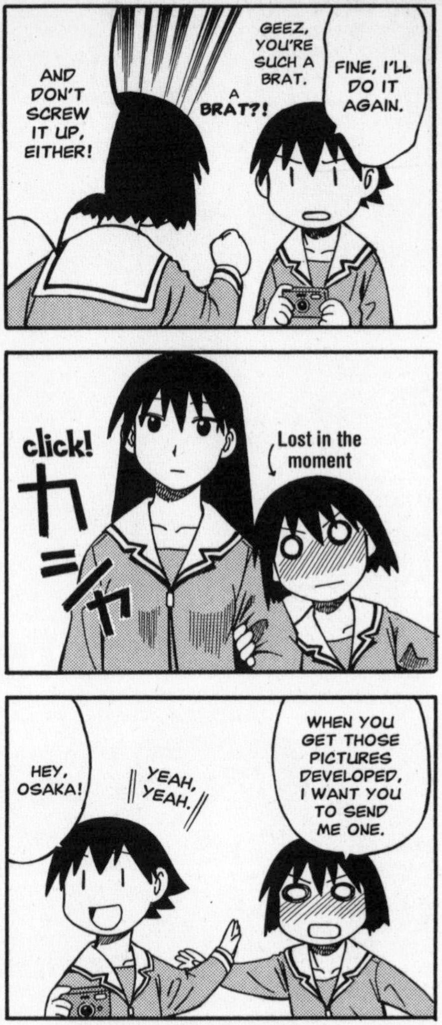
FINE, I'LL DO IT AGAIN.
GEEZ, YOU'RE SUCH A BRAT.
A BRAT?!
AND DON'T SCREW IT UP, EITHER!
Lost in the moment
click!
カシャ
WHEN YOU GET THOSE PICTURES DEVELOPED, I WANT YOU TO SEND ME ONE.
YEAH, YEAH.
HEY, OSAKA!
HEY, ARE YOU LISTENING?!
PLEASE SEND ME A COPY!
I'LL EVEN PAY YOU FOR IT!!
O... OK.

SMILE

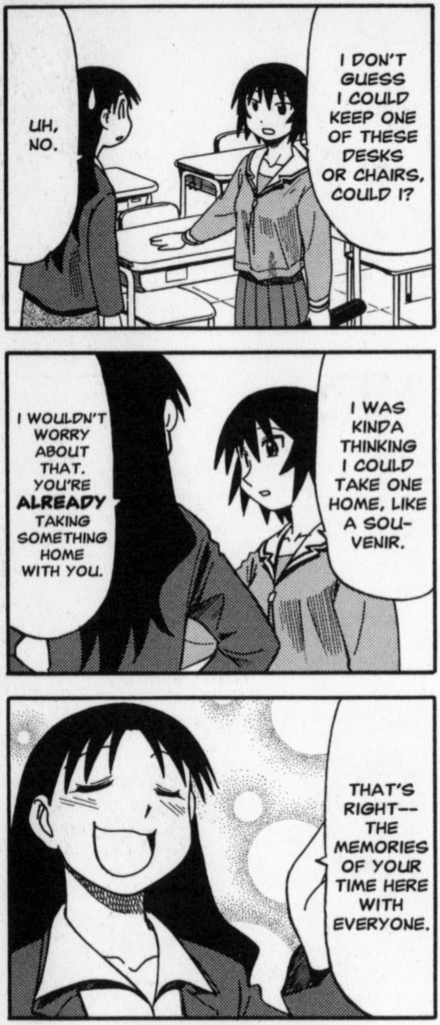
I DON'T GUESS I COULD KEEP ONE OF THESE DESKS OR CHAIRS, COULD I?
UH, NO.
I WAS KINDA THINKING I COULD TAKE ONE HOME, LIKE A SOU-VENIR.
I WOULDN'T WORRY ABOUT THAT. YOU'RE ALREADY TAKING SOMETHING HOME WITH YOU.
THAT'S RIGHT-- THE MEMORIES OF YOUR TIME HERE WITH EVERYONE.
TH... THANK YOU, MISS YUKARI!
drip
ボロボロ
drip
HUH?! UH...

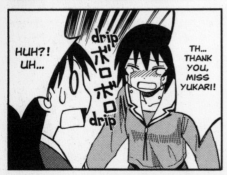

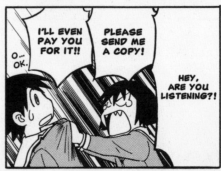

SURE WAS FUN

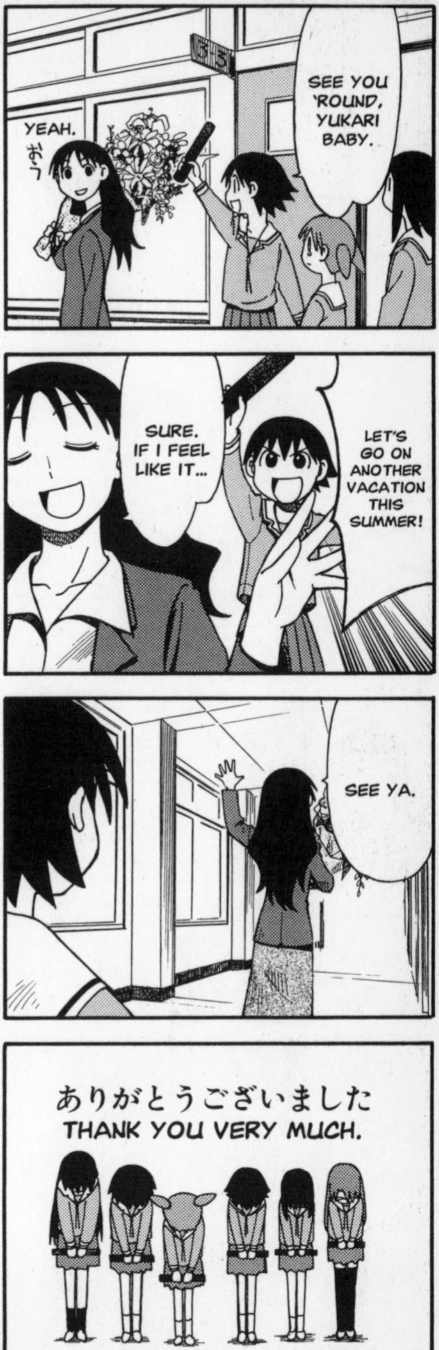
SEE YOU 'ROUND, YUKARI BABY.
YEAH.
おう
LET'S GO ON ANOTHER VACATION THIS SUMMER!
SURE. IF I FEEL LIKE IT...
SEE YA.
ありがとうございました
THANK YOU VERY MUCH.

PREPARATIONS

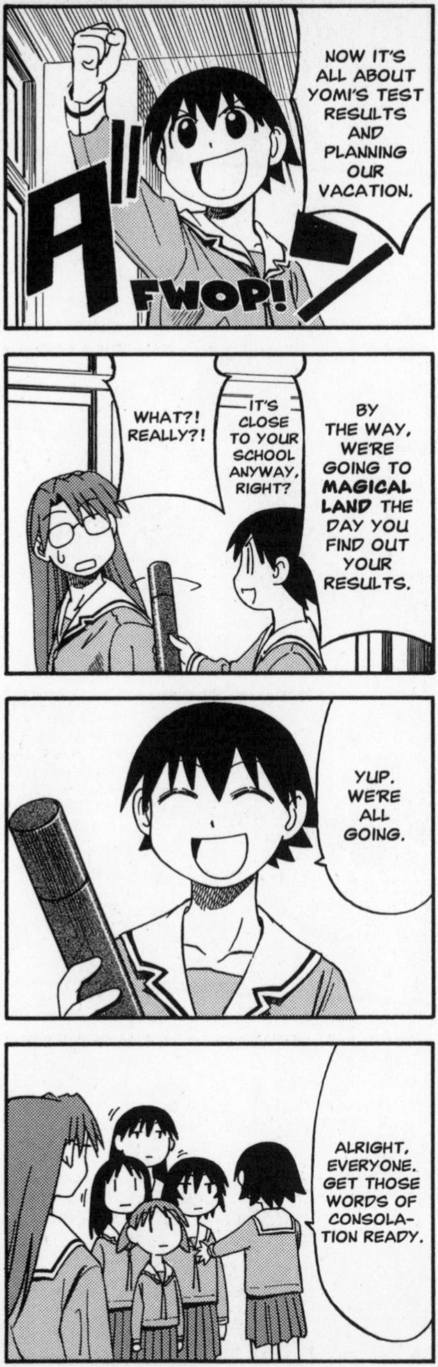
NOW IT'S ALL ABOUT YOMI'S TEST RESULTS AND PLANNING OUR VACATION.
FWOP!
BY THE WAY, WE'RE GOING TO MAGICAL LAND THE DAY YOU FIND OUT YOUR RESULTS.
IT'S CLOSE TO YOUR SCHOOL ANYWAY, RIGHT?
WHAT?! REALLY?!
YUP. WE'RE ALL GOING.
ALRIGHT, EVERYONE. GET THOSE WORDS OF CONSOLATION READY.

THE ALMA MATER

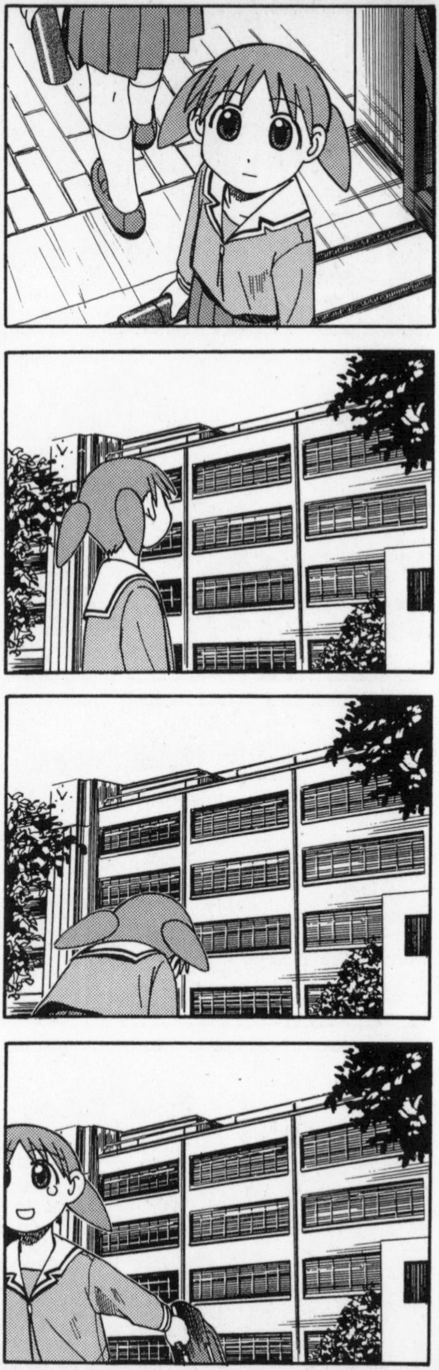

THE DAYTRIP

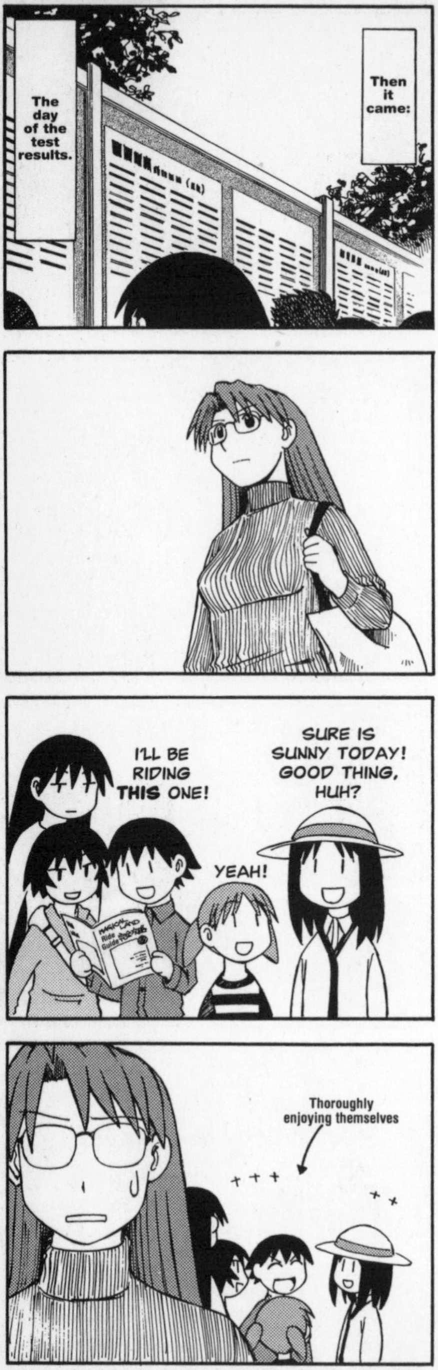
Then it came:
The day of the test results.
SURE IS SUNNY TODAY! GOOD THING, HUH?
I'LL BE RIDING THIS ONE!
MAGICAL LAND Ride Guide
YEAH!
Thoroughly enjoying themselves

THE TEST RESULTS

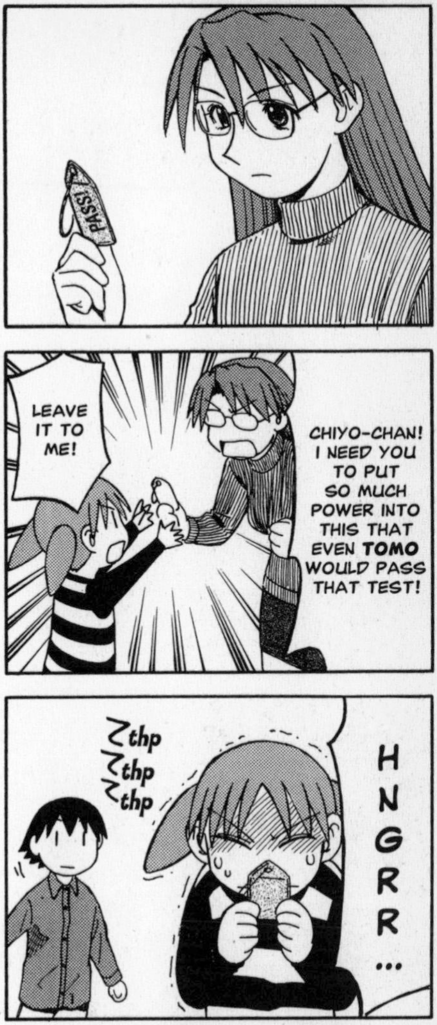
PASS!
CHIYO-CHAN! I NEED YOU TO PUT SO MUCH POWER INTO THIS THAT EVEN **TOMO** WOULD PASS THAT TEST!
LEAVE IT TO ME!
HNGRR...
thp thp thp
HEY, I JUST LOOKED AT THE SIGN-BOARD. YOUR NUMBER WASN'T ON THERE.
WHAT?!

OH.

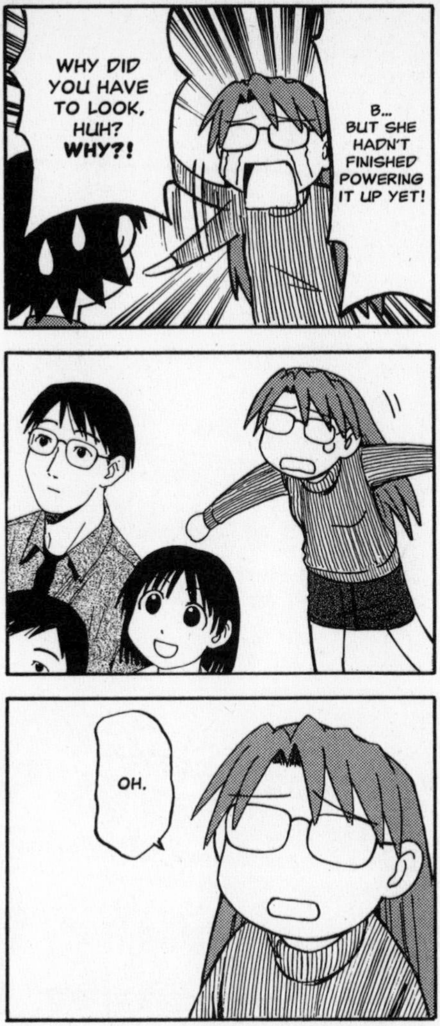
WHY DID YOU HAVE TO LOOK, HUH? **WHY?!**
B... BUT SHE HADN'T FINISHED POWERING IT UP YET!
OH.
UH...
I'M ON THERE.

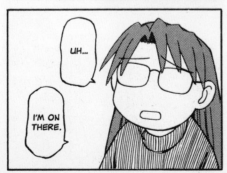

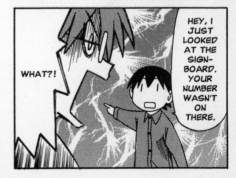

I'M ON THERE!

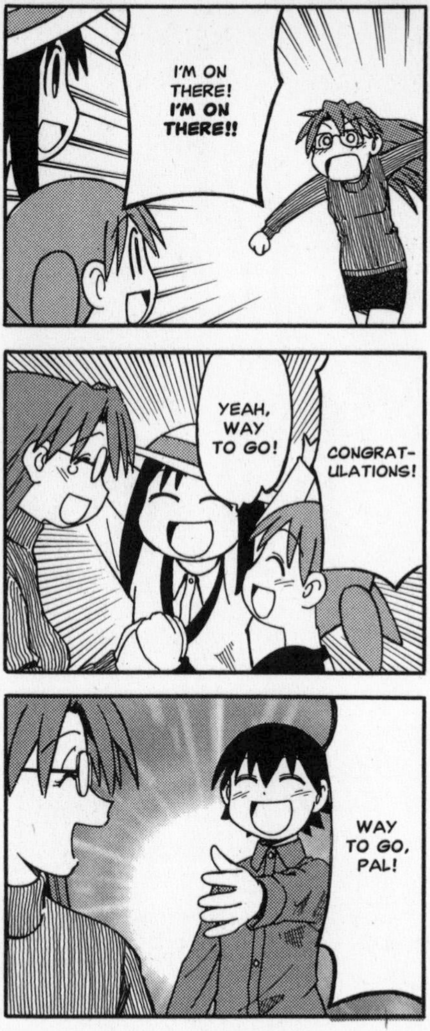

I'M ON THERE! **I'M ON THERE!!**
CONGRATULATIONS!
YEAH, WAY TO GO!
WAY TO GO, PAL!

HIGHER AND HIGHER

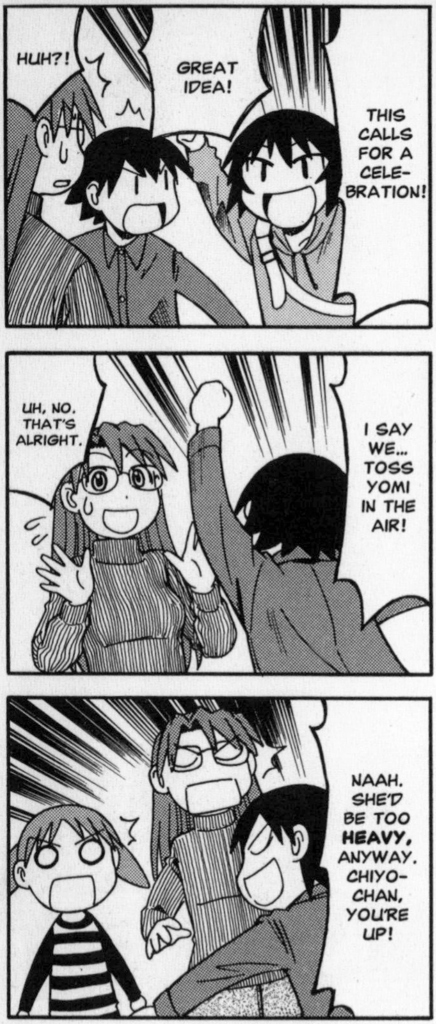

THIS CALLS FOR A CELEBRATION!
GREAT IDEA!
HUH?!
I SAY WE... TOSS YOMI IN THE AIR!
UH, NO. THAT'S ALRIGHT.
NAAH. SHE'D BE TOO **HEAVY,** ANYWAY. CHIYO-CHAN, YOU'RE UP!
AIII!
HELP!!

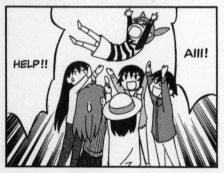

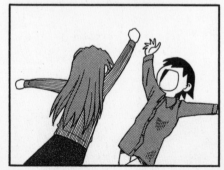

EVERYTHING'S GONNA BE ALRIGHT

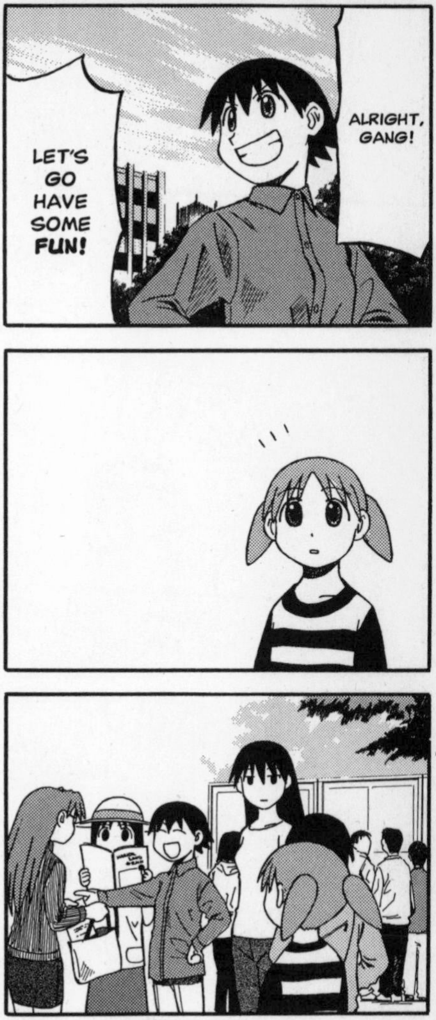
ALRIGHT, GANG!
LET'S GO HAVE SOME **FUN!**
そっか
HEY, YEAH.

US

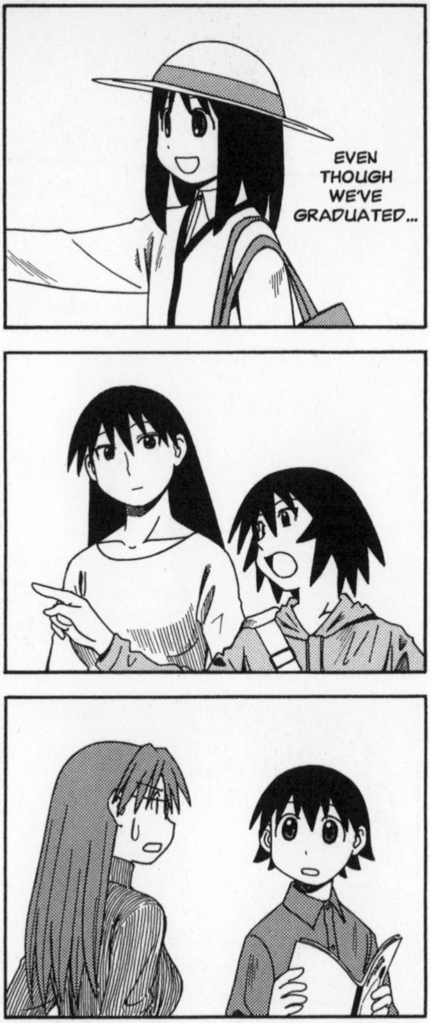
EVEN THOUGH WE'VE GRADUATED...
C'MON! LET'S GO, CHIYO-CHAN!
WE'RE STILL TOGETHER. ALL OF US.
OK!

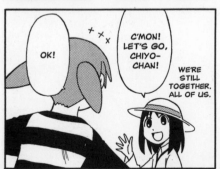

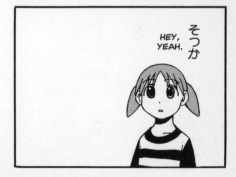

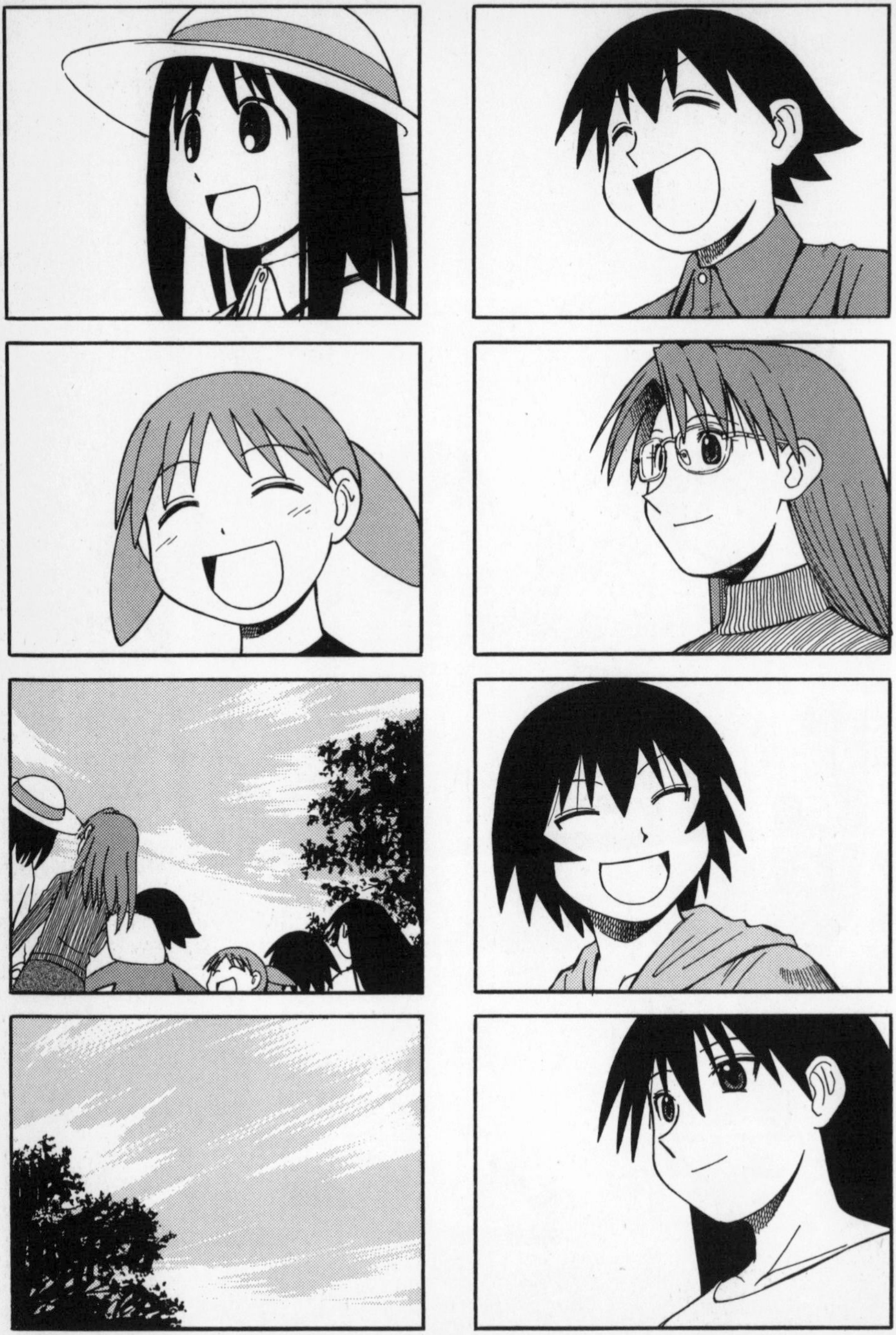

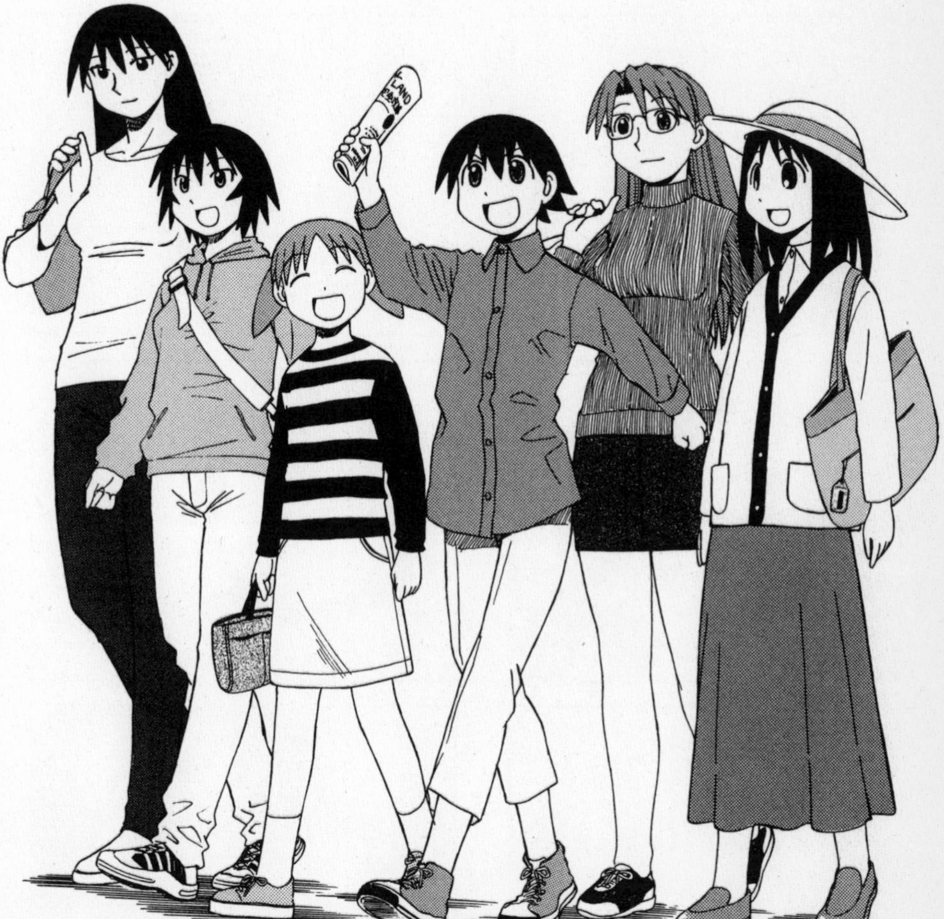
LAND

AZU MANGA DAIOH

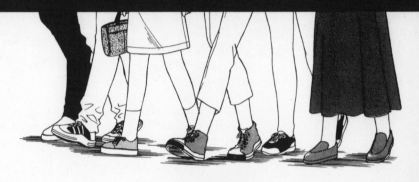

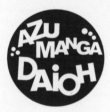

おしまい。

THE END.

Azumanga Daioh Volume Four

© KIYOHIKO AZUMA 2002
First published in 2002 by MEDIA WORKS, Inc., Tokyo, Japan.
English translation rights arranged with MEDIA WORKS, Inc.

Lead Translator/Translator Supervisor	JAVIER LOPEZ
ADV Manga Translation Staff	KAY BERTRAND, AMY FORSYTH, BRENDAN FRAYNE, EIKO McGREGOR
Print Production Manager/Art Studio Manager	LISA PUCKETT
Art Production Manager	RYAN MASON
Sr. Designer/Creative Manager	JORGE ALVARADO
Graphic Designer/Group Leader	SHANNON RASBERRY
Graphic Designer	WINDI MARTIN
Graphic Artists	HEATHER GARY, SHANNA JENSCHKE, KRISTINA MILESKI, NATALIA MORALES, LISA RAPER, CHRIS LAPP, GEORGE REYNOLDS, SCOTT SAVAGE, LANCE SWARTOUT, NANAKO TSUKIHASHI
International Coordinators	TORU IWAKAMI, ATSUSHI KANBAYASHI
Publishing Editor	SUSAN ITIN
Assistant Editor	MARGARET SCHAROLD
Editorial Assistant	VARSHA BHUCHAR
Proofreader	SHERIDAN JACOBS
Traffic Coordinator	MARSHA ARNOLD
President, C.E.O. & Publisher	JOHN LEDFORD

Email: editor@adv-manga.com
www.adv-manga.com
www.advfilms.com
For sales and distribution inquiries please call 1.800.282.7202

ADV MANGA™ is a division of A.D. Vision, Inc.
10114 W. Sam Houston Parkway, Suite 200, Houston, Texas 77099

English text ©2004 by A.D. Vision, Inc. under exclusive license.
ADV MANGA is a trademark of A.D. Vision, Inc.

ISBN: 1-4139-0048-8

First printing, April 2004
10 9 8 7 6 5 4 3 2 1
Printed in Canada

LETTER FROM THE ADV MANGA TRANSLATION STAFF

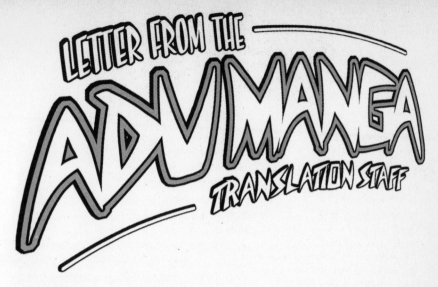

Dear Reader,

On behalf of the ADV Manga translation team, thank you for purchasing an ADV book. We are enthusiastic and committed to our work, and strive to carry our enthusiasm over into the book you hold in your hands.

Our goal is to retain the true spirit of the original Japanese book. While great care has been taken to render a true and accurate translation, some cultural or readability issues may require a line to be adapted for greater accessibility to our readers. At times, manga titles that include culturally-specific concepts will feature a "Translator's Notes" section, which explains noteworthy references to the original text.

We hope our commitment to a faithful translation is evident in every ADV book you purchase.

Sincerely,

Javier Lopez
Lead Translator

Eiko McGregor

Kay Bertrand

Brendan Frayne

Amy Forsyth

ADV Manga™

www.adv-manga.com

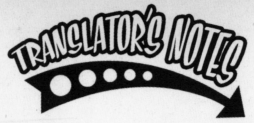

Azumanga Daioh Vol 04

Pg. 27 **(1) Shuri Castle**
Shuri, the former capital of Okinawa, is located just a few miles from the island's current capital of Naha. Shuri Castle is the largest of Okinawa's castles, and an important landmark/tourist attraction.
For more, see the homepage of the Okinawa Prefectural Government at www.wonder-okinawa.jp/001/index-e.html

(2) Shurei Gate
This is the main gate of Shuri Castle. The inscription reads *Shurei no kuni*, or "land or propriety."
For more, see the homepage of the Okinawa Prefectural Government at www.wonder-okinawa.jp/001/001-e/002_03.html

(3) A 2,000 yen note
This note was first unveiled in 2000, to some mixed feedback from consumers (who complained that the new denomination made things too complicated). The note, which features a depiction of Shureimon, was heavily promoted as a tie-in to the G8 summit held in Okinawa the following year.

(4) Shisa
Originally brought over from China, the shisa are a kind of mythological lion believed to ward off evil spirits. Plaster shisa are a staple of Okinawan architecture, and are often found on the gates and roofs of civilian houses.
For a collection of shisa photographs, see the homepage of the Okinawa Prefectural Government at www.wonderokinawa.jp/011/english/meet/visit/mv03/mv03.html

(5) Shiisaa yaibiimi?
Chiyo-chan was correct—in Okinawan, *Shiisaa yaibiimi?* means "Is this a shisa?" Her reply means "Yes, it is a shisa."

Pg. 13 **Fuhgeddaboutit**
So far we've been using "Fuhgeddaboutit" to render *nandeyanen* (Literally, "Why?") because not only does it have comedic and belittling overtones, it is also instantly recognizable as dialectical. In this strip, Osaka was actually using *chau nen* ("nope" or "wrong"), another dialectical phrase that can be delivered to comic effect. Rather than go with something like "Nossiree" (which would have failed to capture the dialectical flavor the strip hinged on), I again used "fuhgeddaboutit."

Student ID
Pg. 18 The Japanese *seito techo* is actually a combination ID and handbook.

(1) I've never been on a school trip before!
Pg. 21 In Japan, the *shugaku ryoko* ("school trip") is only for students in their senior year—hence Yomi's somewhat flustered reaction.

(2) Señora
In the Japanese, Tomo actually used señor, the male form.

Time to get up
Pg. 23 The phrase Tomo used was *okina wa…* which, obviously, is a pun on Okinawa, the destination of their school trip.

Haisai
Pg. 26 Until it was annexed by Japan in 1879, Okinawa was a separate nation with its own distinct language. Today that language survives in two forms—as *uchinaaguchi*, the complete (if increasingly less spoken) language, and as "standard" Japanese that has been influenced by that language. As Osaka pointed out, *haisai* is the Okinawan equivalent of "Hello" or "Good afternoon."

pg. 26 **(1) Island Getaway**

Okinawa is just one island in the Ryukyu chain. There are several others, including Miyako Island (renowned for its crystal blue waters and white sand beaches) and Iriomote Island, where some 90% of the landmass is still unspoiled forest. Iriomote is also home to several unique species of animal, including the rare *Iriomote Yamaneko* ("Iriomote Cat"), which was only discovered in 1964.

(2) UMIN CHU

Kaorin and Mr. Kimura's T-shirt bears the characters for "sea" and "person," a combination that in Okinawan is pronounced *uminchu* and means "fisherman."

pg. 28 **MEOWvelous!**

In Japanese, *nanto* is used to lend a sense of marvel or incredulity. The word appearing in the comic is *nyanto*, a pun which incorporates *nya*, the sound of a cat meowing (note the little cat paw). "Meowvelous" was my attempt to capture this joke. I await the bricks to come smashing through my bedroom window.

pg. 29 **Arauchigawa and Maryudo Falls**

Both Arauchigawa and Maryudo Falls are located on Iriomote Island. According to legend, a giant alligator lives in Maryudo Falls, and will attack anyone who pollutes its waters.

pg. 41 **It's watermelon-splitting time!**

As we've seen previously, putting on a blindfold and attempting to split a watermelon with a bat is a traditional beachside game in Japan.

pg. 42 **Ukon-cha**

Turmeric tea. In Okinawa, it's referred to as "the king of health teas."

pg. 44 **Thank you**

The reason for Kaorin's blushing and use of polite language is (as shown in earlier volumes) she has a mad crush on Sakaki.

pg. 52 **Radio exercises**

Called *rajio taiso* in Japanese, this (along with its television equivalent) is a program of low-impact exercises designed for the elderly, with the aim of improving circulation and promoting overall health.

pg. 28 **(1) Aree, shiisaa aibiran!**

As you've probably guessed, *Aree, shiisaa aibiran!* means "That's not a shisa!"

(2) Osenmikocha

Located on the second floor of Shuri castle, the *osenmikocha* is a prayer room dedicated to the fire god. For some reason, Osaka found the name of this room to be the height of hilarity.

pg. 30 **Champuru**

Arguably the most representative of Okinawan dishes, *champuru* is a kind of stir-fry that mixes a variety of vegetables, meat and/or tofu. The name of the *champuru* dish varies, depending upon the main ingredient—*goya* is bittermelon, *fu* is a kind of wheat-gluten bread and *somin* are noodles.

pg. 31 **(1) Manzamo**

A wide plain in northern Okinawa with a sheer cliff face.

(2) Davy Jones' Locker

The Japanese title of this strip was *umi no mokuzu*, a somewhat poetic-sounding phrase literally meaning "the ocean's seaweed," but referring to drowning. As such, Davy Jones' Locker, an antiquated expression used by sailors to refer to the bottom of the ocean, seemed an appropriate match.

pg. 32 **The fruit of the sea**

The joke of this strip is that all the fish that Tomo, Miss Yukari and Kagura want to "see" are in fact fish they'd like to eat. Osaka one-ups them all by saying she'd like to see *ikura* (salmon roe).

pg. 34 **Chinsuko**

A traditional Okinawan sweet, *chinsuko* is a kind of sugary biscuit in a variety of flavors, such as *goya*, pineapple and yam.

pg. 36 **(1) Sata andagi**

The traditional style of Okinawan donut, *sata andagi* are deep-fried "donut holes" made from flour, vanilla and sugar.

(2) 100 yen

About 90 cents.

PG. 114 Nishihyo Island

Normally, the characters making up the place name Iriomote would be read as *nishi* and *hyo*—hence Kagura's confusion.

PG. 122 Letters in the alphabet

This riddle (and the many to follow) are dependent upon language-specific puns to make them work. In all but one case the joke is lost when translated, requiring the substitution of suitable English-language alternatives.

Originally, this brain teaser went, "What is the fruit of summer?" Chiyo-chan sensibly replied "Watermelon," but Tomo countered that it was actually persimmon. The reason: *kaki* ("persimmon") is a homonym for the word meaning "the summer season."

Birthday / Birth day

PG. 123 In a similar bit of punnery, Tomo asked "What kind of person does nothing but smash cars?" Chiyo-chan responded "A wrecker," to which Tomo declared the answer to be a dentist. When Chiyo-chan protested, Tomo enunciated the words a little differently to get the pun across. While the first time she'd said *ha'isha-san* ("dentist"), the second time she said *hai'sha* ("scrapyard"). Adding *-san* to the end of *hai'sha* gives us, "a person who works in a scrapyard."

PG. 124 (1) Two apples

The original joke went, "What bird doesn't get along well with policemen?" Osaka's (correct) answer was *sagi*, which means "heron" but is also a homonym for "fraud."

(2) Mt. Everest

The trick here is that even before its discovery, Mt. Everest was (and still is) the world's tallest mountain. The original Japanese has a similar trick to it—"If *nihongo* ('Japanese') is the language of Japan, then *eigo* ('English') is the language of what country?" The answer may surprise you. *Kotoba*, the word used in the riddle to mean "language," can also mean "word." Thus, the riddle is really asking, "If the word *nihongo* is Japanese, from what country is the word *eigo*?" Because *eigo* is a Japanese word, the answer is "Japan."

PG. 59 Where's the cup?

This type of vending machine, which most often seems to crop up in bus stations and movie theaters, first dispenses a paper cup, some ice (if applicable) and then the drink itself.

PG. 65 (1) Ichiro and Sasaki

This is a reference to Ichiro Suzuki and Kazuhiro Sasaki, two Japanese baseball players who transferred overseas to join the Seattle Mariners.

(2) You'll get killed

While civilian possession of firearms is illegal in Japan, the fact that they're so accessible in America has helped fuel the belief that if you go to America, there's a good chance you'll get shot.

PG. 68 Now I'm the king of the swingers...

In the original Japanese, Tomo remarked that what Yomi sung was "The Jaian Song." Jaian is a recurring character on the long-running manga/anime **Doraemon**, and his song is filled with such lyrics as "I'm the boss of all the kids/ I am without rival." As such, King Louie's song from **The Jungle Book** seemed the best match for an easily-recognizable reference.

PG. 70 Tight little gym shorts

Also known as bloomers, these shorts are worn from elementary school all the way up through high school. The fact that they're required to be worn for so long (and leave so little to the imagination) is cause enough for Yomi's reaction... as well as Mr. Kimura's.

PG. 77 Chihuahua

In the original Japanese, Chihuahua is "Chiyosuke," a made-up word that takes Chiyo's name and tacks on a male suffix. It has a rather diminutive feel to it—hence Chihuahua.

PG. 78 Criminals!

Fueiho, the original title of this strip, is an abbreviation for the Japanese Amusement Businesses Control and Improvement Law. "Amusement Business" in this case refers to the red light district, including (but not limited to) the sex-for-pay industry. When Tomo saw the two teachers in schoolgirl uniforms, she immediately (whether jokingly or not) accused them of dressing up for the "benefit" of their clients.

PG. 142 Cake

More precisely mille-feuille cake, which is made up of flaky, pastry-like layers, separated by cream custard. It is sometimes topped with fruit.

PG. 146 "I wish I were a bird"

This is a reference to a famous commercial for NOVA, a chain of for-profit English-language schools. In the commercial, a young Japanese girl whose father is a high-school English teacher fixates on a phrase from one of her father's classes. Spreading her arms, the girl cries "I wish I were a bird!"

PG. 147 (1) Former Prime Minister Mori

Yoshiro Mori had a brief stint as Prime Minister following the sudden death of his predecessor, Keizo Obuchi. The spectacularly unpopular Mori served just a single year before resigning his position... and come to think of it, he *does* resemble Chiyo-chan's dad somewhat.

(2) When the cat's away, the mice will play

Originally, Chiyo-chan's "dad" said, " You're a real cat, huh? Well, *I* have a sensitive tongue and can't eat hot food. How about you?" to which Osaka piped up, "I have a sensitive tongue, too!" The pun here is that the word for sensitive to hot foods is *neko-jita*, which literally means "cat's tongue." Unfortunately, this concept doesn't exist in English, and a substitute was required.

PG. 149 Tokyo U

Often called "Japan's Harvard," Tokyo University is *the* top school in Japan.

PG. 174 If we look back on this time...

This is the first verse of "Aogeba Totoshi," a song traditionally performed by the students at graduation. As the language is somewhat archaic, please pardon the rather dry-sounding translation.

PG. 124 (3) The truck

Mercifully, this joke works as-is when translated into English.

PG. 126 Drip, drip

Osaka is referencing the commercial for a skincare product called Domohorn Wrinkle. In the commercial, an elderly woman stares at the steady drip, drip of the product into an awaiting container, while the narrator states, "Domohorn Wrinkle can't be mass produced, because it's made just one drop at a time."

WHOA!

PG. 127

If you've ever spent any time using the pull-apart *waribashi* chopsticks seen on this page, you'll know your chances are about 50-50 that they'll separate the way they're supposed to—hence everyone's stunned reaction.

This is fun

PG. 130

Osaka and Chiyo-chan are performing a ritual for good luck. You're only supposed to ring the bell (that's what they're pulling on the rope for) a couple of times, but Osaka shows no signs of stopping. In her defense, it *does* have a funky, vaguely cowbell-like sound to it...

Omikuji

PG. 133

The *omikuji* is a kind of lottery where fortunes for the upcoming year are drawn at random. Each fortune has a "rank," which ranges from "extremely fortunate" to "beware." Incidentally, Tomo's "ill-fated" (*kyo*) rank is the second-to-lowest.

Gimme some change!

PG. 135

What Tomo was after was *otoshidama*, the New Years' "allowance" typically received up through one's late teens. Apparently she's already forgotten the conversation she had with Chiyo-chan regarding *otoshidama* (see **Azumanga Daioh** vol. 2)

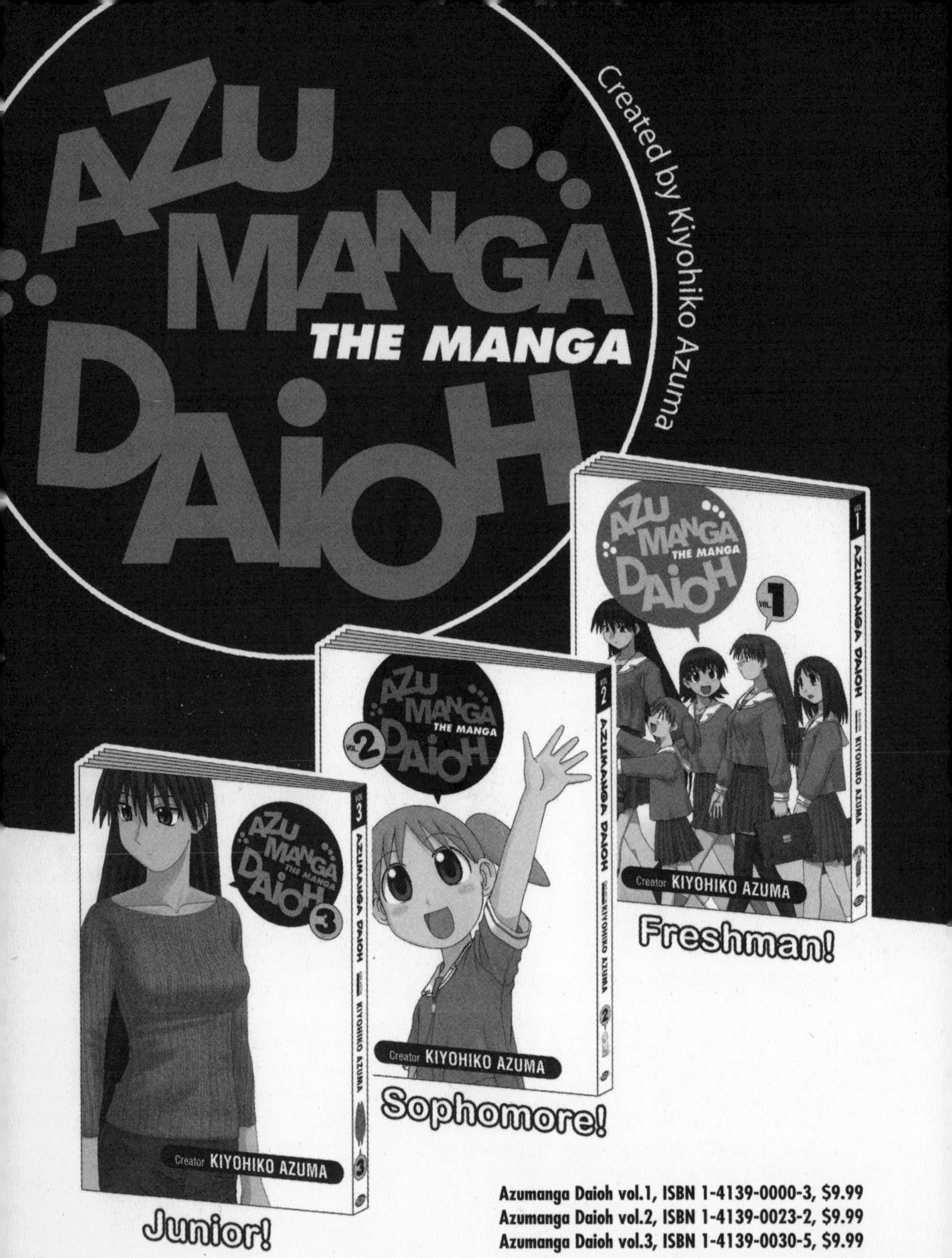
AZUMANGA DAIOH
THE MANGA
Created by Kiyohiko Azuma
Freshman!
Sophomore!
Junior!
Creator KIYOHIKO AZUMA

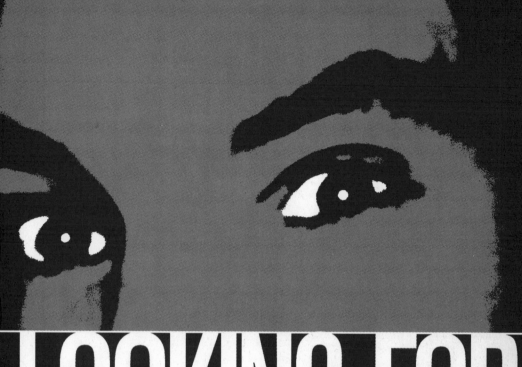
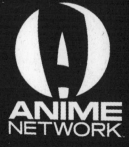

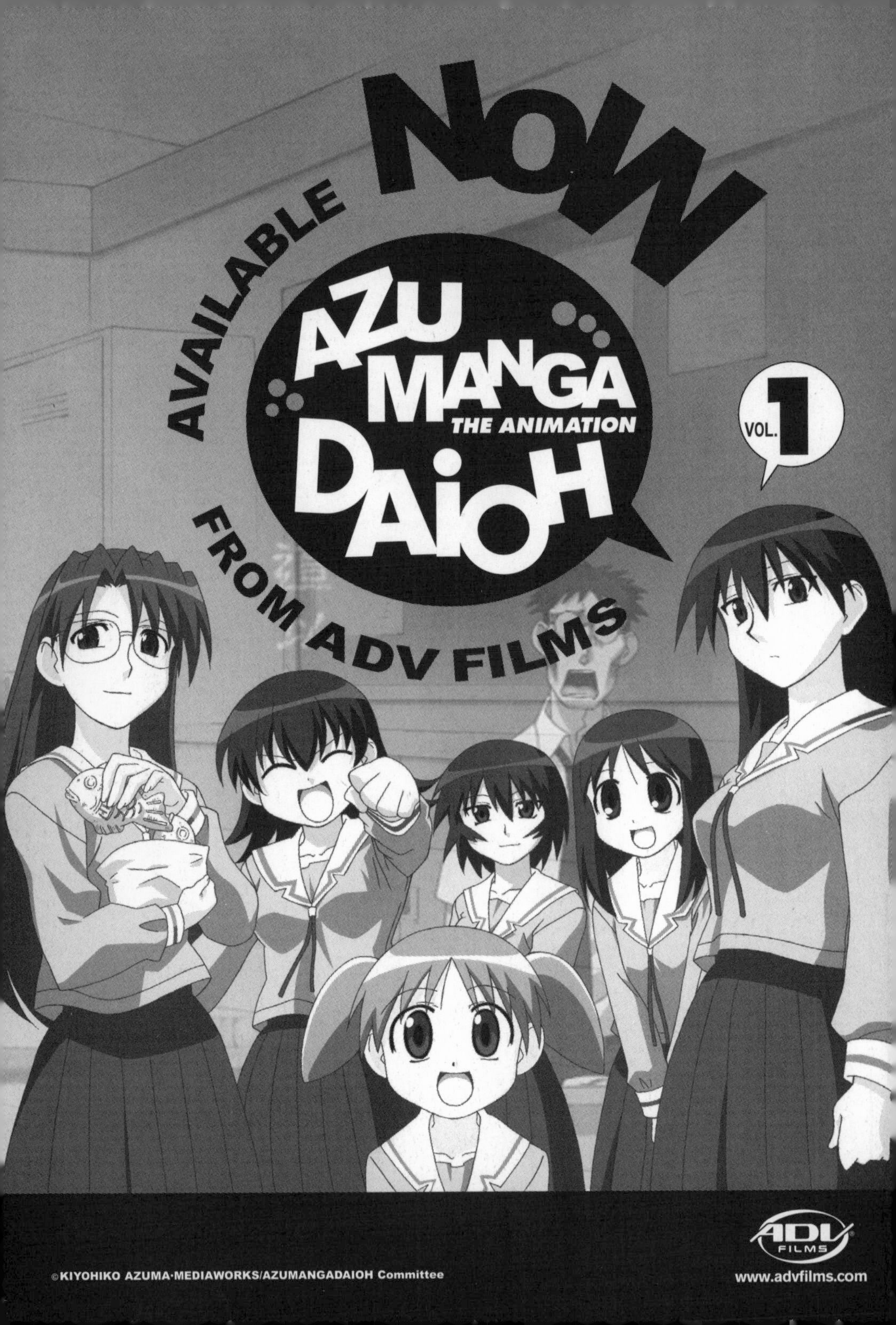

AVAILABLE NOW
AZU MANGA DAIOH
THE ANIMATION
VOL. 1
FROM ADV FILMS
ADV FILMS
©KIYOHIKO AZUMA·MEDIAWORKS/AZUMANGADAIOH Committee
www.advfilms.com

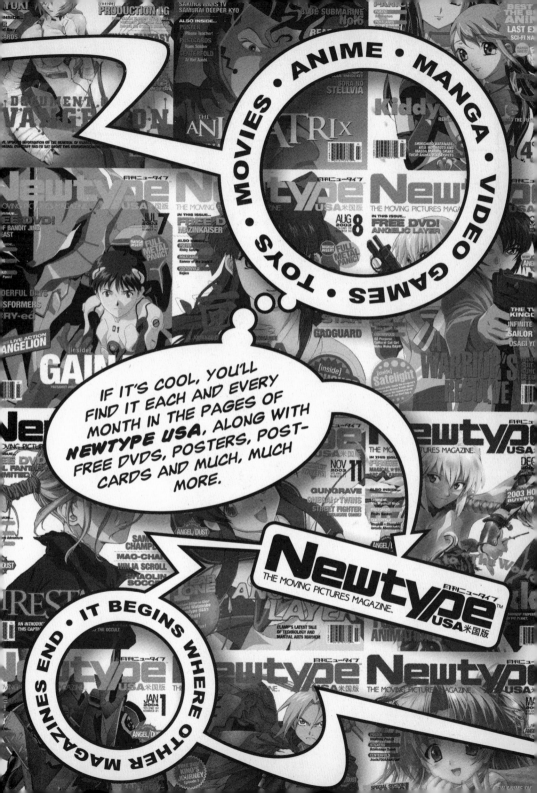

MOVIES • ANIME • MANGA • VIDEO GAMES • TOYS •

IF IT'S COOL, YOU'LL FIND IT EACH AND EVERY MONTH IN THE PAGES OF *NEWTYPE USA*, ALONG WITH FREE DVDS, POSTERS, POST-CARDS AND MUCH, MUCH MORE.

Newtype USA 米国版
THE MOVING PICTURES MAGAZINE.™

IT BEGINS WHERE OTHER MAGAZINES END •